HARDPRESS.NET
HOME OF HARD-TO-FIND BOOKS

Dear Old England: a Description of Our Fatherland
by Jane Anne Winscom

Address:
HardPress
8345 NW 66TH ST #2561
MIAMI FL 33166-2626
USA
Email: info@hardpress.net

WARKWORTH CASTLE.

DEAR OLD ENGLAND:

A DESCRIPTION OF OUR FATHERLAND.

Dedicated to all English Children.

BY

JANE ANNE WINSCOM,

AUTHOR OF "VINEYARD LABOURERS," "ONWARD," "I BELIEVE; OR, THE APOSTLES' CREED EXPLAINED TO CHILDREN," &c., &c.

Fourth Thousand.

LONDON:
JAMES NISBET AND CO., 21 BERNERS STREET.

MDCCCLXXII.

PRINTED BY BALLANTYNE AND COMPANY
EDINBURGH AND LONDON

PREFACE TO THE SECOND EDITION.

THIS new edition of " Dear Old England " has been carefully revised, and many alterations made.

A Map, for the convenience of those who are studying the book, has been prepared, and many foot references, calculated to exercise the reflective faculties of children, have been given. From them they may form comparisons and contrasts, or trace historically what they have learnt geographically.

It is particularly desired that children may know intelligently the geography of their native land—may learn not by memory only, but with heart and understanding. Many tales are mingled—for tales are amongst the joys of childhood, and an anecdote will often impress on the mind a locality or character that with mere names and statistics would pass away.

March 25, 1867.

PREFACE.

"DEAR OLD ENGLAND" is intended either for school or for play-hours. Its object is to interest English children in everything that concerns their dear native land.

Geography should convey ideas, rather than hard names; it should exercise comprehension as well as memory; it should associate places with history, scenery, climate, produce, and inhabitants.

The information in the following pages is intended to stimulate rather than to satisfy inquiry. The volume will be but a stepping-stone to books of far more intrinsic worth and far deeper thought. Ideas are only in embryo here. Future education and after-life must see their development. Something is, however, gained when learning has been made pleasant, when facts have led to thoughts, when the connexion between cause and effect has been observed, and the young mind has endeavoured to solve the riddles that may be extracted from the information each lesson contains.

Amongst the books consulted have been Lewis's " Topographical Dictionary," Knight's " The Land We Live In," " Old England," and especially Murray's excellent " Handbooks of the Southern Counties." As accuracy of information is earnestly aimed at, should mistakes be discovered, the writer would feel deeply indebted for any communications regarding them, addressed to the care of the publishers.

May England's God bless this volume, and permit it to bear its humble share in gladdening children's hearts, in informing their minds, and in increasing their thankfulness to Him who has cast their lot in a land so pleasant, and has given them a heritage so fair as Britain's isle !

December 1860.

CONTENTS.

CONTENTS.

LIST OF ILLUSTRATIONS.

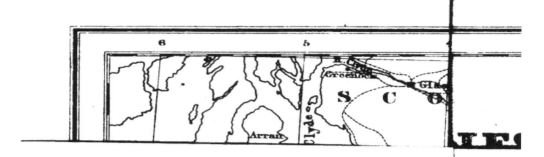

DEAR OLD ENGLAND.

Now I hope the map of England is either hung up on the wall, or laid on the table; for I want your young eyes to be continually looking at it.

Is England an island? No: for the sea does not quite surround it. Here is Scotland, that joins it on the north; and here is Wales, a dear sister country, on the west.

England, Scotland, and Wales, form altogether the island of Great Britain. Dear old Britain! Don't we love it? It is sometimes called our "sea-girt home," because the sea surrounds it like a girdle or belt, and helps to keep us safe from enemies. Yet I think something better than the sea keeps Britain safe, even God's care for our island and our island's queen; and as long as we please Him and ask Him to protect us, our dear country shall be preserved from all dangers.

Why do we love England? Will you try to answer? I will give you four reasons, but, probably, you will think of others.

First, we love it because it is a Bible-land. There are few families in which there is not a Bible. Good King George III., Queen Victoria's grandfather, used to wish

A

that every child in England had this precious book. Any little child may now buy a Bible for sixpence, and the poorest children can go to ragged schools, where they may learn to read it. Being a Bible-land, all who wish may know from God's own book what He desires them to do; and may learn the blessed story about Jesus Christ coming into the world to save sinners.

Secondly, we love England because it is a *free* land. Everybody may do and speak as he likes, and, unless he injures others, no policeman can put him into prison. The Englishman feels his home is his castle; and the rights of the cottager are as sacred as those of the prince. Neither are there any slaves in England . no men, women, boys, or girls, who can be bought or sold.

Thirdly, we love England because it is a *beautiful* land. There are not such grand mountains, and large lakes, and sunny flowers as in some countries; but the fields are very green, and the scenery is sweetly varied; and the cottages, as well as larger houses, are comfortable, and, what is peculiarly an English word, they are " cosy."

Fourthly, we love England because it is our dear *home* land—

"Home, sweet home, there is no place like home."

There are many pleasant countries over the sea ; and we hope the little French, and Swiss, and German children, love their own fatherlands very much, but we know best about dear old England; and don't you like the pretty verse which says,

" I thank the goodness and the grace
Which on my birth have smiled,
And made me in these blessed days
A happy English child " ?

Now, look again at the map, and let us find out what it will tell us about England.

Though the sea goes all round Britain, it is not very far from France in this southern part, and from Ireland here. Ireland is a sister island, and belongs to the same queen as England.

From this coast of France, (look for Calais,) the white cliffs on the shore of England (look for Dover) can be seen ; and so when the Romans first saw England they called it Albion or the White Land. The tribes in Britain were very savage before the arrival of the Romans, I suppose something like the New Zealanders before the English discovered them, only the ancient Britons never ate each other's flesh. Julius Cæsar, the Roman general, and his soldiers crossed over these straits, (the Straits of Dover.) The brave Britons fought with them, but at last were driven back ; and the Romans took possession of Britain, and built large towns and taught the people many useful things.

England is neither very near the equator, nor very near the pole. It is neither burning hot, nor freezing cold. The weather is temperate. There are cold east winds in spring, and often thick fogs in November, but still most of the days are very fine. Being an island, and warmed by a current of water that reaches its western shore, from the Gulf of Mexico, the average warmth is much greater than in other places of the same latitude. More rain falls here than on the Continent, and foreigners are struck with the greenness of England's fields, and the luxuriance of her foliage.

Now observe which coast of England seems the smoothest ; with the fewest bays and headlands. The shape of England is something like a triangle, the most irregular side being on the left hand or west, which is as irregular in its surface as in its shape, almost all the mountains and rough parts being to the west. We will mark a line from this river, the Tees, in Durham, to this one, the Exe, in Devonshire; and on its eastern side, you will find the country generally covered with plains, or gently-sloping fields, and rivers quietly wandering along; whilst on the west side there are mountains and moorlands, deep valleys, clear lakes, and rivers rushing through dells with steep banks on either side. These divisions of the island are also very different in their riches. The beautiful green fields with fine fat cattle, and richly-cultivated land with waving corn, are the riches of the eastern side, whilst minerals of all sorts, lead, iron, tin, coal, or copper, are found in the country to the west of the line.

The greatest length of England, from Berwick-upon-Tweed to the south of Dorset, is 380 miles; and the greatest breadth, from Land's End to Winterton Ness in Norfolk, is 367 miles. Now, it is reckoned that policemen or postmen, whose business it is to walk about, can walk fifteen miles a day. How many weeks of six days each would a man, walking at this rate, be in passing from north to south? How many weeks in going from east to west?

Now. think again: how many miles in one day have you ever walked? Then how many days would you take to walk across England. The narrowest part of England is between the coast of Northumberland and the Solway Frith, there it is only sixty-two miles broad. How long would you take to walk across it?

Now, try and remember all I have told you to-day, for before you hear or read another chapter, I expect you to give me an account of this one.

NORTHUMBERLAND.—PART I.

Now for another geography lesson from me, and eyes and ears from you.

Do you see that dear old England, our sea-girt island, is divided on the map into a number of parts, of all sorts of colours, red, blue, yellow, green, and of all sorts of shapes—this one, Northumberland, like a little England; Buckinghamshire rather like an old woman with a pack on her back; you guess Nottinghamshire, an egg; Westmoreland, an ivy leaf; Somersetshire, a baby's sock; whilst Cornwall always reminds me of a Wellington boot, with a very small toe.

Yorkshire is the largest, and Rutland the smallest county.

Now I must tell you what counties are. They are the forty parts into which England was divided a very long time ago, by the wise king, Alfred the Great. They are not surrounded either by walls or ditches, rivers or hedges. I know a house with one bed-room in Hertfordshire and another in Middlesex; and a garden, with one tree in Gloucestershire and another in Worcestershire. Each county has, however, different officers, appointed by the Queen to keep order; and different members, gentlemen chosen by the people to go up to London to the parliament and consult on the laws by which the English are to be governed. I suppose, in Alfred's time, there were reasons for the different shapes of the counties. Rivers and hills very often partly separate them; and, probably, where there is now nothing at all, there used to be the edge of a forest, or the beginning of a moor.

The division into counties helps us very much to understand the map, and to find out places. Suppose your garden to be divided into flower plots, and each plot to have a name which you know. Charles wants to know where the pretty dark rose has been plucked; the gardener says, "In Flora plot." Mary asks where the geranium is planted; she hears "In Magnificent plot." They then soon discover their favourite flowers.   So, if you remember that this great county is Yorkshire, and you hear that Sheffield, Leeds, and Hull are in Yorkshire, you will not think of looking for those large towns in Cornwall.

Now I wish to tell you about the people who live, the things that are made, the towns that are built in, and the rivers which flow through, each county; and will you listen and try to remember it all?

We will begin with Northumberland, the highest-up county on the map, therefore the most northern, or the furthest away from the part of the heaven where the sun shines.   It is not so warm in Northumberland as in these southern counties; but there are many bright fine days, which in summer are longer, and in winter are shorter than they are on the English Channel.

The German Ocean washes the coast of Northumberland. Generally, the waves beat against soft, bright sands, covered with pretty shells, but in some places high rocks jut out, with perhaps a castle built upon their summit. Sometimes there are deep creeks, or fissures, in these rocks, up which the large waves rush with a great noise; and reaching the end, they throw the spray into the air like a fountain.   It is beautiful to watch it, with the bright sun shining.   It falls down glittering like a shower of pearls and precious stones.

Often there are sad shipwrecks on this coast; but a good Duke of Northumberland provided at several stations between the Tyne and the Tweed life-boats. These are boats made of timber, with a cornice of cork, fitted with air-chambers, and having two bows, so that even if the waves dash over or upset them, they rise to the top of the billows, and right themselves.   If a ship is driven on the rocks, some brave men get into one of these boats, and save, if possible, the shipwrecked sailors.

What can you do to help the sailors when the wind blows hard ? Can't you pray for them ?

Further inland, there are a good many corn-fields, but not nearly so much hay as in the south of England. The grass does not grow quickly in Northumberland, and the farmers take a long time to make it into hay. There are few trees, excepting near the rivers, whose steep banks are often beautifully wooded, the branches of the lowest trees dipping into the clear-running water. In the west of the county there is a great deal of hilly moorland. You may travel for many miles and see hardly any fields or trees; but the moors are covered with the golden flowers of the furze, or the heather's purple blossom ; and even on the soft, spongy bogs are found bright green moss, and rare and beautiful flowers, as pretty as many that grow in the garden. You can see sheep and goats feeding on the hill-sides, and shepherds clothed in plaids, long-checked woollen shawls, taking care of them. Amongst these hills, quite sheltered from the cold east winds, are valleys, where invalids often go for warmer air. The poor people in Northumberland are generally agriculturists ; that is, they work in the fields, sowing, reaping, hoeing. Some are miners, working below the ground in coal-pits or lead mines ; and on the coast there are many fishermen.

They are kind to each other, honest and independent. They seldom beg for money, and have a great deal of common sense. You seldom meet a Northumbrian person who cannot read. They do not like to give up their old customs, whether good or bad. One bad custom is, having only one room for eating, drinking, and sleeping. This is, I hope, giving way a little. Their box beds fastened against the walls with wooden shutters are very unwholesome.

The air, however, is fresh and bracing ; and as the people have good wages, they are able to live on good food,

and are generally tall and stout, with broad shoulders.
They eat brown bread, which is very wise. They often
bake cakes on the girdle, a round, flat, iron plate, hung
over the fire. These are sometimes made of barley, and
pease meal. This is dry food, but quite wholesome, and
soon satisfies hungry children. A better kind is made of
flour, and cream or butter, and currants, and is eaten
quite hot. The pitmen call them "Singing hinnies wi'
sma' co' fizzers." "Hinny" means a good thing, probably
from "honey," and they call the currants small coals,
which sing or fiz with the butter in them.

The Northumbrians have a strange way of speaking,
and use words you would not understand. Perhaps a
mother would tell you her child was a "canny wee bairn,
but somewhat hempy;" which means, a nice little child,
but rather mischievous. Their Rs seem to stick in their
throats. It is very difficult for Northumbrian people to
say, "Around the rugged rocks the ragged rascals ran."

Now what do we get from Northumberland? Some
things so precious that they are called black diamonds.
We neither eat them nor wear them, but only throw them
on the fire. Ah! coals. The best coals in England used
to come from Northumberland, from a place called Wall's
End. The best fish we eat comes also from Northumberland. The Tweed salmon, a red kind of fish, is famous all
over England. Cod, haddocks, oysters, and herrings, are
also plentiful on its coast; but soles and mackerel are
rare; and sprats do not go north of the Tyne.

Very large cattle are fattened in this county.

On the long dreary moorlands many birds are shot, such
as grouse, black-cocks, etc., called moor-game. No one
can shoot them without the Queen's leave, nor before the
12th of August.

Several famous people have been born in Northumberland :—Good old Bishop Ridley, who, in the reign of Queen Mary, was burnt because of his love for the Bible ; Lord Collingwood, who gained a famous victory by sea over the French ; Lord Eldon, a great lawyer; George and Robert Stephenson, the famous engineers. George Stephenson, when a little boy, hoed turnips for twopence a day ; but he was a great thinker ; and his thoughts led to the discovery of the way by which steam-engines could draw railway carriages. Do you like to go on the railway ? Then think of what you owe to the great George Stephenson. Another famous man was once a poor boy in Northumberland— Robert Morrison, who was a shoemaker's apprentice, and afterwards went out as a missionary to China, and translated God's blessed Bible into the difficult Chinese language. Bewick, the inventor of wood-engraving, worked, when a child, in a coal-pit on the Tyne. Now try and think of the country, the people, the produce, and the great men of Northumberland, and to-morrow I will tell you something about the towns and rivers.

NORTHUMBERLAND.—PART II.

Now, look at the map. The Tweed runs between Northumberland and Scotland. It is a pretty, clear river, with beautiful banks, on which are several ruined castles. Long ago the Scotch and English were not good friends, and often fought battles. Then the lords used to have castles, instead of houses, with thick walls and wide ditches or moats all around. Over these ditches were drawbridges—bridges that can be drawn up at pleasure, preventing all passage. Inside the walls were enclosures for the cattle; because if the cows were left in the fields the enemy's soldiers would soon steal them. One of these old castles on the banks of the Tweed, is Norham. It is a ruin now, the walls broken and stones crumbling, but once it was full of armed men, feasting inside and fighting outside. Good Dr Gilly, who wrote about Felix Neff, and cared much for the Protestants among the Alps, lived and died at Norham.

Where the Tweed falls into the sea is Berwick. Berwick is a county of itself, belonging neither to England nor Scotland. It has broad walls all round it; several people could walk abreast along them. The railway station is where the castle once stood. We do not need a castle there now, since there is no fighting between the Scotch and English. Berwick is a famous place for catching salmon. To do so, the fishermen sometimes lay their nets in a half-moon shape from the shore ; they then jump into boats and row round and round between the nets and shore, frightening the salmon, which try to swim away. They, poor things, rush into the nets and are caught. The fishermen then undo the stakes, and draw the nets to land, and take out all the fish they find. Sometimes there are none. Then they have to try again and again. You know there are no gains without pains.

Not very far from Berwick is Holy Island, so called because it was the place where the holy and humble missionary Aidan lived, and also the pastors that, with him, came from Iona in Scotland to preach about Jesus to the heathen Northumbrians. Aidan won them by great meekness and humility. He was much assisted by the good King Oswald, who used to stand by the missionary, translating his words into the people's language. At Holy Island can be seen the ruins of the old monastery. The first church was built of wood and thatched with reeds. Opposite Holy Island is Bamborough. Sometimes you can cross in a carriage from one to the other, because when the tide is low the sand is left dry. At Bamborough is a fine castle, built on a high rock. We read of it 1300 years ago, in the time

Bamborough Castle.

of the Danes and Saxons. It is now appropriated for the good of the poor, and especially for efforts to help the ship-wrecked. In the churchyard is the tomb of Mr Mackenzie, a passenger in the steamer *Pegasus*, which struck on some rocks near, and foundered. As they were sinking, he gathered the passengers round him, and prayed calmly to his God. Here, too, is the tomb of Grace Darling, who lived on one of the Ferne Islands, a group of rocky islets off this coast. They are twenty-five in number when the tide is out, and fifteen when it is in. Hers is a deeply interest-ing story, and I am sure you will love to hear it.

THE STORY OF GRACE DARLING AND THE SHIPWRECK.

More than thirty years since, on the 5th of September, a steamboat left Hull in Yorkshire (which town we will find on the map) for Dundee, in Scotland. Its name was the *Forfarshire*. It had sixty-three people on board—sailors and passengers—men, women, and some little children. The boilers soon began to leak, but the sailors pumped the water out and the vessel went northwards, passed the shores of Yorkshire, Durham, and Northumberland, till it reached St Abb's Head, a rocky cape on the coast of Scotland. Here the engineer said he could not make the engines work any longer, and the captain was obliged to let the vessel drive before the wind. The storm was very high—the waves were lashing, and the white sea foaming. The north wind drove them southward all night, and very early in the morning, when it was quite dark, they found that the foam before them was breaking on a fearful rock, one of these Ferne Islands. They could not manage the helm; so on the ship went, and struck this sharp, high ridge. Loud cries arose—loud cries for God to have mercy. Another tremendous wave struck the ship; it lifted it high above the rock. The wave passed—the ship fell upon the rock's sharp edge, and broke in two. One end was swept into the deep sea, and all the passengers there were buried in a terrible grave of water. Some of the crew now rushed into a little boat that belonged to the ship, and just as it was being pushed off, a farmer took a long leap, jumped in, and was saved; for the men in this boat were afterwards picked up by a ship that met them. Nine others clung to the fore part of the ship, and there they hung, with the waves dashing over them. Amongst them was a poor woman, who had with her two little children. How the waves bruised, and drenched, and chilled, and hurt them! But, ere long, the crying of the poor little ones ceased, for Jesus sent His angel to take their souls to His bright home, where storms and tempests never come. At last morning dawned. Nearly a mile distant was the Longstone lighthouse, built on one of these rocky islets. On this island lived an old man, his wife, and daughter. There was usually a son, too, but he was at the herring fishery. Through the mist of the morning, by the help of a glass, old Darling saw the wreck; he saw the sufferers clinging. Shall we go? thought he. It seemed impossible. The sea was raging fearfully—the current was very strong, and who was there to help to pull the oar? At his side stood his brave daughter, not very tall, not very strong, but with a heart that could trust her God, and that longed to save the perishing creatures. "Father, let us go," she cries, and so the boat is launched, and the mother helps to set them off; and her anxious eye follows those she loved best, and her earnest heart prays God to speed her husband and her child. Grace had not been accustomed to the boat; her father or her brother had always managed it. But God watches from heaven, and He gives her strength and skill. They pull hard, they pull with all their might; the boat reaches the wreck, but a greater danger now awaits it. The billows heave—the boat grazes the rocks, once and again. How easily might it be overturned, or broken in pieces! Still, God protects. The poor mother of the two little children, though herself nearly dead, is removed into it. Then the passengers—one by one— all the nine are saved. The tide is now advancing, the waves becoming each minute stronger. Grace and her father could not, by themselves, have rowed back, but among the sufferers are men that help. God speeds the little boat. It is borne safely across the foaming billows; it has reached the lighthouse island. Is there not heard the voice of thanksgiving to Him who has protected them ? For two days the shipwrecked passengers remained on the little island, and Grace gave up her bed to the suffering woman, and nursed her with the kindest care. When the tale of the shipwreck was known, Grace Darling received many praises, many presents. High and low, all honoured her, but she never seemed to think anything of herself, and only wondered that people were so kind.

For about ten years she continued to live with her father and mother, at the Longstone Lighthouse. Then she became ill of consumption. She knew that she was dying, but was quite willing to depart, and to be with Jesus. She divided amongst her dear friends the presents that had been given her : and, as she grew weaker and weaker, her faith became stronger and stronger, until she was called from all the storms of life, to be safe in heaven's haven. Dear boys and girls, Grace Darling was neither strong, nor rich, nor learned, and yet you see how she served her fellow-creatures. Can you do nothing to assist poor people round you, and to help to bring dying souls to know that Jesus is the Rock of Ages, where only they can find salvation ?

Farther south are the ruins of a large castle, called Dunstanburgh. No one lives there now, excepting during the time when the little lambs are born. Then a shepherd and his dog live inside one of the thick walls. Is not a room in a wall a strange home ? To-morrow we must follow to its source the little river Alne.

NORTHUMBERLAND.—PART III.

You shall hear to-day more tales of the "borders," the name given to those parts of England and Scotland which border on one another. The Alne rises amongst the Cheviots, a range of hills separating the north-west of Northumberland from Scotland and Cumberland. They are famous for the sheep that feed amongst them, which in winter are often buried in the snow. I once saw one which was taken out alive, after being thirty days under the snow : it had eaten all the grass around it, and the wool off its back. The chief town in this wild district is Wooler. Near it is Flodden Field, where, in the reign of Henry VIII., a great battle was fought between the English and Scotch. James IV., the Scotch king, and a great number of his bravest nobility were killed. Not far distant is Chillingham Castle, a fine old place. Here you may see a stone, in the middle of which was found a live toad. In the park are wild cattle which have never been tamed. They are quite white, excepting the ears and tips of the horns, and are handsomely formed.

On this little river, the Alne, there stands an old town, Alnwick. Here the Duke of Northumberland lives in a grand old castle, with thick doorways and spacious courts. The old gates were called portcullises. Instead of shutting from the sides, they fell down from the top of the arches. On the top of the castle walls are strange stone figures ; some seem ready to throw a lance ; some have axes ; others are lifting stones. In this and other castles are deep, dark dungeons, where the unfortunate Scotch prisoners were sometimes thrown. Near Alnwick, one Scotch king, William, called the Lion because he was very brave, was taken prisoner, and another, called Malcolm, was killed. In the Duke's park there are the ruins of a curious old abbey, Hulne. The monks who built it, chose this situation because they thought the slope of the opposite hill, Brizlee, was like Mount Carmel, where they had lived in the Holy Land. At the top of

Brizlee is a high stone tower. Brizlee was one of the hills where, in former days, people used to light beacon-fires, when an enemy approached.* There were then no electric telegraphs, but there were watchers stationed on different heights, who each lighted his fire when he saw one blazing in the distance; and so the presence of an enemy was known for many miles. In the centre of Alnwick, is a curious old archway, which goes by the name of Harry Hotspur's Tower. Hotspur, a son of Lord Percy, was very brave, but very passionate. He fought a battle with King Henry IV. at Battle Field, near Shrews-bury, in Shropshire. The king dressed like a common soldier, and made several of his brave friends dress like the king. Can you tell me of any king of Israel who did the same thing?

Hotspur and other chieftains tried to fight with these mock-kings, and killed several of them. Thousands of Englishmen were slain. At last an arrow went through the brain of Hotspur; and when his friends saw that he was dead, they gave up fighting, and were conquered. This was called a civil war, because all the people who fought on either side belonged to one nation. Are you not glad that there is no civil war now? And won't you pray to God to help all the people in dear old England to keep good friends, and only to fight against what is evil and wicked?

I will tell you another curious story about Alnwick. West of this town is a great moor, in which there are many bogs and morasses.† Once, when King John was travelling across Northumberland, he got into a bog near Alnwick, where he stuck fast. He was very angry, not at his own stupidity, but with the townspeople, and said that no one should ever after have the advantages of free-men of Alnwick, unless they first went through this pond.

* Page 9.   † Page 7.

For hundreds of years this absurd law continued. On the 25th of April those, who wished to become freemen, were obliged to plunge through what was called the "Freeman's Well." Mischievous boys, of course, placed ropes under the water to trip them. But on they must go, head over heels, till, covered with mud, they reached the other side. Afterwards they had feasting: and a green tree was, for the day, placed in front of the doors of the new freemen. Only a very few years since, the people of Alnwick agreed the custom was a very foolish one, and that they would give it up.

The next river south of the Alne is the Coquet, which receives its name because its course is continually winding. It also rises amongst the wild moorlands of the Cheviots. The first small town on its banks is Rothbury —noted for its mild and fresh breezes.* Invalids often go there to breathe the air, and to drink goat's milk, the wild hills around forming pasture for these pretty animals. The waters of the Coquet are very clear, and there the trout jump all day long. You might fancy this is where—

> "Dear mother," said a little fish,
> "Pray is not that a fly?
> I'm very hungry, and I wish
> You'd let me go and try."

On its banks not far from the sea stands a pretty village, called Warkworth, crowned with a beautiful castle. The frontispiece shows you its picture. It is a ruin now. standing on a hill, round which the clear Coquet winds. Further up the river is Warkworth Hermitage, where there are three little rooms, cut out of the solid rock. The story is that a warrior made this his home. He had passionately killed by mistake a lady whom he loved very much; and to make amends for his sin, he determined to

* Page 7.

B

live quite alone in this rock. In one of the windows is roughly carved a lady, with an angel watching her. The hermit had a kitchen, with a wide chimney, so I suppose he kept himself warm, and had good fare. Warkworth, with its ruined castle, and high-spired church, and clear winding river, and curious hermitage, is, I think one of the prettiest places in England.

Opposite the mouth of the river is Coquet Island, where there is a lighthouse. This island used to be full of long-haired white rabbits, with red eyes. On the Ferne and Coquet islands, a number of sea-fowl lay their eggs,—such birds as gulls, and geese, and eider-ducks. The last are noted for the extreme softness of their feathers. Sea-fowls do not make their nests of wool, and hay, and moss, but of stones and sea-weed; and very often they make no nests at all. The eggs are not rounded like those of land birds, but pointed at one end to prevent them rolling.

The country between the Coquet and the Tyne is generally bare and bleak. On a little river, the banks of which can boast of more than one old castle, are Morpeth, the birthplace of Morrison, the Bible translator, and Blythe, a small port for shipping coal. To-morrow we will trace the Tyne, which partly separates Northumberland from Durham.

NORTHUMBERLAND.—Part IV.

THE largest river in Northumberland is the Tyne. It has two principal branches, called the North and South Tyne, which rise in the wild hilly moorlands of South-west Northumberland and East Cumberland, and unite above Hexham.

A railway passes along its banks, between the two large towns of Newcastle and Carlisle. Travelling along this railroad is very pleasant. You continually cross or follow the banks of the river; and you pass through woods, and see pretty castles. One of the peculiar beauties of Northumberland is its many old border castles.* Standing on some hills, you may count from seven to twelve within sight. Nearly on a line with this railway, are the remains of a very old and broad wall. It is called the Picts' Wall, because it was built by the Romans to protect them from the Picts and Scots, rude and savage tribes that lived in the North of Britain. The wall stretched from the Solway Frith to the Tyne. The place where it stopped is still called Wall's End, and is now chiefly famed for its colliery.

Amongst the wild and desolate hills, where the North Tyne and other rivers rise, is Chevy Chase, where very long ago was fought a bloody battle between the English and Scotch. It was not play-work then, as Chevy Chase is with boys now; nor was it song-work as the ballad is with Northumbrians at the present day. This is a verse of it—

> " To drive the deer, with hound and horn,
>   Earl Percy took his way ;
> The child may rue, who is unborn,
>   The slaughter of that day."

In the south-west of Northumberland are many lead mines, very valuable, especially now that a way of extracting silver from lead is discovered.

The first town to note on the Tyne is Hexham, where there is a beautiful church almost like a cathedral. In its windows was fixed the first glass used in England, and near it was fought a battle in which Margaret of Anjou was defeated.

Above Newcastle, on the Tyne, are villages, where are foundries for smelting and working iron. It is wonderful

* Pp. 9, 10, 11, 14, 15, 17, 18.

to see these great furnaces at night. You would think that the buildings were on fire; the flames rising high above the chimneys, and the sky quite red with the reflection of the light.

Newcastle is an extremely smoky town. There are so many collieries near it, (these are places where the coals are brought from below ground,) and in it so many manufactories of iron or glass, all having tall chimneys, from which smoke is poured forth in clouds, that the whole place seems to be in an atmosphere of smoke. The town is, however, in the new part extremely well built;—the streets, monuments, and public rooms are very handsome, and the markets, covered with stone and glass, amongst the finest in Europe. There is a very old castle here, which was built by Robert the son of William the Conqueror. It must have been then that the town got the name of Newcastle, which it still keeps. In this old castle are many strange things, once belonging to the Romans, which have been found under or near the Picts' wall.

The Northumberland Newcastle is always called Newcastle-on-Tyne, to distinguish it from a large town in Staffordshire, which has the name of Newcastle-under-Lyne. Across the Tyne is a splendid railway bridge, very, very high. On the top of the arches is a road for passengers and carriages, and above it is an iron road for the railway trains. Though Newcastle is so smoky, the people who live there like it very much, and talk about " canny Newcastle." Large flat-bottomed boats come up the river, called keels, to be filled with coals. The boatmen have a very favourite song, with a pretty tune, the chorus of which is—

" Weel may the keel row, the keel row, the keel row,"

which nearly all Northumberland people sing.

Near Newcastle are lead-works, where shot and bullets and various leaden things are made, and where silver is extracted from the molten lead. The shot, to be round, must fall through sieves at a great height; so the shot tower is made very high, and you see it far off. White lead, which is used in painting, is also made at these works; but they are so unwholesome, that the poor work-people seldom live long. At Newcastle the celebrated Armstrong guns are partly made. They can carry cannon-balls a distance of nearly five miles. Pleasanter works than these, for they speak of peace and not of war, are the Wylam Iron-works, which belonged to George and Robert Stephenson.* There, is shown the first moving steam-engine that ever drew a train. At Newcastle is the largest manufactory in England for these engines called locomotives. They are sent hence to France, and Russia, and Egypt, and India, and to all parts of the world.

From Newcastle to North Shields the river presents a lively scene—potteries, iron-works, wharves, shipbuilding, and collieries. The smoke and business thicken, as North and South Shields on the opposite sides of the river are approached. These two towns are connected by a steam ferry, into which boat you may drive, and if you choose, look out of the carriage window on the water below, and the many ships around. More vessels sail from the Tyne than the Thames, only they are not so large. It is very pleasant to see them passing, each drawn by a busy steam-tug. The little tug often draws a large three-masted ship; and even so, little children may do for themselves and others great things if they will but try. At the mouth of the river is Tynemouth, a pleasant bathing-place, where there is a great rock, on which are the ruins of a beautiful old priory. Monks once lived there, but now soldiers.

* Page 9.

When the north and east winds blow hard, the sea is very rough off Tynemouth rocks, and ships coming into the Tyne are often dashed to pieces. To see the cliffs crowded with the sailors' anxious wives and children, to watch the vessels driven onwards to destruction, to hear, perhaps, the sailors' cry, and to discover them clinging to the masts and rigging, and yet not to be able to help them, is indeed a sad sight. Another time you shall hear of the efforts made to improve the entrance of the river; and, after you have told me all you can remember about Northumberland, we will cross the Tyne and enter Durham.

———

The teacher will find it a good plan on the following day, to rehearse the various places that have been mentioned, tracing the rivers from the hills to the ocean, and talking about the towns and castles on their banks. The teacher might imagine meeting boats or ships, and make the children guess with what produce they may be laden, as, for instance, salmon in the Tweed, smaller trout or coals in the Coquet, iron, glass, coals, pottery-ware, etc., in the Tyne. This might be varied by taking the line of rail between Berwick and Newcastle, and leading the children to think of the various articles or people that may fill the trucks and carriages. Thus, at Berwick, salmon; between that place and Alnwick, Cheviot sheep and cows; at Alnwick and Warkworth, excursionists who have been viewing the castles, whilst, nearer to Newcastle trucks of coal should be added to the train.

Then the teacher might go along the Newcastle and Carlisle Railway, making the children think of what they would see, such as the river Tyne, bridges, castles, the abbey-church at Hexham, the iron-foundries, trucks of lead ore—of iron, of coal, of coke; as the train went westward, heathery hills, and the sportsman with his gun, and grouse, with here and there a peep of the Picts' wall. Or, again, there might be an imaginary sail, between the Tweed and the Tyne ;—Holy Island and the Ferne Islands viewed, the name of Grace Darling recalled, the sea-fowls observed, Bamborough, Dunstanborough, and Warkworth castles pointed out, the mouth of the Alne and Coquet passed, Coquet Island touched at, Tynemouth rocks and priory, marking the entrance of the Tyne, described.

These are merely suggestions, to make the recapitulation more interesting than a regular routine of question and answer.

DURHAM.—Part I.

On the south side of the Tyne lies the county of Durham. Though not nearly so large as Northumberland, more people live in it. There are not so many farmers, nor labourers who are called agriculturalists; but there are more colliers, more shipwrights,—that is, men who make ships,—more sailors, and more manufacturers. The roads in the county of Durham never look white, but are black with coal dust; and in the eastern districts, the trees and hedges are very sooty.

There are fine cliffs along the coast, especially those called the Marsden Rocks, and there are frequently tall, massive blocks standing solitary, a little distance from the shore. Inland, the country is very bleak and bare. There are, however, pretty valleys along the banks of the rivers. The grass grows richly along the lower course of the Tees; and the cattle feeding on it, called the "Durham Shorthorns," are reckoned the finest in the kingdom. In the west, there are desolate, hilly moors. If you were travelling through Durham, you would be most struck by the coal-pits; so I shall here give you the description of one.

DESCRIPTION OF A DURHAM COAL-PIT.

Above ground you see a tall chimney with a quantity of smoke pouring out, an engine-house where the steam-engine is very busy winding up the coal, low sheds, and large heaps of small coal. Sometimes these great heaps are on fire. Formerly, they used to light the country all round; but now the small coal is consumed in glass-houses and manufactories.

Coal-mine.

If you wanted to go down a shaft, that is, the hole of the pit, something like a very wide and long chimney, you would have to be dressed like a pitman, in wide begrimed trousers, loose flannel jacket, and round leather cap with a broad brim. Then you would have to get into a cage, or a basket, and keep your legs and arms very steady; and in four or five minutes, you may descend about a thousand feet, as deep as three St Paul's Cathedrals would be high.

At the bottom of the shaft or chimney, you meet passages, the walls of which are made of coal. There is generally one main passage, and several others turning right and left, like one long street, and small ones stretching away on either side. If you went down one of these, you would find it gradually get narrower and lower, till at length you reached the part where the hewers are, knocking the coal in lumps out of the face of the coal wall that is before them. They seem strange black-looking men, some kneeling, some stooping, some lying upon their backs, but all pick, picking away. It is, of course, quite dark, excepting the light from the lamps or candles which the men are burning. Baskets filled with the coals are placed on little trucks and moved along an underground railway to the bottom of the shaft. Little ponies, strong, but generally blind, draw these trucks, and boys, as young as ten or twelve years old, drive them. The pitmen generally fasten themselves very fast in the loop of a rope to be drawn up the shaft, and the men take the little boys on their knees, or hold them tight in their arms. Poor fellows, how seldom they see the sun, working down in the dark regions all day long.

The pitmen live in long straight rows of houses near the pits. They call them "Shiney Rows," and that in which the chief men of the pit live is known as "Quality Row." When the men reach home they wash themselves, and then sit down to their tea and "singing hinnies." Don't you think the wives should make the houses very comfortable, when their husbands have to work for them in such dark and dreary places?

Sometimes there are very sad accidents. The air in the pits becomes foul, or full of a gas which is called fire-damp. This easily catches fire, and makes a tremendous explosion. Some of the men are burnt, others suffocated, whilst some are killed by the falling in of the ground, or perhaps drowned, by the bursting of the wells of water. The noise of the explosion brings to the pit's mouth the wives of the poor men, feeling anxious lest their husbands should be killed. As the bodies are brought up, there is great weeping. Sometimes a poor woman may lose her husband and all her sons at once.

I will tell you the story of a little boy, who, with thirty-five men and forty-one boys, was, in consequence of one of these sad accidents, either starved or suffocated. He was found dead, with a Bible and a tin box at his side. Inside the box lid, he had, with a sort of nail, scratched these words, " Fret not, dear mother, for we are singing the praises of God, whilst we have time. Mother, follow God more than ever I did. Joseph, think of God, and be kind to poor mother."

The pitmen have generally large families. Many boys are great riches to a poor pitman, because, as soon as a boy is ten years old, he may work in the mines and get wages. Dear children, you may all be riches to your parents, if you bring them a good name on earth, and be like jewels for them to present to God in heaven.

Durham is a rich county, but its riches are all under ground, in these coal-mines and in the lead-mines that are worked in the west. It also produces a valuable hard sandstone used for grinding. Several things we use have probably come from the county of Durham. Perhaps the coals, perhaps the lead with which the spouts are lined; very probably the glass of the mirrors, and the glass of the window-panes too, if they are large ones. Then the soda that the washerwoman uses, or that the chemist sells for seidlitz powders; and magnesia for Gregory's Mixture.

Mustard for dinner is called Durham Mustard; but it really comes from York.

I must now tell you about some great and good people born in this county.

Have you heard of the brave Sir Henry Havelock, who feared God, but did not fear all the wicked mutineers in India, and marched up to Lucknow, to save the poor English there from ten thousands of their enemies? That brave Sir Henry was born near Sunderland.

At South Shields lived Mr Greathead, who invented lifeboats.

At a small village further up the Tyne, there lived a very long time ago, a little boy, of the name of Bede; he was an orphan, and when six years old was taken to a religious house to be educated. As he grew older, he learnt to read Latin; and then he loved to read the Bible, for, in those days, there were no English Bibles. He wrote several books; and when he was an old man, translated St John's Gospel into English. On the day he died, having finished its last sentence, he begged the young man who had written what he had dictated to support his head a little while. He soon sank to the ground, saying, "Glory be to the Father, and to the Son, and to the Holy Ghost!" Bede's tomb is in the cathedral of Durham, and he is always called "The Venerable Bede." His chair may still be seen at Jarrow, where he was born. With one more story about a good man, who had a parish in this county, in the time of Queen Mary, we must finish to-day's lesson. His name was Bernard Gilpin. He was a Protestant, loved the Bible, and worked very hard, preaching about Jesus in the North of England. The wicked Bishop Bonner heard of him, and threatened that he should be burnt in a fortnight.* So the judges sent for him to come

* Page 9.

to London. Gilpin used always to say, that whatever
happened was intended for good. As he travelled to
London, he broke his leg. Some that were with him said,
"Well, is this meant for your good?" He said, "I have
no doubt of it." And before his leg was better, a message
came down to say that Queen Mary was dead, and that he
was at liberty. Try always to trust God like good Bernard Gilpin.

DURHAM—Part II.

You know something about the Tyne on the north side.
We will now follow it on the Durham side. This little
river that runs into it is called the Derwent. The valley
through which it flows is very pretty. There are manufacturing villages all down the Tyne till you reach Gateshead. At one of these, very near Gateshead, wire ropes
are made and telegraph wires. Gateshead is a large town
immediately opposite Newcastle; the High Level Bridge,
of which I told you before, and another bridge, connecting
the two towns.* At Gateshead there are large soap-works
and glass manufactories, where the glass is cut, and where
the mirrors are polished that look so bright in drawing-
rooms. A few years ago, there was a very great fire in Gateshead. After it had burnt a little while, tremendous explosions took place. A building full of something like
gunpowder had taken fire. Every window in Gateshead
and Newcastle shook; many were broken; and all the
people were startled out of their beds. Then great burning pieces of timber fell in the streets, injuring many of
the people and setting fire to a great many more houses,
How the fire-engines did play, and the brave firemen work.
At last, through God's mercy, the fire was stopped. Some
parts of Newcastle and Gateshead are very dirty, and

* Page 20.

when the cholera has been in England it has been worse here than anywhere.

Further down the river is Jarrow, where the Venerable Bede lived. It is not now a place for study, but a busy, bustling town, where many ships are built, and where there are docks in which they are laden or unladen, sheltered or repaired.

The south side of the Tyne is as busy as the north side. A great deal of shipbuilding goes forward, and there are many manufactories. Below Jarrow is South Shields, which is even more smoky than Newcastle. A colliery is in the centre of the town, and many chimneys continually send forth clouds of smoke. The highest chimneys belong to the alkali or soda works, where soda is made from salt and sulphur and charcoal. The lower ones, wider at the bottom and narrowing upwards, belong to the glass works. Here it is that sand and flint are melted into glass. When these have been molten for a long time, the fiery liquid is poured into a caldron. This huge vessel is pushed on wheels along the dark stone passages, then raised on a hook and swung in the air till it is exactly at the proper place. Then it is turned over, and the red-hot glass is poured on iron tables surrounded with a rim as high as the glass is to be thick, to prevent the liquid from running over. After being smoothed, the glass is drawn into a hot place to cool. It must be hot at first, or it would get too quickly cold and would crack. In this way plate glass is made ; common glass is blown. The workmen seem half dried up with the heat. They wear thin woollen veils, lest the sparks should burn their eyes.

Along the banks of the Tyne, are mounds 200 or 300 feet high, formed of gravel and earth, brought from the bottom of the Thames, or from foreign places. Why is it brought, for it does no good there, and looks very unsightly ?

It is brought as ballast; something heavy to weigh down the ships instead of the coals that they take away. The ballast is thrown out, as much as 10,000 tons in a week, and the coal is taken in.

On each side of the Tyne, handsome stone piers are built, which makes the entrance of the river much safer for ships.

Now, we will leave the Tyne, and follow the course of the Wear. The first interesting place on its banks is Bishop Auckland, where the Bishop of Durham lives. Afterwards, we reach Durham. It is a curious old town, with very steep narrow streets. On the top of the banks are the beautiful cathedral, and the castle which is now used as a college. The cathedral is built of stone, and is very massive and grand-looking. Do you remember whose tomb is there?

Durham is not full of manufactories, like Shields and Newcastle. There are beautiful woods and gardens stretching down to the river side; and on the water there is a great number of skiffs. Once the Wear was on fire. Some gas escaped from the coal-mines below the river, through cracks in its bed. When this was found out, funnels were placed over the cracks, with pipes fastened to them long enough to reach the surface. These were lighted and brilliant flames burnt, thousands of people going to see the river on fire.

A great battle was fought at a place near Durham called Neville's Cross. It was between the English and Scotch.* Edward III. was away at the time; but when his brave queen heard that the Scotch king, David, was marching into England, she collected a small army, and went to meet him. After a hard-fought battle, David was wounded and made prisoner. It is said that before the

* Pp. 9, 15, 19.

battle began, the brave queen, Philippa, begged the soldiers to fight manfully, and then went to a quiet place, that she might pray for them.

Not far distant is Witton-Gilbert, where we read of the longest snow-storm ever known in England. It is more than two hundred years ago. It began to snow on January 5, and snowed, more or less, every day till March 12, causing both men and cattle to lose their lives.

Further down the Wear, which runs between prettily-wooded banks, is a ruined abbey, called Finchall, where very long ago, a foolish man, named St Godric, lived. Instead of enjoying the good things that God had kindly given him, he put himself to torture by wearing an iron shirt, eating bread mixed with ashes three or four months old, standing, during the cold winter, up to his neck in water to pray, and doing many other senseless things; imagining, like the poor Hindoos, that God was pleased to see him tortured. Below Finchall, is Chester-le-Street, with a fine old church and very curious monuments. It is supposed to have been a Roman station. Along the Wear are several castles; some inhabited by noblemen, and some in ruins. There are many collieries, and as the river approaches the sea, a great deal of shipbuilding. There are also manufactories for various things; such as paper, glass, copperas, and earthenware. At the mouth of the river is a large town called Sunderland, where there are glass-houses and potteries, and shipbuilding yards, and docks for ships, besides a great deal of commerce. Such towns are called commercial. A very handsome iron bridge, the second ever made in England, connects Sunderland with Monk-Wearmouth, an old town where there used to be a monastery.

Some of the little rivers which fall into the sea, south of the Wear, run through beautiful dells. One of these,

Castle Eden Dean, is extremely pretty; the deep glen, the over-hanging trees, and the brawling stream, making a very picturesque scene.

In the south, on the coast, is Hartlepool, another commercial town. Long, long ago, before commerce and steam were so busy, this town stood beside a pond, where the deer used to come and cool themselves; and so it was called Hart-le-pol, or, The Deer's Pond. In St Hilda's church, at Hartlepool, there is a fine old tomb, to the memory of some person unknown; perhaps a great warrior, or a beautiful lady, or a rich lord; but all forgotten now. Will you ask God to write your names in heaven? There they shall never be forgotten, for God has said, "Their names are continually before me."

The river, which separates Durham from Yorkshire, is called the Tees. It rises in Cumberland. As it leaves the dreary moorland, it rushes over great precipices, looking very grand, and forming two beautiful waterfalls—the Caldron Shoot, and the High Force. The Caldron Shoot is a succession of precipices, over which the water rushes and foams, seeming in haste to escape from its former desolate region, to the prettier one beyond. The High Force is nearly perpendicular. You may there stand on the rock, which divides the river in the centre, and see the water come foaming and splashing on each side of you. High rocks form the river banks. They are covered with beautiful old oak-trees, and elegant mountain-ashes. When the sun shines, it forms rainbow colours on the spray that rises very high. Is not God kind to make so many pretty scenes in our native land?

The first town on the Tees is Barnard Castle. Here, there are beautiful ruins of an ivy-covered castle. Along the banks of the river are mills for spinning thread. On a little stream, which joins the Tees from the north, is Darlington. There are several small manufactories here for carpets and linen, and fairs for all sorts of cattle, and a large railway station. Further along the Tees are pretty villages, such as Dinsdale and Middleton, where there are iron waters, which invalids drink to strengthen themselves. Stockton is a well-built commercial town, whence ships take away coal, iron, and the various things manufactured in the neighbourhood. Between Stockton and Darlington, the second railway made in England was constructed.

Now my relation of the somewhat grimy, but very useful county of Durham is over, I shall look to you to tell me, to-morrow, of its coal-pits, manufactures, and scenery.

These chapters may be revised by tracing the rivers from their sources, or by coasting the county from the Tyne to the Tees.

In tracing the Tyne, part of the old lesson on Northumberland should not be forgotten. The shipbuilding going forward on all the rivers of Durham, must be especially mentioned; as it may be termed the characteristic of the rivers of that county.

The journey along the railroad may also be followed, as in the county of Northumberland.

Again, the children might imagine they were visiting the county under different characters. One party as archæologists, fond of old remains; the second as mineralogists, engaged in mines; the third, as commercial men, inquiring into the manufactories, &c.; and the fourth, as tourists, in search of picturesque scenery. In this case, the archæologist would endeavour to search out the old monastery at Jarrow; especially notice the cathedral and castle at Durham; Venerable Bede's tomb, his chair, &c.; Neville's

Cross; Finchall Abbey; Barnard Castle; St Hilda's at Hartlepool; and, though not exactly a subject for archæology, the rectory of Houghton-le-Spring, good Bernard Gilpin's home, might be pointed out.

The mineralogists would descend the coal-mines, each child mentioning something he remembers. They would likewise visit the lead-mines in the west.

The commercial men would order goods from the glassworks at Sunderland, South Shields, or Gateshead: from the potteries, at these several places; the alkali or soda-works, at South Shields; the telegraph and wire roperies, at Gateshead; they would order linen from Darlington, and thread from the banks of the Tees. They must arrange concerning transit at the railway stations (point on the map) and at the sea-ports, South Shields, Sunderland, Hartlepool, and Stockton.

The tourists would delight to visit the Tees in its upper course; they would also see Durham, situated so beautifully on the steep banks of the Wear, and not forget the precipitous cliffs of Marsden rocks, and the beauties of Castle Eden Dean.

All might unite as biographers of the great and good, and recall the names of Sir Henry Havelock, Greathead, Bede, and Gilpin.

YORKSHIRE.—PART I.

WE have now come to the largest county in all England —great, big Yorkshire. It is as large as half-a-dozen of the central counties. There are seven counties touching Yorkshire. You remember Durham with its coal-mines; and here is pretty little Westmoreland, and manufacturing Lancashire, about which I shall soon tell you; and here is Cheshire, the county for cheeses; and Derbyshire; and

Nottinghamshire, the county like an egg; and this large county on the coast, Lincolnshire. On the east, it has the same wide sea, the German ocean, as washes the coasts of Northumberland and Durham.

Several large rivers run through Yorkshire, making a great part of the county very fertile. They rise amongst the mountains in the west, and generally run south-'east to join the Ouse. This unites with other long rivers from the middle of England, such as this one, the Trent; and they together all form the broad Humber, on which many ships continually sail.

The west of Yorkshire is very mountainous. Some of the highest mountains of England's backbone, which you may trace from the Cheviots * to Derbyshire, are there; and through them are cut the longest railway tunnels in all England; and across one of them passes the highest railway. These mountains are formed of limestone; and there are in them most wonderful caverns, of which I shall tell you soon.

There are some tarns, or large mountain-ponds, amongst them; but no beautiful lakes, as in Cumberland and Westmoreland. Some of the bases or bottoms of these mountains are very wide, that of Ingleborough being thirty miles round. In the north-east of Yorkshire, nearer the sea, there are likewise considerable hills and moorlands, where the weather is very cold. These hills stretch quite to the sea between Flamborough Head and the mouth of the Tees, and form a splendid bold coast. There is a place near Whitby called Stoupe Brow, where the cliff is nearly 900 feet high. How far can you walk along the road in three minutes? Then fancy that distance straight up like the wall of a house.

There are two capes on the coast of Yorkshire—Flamborough Head and Spurn Head. Flamborough Head, or

* Page 15.

the head with a flame, so called on account of the beacon-fire that used to burn there, is very high, and formed of brilliant white chalk ;* whilst Spurn Head is a low ridge of sand and shingle, tapering to a point. The sea washes away every year about two yards and a half of the shore all the way between Bridlington Bay and Spurn Head, and then it washes back all this soil into the Humber; so that some land, called Sunk Island—which, 200 years ago in the reign of Charles I., was a mud bank in the middle of the river—now forms a part of the land, and is covered with corn-fields and meadows, farm-buildings and cottages, and in the midst there is a church.

The part of Yorkshire between the western hills and the eastern moorlands, is generally full of valleys and green fields. From the west flow the Swale, the Ure, the Wharfe, the Nidd, the Aire, and the Don. Can you trace them on the map? The country between them is frequently flat. In Yorkshire, we find the largest vale in England. It is called the vale of York, and is about sixty miles in length. It is full of beautiful green fields, and hedgerows with fine tall trees. Though there are many pretty cottages, and the quiet wandering rivers look like strings of silver, the scenery is not grand, and if you lived there, you would, I think, long to see high hills and to run down steep slopes. In the south-west of Yorkshire the country is very beautiful, with wooded hills, valleys, and rivers. Altogether, Yorkshire is one of the finest counties of England, as well as the largest. It is divided into three parts—called the North, the East, and the West Ridings. The North-Riding stretches from the county of Westmoreland to the sea. The west is a very large division, from the mountains to the Ouse; and the east contains all the rich, flat land from

* Page 16.

the Humber in the south, to* the Derwent in the north.

In the east of Yorkshire, a great deal of corn is grown; and in thê west, the fields are principally pasture, where you would see many long-horned cattle and horned sheep too.* In some parts of Yorkshire, you would see fields covered with a plant, having a beautiful blue flower in July, and afterwards a head of silky seeds. This is flax, of which linen is made. Near York, are large fields of a yellow flower—mustard;† and there are also fields of another yellow flower—teasel, which is used in dressing cloth for jackets. A great many very thin cattle are brought into Yorkshire, every year, from Scotland, and sold to the farmers, who soon fatten them on their rich grass, and then sell them to the butchers, in Leeds, Sheffield, Manchester, and all the many manufacturing towns. A great number of beautiful horses are reared in the north and east of the county. There is, too, a busy, useful little insect, that you would often see; I mean the busy bee,

" Gathering honey all the day
From many an opening flower."

The oak-trees are not large, but the wood is very hard and good. Little and good, is better than much and bad It is almost all made into butter firkins.

In some parts of this county, a great deal of coal is found; but not so good as in Northumberland and Durham. There are also iron and lead, and stone for building, and a kind of blue clay, which makes beautiful white brick; near Whitby is found alum, a useful white mineral, and jet, which makes very pretty black ornaments.

Amongst the clay and gravel, near the east coast of Yorkshire, have been found curious fossils of enormous

* Pages 8, 23. † Page 27.

animals, with teeth ten inches round, and a great many fossil-shells and snake-stones. Beautiful crystals have also been discovered.

Now we must think of some of the things that you use, which have probably come from Yorkshire, for, in many parts, it is a busy, manufacturing county. At one town, Sheffield, rough iron is turned into knives, scissors, tools, nails, and scythes; and there, too, tea-pots, coffee-pots, dish-covers, and many articles of metal covered over with silver, called plated goods, are made. At another town, Leeds, and at Bradford, and several other places, you would find large manufactories full of people and machines making woollen goods, particularly cloth for little boys' jackets, stuffs for their sisters' frocks, shawls, blankets, and many other comfortable things. It has been said of Yorkshire, that it clothes one-third of civilised men in wool, and finds them in files and penknives. It furnishes our ward-robes, our dinner-tables, and our armouries. Now look round this room and think what may have come from Yorkshire. Is there anything in Johnny's pocket or in Amy's work-box? Anything that Charlie or Mary wears?

The people in Yorkshire are generally strong in body, and hearty, independent and sensible in their ways. They are fond of making money, and think a great deal of their beautiful large county. They have good wages and good food. They are not so polite and polished as the people farther south, and have generally a very ugly tone of voice. In some parts, they talk something like the Dutch, according to the following rhyme :—

> " Gooid brede, botter, and cheese,
> Is gooid Yorkshire and gooid Friese."

This refers to Friesland, a part of Holland.

There have been many famous men born in this county

—such as Captain Cook, who sailed all round the world; Miles Coverdale, who translated the Bible into English; Wycliffe, the great and good reformer; and others, about whom I will tell you, when we come to the towns where they were born.

There are many beautiful churches and old ruined abbeys. Indeed, I think if Northumberland is the county for castles,* Yorkshire is for churches and abbeys. But I fancy you have heard quite enough of great Yorkshire for one day; or the account to-morrow will be large and bad, instead of little and good.

YORKSHIRE.—Part II.

THE most interesting way of learning about Yorkshire, will be to follow its beautiful rivers from the mountains to the sea. You know the name of the river that separates it from Durham, and you can remember about the fine waterfalls in the upper part of its course. As we follow it on the Yorkshire side, we find the scenery wild and beautiful, and we pass two celebrated places—Rokeby and Wycliffe. Sir Walter Scott has written a long poem about Rokeby, and described its pretty scenery and old abbey; and Wycliffe is said, by some, to be the birthplace of the good reformer, John Wycliffe, who translated the Bible into English, and is called the Morning Star of the Reformation. Why? Because he lived some time before Luther, who was like its sun; he shone when all was in Popish darkness round about, and he was a forerunner of the brighter light.

Wycliffe's Bible was not printed or spelt like ours. The printing was in black letter. Can you read the Lord's Prayer as it was then written :—

* Pages 9, 19.

" Our Fadir that art in hevengs; halewid be thi name.
Thy kingdom come to, be thi wil done in the erthe as in hebene.
Gibe to us this day oure breede obir othir substance.
And forgibe to us our dettis as we forgibe to our detteris.
And lede us not into temptacion; but delyber us from ybel.
Amen."

A small town on the south bank of the Tees is Croft,
with mineral waters, and another is Yarm, where many
cheeses are sold. Between the eastern mountains and
the Tees is a beautiful fertile valley, called the Vale of
Cleveland.

Here is Marton, where Captain Cook was born. He
was born in a poor little cottage, with only two rooms,
and was taught to read by the mistress, in whose service
he was. Her name Mary Walker is on one of the tombstones of the little churchyard. How little she thought
that the poor child to whom she was so kind, would become so celebrated a navigator.

Another place on the Tees is Middlesborough, which has
grown large all at once, where thousands of tons of iron,
dug from the Cleveland hills, are smelted, so that the pure
iron is separated from the iron ore.

In this neighbourhood is Rosebury Topping, a famous
hill, from which we may look, for the last time, into old
Northumberland; it was in this district that Robert the
Bruce, the famous Scottish king, was born.

Now, let us return to the mountains, and find the
Swale, the next river south of the Tees. Between it and
the Tees is Mickle Fell, the highest mountain in Yorkshire, 2600 feet. You do not see the sea from this mountain ; but the view is very fine—the lake mountains in the
west—the valleys opening to receive the Yorkshire rivers—
the Cleveland hills far away to the east, and all round by

the south-west the massy mountains of Penyghent, Whernside, and Ingleborough.

Following the Swale, after passing many lead mines, we reach Richmond. This is an old town, with an old castle, very famous for its beautiful situation. It was built in William the Conqueror's time, by Alan the Red. Here King Arthur and his knights are said to be asleep, in some mysterious room, waiting till a great peril of England shall awaken them.

Further down the river is Catterick, to which the Romans gave the dreadfully long name of Catteractorium.

Further down, on a branch of the river, you see Northallerton marked. About three miles from this is a hill called Standard Hill, where the Yorkshire men fought a great battle with David, king of Scotland. The bishops, in those days, were often soldiers; and a very warrior-like bishop, called Thurston, led the army. To encourage the men, Thurston had mounted upon wheels a great pole headed with a cross, and from it hung three large standards of three celebrated saints. The Scotch king and his soldiers were afraid when they saw this, and were quite defeated—10,000, it is said, being killed. This was called the Battle of the Standard.*

Below Northallerton is Thirsk, a good-sized town. These are all agricultural towns, more celebrated for their markets than for their manufactures.

At last the Swale joins the Ure, and the two form the Ouse, at a small town, Boroughbridge. Near to it stand three enormous stones, eighteen and twenty feet high. They are called the Devil's Arrows, because a foolish story says he shot them to destroy a city. They were probably placed there by the early Britons, though we wonder how, in their savage state, they were able to move such immense stones.

Now, we must return to the next river we see in the

* Pages 9, 15, 19, 30.

north-west of Yorkshire ; it is the Ure, and flows through a beautiful valley called Wensleydale. Near its source are desolate moors* and wild leaping waterfalls. Below one of these, during a very hard frost, the water froze. The spring from above, continued supplying it with water, which formed a cone that rose higher and higher, till at last it was as high as a church steeple, and thirty yards round at the bottom—an icy pyramid. These moors are so large that the many-scattered sheep appear very few.

At an old village in this wild country, a horn is still blown during winter at ten o'clock at night. It used to be a signal for benighted travellers in the forests, to know where they might find a shelter.

On the banks of the Ure are ruins of old castles and abbeys. At Bolton Castle, the unfortunate Mary, Queen of Scotland, was a prisoner. Below it is Coverdale, where Miles Coverdale, who translated and printed the Bible, in the reign of Henry VIII., was born.

The Ure soon rushes over a great waterfall, Aysgarth Force. The view of the foaming water, and the bridge stretching over from the rock on either side, is very beautiful.+

We may now follow the Ure for some distance, during which the narrow glen widens into an extensive fertile valley, till we come to Ripon. Here there is a cathedral, built about 700 years ago. Under it are chambers called catacombs, where the bones and skulls of the dead are curiously preserved and arranged. At Ripon, at nine o'clock every night, a horn is blown three times at the Mayor's door, and again at the Market Cross. This has been done ever since the time of Alfred the Great, or for 1000 years.

About three miles from Ripon are the ruins of one of the most beautiful abbeys in England, called Fountain's

* Pages 7, 23.   + Page 32.

Abbey. The first monks were very poor, and lived under some straw thatching placed amongst the branches of seven yew trees, eating at times boiled leaves of trees and wild plants. It is said that once when the monks had only two loaves and a half of bread, a stranger asked for food. The

Fountain's Abbey.

abbot or chief said, " Give him one loaf, God will provide for us ; " and soon a cart-load of bread arrived, sent by a neighbouring baron. Afterwards rich people left the monks a great deal of money, and then they built the beautiful abbey and lived on rich fare.

Now we may follow the Ure to Boroughbridge, where the great stones are, and you must tell me with what river it there unites.

Now return to the next river, south of the Ure. It is called the Nidd. I shall only tell you of one place on its banks, the old town of Knaresborough, with houses on the steep hill-side, the door-steps of one being as high as the chimney-tops of another. There is, above them all, a fine old ruined castle. The great curiosity of Knaresborough is the Dropping Well. Near the beautiful river is a limestone rock, thirty feet high; over this water constantly drops. This water is full of particles of lime, with which it incrusts whatever is placed below, so that plants, birds' nests, twigs, and all kinds of things, seem, in a few weeks, to be petrified or turned to stone.

Near this is a chapel, called St Robert's, with hideous faces carved on the wall, and outside the door an immense stone figure, drawing a sword. A mile off is St Robert's Cave, where a frightful murder was committed more than a hundred years ago; but after thirteen years, discovered by the providence of God. The wicked murderer, Eugene Aram, a schoolmaster, was an extremely clever man, wrote poetry, was a good· historian, understood botany, and had studied a number of languages; but you know a clever head does not make a good heart, and the love of money led him to this frightful sin.. Do you remember a verse in the Bible about the love of money?

Enough for to-day; but we still. have more rivers in great Yorkshire to trace.

YORKSHIRE.—Part III.

BEFORE we search the source of the next river, we must visit the large ancient and celebrated city which stands on the Ouse, between the Nidd and the Wharfe. It is York, the county town of Yorkshire. It is one of the very oldest towns in England; there was a little collection of huts, where British chieftains lived, even before the Romans came. When the Romans took possession of England, they made York their capital town. Here two of their emperors died, and it is said to have been the birthplace of the famous Constantine the Great. York has a very old castle, and an exceedingly grand cathedral, reckoned the finest in England.* Its towers are so high, its arches so many, its clustered pillars so elegant, and its windows so beautiful, that everybody admires it; and we are glad that a place so magnificent is for the best of uses, the worship of God. Twice, however, within the last fifty years, it has been very nearly burnt down—once by a madman, to make himself famous, and another time by the carelessness of a workman. What untold harm, foolishness and carelessness will often cause!

The old castle of York is now used as a jail.† In King John's time, some hundreds of Jews were barbarously shut up in this castle, that the wicked king might extort their money, and when they would not give it up, it is said, he ordered the only well in the castle to be poisoned, so that they all died. There is a beautiful ruined abbey, St Mary's, and the remains of an old hospital, but many years ago these ruins were used as a quarry, and the stones were taken away to build houses, and great heaps were burnt in a lime-kiln. Near the city are several battlefields; Stamford Brig, where King Harold conquered the King of Norway, just before he went to Hastings to be conquered by the Duke of Normandy; Marston Moor, where Prince Rupert, leading King Charles's army, was defeated; and Towton, the scene of one of the bloody battles of the Roses.

The city is surrounded by walls, which were first built in the time of the Romans. These have four bars or gates.

Who *do* you think was born near York? Guy Fawkes.

Etty, a celebrated painter, and Flaxman, a famous sculptor, were also born here, besides other distinguished people.

The Wharfe, the next river that we reach, has a much longer course to run than the Nidd. It rises far away in

* Page 30.　　† Compare castles, pp. 10, 11, 15, 20, 30.

the west, in the great mountain of Ingleborough. And now, before I tell you any more about the river, you shall hear of some splendid caverns that are found in the side of this hill. Some of them have strange names, such as Cat-Knot-Hole, Long Churn, Dicken Pot. The first I will describe is Weathercote Cave, in the pretty valley of Chapel-le-Dale. You go down a rough flight of steps into a narrow rocky chasm, covered with ferns and mosses; you pass a spring, which, like the dropping-well at Knaresborough, turns the moss to stone; and soon you see, at the farthest end, a white column of water rushing and roaring over the rock, eighty feet high. You cannot see the sky, for the bushes on the top of the narrow crevice meet. The water is swallowed up in the bed of pebbles on which it falls. Would you like to wander along that dark cave, and hear the tremendous roar of the foaming waterfall?

But now you shall hear of the still more famous cave of Ingleborough, through which you may go half a mile into the centre of the mountain. It is near the little village of Clapham.

The entrance is a low wide passage that gradually becomes narrower. The guide gives each person a lighted candle, and unlocks an iron gate, which is the entrance of a cavern, called "The Inverted Forest," for all the vegetation grows down instead of up; immense fungi hanging from the roof. Then is reached a narrow passage cut through a wall of stone, which divides the old from the new cave; the inside one being called new, having been discovered only a few years. As one enters it, it appears almost like a fairy palace. The walls are of snowy whiteness, and over the ground are spread white mounds, which seem to glitter as with millions of diamonds.

Beyond this is a wider cavern, called Pillar Hall. Here

thousands of the white crystals, called stalactites, hang from the roof; others grow upwards from the floor. At length, owing to the constant trickling water, the ends meet, and form the beautiful crystal pillars, some of which are fantastically twisted. Frequently, where there is a thin long crack in the roof, the stalactite looks like a curtain suspended gracefully in this fairy hall. Some are like a bee-hive; one of the largest, called the Jockey Cap, is supposed to have taken 259 years to reach its present size. Little drops of water full of grains of lime form these beautiful things; and, in like manner, may not little children take their tiny share in doing things that are beautiful, because they are good?

Farther on is a low, narrow passage, through which, with the help of a scrubbing-brush to keep the hand from the slippery rock, the visitor is obliged to creep. Thus is entered the "Cellar Gallery," a long sort of tunnel, with no pretty stalactites shining. This, however, leads to the Giant's Hall, with its lofty roof, and the stalactites and curtains hanging as before. On one side you may look down two holes, at the bottom of one of which is a deep pool, into which water is ever falling. A gentleman once swam across this dark little lake, but it was all wall at the other side; he could go no farther. The noise of the waterfall, plunging night and day, in the deep darkness, is said to be very awful. Yet, would you not like to see those fairy caverns, and to peep down those dark holes?

The other chief mountains in this part of Yorkshire are Whernside and Penyghent. There are both a Great and Little Whernside, one being 300 feet less than the other.

Now, let us descend the Wharfe, with its savage, wild, and beautiful scenery. There are more cliffs and crags on its banks than on any of the other rivers.

Here Bolton Abbey stands. Have you ever seen Landseer's beautiful picture of this abbey in the olden time, with the old monks receiving all kinds of provision,— venison, game, fish?

The story of the lady who built Bolton Abbey is a very sad one. She was a widow with two sons. The elder died, and the younger, Romilly, the Boy of Egremont, for he was born at that town in Cumberland, was the only hope of his poor mother. A little above the Abbey is a part of the river called "The Strid," because it is so narrow that people can stride across it. Here the water rushes madly and impetuously between the high rocks. Poor Romilly tried to cross this one day—his greyhound pulled him back—he fell, and perished in the stream.

> "And the lady pray'd in heaviness,
> That look'd not for relief,
> But slowly did the succour come,
> And a patience to her grief."

In remembrance of this unfortunate son, she built the beautiful priory, the ruins of which still stand. There is, also, a pretty story about the White Doe, of which Wordsworth wrote in sweet poetry. It is said, the poor little white doe regularly came from Rylstone, over the hills, on Sundays, during service, and wandered gently and timidly among the tombstones. Not far from Bolton is Skipton Castle, which once belonged to the Shepherd Lord Clifford, so-called, because for twenty-five years he lived in the savage valley of Borrowdale.

Between the Wharfe and the Nidd lies Harrogate, where is a famous well for medicinal water. It tastes and smells of rotten eggs and sulphur. The Wharfe continues its beautiful course, passing Tadcaster, where there are famous Roman ruins, and then enters the Ouse a little above Selby, a small town, with a very beautiful church.

Leaving the more picturesque part of Yorkshire, we shall to-morrow travel to the manufacturing districts.

YORKSHIRE.—Part IV.

IN the very west of Yorkshire, is a fertile district called Craven, through which the Ribble flows, before it enters Lancashire, passing westward to the Irish Sea. There are beautiful cliffs in this district, and a very fine waterfall, called Gordale Scar. The principal town is Settle.

Now we must again follow the rivers running east. At the foot of one of the grandest cliffs, from a low, flat arch, the Aire rushes out, clear as crystal, very different from what it is after passing Bradford and Leeds. Very soon, the manufacturing towns and villages begin. Keighley is one of the first. Then comes Shipley, near which is Saltaire, a model town built by Sir Titus Salt. The houses are built so as to make the work-people comfortable, cleanly, and healthy. There is no public-house; but there is a chapel for the worship of God, and a hall for music and lectures. The manufactory is like a palace, and the chimney, of immense height, is quite ornamental. 30,000 yards of stuff for dresses can be made there in one day. The machinery is beautiful; if you saw it at work, you would almost fancy the iron was alive and thinking.

The principal town for stuff manufactories is Bradford, and for broad-cloth Leeds, nine miles distant. The Bradford and Leeds people are each anxious that *their* town should be the greatest; and if a new institution is built in one place, a similar one is built in the other. Besides the people employed at the looms, many are engaged in

D

dyeing. It is curious to pass through some of the neigh-bouring villages, and see the people with blue arms and legs. The factory men often wear long pinafores from the throat to the foot, to keep off the fluff that blows about from the wool. Much of the cloth is woven in the poor people's cottages. The rooms up-stairs are filled with the looms, whilst those below are for cooking and sleeping. Though they have not much furniture, there is often a mahogany chest of drawers and an eight-day clock. In Leeds about 50,000 people are employed in manufactories. There are railways and canals, besides the river, by which to send off the woollen and linen goods. The town is generally smoky, and has many chimneys. There is a very large school for 400 ragged children, with a large dining hall, and sleeping rooms for many of them.

Now leaving the Aire for a little while, we must follow the course of the Calder, a small river that joins it. The first large town near the Calder that we reach is Halifax, like Leeds, full of woollen cloth manufactories. Here there is the largest carpet factory in England. Halifax is one of the largest parishes in Great Britain, about 150,000 people living in it.

Further on is Batley, a place famous for making "shoddy." "What is shoddy?" I daresay you inquire. It is a kind of cloth made out of old clothes. Perhaps you wear shoddy; for many gentlemen's topcoats and ladies' Linseys are made of it, but fine broad-cloth is not shoddy. Old clothes are sent to Batley from all parts of Europe; soldiers' coats and monks' gowns, worsted stock-ings and tattered scarecrows. Tremendously powerful machines pull them all to pieces, then the fibres are drawn out, then they are woven, and frequently dyed. Shoddy is also made at Dewsbury, which, perhaps, you will see on the map. Huddersfield, not far distant, is a well-built town, where a number of dresses, partly wool, partly silk, and partly cotton, are woven.

On the Calder is the churchyard where Robin Hood's grave is shown; and further down is Wakefield, a well built town with a famous old church. This town is for farmers as well as for manufacturers, as here there is one of the largest corn markets in the kingdom. Near Wakefield was fought a battle during the wars between the houses of York and Lancaster.* Below the junction of the Calder and Aire, we find another town, Pontefract or Pomfret. Its castle still stands, where the unhappy Richard II. was murdered. There is a famous liquorice manufactory here, the plant being grown in surrounding gardens. Have you ever tasted Pomfret cakes,—small liquorice lozenges, with a castle stamped on them ?

Now, having told you of the chief woollen manufactories in Yorkshire, we will follow the Don, its most southern river, with the smaller streams that flow into it. Near a northern branch of it is Barnsley, where the chief manufactories are for linen goods, such as towels, sheetings, and damask table-cloths. Several collieries are near it, where the most fearful explosions have been. The worst that ever occurred was in 1866, when nearly 350 strong workmen found a grave in the deep coal-pit, and about 20 brave men, who sought to rescue them, perished too. On the Don is a very large town, Sheffield, full of smoking chimneys and of noisy hammers. Can you remember what is made at Sheffield ? If you look at one of the table-knives, you will possibly see the name of Rogers, Sheffield. Some of the cutlery made there is reckoned the finest in the world. It requires intense heat and great care to convert iron into steel; and it

* Page 45.

is wonderful to think how a little bit of coarse iron can
become a valuable blade of steel. The iron of which
steel is made comes from Sweden. Chantrey, the famous
sculptor, and Montgomery, the Christian poet, belonged to
Sheffield. Very probably you know one of Montgomery's
pretty hymns—

> " Prayer is the soul's sincere desire,
> Uttered or unexpressed,
> The motion of a hidden fire
> That trembles in the breast."

There is another large town further down the river,
Rotherham, where there are large iron and chemical works;
and below it again is Doncaster, in which are only a few
manufactories. Doncaster is a very healthy town, and
beautifully situated. One of its churches is particularly
handsome, and there is an excellent institution for teaching
the deaf and dumb children of Yorkshire. You see, towns
are very thick in the south-west of Yorkshire. They are
growing larger every day. During the last ten years more
than 300,000 people have been added to the population of
the West Riding; and the quantity of woollen goods they
manufacture has very much increased.

Now I will make a list of the manufacturing towns we
have mentioned to-day :—Keighley, Shipley, Saltaire, Bradford, Leeds, Halifax, Batley, Dewsbury, Huddersfield, Wakefield, (look back and see what kind of woollen fabric is made
at each town.)—Barnsley, famous for linen, with collieries
near it; Sheffield and Rotherham, for iron goods. You must
try and get these hard names woven into your young heads.

YORKSHIRE.—Part V.

We have still a large portion of Yorkshire to talk about,
so you may expect a long chapter. We must trace this river,
the Derwent, that joins the Ouse from the north-east; and
then we must suppose that we sail down the Humber, and

along the Yorkshire coast northwards to the mouth of the Tees. The Derwent rises only a few miles from the coast; but though "rivers to the ocean run," they cannot run up hill; and so, if you look on the map, you will see the Derwent has to run many miles before it reaches the sea. On one of its little branches is Kirby Moorside, where the once witty and wealthy Duke of Buckingham died, not in a grand palace, but in a little cottage. He had loved the world, and forgotten God; and when he came to die in what has been described as the " worst inn's worst room," uncared for and uncomforted, he felt the wretchedness of the choice he had made. Near this is Kirkdale, where, in digging a quarry, the workmen discovered a cave, the floor of which was covered with dried mud. In this mud were found the bones of all kinds of animals—elephants, hippopotami, horses, tigers, bears, wolves, oxen, deer, hares, rabbits, mice, larks, ducks. From this we know that many thousand years ago, hyenas, tigers, and elephants must have lived in dear old England. I could tell you of several more old abbeys and castles; but I am sure you would forget their names. There is one beautiful old ruin, Rivaulx Abbey, on the banks of the Rye, a branch of the Derwent. It is covered with ivy, and is beautifully situated in a narrow dale.*

The Derwent flows through a pretty green fertile country, but there are no large towns upon its banks—no coal-mines—no tall smoking chimneys. It enters the Ouse just opposite the Aire, and their united waters form the Humber. A little below this junction is Goole, a seaport town, where there are large docks.† These are safe homes for ships, when they return from their voyages, and where they can be loaded and unloaded. Goole is at the entrance of a canal, that is cut across England, connecting the Humber with the Mersey.

* Pages 15, 31, 39, 42, 45, 48.   † Pages 29, 31.

The Humber is a very broad river, almost like a part of the sea, only the waters are earthy coloured instead of sea-green. The largest town that stands on it is Kingston-on-Hull, always called Hull, the name of the little river which here enters the Humber. It is a busy, but melancholy-looking town, perhaps because it is on a dead level and somewhat dingy in colour. Etty, the painter, used to say it was memorable for "mud and train-oil." This was when a great many of its ships sailed to Greenland to catch whales. Now, most whale-ships sail from Peter-head, in Scotland. From Hull are sent cotton and woollen and hardware goods to all parts of the world, whilst, into Hull, ships bring iron for Sheffield, wool for Leeds, rags for Batley, cattle and corn, oil, bones, German yeast, and annually about £100,000 worth of children's toys, including fifteen tons of boys' marbles.

Here William Wilberforce, the good man who persuaded Parliament to set the poor negroes free, was born; and from Hull, according to the famous story, Robinson Crusoe set sail.

The south-east part of Yorkshire is called Holderness. It is a district flat and fat. It is quite level, but the soil is so rich that everything grows abundantly Once it was, in many parts, an unwholesome, useless swamp, but now the land has been well drained. There was discovered under the water an old forest of all sorts of trees, which must have been buried there for very many years.

On the north of Holderness is Beverley, an ancient town, where there stands a very beautiful minster. Amongst the many interesting stories of this neighbour-hood, is the account of a meeting between Paulinus and Coifi, which took place in one of its green forests, in the presence of Edwin, the Saxon king of Northumberland, and his queen, Ethelburga. Paulinus, the Christian missionary, spoke for Christianity; whilst Coifi, the

Saxon high-priest, defended Paganism. Coifi was convinced; and mounting the king's charger, with a spear in his hand, he rode to the principal temple, hurled his spear into the image, sent it quivering to the ground, whilst his followers broke down the wall, and set the building on fire. Such, according to story, was the end of Paganism in Northumbria.*

Leaving the Humber, we must round Spurn Head. Is it a high or low promontory? Here there used to stand a town, Ravenspur. It was once so large that it sent members to Parliament, and was the landing-place of Henry IV. But it is all swept away and gone; the advancing waves covering it. Other villages are gone or going.

Towards Bridlington, the clay cliffs cease and chalk ones appear. These being harder, resist the sea better, and so the land stretches out into the noble promontory of Flamborough Head.† Bridlington is a pleasant, quiet bathing place, with a church that once was almost as beautiful as Beverley minster. Pleasant excursions may be taken from Bridlington, in small boats round Flamborough Head.

Now shall we press onwards, or stop and listen to a story about a good old Flamborough fisherman? I think you choose the story; but if not we will pass it over.

THE STORY OF JACK NORMIDALE, THE FISHERMAN.

Jack was a very poor man, and neither able to read nor write, but he knew and loved the Lord Jesus Christ; and this made him love his fellow-creatures.

Jack's wife was called Molly, and soon after they were married, a poor fisherman was drowned, and his wife and four children were left without anything to support them. Jack said to the poor widow, "Come to my cabin, I'll make a room ready for you, and you shall share the good

* Page 10. † Page 36.

of my bit of garden, and only pay your rent as you have it." Molly took care of the children when Sally, the widow, went out working. Her little boy was brought up altogether at Jack's expense—fed, clothed, and sent to school; and when he grew up, he bought him a boat and tackle for fishing. Was the boy grateful to his good friend? No, I am sorry to say, no. He never seemed to care for him at all. His sister Mary married a fisherman, called William, and they had five little children. One day William went out to sea, taking his dear son with him. As they returned, a storm arose; the boat upset when very near the land. Brave Jack plunged into the sea, caught one of the drowning men, and pulled him to the shore. He had hoped it might be William, but it was his partner. Poor William and the boy were both drowned. Again did Jack take the widow and her children to his home; again did he adopt one of them, and he and Molly cared for them as much as was in their power. The old man shared his meals with the fatherless little girl, and nursed her when she was sick. At last, old Molly died; and her good old husband had scarcely sixpence in the house to bury her. Who then helped? The widowed Mary and her children, even little Mary, the adopted child, gave a shilling that had been given her; and when Jack would have been left quite alone, they took care of him, and sought to make him comfortable. Jack is, no doubt, dead now; but did he not gain the blessing spoken of in the Bible, "Blessed is he that considereth the poor and needy, the Lord will deliver him in the day of trouble"?

Now, leaving this old fisherman, poor but rich, we will proceed along the sea-shore of Yorkshire.

A little to the north of Flamborough Head, stands Scarborough. This place is called the "Queen of English

Watering Places," the sands and scenery are so beautiful and the visitors so many. There is a fine old church here on the top of a steep cliff, and a castle, about which there are several stories in the history of England. There are waters also for invalids to drink, tasting of rusty nails and salt.*

The next place of consequence is Whitby, a most pleasant bathing-place. The scenery is beautiful, especially up the little river Eske, which flows through a wooded valley, and then widens to receive all the ships that trade with

Scarborough.

Whitby, whilst the houses rise on the steep bank, appearing to rest one on the top of another. It was from Whitby that Captain Cook sailed, when he went all round the world.

Here are the remains of an ancient abbey, where a meeting between the bishops of the ancient British churches, and the bishops sent over in Gregory's time from Rome, was

* Page 48.   † Page 40.

held.   We must not forget that though the Saxons were heathen, many of the ancient Britons had long before been converted to Christianity.*

Whitby used to be a great place for the whale-fishery. Mr Scoresby, whose son wrote some very interesting accounts of the Polar Regions, brought back, in twenty-eight voyages, 540 whales.   It is now famous for its jet and alum works, and beautiful fossils.   The jet is found in small pieces, from half an inch to two inches thick.   It is cut and polished.   The ammonites, or snake-stones, being polished too, are used with the jet for ornaments, a very small one being chosen for the middle of a brooch, or a large one for the bottom of a candlestick.

Near Whitby have been found the bones of tremendously large creatures, far larger than crocodiles, which may have lived when God first bade " the waters bring forth abundantly the large moving creatures which had life."   The alum works were commenced in the reign of Charles I.   A gentleman, who had travelled in Italy, observed that the colour of the foliage was, on his estate in Yorkshire, the same as in the alum districts in Italy.   Such is the good of using one's eyes.   He determined to begin alum works; but as the Pope did not wish that there should be any alum works in the world except his own, the Yorkshire knight was obliged to have the workmen hidden in casks, or they could not have left Italy.   Alum is a kind of earth, very useful in dyeing, in hardening tallow candles, and in preventing the wood or the paper soaked in it from taking fire.   It is also used as a medicine; and often the bakers very improperly put it into their bread to make it appear white.

Further north, very near the mouth of the Tees, is Redcar, rather a dreary bathing-place.   Now, when I tell you

* Page 10.

that many of the fishermen's villages on this coast are like clusters of martins' nests hanging to the high cliffs, and that some of the scenery between Whitby and Pickering is compared to that of Switzerland, I think you will have heard enough about Yorkshire to wish to go and travel there, if you do not already live in that great big county. And perhaps this evening we may play at the following Yorkshire game :—

THE GAME OF YORKSHIRE.

The children are seated round the room, and the teacher in the centre is telling a story, or imagining that she is shopping. The children each choose the name of a Yorkshire town, and as the article characteristic of the place is mentioned, the child turns round or pays a forfeit. Thus Willie is Bradford; Amy, Leeds; Edith, Hull; Laura, Wakefield; Cave, Whitby; Robin, Sheffield; Kate, Huddersfield; Harriet, York; Charlotte, Batley; Arthur, Scarborough; and Algernon, Barnsley.

The teacher goes out a day's shopping with Edward and Mary. First she goes to a clothier's, and buys cloth to make Edward a jacket. Amy turns round for Leeds. She gets a great coat for him of a coarser material. Charlotte jumps up for Batley. Then the teacher goes to a linen draper's and buys a stuff dress for Mary. Willie turns round for Bradford. She also purchases a silk mohair, a mixture of wool and silk, for herself. Now it is Kate's turn for Huddersfield. Then she asks for table-cloths and sheetings, upon which Algernon rises for Barnsley. Passing a print shop, she is struck with the view of a beautiful cathedral (Harriet turns round for York,) and also sea-pieces with grand towering rocks and foaming sea. Cave and Arthur both jump up for Scarborough and Whitby. Then a cutler's shop is entered, and Robin turns round;

and then a fancy shop, where toys are bought, which have come from Holland to a large seaport, Edith rises for Hull; and jet ornaments are inquired for, on which Cave again turns himself round for Whitby.

With fewer children, rivers might be taken instead of places, and the river must give a turn as any town or place of interest upon its banks is mentioned.

CUMBERLAND.—Part I.

TO-DAY we will cross England and visit the western coast, and you shall hear of Cumberland, one of the prettiest counties in the whole of dear old England. Part of this county, and part of Westmoreland, with a little bit of Lancashire, form what is called the lake district. Cumberland is, you see, like Northumberland, a border county touching Scotland on the north. What are the English counties which join it? The arm of the sea that runs up between Scotland and Cumberland is called the Solway Frith. When the tide is out, a quantity of sand is left dry, and the water often has a whitish hue. The north part of Cumberland is hilly, with large moorlands and extensive peat-bogs, or mosses, as they are frequently called. The mountains in the north-east are high and massive, but not nearly so beautiful and picturesque as those near the lakes. They are composed of a different kind of stone, called lime-stone, and are generally covered with heath and furze bushes ; but the lake mountains are chiefly formed of slate and granite, which rise into steep and rugged heights. In one part of Cumberland, the stone is of a reddish colour, so the houses are nearly as red as if built of brick. You seldom see tiled houses in Cumberland or Westmoreland.

Being a slate district, slates are the cheapest things with which to roof the cottages.

The rivers in Cumberland are very pretty, clear, and sparkling. ' They have generally rocky beds, over which they foam and gurgle, and play and leap. There are also beautiful cascades, or waterfalls, which rush down the mountain sides. And then there are the lovely lakes, sometimes sleeping calmly, with the mountains watching over them, and reflecting all the beautiful sky and passing clouds of heaven ; and sometimes becoming stormy. Then the water grows dark, and waves rise, and the bottom is stirred up, and the sky is no longer seen in the water. I think our hearts are very like lakes— when angry and passionate, with evil tempers stirred up, they are like the stormy lake ; but when they are gentle and kind, when God's Spirit calms them with love, then heaven is reflected, and Christ, heaven's best Sun, shines in them.

In Cumberland there is a great deal of rain, so the farmers do not grow much corn or hay; but they keep a great many cows and sheep, which feed on the beautiful green pastures. The dairy-maids make excellent butter. Turnips, which like rain very much, grow well in Cumberland. Along the rivers, there are a great many trees. The trees are generally larger in Cumberland than in Northumberland, Durham, or Yorkshire, because the cold east wind does not blow so much.*

Cumberland is chiefly inhabited by farmers. The people are honest and industrious. They pronounce their words strangely. Most of them work in the fields. The only coal mines in the county are at Whitehaven and Workington, and these extend under the sea.† Some of the people work at the slate quarries, and others in manufactories at Carlisle and different towns. Cumberland is a very

* Pages 7, 23, 37.   † Pages 20, 24, 29, 30, 51.

healthy county, where people generally live a long time. The country people are very simple in their habits. Butchers' meat, poultry, fish, and vegetables, are cheap.

You have often heard of an eruption from a burning mountain or volcano. Now I am going to tell you of an eruption that happened in Cumberland about one hundred years ago; but it was an eruption of mud, and not of fire—black, not red—an eruption from a bog, not from a crater. Amongst the mountains in the north of the county, was a very large bog called Solway Moss. The earth was peat, which is a sort of half-made coal, quite black, and used for firing. It surrounded it, like a saucer keeping in the water; but the people had cut it too near the bog. A heavy rain, for three days, increased the quantity of water very much, till, at length, it burst the shell of peat, and came rushing down towards the plain. A farmer, who lived near, heard that night an extraordinary noise. He took out his lantern, and thought at first it was the manure-heap in the farm-yard moving, he knew not how, towards him. As soon as he found out his mistake, he called on the neighbours to escape. Some of them did so; others got on the roofs of their cottages, and there remained till the morning, the black mud filling the rooms below. The poor sheep and most of the cows were suffocated. In one cow-house were eight cows. All were killed but one, which, for two hours, stood up to the neck in mud and water. When set free, it would eat, but seemed horrified if offered water. After three days, the bog had emptied itself, and that part of the hill which it had filled had become a hollow, and the corn and grass over which it flowed were all destroyed; but now the land is covered again with fresh trees and herbage.

I can tell you another story about this Solway Moss. There was in Henry VIII.'s reign a battle between the

English and Scotch, called the battle of the Solway. The Scots were defeated, and fled. In their alarm, a troop of five horses plunged into the Moss, which closed over them, and they were seen no more. This story was for long hardly believed; but a few labourers were some time since digging peat at the place where it was said this frightful accident happened, and they dug out a man and his horse thoroughly armed.

There are eagles among the highest mountains of Cumberland; and I have heard, too, that wild cats inhabit some of the wildest parts. Amongst other minerals that are dug out of the earth, is the black lead of which the pencils with which you draw are made. Common kinds, such as the housemaid uses for the grates, occur in various parts of the world, but the best black lead for pencils is found in the valley of Borrowdale. Though it has the name of black lead, it is not a species of lead at all. It is very valuable, and for fear of robbery the men's clothes are always searched before they leave the works. The mine is occasionally closed for some years.

A good many fish are caught on the coast—salmon, herrings, and others. Excellent cockles are found in the Solway Frith; and on the wild moors, the same kind of birds are caught as on the moors of Northumberland and Durham. What? Fresh-water fish, too, are found in the lakes, such as trout, char, pike, &c.

To-morrow, I hope to tell you more of the towns and beautiful places that are seen in the county of Cumberland, and will you try and remember about the mountains, the castles, the people, the moving bog, and the black-lead mine?

CUMBERLAND.—PART II.

THE chief river in Cumberland is the Eden. It enters the

county from Westmoreland, and is joined by the Eamont, which flows from the beautiful lake of Ulleswater, and separates Cumberland from Westmoreland. Near Ulleswater rises Helvellyn, the second highest mountain in England. From its summit there is a splendid view; the mountains lying around and beneath you, in the magnificent confusion that God's own hand has cast. A few hundred feet below the top of Helvellyn is a little lake, called Red Tarn. On one side is the Striding Edge, a ridge of rocks, only six feet wide, with deep precipices on either side. An unfortunate young traveller, Gough, once tried to go this way, and fell. Three months passed before his body could be found. At length it was discovered, and beside it lay his faithful dog, still guarding his poor master's corpse. Wordsworth, the poet, wrote these beautiful lines about this good animal—

> " This dog had been through three months' space
> A dweller in that savage place ;
> Yes, proof was plain, that since the day
> On which the trav'ller thus had died,
> The dog had watched about the spot,
> Or by his master's side.
> How nourished there, through such long time,
> *He* knows, who gave that love sublime,
> And gave that strength of feeling great,
> Beyond all human estimate."

Ulleswater is, excepting Keswick, the most beautiful of all English lakes, excepting Windermere, the largest, and, excepting Wast-water, the deepest. The mountains, jutting out on either side, appear almost to divide it into three parts, and the beauty of the highest reach, or expanse, is very great. Everything that is pretty is seen at Ulleswater ; towering mountains, rugged crags, foaming cataracts, soft clear water, peaceful islands, wooded banks. A little to the north of the lake is a beautiful waterfall, called Airey Force.* A wooden bridge crosses it above, and another below. The overhanging trees form arches over the stream, and the water hurries thundering onwards to the deep pool below.

In the midst of all this splendid scenery are some fine parks and old castles; and, following the Eamont a little way we approach Penrith. Penrith means Red Hill; perhaps it has this name from the houses having been always built of the red sandstone, which abounds in the neighbourhood.† The town stands in a valley, but there are beautiful hills all round. From one of them, Beacon Hill, where signal fires used once to be lighted, ‡ there is a splendid view; castles, parks, hills, Ulleswater Lake, the river Eden, the massive mountain of Crossfell on one side, and the varied heights of Helvellyn, Blencathara, and Skiddaw, on the other. Near Penrith are Roman remains, the ruins of the old castle, and giants' caves where strange stories are told of the giant Isis. In the churchyard there are two very old stone monuments, which are called "The Giant's Legs."

Following the Eden is Great Salkeld, where there are some of the most wonderful remains of olden times, a large Druidical circle. This is a collection of sixty-seven enormous stones, placed in a circular form, and supposed to have been a temple used by the Druids, before any missionaries came to tell the poor Britons of the great God and His Son Jesus Christ. These stones go by the name of "Long Meg and her daughters." Long Meg is very tall, eighteen feet high, and many of her daughters measure ten feet, as high as sitting-rooms are usually. The Eden receives several streams on the right, from hills which form the part of England's back-bone between the

* Pages 32, 42, 46. † Page 60. ‡ Pages 16, 36.

E

Cheviots and the Yorkshire mountains.* The highest of
these is Crossfell; and from a swamp on its eastern side,
the Tyne and Tees flow.† On the top of Crossfell the
clouds and the winds blow in a very peculiar manner.
They are called Helm, because the clouds assume a
helmet-shape. They look very dark and awful, and spread
a shadow almost like the approach of night. The darkness is all in the east; in the west, the sky is probably
clear and the mountains distinct. The dark helmet-
shaped cloud rises from the mountain-top, and another
cloud spreads itself across like a bar, leaving a space
between of clear sky. From this there rushes a very
strong wind, which sometimes overthrows waggons, and
scatters stacks of corn and hay. Sometimes it lasts for
a few hours, or sometimes for a few days. It cannot be
pleasant, but it is said to be very healthy; and, perhaps,
the purity of the air which it causes is one reason why
the inhabitants of Cumberland live so long. These strange
tumults in the air, when the reason of them could not be
explained, gave rise to curious superstitions. The mountain was thought to be inhabited by demons, and was
called Fiend-fell. St Cuthbert said he would expel them,
and he planted the cross on the highest point. The
demons then took flight, with all their goods; but in the
hurry of their departure they dropped a golden cradle
into a tarn on Saddleback. This cradle is sometimes
seen, but it cannot be fished out! Can you guess what
it is? The reflection of the crescent moon at mid-day,
which, in certain states of the weather, may be observed.
From this legend the hill received the name of Cross-fell.
The Eden continues flowing north till it reaches Wetheral,
passing beneath the walls of its quiet churchyard. Opposite are the woods of Corby; and on the Wetheral side are

* Pages 15, 35.　　　　　† Pages 18, 32.

steep banks covered with trees, and rocks containing caverns, used in former days for hiding treasure. The mouths of the caves are in the face of perpendicular rocks overgrown with ivy. Men who wished to enter them were lowered by ropes from above, and the enemy could not discover so well-concealed a hiding-place.

Below Wetheral, the Eden is joined by the Irthing, parallel to which the Picts' wall was built.* On its banks stand Naworth Castle and Lanercost Priory. The former is a strange old castle, where there lived, in Queen Elizabeth's time, "Belted Will," in other words, Lord William Howard, the terror of the border robbers.† He had a snug little library up a steep narrow staircase, where, when at study, he did not like to be disturbed. Once, a servant came to tell him that a prisoner had been brought in. Belted Will answered crossly, "Hang him." When he had finished his study, he ordered that the man should be brought for examination, but was told that his orders had been obeyed. The poor man was already hung, and thus a hasty word was the death of a fellow-creature. The old priory at Lanercost is in ruins now, but part of it is preserved and used as a church. It is a good change when old monasteries are turned into churches. The towers of several of the old churches in Cumberland have been used for defence against the Scotch, and have, no doubt, been places of retreat for the women and children who inhabited the villages. Near a little river, the Gelt, that runs into the Irthing, is a hill, called the Written Mountain. The face of the rock is covered with inscriptions, carved by the Romans. They are, however, so high, that you must use a telescope to read them. This is a very old custom. In the desert of Sinai, in Arabia, is a valley, called the "Written Valley."

There the steep rocks on each side are covered with writings, so numerous, and so ancient, that they are supposed to have been carved by the Israelites during the forty years of their wanderings.

A little lower down the Eden is Carlisle, the chief town of the county, which often goes by the name of "Merry Carlisle." The cathedral, built of red sandstone, is not nearly so large as those of York and Durham. Milner, who wrote a history of the Church, was dean of this cathedral some time ago. Not far distant is the castle, which was built by William Rufus. The Scotch and English have often fought for this strong fortress. Not much more than one hundred years since, it was besieged by Prince Charles, called the Pretender, a grandson of James II. He took it after three days' fighting; and when he marched back to Scotland, left there most of the Englishmen who had followed him. Soon afterwards, the army of the king, George II., besieged it again, and made prisoners its 400 unfortunate inhabitants, many of whom were beheaded. In Carlisle are dye-works, and manufactories for ginghams, for woollen goods, for whips, and fish-hooks, but perhaps the most famous is Carr's, for making biscuits by steam. The dough is cut, and kneaded, and beaten, by this wonderful power. Here another little river joins the Eden from the south, passing Dalston, where, also, there are manufactories. After leaving Carlisle, no other place of importance marks the Eden till it enters the Solway Frith.

CUMBERLAND.—Part III.

WE must leave several old castles and Druidical circles, which are found in the north of Cumberland, and hear something of its seaports.

The first town of note on the coast is Maryport, a busy, flourishing place, which, about one hundred years ago, was only a collection of a few small huts.* Now ships come and go, bringing timber from America, and flax from Ireland, and taking away coal, limestone, and red sandstone.† Once a great Roman encampment stood here, intended, no doubt, to keep away the Picts and Scots, who might land either from Ireland or Scotland.‡ Further south, at the mouth of the Derwent, is Workington, where there is a good deal of trade and ship-building, and where there are some of the sub-marine, or under-the-sea, coal mines. To track the Derwent from its source will bring us through the midst of the lake district, so now let there be great attention, and you shall hear more of the wonders and beauties of the Cumberland mountains, lakes, and valleys.

The lake hills do not form part of the backbone, or Pennine Chain of England. They stretch from the Eden in Westmoreland very nearly as far as the Irish Sea, and form parts of Cumberland, Westmoreland, and Lancashire. They are principally composed of slate; but there are also among them granite and other very old rocks. They are far older than the Alps, and indeed are amongst the oldest hills in the world.

The Derwent rises in Sca-fell, the highest hill in England. It is 3166 feet, or more than half a mile in height —far above the clouds. On the top there is a great heap of stones and wood. These piles, which are seen on the summit of every hill, are, in Cumberland, called " Men." Climbing to the top of Sca-fell Pikes is a work of great labour, but when there, if the day be clear, one has a most beautiful view,§—all the west coast from Anglesea, in

Wales, to the Mull of Galloway, in Scotland.—far across the sea, the soft blue hills of the Isle of Man; and should the day be remarkably clear, the very distant outline of the Irish coast. The top of the mountain is bare rock, with a few tufts of moss between the huge stones. No sheep browse there, no bird flies there; no sound breaks there. You are above all the surrounding earth; but far above is the heaven, where God especially dwells, and trusting and loving God, His children may raise to Him the eye which has been gazing around, and with thankful, joyful hearts, may say, "My Father made it all."

In this mountain is a wonderful pass called Sty Head, where the voice echoes from rock to rock. One side is called Great Gable, and the other Great End. A little stream passes through the grand and awe-striking valley of Borrowdale. It has been described as "the finest imaginable assemblage of rocks and rocky hills, all wildly wooded." The rocks hang overhead, and appear ready to fall down and crush you in a moment. Here, during the wars of the Roses, was concealed the Shepherd Lord Clifford, of whom I told you in Yorkshire. He lived here for twenty-four years, had no opportunity of learning to read or write, and grew up hard and savage as the rocks.* In Borrowdale is the famous mine for black lead. The mineral is not found in veins like copper, but in lumps, which sometimes weigh a few ounces and sometimes fifty pounds. Their shape is that of a tree, the trunk being usually of a much better quality than the branches. The Derwent now passes the largest stone in England, called the Bowder-stone. It is an immense block, like a "stranded ship with keel upturned." There is a ladder to ascend it, and from the top you have a beautiful view. It must, in ages past, have rolled down from the steep hills above. Just before the

* Page 48.

Derwent river enters Derwent-water, or Keswick-lake, is Grange, near which is a fish-nursery, where little trout and char are born and fed. They do not grow nearly so quickly as kittens or sparrows. On the right of the lake is the cataract of Lodore, not rolling in one stupendous fall, but leaping and foaming over a number of projecting rocks.* Southey has written a curious poem about it, which all children like to read. Just now you must be content to hear a very little bit—

> " Here it comes sparkling,
> And there it lies darkling ;
> Here smoking and frothing,
> Its tumult and wrath in.
> " It hastens along, conflicting, strong,
> Now striking and raging,
> As if a war waging,
> The caverns and rocks among."

Derwent-water is a lovely lake, studded with islands, which look like gems set in the clear silvery water. It is the shallowest of the lakes, and sometimes the surface is rough when not a breath of wind blows. Amongst its islands is one covered with reeds and water-plants, called the Floating Island. It sometimes rises to the surface, and sometimes sinks to the bottom. Probably both these strange phenomena, for such we call things in nature not easily explained, are caused by the expansion of gases below the water as they rise to the surface.†

Near Derwent-water, lovelily situated, is Keswick, sheltered by the lofty Skiddaw from the north. Here is a manufactory for black-lead pencils ; and in the Town Hall a beautiful model of the lake district.

After leaving the lake, the Derwent receives the little river Greta, which passes through the lake of Thirlsmere, and a lovely valley called St John's Vale, where is a rock, which, from the time of King Arthur, has been continually mistaken for a castle. Thirlsmere, a very narrow lake, is

Pages 32, 42, 46, 64.   † Page 30.

in the midst of mountains,—Helvellyn rising from its waters, and the "Eagle's Crag," and other grand precipices frowning darkly over it. A wooden bridge crosses the narrow centre of the lake. From a tarn in Blencathara, probably the one of the Golden Cradle, the Greta receives another stream.* Blencathara is also called Saddleback, on account of its shape. Adjoining it is Skiddaw, the third mountain in height, a splendid-looking hill; standing more by itself than either Scafell or Helvellyn, it seems like a monarch among the rest. Skiddaw Forest is at the foot of the mount. Do not you imagine it full of trees? There is not one; it is a bleak uncultivated plain. The Derwent next enters Bassenthwaite Water, surrounded by beautifully-wooded banks. Mountains tower one above another on the south side; but towards the north-west the great hills cease, and the Derwent flows on through a comparatively plain country, passing low hills made of fossil shells, to Cockermouth, where it is joined by the Cocker. Cockermouth is a busy little place, with various manufactures. It has a ruined castle, beautifully situated, overhanging the junction of the rivers, and is noted as the birthplace of Wordsworth the poet.† Let us now seek the source of the Cocker.

It rises close to Honister Crag, a rampart of almost perpendicular rock, 1580 feet high.‡ How many steps are there to the top of this house? Find that out before to-morrow, and then, if we reckon one step to a foot, we shall have an idea of the height of this crag. The little stream soon enters Buttermere, a small lake, surrounded by such grand and steep mountains, that you would feel it almost awful to wander there alone. Still it is very beautiful to see the steep rocky crags, and the quiet peaceful lake, and to remember that it is made by the great God, who cares so

* Page 66. † Pages 48, 64. ‡ Page 35.

much for us. The sight of the little churches in the lovely valleys is here peculiarly pleasant. Crummock-water, with three islands near the head of it, is also very beautiful, being surrounded by splendid mountains.

Over these heights are waterfalls. One has a strange name, Sour-milk Force. Another, Scale Force, is the deepest in Cumberland, 156 feet. Fancy three or four three-storied houses, placed one on the top of another, and

Scale Force.

you will have an idea of the height from which the water falls. It is a grand sight, after much rain, to see the angry torrent of water, come splashing and dashing furiously from the hill into the valley; the dark hue of the steep grand rocks on either side contrasting with the water's white foam.

These lakes are all famous for their fish, especially char, a kind of trout generally caught in nets. No particular place marks the Derwent between Cockermouth and Workington.

Further south is Whitehaven, with coal mines like those at Workington. The entrances to these mines are called "Bear Mouths." They open at the bottom of a hill, and you pass through steep passages to the galleries, where, far below the sea, the men work the coal. The great danger used to be fire-damp; but the safety lamps that are now used preserve the miners from many accidents.*

Beyond Whitehaven is St Bees' Head, a prominent red-sandstone cape. Here there is a college to prepare young men for being clergymen.

Further south, is the mouth of another little river, the Ehen, which may be traced to Enerdale Water, with its wild and savage banks. This lake has no wooded islands, nor beautiful trees, nor magnificent mountains; but the whole scenery is stern and lonely, but beautiful even in its lonely wildness. On the Ehen stands Egremont, with an ancient castle on a height, and old houses fronted with piazzas. Egremont has grown small, whilst Whitehaven has grown large. Do you remember anything of the Boy of Egremont?

The next little river is the Calder, on which are the ruins of the ivy-covered Calder Abbey; and in its neighbourhood is a hill called "Wo-to-bank." Would you like to know the story which accounts for this strange name? In the days when wolves and bears prowled in England, a nobleman was out hunting with his wife and servants.

* Pages 26, 51.

Suddenly the lady was missed. She was sought for, and soon discovered slain by a wolf, which was in the very act of tearing her to pieces. The husband beheld the scene in agony, and in his grief exclaimed, " Woe to this bank !"

" ' Woe to this bank ! ' the attendants echoed round,
And pitying shepherds caught the grief-fraught sound."

And to this day, Wo-to-bank has been the name of that fair green hill.

The last little river I will mention is the Irt, which flows through Wast-water, the deepest of the Cumberland lakes, whose waters have never been known to freeze. It is surrounded by very high and grand mountains.

Will you try and remember the names of the Cumberland Lakes ?

Ulles-water, with its three beautiful reaches.   P. 64.

Derwent-water, with its floating island.   P. 71.

Bassenthwaite-water, with its high wooded banks. P. 72.

Buttermere, with its steep rocky shores.   P. 72.

Crummock-water, with its three islands and its water-falls.   P. 73.

Enerdale Lake, wild and desolate ; and

Wast-water, so deep that it never freezes.   Pp. 74, 75.

And now we must leave beautiful Cumberland ; but only to enter a little county of equal interest—Westmoreland.

———

In rehearsing Cumberland, each child might relate a story that he has heard.

For instance, Charles might tell of the moving of Solway bog, and Arthur the story of Carlisle Castle, and Willie of Naworth Castle and Belted Will. Amy might tell about the Helm wind, and Laura about the unfortunate traveller and his faithful dog, whilst little Frankie might relate the sad story of " Wo-to-bank."

Or again, Willie might suppose that he lived in the time of the Romans. Then he might see the carving of the inscriptions on the written mountain, the building of the Picts' Wall, the great encampment near Maryport, or the red sand-stone buildings near Penrith. Even as an ancient Roman, he might stop and wonder at the Druidical remains, at the Giant Isis' Cave and the Giant's Legs in the churchyard at Penrith, taking note of the wolves at Wo-to-bank. Then Charles might live in the middle ages, and mark the struggles between the Scotch and English, the sieges of Carlisle Castle, the attacks on the villages, and the unprotected people taking shelter in the towers of the churches, describe an attack on Naworth, and Belted Will's exploits, or on Corby and the hiding of the treasure in the caves of Wetheral. Amy might think of the monasteries built at the same time, Lanercost Priory, Calder Abbey, and not forget the young Lord Clifford in savage Borrowdale. Arthur might be the traveller of the present century, and describe the present state of the principal towns, such as Carlisle, Whitehaven, Penrith, Keswick, Maryport, &c., visiting the cathedral and manufactories in Carlisle, the coal-pits at Whitehaven, the lead-mine at Borrowdale, the slate quarries amongst the mountains, and the college at St Bees.

The tour of the lakes might be deferred till the remainder of the lake country is described.

WESTMORELAND.—Part I.

THIS is one of the smallest counties of England, and the only one of the six northern counties that is an inland one.

Tell me the counties that border on it. Though an inland county, one little corner of Westmoreland touches this arm of the sea, Morecambe Bay, where there is a small seaport, Milnethorpe.

Westmoreland is a county that is very full of lakes and mountains. So much of the surface being mountainous a great deal of the ground is uncultivated, not divided into fields, and never cut by the ploughshare. You frequently meet with huge masses of stone on the low hills, and even in the plain country. There is not much corn grown in Westmoreland, but turnips, clover, hay, and, near Kendal, a great many potatoes. During summer, the farmers can keep a quantity of cattle on the hill-sides and moorlands; so what they chiefly want are hay or turnips with which to feed them during winter. A great many cows are kept in this county; but butter, not cheese, is made from their milk, the butter being sent to Liverpool, Manchester, or London, for sale.* The sheep that feed on the mountains have horns, dark-gray faces, and thick hairy wool.† There are also a great many pigs, the bacon of which is packed in hogsheads and exported. In some parts of Westmoreland, a great deal of young wood is grown. The trees are cut down when about sixteen years old, and made into hoops for barrels and tubs, and for what else? For little children to play with? I suppose so.‡ The tree that grows best in Westmoreland is the larch, a kind of fir-tree. A great many fish are found in the rivers and lakes like those found in Cumberland. § In Lake Windermere is what is called the gray trout, a very large fish which sometimes weighs two stone.

There is hardly any coal found in Westmoreland, and in many parts the cottagers have peat for their fires. Peat is found generally in boggy moors. It is a black kind of

* Page 61.   † Pages 15, 37.   ‡ Page 37.   § Page 63.

earth, a sort of half-made coal. It is cut out of the bogs, dried, and packed in stacks, and the square pieces into which it is cut are laid on the fire as we place coal.*

In Westmoreland there are many slates found, of different shades of hue, some greenish, and others almost black. The latter are the school-room slates. There has also been discovered a great deal of beautiful marble; one kind is white veined with red, another a dull green veined with white, and another, black. Copper, lead, and iron are also found. The people in this county are principally agriculturists. The women used to be much employed in knitting stockings. There are very few manufactories; but at Kendal a good deal of coarse woollen cloth is made. Some of the people are employed in making hoops, or in burning charcoal for the ironworks, in tanning leather, or in cutting slates in the quarries.

In Westmoreland, people have still a great many old-fashioned customs. Both men and women wear, in winter, clogs, shoes with wooden soles. These are very noisy, but keep the feet free from wet and dirt. They often make oaten cakes, which they call haver-bread.† Would you like to hear the story of a little cottage girl, who lived on one of the Westmoreland mountains?

THE STORY OF AGNES GREEN AND THE SNOW-STORM.

Many years have now passed since six little children sat round a peat fire in a little cottage at Blantern Ghyll. Their parents were gone to Langdale, but they had intended soon to return home. The snow was falling heavily, very heavily; but still the little ones watched and listened —they listened and watched. Night came on; but no parents returned. Then little Agnes, who was only nine years old, grew very sad; she, however, put the younger

* Page 62.   † Page 8.

ones to bed, and soon they all lay down and slept. When they woke in the morning, it seemed as if the light was never coming. They were in a snow prison. Their little cottage was buried in the snow. No father, nor mother, nor friend could reach them now. Poor little Agnes bade her brothers and sisters pray, and they all knelt down and asked God to care for them. Then Agnes was as a mother to the little ones. See dressed them in the morning, and when night came she sang them to sleep. She made them porridge with some oatmeal, and baked cakes on the "girdle" with flour that she found. At one side of the house, the wind must have blown the snow away ; and so she was able to go into the yard for peat, and to go to the byre to milk the cow. She climbed, too, into the hay loft, and with a great deal of difficulty, pushed down the hay, that the good cow might not starve. Another day passed ; and though Agnes kept awake till midnight, she could not hear any sound or any cry for help. At last the snow ceased ; the weather changed, and after a little while Agnes was able to go to the nearest cottage, and tell how sad they were without their dear parents, but also how safely God had kept the little ones. They sought the poor, lost parents, and at last they found them, cold, and stiff, and dead, all covered with the snow.

Dear orphan children ! God watched over them. He put it into the hearts of people to be kind to them; and they were taken from their solitary little cottage to a comfortable home.

Now, I will ask you a question that has already been put to other children :   "What would you have done, had you been in the place of Agnes Green ?   Would you have known what to do with the milk and meal and corn and hay ?   Or would you have sat down and cried, and been cross to the little ones and forgotten to pray ? "

WESTMORELAND.—Part II.

The Eden, which we traced in Cumberland, rises in the great mountains which separate Westmoreland from Yorkshire. It flows through a wild moorland country, passing Kirby-Stephen, Brough, and other pretty mountain-towns, and then reaches Appleby, a very small place, though the county town of Westmoreland. Formerly it was of consequence, and is prettily situated, the castle standing on the top of a hill, the church at the other end of the town, and the clear waters of the Eden flowing nearly all round it During the terrible Border wars in olden times, Appleby Castle was twice destroyed. It never recovered the devastation it suffered from the Scotch in Richard II.'s reign ;* and in Queen Elizabeth's time it was visited by a plague, in which most of the inhabitants perished. There is an hospital here for thirteen aged widows. Their tidy cottages form a square, and they have a neat little chapel for service.

The country south of Ulleswater, which separates Westmoreland from Cumberland, is very fine. There are beautiful dales ; one much admired is called Patterdale. Then there are deep coves, with clear streams hastening from their dark shades. A beautiful little lake has the name of Brothers' Water ; for it twice happened that there two brothers were drowned together. A rivulet, the Eamont received from the south, flows through Hawes Water ; whose eastern shore is thickly wooded, and its western surmounted by a rugged cliff, called Wallow Crag. The Lowther passes through beautiful parks, Lowther Park and Brougham Castle.

Now we must look for the little streams running south,

* Pages 9, 67, 68.

The first of which I tell you, passes through, perhaps, the most beautiful of all the beautiful scenery. It runs through the lakes of Grasmere and Rydal Water, small but very lovely. Behind the town of Grasmere rises a curiously-shaped rocky mountain, called Helm Crag, looking like an old ruin on the top of a hill, or, as Wordsworth fancied, " like an ancient woman and an old astrologer

Windermere Lake.

sitting there in spite of wind and weather." Near Rydal is the house where Wordsworth lived.* Only a few years ago, several famous poets, Wordsworth, Coleridge, Southey, Wilson, used to spend a part or the whole of the year in this beautiful neighbourhood. They have all passed away now; but the glens, and lakes, and mountains, where they loved to ramble, still remain. The Rydal waterfalls are

* Page 72.

F

very famous, and grand to behold. Ambleside stands where the Rothsay enters the splendid lake of Windermere, which is eleven miles long and one or two wide, and the largest of all the English lakes. It is studded with thirteen islands, which are generally wooded. The banks of the lake are covered with trees and cottages. The grand mountains lying beyond these are often capped with clouds. Near Ambleside is a beautiful waterfall, called Stock Gill Force. It rushes down a narrow ravine overhung with wood, taking, as it were, four bounds over its rugged rocky bed.* The large stones in the stream are covered with dark-green moss, and the rocks, at the side, are full of little caves, hidden by the interlaced roots of trees. The stream rises below Kirkstone pass, a very high road crossing a mountain between Windermere and Ulleswater. Near the top of it is a small inn, on which is written, "This is the highest inhabited house in England." I think we should like better to see it than to live in it, for high lands are always cold lands. East of Lake Windermere is Troutbeck Valley, a wild district, through which a little stream passes. There are strange stories about this vale. One is, that there lived here a giant who used to eat a sheep at one meal; and the people talk about the 300 bulls, the 300 bridges, and the 300 constables of Troutbeck. This sounds very strange; but the meaning is, the parish being divided into three parts, called hundreds, each part had a bull, a bridge, a constable, so all the difference between three and three hundred, lies in the apostrophe ('s.) Bowness, further south, is, like Ambleside, a pretty village on the lake, filled during the summer with tourists. Many skiffs are on the water, in which it is pleasant to row, with the bright sky

* Pages 32, 42, 46, 64, 70, 72.

above, and the clear waters below. The south part of Windermere belongs to Lancashire.

The next little river is the Ken, which rises in Kentmere Tarn, below a very high mountain, called High Street. The Romans made a road, which crossed it almost at its summit. They called roads streets, and so the mountain has that name to the present day. In Kentmere Vale, Bernard Gilpin, the good vicar of Houghton-le-Spring, was born.* Kendal, past which the Ken flows, is the largest town in Westmoreland. It is beautifully situated, with an old castle, where Queen Catherine Parr, the last of Henry the Eighth's six wives, was born. It is pleasant to stand there, looking on the town and valley below, and viewing the beautiful hills around. The old church is a very large one, with five aisles. In it there is the following curious epitaph on the tombstone of a vicar, who died more than two hundred years ago :—

> " London bredd me,   Westminster fedd me ;
>   Cambridge spedd me,   My sister wedd me ;
>   Study taught me,   Kendal caught me ;
>   Labour pressed me,   Sickness distressed me ;
>   Death oppressed me,   The grave possessed me ;
>   God first gave me,   Christ did save me ;
>   Earth did crave me,   Heaven would have me."

In the town is a museum, where there is an old brass clock, one of the first ever made with a pendulum. Two hundred years ago, the mayor presented it to the town for the use of his successors. It has this inscription, which we should always try to remember :—

> " Time runneth :—Your work is before you."

At the mouth of the Ken is Milnthorpe, the only com-

------

* Page 27.

mercial town in Westmoreland. In the extreme east of Westmoreland is the Lune. On it stands Kirkby Lonsdale, a well-built town, standing in a lovely valley. The church is very ancient and handsome; and, from the churchyard, there is a magnificent view. Near it, there is a school for the daughters of clergymen. Many places, especially in the north of England, have the name of Kirkby.* Kirk means a church; so Kirkby Lonsdale means church in the dale of the Lon or Lone.

Now we must leave pretty little Westmoreland, but we shall yet, in the north of Lancashire, hear something more of lakes and mountains.

Westmoreland might be reviewed on any of the previous plans suggested; or the teacher might pass over to page 88, and taking the north of Lancashire, finish the lake district. Then the pupils, if old enough, might each write a little tour of the lakes, either in the form of a journal or of letters. They might choose for themselves, whether the journey should be on foot, on horseback, or in a carriage, and they might amuse themselves by interspersing characteristic imaginary adventures. Or, again, a description might be given of the lake scenery, one child selecting the mountains, another the lakes, another the towns, another following the Eden, or another the Derwent.

Such exercises would impress the scenes strongly on the memory, besides exercising various powers of composition.

LANCASHIRE.—Part I.

WE have now reached the last of the six northern counties,—busy, manufacturing Lancashire.

We must, however, first hear what the county is like,

* Pages 53, 80.

the good things that God has wrought by the hand of nature, and then what He has wrought by the hands of man.

It is a county that borders on the Irish Sea, forming part of the west coast of England. It is not an even shore, like that of the eastern counties; but it is full of deep bays.* The principal are Morecambe Bay in the north, the mouth of the Ribble in the centre, and the mouth of the Mersey in the south. The coast is very flat and sandy towards the south-west. In the north is Walney Island, long and narrow, but only inhabited by great numbers of sea-gulls.† North of the Ribble, is a tract which is fertile ; whilst north of Morecambe Bay, is, as I hope you remember, a portion of the lake district. In the east of Lancashire, near Yorkshire, we find again the backbone of England. ‡

Lancashire is not a cold county, but the weather is often very rainy. Corn and turnips are both grown in Lancashire, but it is chiefly famous for potatoes. There are very large peat mosses in this county ; one, called Chat Moss, not far from Manchester, is five miles long and three broad, about twelve yards deep, and overgrown with coarse grass. § A good deal of coal is found in the south, which is very valuable for the many manufactories. Good stone is quarried for building houses, and slate for roofing them is found in the mountains. Near Wigan is obtained what is called cannel, or candle-coal. If you put a flame to it, it takes fire at once. It can be polished like jet, and you may take hold of it in your fingers, and not dirty them in the least. Sometimes it is made into snuff-boxes and candlesticks.‖

The manufactures of Lancashire are, however, what

* Page 3.   † Page 18.   ‡ Pages 35, 65.
§ Pages 62, 77.   ‖ Page 58.

mark it from all other counties. Nowhere are there so many cotton factories. We may say it is the principal place for supplying the whole world with white and coloured calico.* The cotton is brought in ships from America or India to Liverpool on the Mersey, and then it is sent by canal or railway to Manchester and many other towns. The railways form quite a network amongst these busy towns, crossing each other in all directions. In this county, much silk and wool are also spun and woven, but of the latter not nearly so much as in Yorkshire. Here are also paper and hat manufactories, and near Liverpool a great quantity of soap is made. What is soap made of? Tallow and soda.

Lancashire is a county where the industrious and sensible poor have frequently become rich. I will tell you a story about a farmer, his son, and his grandson :—

About a hundred years ago, there lived at Blackburn a farmer, who had not a great deal of money. He was much interested in the manufactories around him, and, at last, gave up farming and became a calico printer, that is, a stamper of patterns in different colours on plain calico. Having traced and cut out a parsley-leaf on a bit of wood, he wetted it with some colouring mixture, and then stretched the calico tight over it, striking it with a little hammer, so that the print of the parsley-leaf was left. When it was stamped all over, his active wife and daughters helped him by ironing it. To iron long webs of calico, took, however, a long time, so the clever farmer invented a mangle. Mangles had never been thought of before. The calico he printed was quickly bought, and the farmer soon became a rich man. His eldest son, Robert, joined him in his printing business, and grew still richer. When England wanted soldiers, he sent out a regiment of horse

* Page 38.

at his own expense. The king then made him a baronet, so the farmer's son became Sir Robert.

He, again, had a son, who was sent to Parliament, and often gave such wise counsel, that, at last, he became Prime Minister, or chief adviser, first of William IV. and then of Victoria. He was one of the cleverest men of dear old England. The Blackburn farmer's grandson was the celebrated Sir Robert Peel.

I will make a list of some of the famous people born in Lancashire. John Bradford, a good and holy man, who, in the reign of Queen Mary, was burnt to death, for he would not give up the Bible.* He sold all his jewels to give to Christ's poor people; and was so humble, that when he saw a thief, or a murderer, led to be hung, he would say : "There goes John Bradford, but for the grace of God." Sir Richard Arkwright, once a poor barber, who improved spinning jennies, the machinery which draws out cotton into the fine threads, from which it is afterwards woven. Roscoe, a talented man, who tried, like Wilberforce, to free poor slaves.† Mrs Hemans, who wrote beautiful poetry. Do you know her pretty hymn?—

"I hear thee speak of a better land."

Edward Baines, a great friend of the poor, and of Sunday schools. Legh Richmond, the author of " Jane, the Young Cottager;" and good Edward Bickersteth, whose heart was very full of love to God.

The first railway, and the first canal in England, were both made in Lancashire. The first canal was about eleven miles long; but a more famous one was soon afterwards cut by the Duke of Bridgewater, between his collieries at Worsley and Manchester. There were about three miles of it underground, the tunnel being arched with the natural

* Pages 9, 27, 39.   † Page 54.

rock when possible, or with brick where coal or loose earth was above.

The first railway was between Liverpool and Manchester.* It was only thirty-one miles long, but there were thought to be difficulties that could never be surmounted. First, there was, under Liverpool, a tunnel to be made, more than a mile in length. Then there was a viaduct, or a road on arches over a valley, for about one hundred and fifty yards. Then there was the great bog, Chat Moss, to pass over, where the ground was so soft that the iron rails sank twelve yards. This difficulty was overcome by throwing thousands of cart-loads of earth into the moss, which at length made it sufficiently firm. The 15th of September, 1830, was the day on which George Stephenson, the great engineer from Northumberland, was to try his locomotive, or moving steam-engine.† The Duke of Wellington, Sir Robert Peel, and others were present. The engine did all that was expected; but a sad accident happened. Mr Huskisson—who, seeing what a great benefit railroads would some day be to the country, had used all his influence to help them forward—stepped out of the carriage. Another train came up more quickly than, in those early days, could be well understood. Mr Huskisson grew confused, fell, and the wheels passed over him. Notwithstanding the triumph of the steam-engine, Stephenson and every person felt sad to think of the death of this worthy man. To-morrow we hope to talk more of Lancashire.

LANCASHIRE.—PART II.

ONCE more for lakes and mountains. We will commence this morning with a description of the north part of Lancashire, and an interesting story about Morecambe Bay.

* Page 33.   † Page 9.

This district is separated from the rest of its own county by the bay just mentioned, and a part of Westmoreland. It is formed of the same kind of rocks as the lake district of Cumberland and Westmoreland, and has the same high mountains and clear lakes.*

The coast is deeply indented with salt-water inlets. The rugged promontory overgrown with underwood, situated between Morecambe Bay and Duddon River, is that of Furness, where there are beautiful ruins of an old abbey. Near this is Barrow, which, from a small village, has grown in ten years as large as Lancaster. The river to the east of this issues from Coniston Water, on whose northern side is a fine mountain called Coniston Old Man.† The summit is granite; but the mountain is, in a great measure, composed of slate, and has many slate quarries, and also a copper-mine. The lake is famous for its fish, especially its char.‡ A railway conveys the slates and copper on to Barrow. Ulverstone is a small seaport on Morecambe Bay, where there is a beautiful old church, from which there is a good view of all the surrounding country. It is pleasant to see houses built for the worship of God, where He has made such lovely scenery for the happiness of man.§

There is another little lake in north Lancashire to the west of Windermere—Esthwaite Water; but though pretty, it is not so beautiful as Windermere, or Coniston. Stones are used here for almost everything; even the gate posts are formed of high flat stones.

The water of Morecambe Bay is shallow; so, when the tide is out, a quantity of sand is left dry, as at Holy Island, on the Northumbrian coast. It is, however, dangerous to cross, as the sands are wide and the tide comes in very quickly.

I will tell you the story of a traveller, who was nearly lost amid the rapidly-advancing billows. I think, that

* Pages 60, 69.　　† Page 69.　　‡ Page 73.　　§ Page 72.

from it, you may learn a lesson of trust in the kind providence of our heavenly Father.

THE DOCTOR AND THE COMPASS. *

Several years ago, a medical gentleman was called on by a messenger, who told him that a lady, living on the opposite side of Morecambe Bay, was dangerously ill, and wished him to visit her immediately. He added that he had a chaise ready, and that he thought there was just time to cross the sands, so as to save driving several miles round. The physician consented, for the day was beautiful, the sun shone brightly, and the post-boy assured him that he knew the way. The sands were not half crossed, when the sky became overclouded, the sun seemed like a yellow ball, and then disappeared, and a thick fog spread around, so that the driver could not see beyond a few yards. The doctor became much alarmed, for he knew that the tide was turned, and that the waves would soon rush over the spot where they were. "Drive on, drive faster," he exclaimed. The man urged on the horses, but soon they stopped; the way was lost. He thought he was driving towards the sea, for he heard the rolling of the waves. The carriage is turned, but soon it stops again, for they distinctly hear the mighty waves approaching. They fear they are lost, the fog hides every landmark; if they advance, they seem to be rushing to death; if they remain, the waves must cover them. What a moment for prayer! How blessed, then, to feel, that living or dying they were safe in Jesus!

Suddenly, the doctor exclaimed, "Thank God, we may yet be saved; I put in my pocket, this morning, a compass, which was lying on the table." He pulled it out; examined it; was able to tell the driver which way to turn;

* Churchman's Penny Magazine, 1849.

and in a short time, to their inexpressible joy and thankfulness, they arrived safely on the other side.

Which shows more the love of God—the beautiful lakes and mountains, or His kind care of this poor traveller?

Do not both creation and providence say that God is love?

And now we must talk about the towns of Lancashire. The most northerly one is Lancaster, which is also the oldest, and was once the most important. You may always know that towns which end with "cestor," "chester," or "caster," are old; for they were called so by the Saxons on account of their Roman castles. Lancaster is on this little river, the Lune. Do you remember our talking of it, when we visited Kirkby Lonsdale, a pretty little village in Westmoreland? * Lancaster has a fine old castle, on the top of a rock, which is well seen from the railway. It is now used as a prison. The town is noted for the making of excellent mahogany furniture—Gillow, the famous upholsterer, having belonged to this place. There are cotton mills here; but few compared with other Lancashire towns. The next river southwards that you see is the Ribble. We heard of it, if you remember, as running through the rich district of Craven, in the west of Yorkshire.† On one of its branches is Burnley, where there are many cotton-mills. Further down the river, stands Preston. It, too, has a great many tall chimneys, which mark the mills, and is a large and busy town. It is commercial as well as manufacturing, for small ships can come up the river. Its first name was "Priest's Town," because there were so many monasteries in it. Now, I am glad to say, there are many churches and schools. Near Preston, there was fought, nearly 150 years ago, a great battle between the troops of King George I. and the followers of the Pretender, King James II.'s son. ‡

* Page 84.   † Page 49.   ‡ Page 68.

South of Preston, and approaching Manchester, are several very large towns, some containing from 60,000 to 100,000 people. The largest are called Blackburn, Bury, Bolton, Oldham, Rochdale, and Wigan. Most of these places were hardly larger than villages, sixty years since; but now they are full of cotton-mills, besides other factories. Blackburn is the place where, I hope you remember, Sir R. Peel's father and grandfather lived; whilst in the parish of Bury is the spot where he was born. Bury was famous in the reign of Edward III., for its worsted manufactures, and here, there still are more woollen than cotton goods made.* In Bolton the manufactories are chiefly for cotton goods, muslins, calicos, and quilts; and there are likewise immense bleaching grounds. I have read that every year 10,000,000 pieces of long cloth are bleached in this parish.

One hundred years ago, there were in Oldham sixty cottages, mostly thatched with straw. Now, there are about 160 mills, and in the borough more than 113,000 people. Most of the mills are for spinning cotton, not for weaving calico; corduroys and velveteens are principally made here. The town has increased thus greatly, because the valuable coal-mines near it supply coal for the factories.

Rochdale is a very old place. The church stands on a great height, and you must climb 122 steps, from the lower part of the town, to reach its door. The houses are roofed with stones, not with slates.† The factories here, like those in Yorkshire, are chiefly for woollen goods; not, however, broadcloth, but such as baizes, blankets, and flannels. Calicos are also made here, and so are hats.

Wigan is divided into two parts, old and new; but it is not at all a pleasant-looking town. There are collieries

Page 86.   † Page 89

round it, and in it all sorts of manufactories ;* not only for cotton goods, but for paper, spades, and carpenters' tools, brass, and pewter things.

Ormskirk is a decreasing town; but for what do you think it is famous? For its gingerbread. In the south of Lancashire, near Liverpool, is Everton, noted for toffee.

To-morrow, you shall hear of the two second largest cities in England.

Manchester.

LANCASHIRE.—Part III.

To-DAY I must tell you of two towns which, next to London, are the largest and most populous in England—I mean Manchester and Liverpool. Manchester is situated on three

* Pages 20, 29, 51.

little rivers, the Irwell being the chief one; and is connected
with all the other towns, of which I have been speaking, by
canals and railways.   It contains, with Salford, more than
half a million of people, and is the centre of the great
cotton factories.   It has a fine old cathedral, full of very
beautiful carvings.   There are many good public buildings;
the exchange, where very many bales of cotton are bought,
and orders received for many pieces of calico; the Free-
Trade Hall, an immense building for holding meetings, and
speaking to the people; a very good museum; a college for
eighty boys, dressed like the blue-coat boys in London;
and many other schools, and churches, and public buildings.
In the year 1856, there was, in Manchester, a great exhibition of beautiful pictures; so, you see, though the people
have to think so much about their cotton, they can care for
other things.   One very good thing is, that the shops and
factories all close early: so that the men employed have
the evenings for being at home, for reading, for lectures, or
for whatever they like.   Once the factories employed men,
women, and even children, for twelve or sixteen hours in
the day; but a good nobleman, Lord Shaftesbury, then
called Lord Ashley, got a law passed, limiting the labour
to ten hours a day, and obliging the parents to send their
children to school.

More than 30,000 people are employed in the cotton-
mills alone; besides a great many in silk and woollen
manufactories.   There are beautiful parks near Manchester, where the people may walk, and children play.
Clergymen, ministers, and missionaries do a great deal of
good among the poor.   There are a great many Sunday
Schools.   In the year 1851, Queen Victoria paid the people
a visit, and the Sunday-School children, numbering 80,000,
were arranged to give their dear Queen a welcome.   It was
beautiful to see the many young and happy faces, and to

hear their sweet voices singing, " God save the Queen ! "
Queen Victoria stopped, and could not help shedding tears,
for the sight was exceedingly touching.   Adjoining Manchester, on the opposite side of the Irwell, is Salford, a
many-peopled borough, with the same characteristics as
its populous neighbour.

In almost all these Lancashire towns, we have talked
of cotton-factories.   Would you like to hear a little more
about them ?   I once went through a very large one, and
I think if you did the same, you would never forget the
noise, and yet the order; the quantity, and yet the regu-
larity of the work.   The machines seemed as if they
knew their business, and one could not help thinking how
very clever the men were that invented them.   And must
not God be wise, who made man's brain, and invented the
hand, the eye, the ear, which all know their business
without our teaching them ?

Cotton grows in the pod of a tree, which is cultivated in America, Africa, India, and other parts of
Asia ; but principally in America.   It comes over in
large sacks, and then it looks very dirty · but it is put
into a machine that pulls it to pieces and combs it, leaving all the rough bits.   It is then pressed between rollers,
and comes out like the finest softest wool.   This, gummed
at the back, is what is called wadding.   Another machine
divides it, and rolls each part more closely in the form
of a very soft cord.   This is gradually spun finer and
finer, till it becomes fit for weaving.   It is spun by the
spinning jennies, or similar machines.   It is curious to see
them marching, as it were, in and out, more regularly
than soldiers, and without any orders.   Children often
watch these machines, mending the broken threads.   In
another part of the mill all the looms are at work.   I
have seen 1300 in one manufactory.   The noise was deafen-

ing, and it was some time before it was possible to hear another person speak. The webs of cotton are afterwards passed through large vats of boiling sago, that the fibres may be fixed.

Wherever British ships go, purchasers are found for Manchester cottons. I remember seeing, in Scotland, dye-works, where a quantity of very thin calico was coloured Turkey-red and bright yellow, to be sold among the ladies of Chili and Peru.

And now we must follow the Mersey, and talk of busy commercial, as well as of busy manufacturing, Lancashire. But first, I will tell you a little more of manufacturing towns. On the Mersey is Warrington, with a very large railway station. Here cotton is spun, and glass and pins are made. To the north of Warrington, at Newton, there is a large manufactory of lucifer matches; and at Prescot and St Helen's, the fine movement works and the delicate hands of watches are made. At St Helen's, too, you would see, as at Newcastle, broad glass-work chimneys, and also furnaces for smelting copper.*

But we must hasten on to Liverpool, with all its ships and its miles of docks.

Liverpool is, next to London, the largest port in Great Britain. The value of the cargoes, brought from, or sent to, foreign countries, is more than double that of London; so Liverpool, in its foreign commerce, stands the greatest port in the world. A great many ships come from America laden with raw cotton, corn, and sugar; others from China, with tea; others from India, with sugar and indigo; or from Australia, with gold and wool: and many others, with goods more diverse than I can tell you. Then, heavily-laden ships go out to all parts of the world, with linen and cotton fabrics from Manchester, and the towns

* Pages 20, 29.

of which I have told you; broadcloth from Leeds, and other Yorkshire towns; cutlery from Sheffield; hardware from Birmingham; and earthenware from Staffordshire, of which I shall tell you more afterwards; also, with salt and cheese from Cheshire; and soda and soap—a great deal of soap being made, as I mentioned before, in or near Liverpool. Immense steamers are also continually starting for America, crossing the wide Atlantic in about twelve days; and others leave for Africa and for Australia. Besides these, many ships sail full of emigrants. These are people who leave their own land to try and gain a livelihood in another part of the world. They reach Liverpool from all parts of England, Scotland, and Ireland; and many likewise come from Germany, crossing by railway from, what port do you think on the eastern coast? *

The emigrants are mostly bound for Canada, the United States, or Australia. Some are for New Zealand, or the Cape of Good Hope. Many little children go with their parents, crossing the wide, wide sea in the large ships. They often feel sad to leave dear old England; but they hope to find a bright young England far away; and we must ask God to speed the emigrants, and give them happy homes, and help them to please Him wherever they go.

These ships require a great many docks, the walls of which extend for five miles along the Mersey.† Some of these are dry and some are wet docks. The wet docks are always full of water, in which ships can float; but dry docks have only water let in when a ship is to enter or to depart. Ships go into dry docks when the keel or lower part requires mending.

Liverpool is not an old town. In the reign of Queen Elizabeth it was a little fishing village, with 800 people in

* Page 54.   † Pages 29, 31, 53.

G

it. In Queen Anne's reign, it was a small town, with
about 8000 people; whilst in Queen Victoria's reign, it is
the mighty port that I have been describing, with nearly
600,000 people.*

There are many handsome buildings, churches, and halls,
the chief of which is St George's Hall, very grand, with
beautiful pillars. But I must leave these, and tell you of
a little church, not built of stone, not built on the ground,
and without either tower or spire. It is the Mariners'
Church, a ship made into a church, which lies in a small
dock. It is in the midst of the other ships, so many sailors ·
go to it, and hear, perhaps, the story of Jesus walking on
the waters, and stilling the waves.

There is also a home for the sailors, a comfortable house
for them to go to when their ship reaches port. The good
Prince Albert laid its foundation-stone.

Near Liverpool is a curious burial-place, made in a deep
quarry. Many of the graves are in the side of the rock,
like the tombs we read of near Jerusalem.

Southport, Blackpool, and Fleetwood, are all bathing
towns on the Lancashire coast ; and in summer they
are very pleasant places of resort for the many people
from Manchester and Liverpool, who, during the rest of
the year, see little but the busy thoroughfares and smoky
chimneys of those large towns. Many go over to the Isle
of Man, a pretty island in the Irish Sea; nearly equally
distant from England, Scotland, Ireland, and Wales.

The children might rehearse Lancashire, by making lists
of the towns, the manufactures, the public works, the
remarkable places, and the famous persons born in that
county. When a sufficiently accurate knowledge has been
acquired, the following game might enliven an evening :—

* Pages 40, 92. This includes West Derby, which now forms part of
Liverpool.

THE GAME OF LANCASHIRE.

The narrator is seated in the centre, and the children arranged on the right hand and left.

The story commences.

"Brother George is expected home this evening, and he means to bring "——   There is a pause, and the child seated first on the right hand mentions some article manufactured in Lancashire.   The child first on the left hand mentions a town in which it is made.   Thus—

> No. 1 Right-hand says—A silk dress for mamma.
> No. 1 Left-hand adds—From Manchester.
> No. 2 Right-hand says—And a watch for papa.
> No. 2 Left-hand adds—Its works from Prescot.
> No. 3 Right-hand says—A hat for Charles.
> No. 3 Left-hand adds—From Rochdale.
> No. 4 Right-hand—A muslin frock for baby.
> No. 4 Left-hand—From Bolton or Manchester.
> No. 5 Right-hand—Blankets for Annie's bed.
> No. 5 Left-hand—Blackburn or Rochdale.
> No. 6 Right-hand—A Box of soap for the washerwoman.
> No. 6 Left-hand—From Liverpool.
> No. 7 Right-hand—A spade for the gardener.
> No. 7 Left-hand—From Wigan.

This, after once going round, may be reversed, the left-hand mentioning the articles, and those on the right-hand the places.   When either is at fault, a forfeit should be paid.

CHESHIRE.—Part I.

CHESHIRE, the county that we commence to-day, is a very beautiful, fertile district.   King Edward III. named it "The Vale Royal of England," and one of the titles given to the Prince of Wales is Earl of Chester.   There are several parks belonging to different noblemen and gentlemen, and the fields are beautifully green, and covered with the richest grass.

A small portion of Cheshire touches the Irish Sea, and that part has, as you may observe, an arm of the sea on each side; the upper one being the mouth of the Mersey, the other, the mouth of the Dee. The shore of the Mersey is covered with merchandise, and there are large docks on the Cheshire as well as the Lancashire side of the river; but the shore of the Dee is very quiet, most of the ships taking their cargoes to the Mersey. Two Welsh counties touch Cheshire, Flint and Denbigh, and five English ones —try and name them—Lancashire, Yorkshire, Derbyshire, Staffordshire, and Shropshire.

In the north and east, Cheshire borrows something of the character of Lancashire, Birkenhead being like a small Liverpool, and Stockport like a small Manchester; but still Cheshire is more famous for its dairies than for its manufactures.

There were 90,000 cows feeding in this country, but the cattle disease raged sadly here. These eat such beautiful grass, that they give very rich milk, and the good milk makes good cheese; and so Cheshire cheeses are known all over the world. To London alone 14,000 tons are taken every year. A ton is as much as is generally drawn in a two-horse cart-load of coals. Cheshire cheeses are also sent to America, France, and Russia. As there are so many cows, most of the fields are full of grass, and not of corn.*

Underneath the ground are found coal, copper, lead, and cobalt,—the last is a beautifully blue earth, much used in painting; but what is of more consequence in Cheshire than these minerals, are the mines of rock salt.

A quantity of this is every year dug out of the ground,

* Pages 61, 77.

and is principally used in salting fish. Would you like to hear about a salt-mine? Though not more curious, it is far more beautiful than the coal mines of Northumberland and Durham.

Descending in a tub, which is let down by chains, you would soon reach a large apartment, perhaps too large for any light to show its full extent. The ceiling and walls and floors are all of salt, and the crystallised particles sparkle very beautifully. Salt pillars are left to support the roof, not soft salt as you see at table, but salt as hard as the stone of which the house may be built. The floor is covered with crushed salt, something like the ice on a pond, where many people have been skating. In one large mine near Northwich, is an opening two hundred yards long, called Regent Street. Here, people have often picnics, and when they are gone, the little mice that have chosen these spacious halls for their homes, peep out and eat the remnants. Horses sometimes live in salt-mines, like the ponies in coal-pits, but the horses thrive better than the ponies, the salt being very wholesome.* A few years ago, the ground above a mine, about an acre in extent, with the engine house, stables, and some cottages, fell in, sinking about fifteen or twenty yards. Several people were hurt and some were killed. How dreadful it must have been to feel the ground breaking and sinking beneath one's feet. It is supposed, that, very long ago, the sea covered this part of Cheshire, and that the deposits of salt were once hollows covered with sea-water. Near the mines are many salt springs, and the finer salt is obtained from these by evaporation. For this purpose, the water is boiled again and again; and as it boils, the salt falls to the bottom of the iron pan, and the water goes off in steam. When the pan is full of salt crystals, they are taken out

* Page 25.

and dried. Salt is a very necessary ar.d very common thing. Have you ever thought how kind it is of God to make necessary things common also?

Cheshire is generally a flat country, but towards the east are several hills, from which there are beautiful views. Over the rich and fertile plains, clouds of smoke are seen resting here and there on such towns as Stockport, Macclesfield, or, in the far distance, Manchester. Alderley Edge is a pleasant rise of this kind, wooded to its summit. It is not many miles from Stockport, and, being near the railway, people from the busy manufacturing towns often visit it for the day, and breathe its fresh air. Another hill is called the "Nab," and another "White Nanny." On the very borders of Cheshire, Derbyshire, and Yorkshire, is a very elevated peat moss, over which one of the highest roads in England passes.* Amongst the good and great people born in Cheshire are Matthew Henry, who wrote an excellent Commentary on the Bible, and Bishop Heber, who was sent as Bishop to Calcutta, and wrote the beautiful missionary hymn, "From Greenland's icy mountains." They were both born in the parish of Malpas.

Many houses in Cheshire are built of stone, with black beams of timber put crosswise. In the time of William the Conqueror, a great deal of the land was desolated, because Earl Edwin, a Saxon nobleman from the neighbourhood, struggled against the fierce Norman's power. On this desolate land, great forests afterwards grew, in which lived the injured Saxons, robbing and taxing the Norman lords. In the centre of one of these woods, Delamere Forest, is a waste spot, called "The Chamber of the Forest," where, it is said, that a large town once stood.

Many of the gentlemen's families in Cheshire have lived there for hundreds of years. The farmers are very

* Pages 35, 81, 83, 85.

hospitable. They often regale their friends with a dish called "furmity," made of boiled wheat, milk, spice, and sugar. Great quantities of potatoes grow in this county.*

Three rivers water Cheshire; the Mersey, separating it from Lancashire; the Weaver, running through the centre; and the Dee, dividing it from Wales. Do you remember an eastern county divided in this way?

CHESHIRE.—Part II.

Now let us begin with the south of Cheshire, and follow the Mersey and its tributaries. The first large town with which we meet is Stockport, where a quantity of calico is woven and bleached or printed. Here is a large Sunday school, where more than 3000 children can assemble. South of Stockport, on the Bollin, is Macclesfield. Near this there are stone and slate quarries, but the town is more famous for its silk manufactories.† The kinds of silk generally made here are sarsenets, Persians, shawls, and handkerchiefs. Beautiful silk velvets are also woven, and there are likewise manufactories for buttons, and large-dye-houses.

There have been some curious customs in this town. One was furious driving at a wedding; and, to this day, there are people who, if they can afford it, hire a carriage to drive as quickly as possible through the streets. The holidays of Macclesfield are not Easter or Whitsuntide, but St Barnabas day, June 11th, and they sing their wakes not at Christmas but at Michaelmas. On the banks of the Mersey, at the entrance of the canal from the Mersey to the Irwell, is Runcorn, a thriving port, where iron ships are built, soap is made,‡ and from which

* Page 85.   † Page 94.   ‡ Page 97.

a great deal of Cheshire salt is exported. Many people also go there for bathing.

We must now follow the banks of the Weaver. Near it most of the salt-mines are worked, and in this district the best cheeses are made. It passes through a very rich country. Over it is built the Vale Royal Viaduct, a fine bridge of five arches, each twenty-one yards across.* On one of its branches, close to the borders of Staffordshire, stands the old town of Congleton. Here the chief manufacture is silk, principally black. You know how a caterpillar spins the silken thread, afterwards woven into beautiful textures. This comes to England from warmer climates, wound off the cocoons into hanks. The process of twisting, cleaning, and preparing it for the loom, is called throwing, or throwsting. In twisting two threads together, if one breaks, the work is undone. To prevent this, each thread passes through a fine wire loop, which the thread holds up. If it breaks, the wire falls, touches a little lever, sinking one end of it, and raising the other. This catches the wheel, and stops the machine, till the attendant mends the broken thread. I cannot explain to you the weaving of the silk; but the pattern is drawn in some peculiar way on cards, which the weaver reads, as a musician would the music of his book. M. Jacquard, a clever Frenchman, invented the best kind of silk-weaving machine.†

On the Weaver, or some of the canals connected with it, are Northwich, Nantwich, Middlewich, Sandbach. Near to all these towns are found salt-mines, or salt-water springs. You may always know that salt is found near the towns that end with "wich." In this district is Crewe, a town of wonderfully quick growth, built within the last few years; six lines of railway start hence, and its importance is entirely owing to railway traffic.

* Page 20.   † Page 86, 87.

There is a ruined castle near the Weaver, taken in King Charles's time by the Royalists. It was done very suddenly, in the pitch darkness of midnight, by only a handful of brave men. The soldiers inside thinking there was no danger, were not watching; but the Royalists entered, and, to the astonishment of all around, King Charles's flag was seen waving there the following morning.

Passing Frodsham, where you still meet salt-works, we must now look on the map for Birkenhead, exactly opposite Liverpool, a child of Liverpool, promising to be as tall as its mother. In 1821, there were only two hundred people living in the little village of Birkenhead. Fifty years afterwards, there were 65,000. Birkenhead has become famous for its docks; a bog at the mouth of a very small river having been converted into very large ones. This great floating harbour is surrounded by warehouses admirably built, and all round the docks is carried a railway, so that the goods brought by the ships require no carting before they are sent, perhaps to the heart of England. In Birkenhead there are a number of houses built for workmen, with every regard to their comfort. They are not cottages, but high houses; on each floor live two families. The door of each dwelling does not open on the street, but on the stairs. The houses are well drained, and the rooms of a good size, so as to make them as healthy as possible. There are several churches, with earnest clergy, a good market, and a noble park. If you stood on the pier, you would see steamboat ferries going ceaselessly across the Mersey, to and from Liverpool.* Near Birkenhead, many of the rich Liverpool merchants live. There is here a college for preparing young men to be clergymen and missionaries.† It is called St Aidan's College, after the good missionary

* Page 21.   † Pages 30, 74.

who left Scotland, and came to Holy Island, to teach the
Northumbrians about the great God and Jesus Christ.*   We
like to hear that there is a college for training missionaries
near that river where so many ships are floating, carrying
merchandise to all parts of the world.

Now, do you remember the name of the river on the
west side of Cheshire ?   I shall only tell you of one town
on the Dee, Chester.   It is as remarkable for being old as
Birkenhead is for being new.   Its name marks it as a
Roman camp.†   Formerly there was a great deal of commerce with Chester; but the Dee has become so shallow
with mud and sand banks, that large ships can no longer
sail up it; and thus almost all its traffic has been trans-
ferred to Liverpool and Birkenhead, on the broad and
deep Mersey.   Industrious man has, however, deepened
the river, so that now many smaller vessels trade with
Chester ; and commerce is rapidly increasing.

Round the town still extend the old Roman walls.‡   It
is very pleasant to walk along them, without any fear of
being shot by either arrows or guns.   The streets are very
strangely built.   The carriage-road is a good deal below
the inhabited parts of the houses, having on each side of it
small shops or warehouses.   *Above* the shops is the covered
footpath, at the side of which is another row of shops.
These upper paths are called "The Rows."   Stone steps
are frequent to lead the foot passengers from them into the
carriage-roads.   There is a good deal of wood mixed with
the stone of these houses, and the carving is very old and
curious.   Concerning one old house, which is still standing, I will tell you a very interesting story.

Near the end of Queen Mary's reign, an order was signed
for the persecution of the Irish Protestants.   Dr Cole, a
zealous Romanist, was the bearer of the order, and whilst

* Page 10.   † Pages 31, 91.   ‡ Pages 10, 19, 45.

stopping at this house, which was then an inn, before he
embarked for Dublin, he was visited by the Mayor, to
whom Dr Cole told the object of his mission, showing a
little leather box, containing papers.

Soon afterwards, he escorted the Mayor to the door. The
Protestant mistress of the inn had been present during the
conversation. She took advantage of the few minutes of
the doctor's absence to change the papers for a dirty pack
of cards. Soon Dr Cole, with his little leather box, sailed,
reached Dublin, opened it before the Viceroy, presented
his commission for the persecution of the Protestants, and

The Rows in Chester.

behold! it was a pack of cards! He instantly returned
to London, and again left for Chester, with a renewed
order. But now the wind did not blow favourably; and
as he waited for it to change, news arrived that the Queen
was dead, and that the Protestant Elizabeth ruled.*

* Page 27.

When the plague raged in Chester, only one house escaped.* It still stands, and over it is written, "God's providence is my inheritance." There is here an old cathedral, built of red sandstone, but not so handsome as several others in England.† Though Chester is not a *manufacturing* town, shot, lead pipes, paint, and other articles are made in it; and shipbuilding is again going on vigorously.

Cheshire might be reviewed as follows :—When each child has been furnished with a slate, or paper and pencil, let the teacher furnish some names of places, from which each may select what he chooses, writing under each name what he could there see. Thus, Chester, Birkenhead, Northwich, the river Weaver, Stockport, are named. Under Chester might be written, the river Dee, old walls, a few ships, cathedral, the Rows, the old house where Dr Cole lodged, the house that escaped the plague, shot-tower. Under Birkenhead might be written, docks, many ships, steam-ferry, model-houses, noble park, St Aidan's College. Under "Northwich," salt mines. Under "the Weaver," salt mines, dairies for cheeses, rich grass, good cows, towns ending with "wich," Vale Royal Viaduct. Under Stockport might be written, cotton mills, bleaching grounds, printing and dye-works, large Sunday school.

STAFFORDSHIRE.—PART I.

Now we go into a new county, Staffordshire. If you look at the principal river in it, the Trent, and trace its course, you will see that it will lead us through several other counties, until it reaches our old friend, the Humber, in the south of Yorkshire. Of all these counties, I hope to tell

* Page 80.　　　　　　　† Page 63.

you very interesting stories. Now look again at Staffordshire, and tell me the names of all the counties that border
on it. You see it is an inland county, no sea washing its
shores.* There is not such beautiful scenery in it as in
many others; but it is one of the most useful counties in
dear old England.

The north-eastern part is rather bleak, consisting of
high moorlands, the end of the great chain of hills from
the Cheviots southwards.† In the north-west, clay is found
suitable for earthenware; so there is an extensive district,
with various manufactories, or "banks," as they are called,
for making china. Across the middle of Staffordshire the
land is not rich, such as we heard of in Cheshire and
Yorkshire, but poor soil, where moorland oats are sown.
However, in the valleys near the rivers, grass grows abundantly. The south of Staffordshire is called the Black
Country, and it well deserves the name, as throughout it
bright-green fields are almost unknown. The earth there
is rich below, rather than above ground, immense quantities of coal and iron being imbedded.‡ These are needed
for the service of man, for the iron must be melted in immense iron furnaces, supplied abundantly by the coal. How
wisely God has ordered that coal and iron should be so
frequently found together. Collieries and ironworks consequently cover all the country, the overhanging smoke
causing a sort of perpetual twilight by day, and the enormous furnaces reflecting their fiery flame by night. No
fish swim in the streams, which, like everything else, are
black. The cottages and houses are of grimy brick, whilst
the large towns lie very near one another, filled with great
numbers of people.

Are the people black, too? Yes, they look so; for clean
faces and clean clothes are quite impossible when so much

* Page 76.   † Pages 15, 35, 65, 102.   ‡ Pages 4, 8, 26, 37, 85.

soot fills the air. But their minds are not so black. They are very rough, but some are intelligent and industrious, sending their children to school, attending lectures about poetry, geology, or history; and, what is better still, a great many go to church or chapel.

The women often wear their husbands' linsey coats and felt hats, and may be seen driving donkeys laden either with coal, or with bars of iron to be made into nails.

In the north of the county, among the potteries, the dress of the people is all a sort of gray or whitey-brown; and they wear round gray hats, with the brims turned up.

A peculiar custom in Staffordshire is, that the youngest instead of the eldest son succeeds to his father's property.

The district called the potteries is a collection of towns and large villages, which extend, like a manufacturing street, about eight miles along the road, the most central one being Burslem, which is sometimes called "the mother of the potteries," and the largest is Stoke-upon-Trent. The fields around are green and pleasant, whilst at a distance, the buildings, with their high walls, and chimneys narrowing upwards, and huge rounded furnaces, have almost the effect of a line of fortifications. It is from these that most of the common ware is sent, which provides so many comforts for English homes. In no country abroad are there such nice basins and jugs and footbaths, or such pretty common cups and saucers, as in England. Would you like to hear something about the manufacturing of these things, how the mug is made on which Charles or Mary is written in gold letters, or the plate with its pretty wreath of flowers?

The material of which fine china is formed is a mixture of flint and bones and Cornish clay. Flint prevents its breaking, though made very thin. First of all, the flint is calcined or burnt, till it is as white as possible, and with

the bones and clay is crushed or ground by the power of
steam. The mixture, which is then about as thick as
cream, is passed through a very fine sieve. It gradually
hardens by evaporation, till it is as thick as dough, and
then by the quick turning round of the potter's wheel, the
shapeless lumps of clay are formed into whatever shape
he chooses. Cup handles, jug spouts, &c., are made sepa-
rately in little moulds, and before they are baked, are

Scene in the Potteries.—Potter's Wheel.

cemented on by "slip," the material in its fluid state.
After being baked, the article is called biscuit, and has, if
made of very fine clay, almost the appearance of empy-
rean marble, being dull white, and porous. Porous means
that water can ooze through it. To prevent this, and to
make it bright, the china must be glazed. If it is common

china, the pattern must be printed first; but if it is the best china, glazing is the next process.   This is done by dipping the biscuit china into a mixture of water, lead, and glass, the latter two being ground to the finest powder. After glazing, it is baked; and if it is painted or gilt, it must be baked again and again, as often as any fresh touches are needed ; otherwise, the paint would wear off. The ovens are filled when the fires are out.   The various articles are put in large earthenware vessels, something like footbaths, called " saggars," and piled one upon another till the oven is full.   Then the furnaces all round are lighted.   Such red-hot furnaces they are ! and are kept burning for about fifty hours.   It is sometime before the oven is sufficiently cool to allow the saggars to be taken out.*   All the china that is not round is made in moulds, the clay being either pressed or poured into them.   The making of these moulds, and painting the beautiful pictures you see on china, require clever fingers ; and the designing of the shapes and patterns requires clever heads. The pretty little china brooches, which, perhaps, mamma wears, are made by workmen as neatly, and far more quickly than any lady could model wax flowers.   Do you think you could design anything?   After lessons try with a pencil and paper what you can do.

In this district of the potteries are Minton's celebrated works for the Mosaic pavement, which you often see in churches and in public rooms.   The patterns and colours are very beautiful.   How to make this kind of ware has only been discovered in the last few years.   The man who did most to increase the value of Staffordshire pottery was Josiah Wedgewood.   He lived about a hundred years ago.   He invented several new kinds of china, and copied the beautiful old ornaments used by the Greeks and

* Page 29.

Romans. Porcelain, or the kind of china, which is almost transparent, was not made in England till 1777. The curious old china ornaments, often seen in drawing-rooms, come from China, and so the name of that country is given to all such ware.

Staffordshire pottery is now sent to all parts of the world. I have heard of some being packed in peculiar shaped cases to fit the backs of the llamas, which were to carry them across the hills of central America.*

I must not tell you more to-day, but I hope one of you will bring me to-morrow the design of a vase, or of a jug, and that another will try to draw a bunch of grapes for the centre of a plate; or a wreath of vine leaves for the border.

STAFFORDSHIRE.—PART II.

I TOLD you in Cheshire of two silk towns. Name them. Now I will tell you of one in Staffordshire. They are all on the road between Manchester and Derby, the chief seats of the silk manufacture. Leek, in the north of the county, is the Staffordshire silk town, where ribbons are chiefly made.

A little to the west of the Potteries, is Newcastle-under-Lyne, which rhymes with Newcastle-upon-Tyne. Where is that?

Large collieries are near both the Newcastles. Lyne or Lyme, is an old name for a forest. There was a large one between Staffordshire and Cheshire, on the borders of which this Newcastle probably stood, and so received its name.†
There are manufactories for hats, silk, and cotton; but it is not nearly so large a town as the Northumberland New-castle.

* Pages 38, 95.   † Page 102.

II

Further down, on the Trent, is a splendid palace belonging to the Duke of Sutherland; and still further is Stone, where was once a very old monastery built by a Saxon king in honour of two sons, whom, whilst a pagan, he had murdered, because they had become believers in Jesus. Stone was the birthplace of Earl St Vincent, who fought a great naval battle. On the Stour, a branch of the Trent, is Stafford, a well-built town. There are here several tanneries, where leather is prepared, and here many boots and shoes are made. On the top of a high hill covered with trees is a fine old castle.

On another branch of this river is the seat of Lord Hatherton, which is said to have as many windows as there are days in the year.

About fifteen miles from Stafford is Lichfield, one of England's cathedral towns. The cathedral is built on a hill, and has three spires. Dr Johnson, who wrote the great dictionary, was born here. We are now within a very short distance of the hardware manufactories of the south of Staffordshire; the Black country, as it is called.

This is a very populous district; the largest towns are Wolverhampton, Walsall, Dudley, Sedgeley, Wednesbury, and West Bromwich.*

At Wolverhampton, all kinds of iron-work are made. The rough iron is smelted and converted into pigs, bars, hoops, and plates; and from these again are made grates, fire-irons, and garden tools. As Wolverhampton is famous for its locks and keys, its hinges and its latches, very possibly our doors are fastened with Wolverhampton locks. There is here a beautiful orphanage, founded by Mr Lees, of the little children who have no father nor mother. Walsall is on the eastern edge of the Black country.

* Page 92.

Here, too, are great iron-foundries, and manufactories for making saddles, harness, buckles, snuffers, firearms, and other things. Walsall has a famous market for pigs; not iron pigs, but living, squeaking, grunting ones.

Now we must visit Dudley, where, besides iron-works for boilers, cables, spades, and nails, there is a fine old castle, and also great caverns in the limestone rocks near the town. Do you observe how caverns and limestone generally go together?* The castle was first built more than a thousand years ago, by Dodo, a Saxon. If walls could speak, these old castles could all tell tales of wars and sieges. We thank God, that the noise now heard is not that of cannons firing, but of hammers beating out many useful things. Some nails are made by steam-machinery; but a great many by the strength and industry of man, and, I am sorry to say, of woman too; for you will be surprised to hear, that in this neighbourhood the women work hard at the hammer, with their fathers, brothers, and husbands. The work is done wonderfully quickly. I have heard of one man making 34,000 large nails in a fortnight. In the neighbourhood of Sedgeley, nothing but nails are made. Wednesfield, another town, supplies traps for catching rats, mice, and foxes. At Wednesbury, various kinds of iron-work are done, principally railway carriages, and springs for coaches, hinges, and gun-locks.

Between Birmingham, and either Dudley or Wolverhampton, the roads pass through a continuous town, under clouds of smoke. The ground below is quite like a honeycomb; it has been so searched for coal and iron. Often portions of it sink, and the road has to be altered, or the houses removed.† This is a short chapter, but I think you have heard the names of plenty of places to-day. To-morrow, I hope to tell you about the manufactories of

* Page 44, 46. † Page 101.

Birmingham, one of the most wonderful towns in England, which stands partly in Staffordshire, but principally in Warwickshire.

WARWICKSHIRE.—PART I.

BEFORE I tell you of Warwickshire as a county, I must tell you of Birmingham as a town; for if you look on the map, you will see it stands on the borders of—which counties? It is, as it were, the parent of the busy, smoking district of which I so lately told you—namely, the Black country. The coal and iron, which its many manufactories require, are easily brought from this district, either by canals or railways, with which it is well supplied.* There is no river near, which is rather singular, as almost all great towns are on rivers. Can you tell me why? Birmingham is the fourth largest town in England. What towns are larger? It stands on several low hills, and being well drained is very healthy, although nearly 350,000 people live in it. Several of its inhabitants have lived to be ninety or a hundred years old. There is a fine town-hall, built of marble from the Isle-of-Man, and a very large market-hall, with six hundred stalls, where beef and toys, potatoes and necklaces, ducks and geese, pigs and cabbages are sold. There is a School of Art, for teaching men and boys to make models and draw designs, and there are many other schools; and hospitals for the sick; and churches, where there have been and still are excellent clergy and other persons, who have spent their lives in doing good among the many thousand people.

In almost every street of Birmingham are high chimneys, beneath which are boilers and steam-engines, all hard at work, making an immense number of useful things. There

* Page 50, 86.

is hardly anything into which metals can be made, which is not manufactured in Birmingham.* You are always using some of its ware. Your clothes may come from Leeds or Manchester; but the buttons are probably made in Birmingham. Your tea may come from China; but the tea-kettle from Birmingham. The timbers of your house may be from Norway; but the nails from Birmingham. I cannot tell you of all the things made in its great manufactories. There are mighty steam-engines, and little pins; there are the iron and glass of the great crystal palaces, and multitudes of hooks and eyes; there are glittering swords, and golden chains; enormous guns, and an incredible number of steel pens; glass chandeliers, and pots and pans; papier-maché trays, and silver tea-pots. Would you not like to see some of these things made? I will tell you a little about hooks and eyes, for they are useful; about cut-glass, for it is beautiful; about the great iron-works of Messrs Fox and Henderson, who built the Crystal Palace, for they are stupendous; and about buttons, too, for they are little.

The wire for the hook or eye is unwound by a small machine from a wheel, round which it has been coiled, and in less than a second it is thrown into a drawer beneath, *finished.* The little machine is about the size of a writing-desk. It draws in the wire; at a certain point, it snips off the right length of wire; small steel hooks at this moment descend, they clasp the wire round them at each end, and bend it in the centre, circular for an eye, or double for a hook; but it must not stop there, as others are to be made, so a little spider-looking claw springs forward, catches it as a cat would a mouse, and throws it into a drawer. From 4000 to 6000 of these can be made in an hour.

* Page 51.

Now for a little about cut-glass, which is used for decanters, wine-glasses, chandeliers, and other ornamental things. It is made of flint-glass, a little different in the materials of which it is composed from the plate-glass of which I told you at Shields. A tube is put into the hot liquid glass, which collects a little of the metal. If the workman wishes to make a bottle, he whirls this round and round, then rolls it on a flat slab, and afterwards blows into it to make it hollow. With a little iron tool he flattens the bottom of the vessel, and to this he fastens an iron wire, and keeping the other part hot, he cuts off, with a pair of scissors, what glass he does not want, and gives the remainder what shape he chooses. There are no knives employed in cutting glass ; but the sharp edges which you feel, and which are so ornamental, are made by grinding the surface of the article upon wheels, sometimes with sharp, sometimes with round edges, and always kept wet with sand and water, which drips from funnels placed above them. Here, too, with very narrow wheels are engraved the beautiful flowers, stars, or crests you sometimes see drawn on glass.

Now for a little about the monster iron works. Here are made engine boilers, railway carriage wheels, iron axes, iron girders, cannons, rifles, bedsteads, and more things than I can mention.* Here was made all the iron-work of Sydenham Palace, and of most of the railway stations. The noise and din are terrible. The iron is forged, not by the strength of the blacksmith's brawny arm, but by steam, which, with enormous shears, cuts plates of iron as easily as you would cut a sheet of paper; and with sharp tools pierces large round holes, as easily as the cook would cut out the little cakes from gingerbread dough. Here is used Nasmyth's famous hammer, worked by steam, which can

* Page 21.

come down with force sufficient to rivet the largest blocks
of iron, or with such gentleness that it could break a nut-
shell without hurting the kernel.

Now, lastly, for a little about buttons. I have not time
to tell how all the various kinds are made, such as pearl,
metallic, tailors', shirt, and the different ornamental
ones. In making pearl buttons alone, more than 2000
people are engaged. Many tons weight of mother-of-pearl
are brought from London, having been conveyed there by
ships from India. A little tubular saw, worked in a lathe,
cuts them round out of the oyster shell, then women make
the holes, by means of a sharp iron pointer called a "drill,"
and afterwards they are polished with soap and rotten
stone. The tailors' buttons, such as are seen on coats, are
made of five pieces, the metal plate, the perforated bottoms,
a piece of paper to fill up between these, the silk cover,
and a coarse bit of cloth between the paper stuffings, and
the bottoms. These, properly placed, are all fastened together in a moment, by a sudden pressure, and they cannot
be separated. Ask for a button, such as papa wears, cut
it up, and see if the five pieces are there.

The electro-plating in Birmingham is also very curious.*
An article, perhaps a tea-pot, made of German silver, or
nickel, is placed in a vat for less than a minute, and comes
out coated entirely with silver, which, after being polished,
is ready for sale, looking as bright and beautiful as possible. When you are older you will understand how this
is done.

I will just tell you of one thing more—papier-maché
work. The best trays are made of this, and also the pretty
workboxes, and portfolios, with flowers and birds painted
on a black ground, which you see in the drawing-room, and
sometimes the tops of tables, or even sofas and chairs

* Page 38.

are of this material. Now what do you think papier-maché is made of ? Paper; sheets of brown paper pasted together, and then japanned, painted, gilded, varnished. I daresay when you were little, you often made paper chairs, tables, and sofas, for the baby house; but perhaps you never thought there were real paper ones for grown-up people.

Near Birmingham are the Soho Works, where the famous James Watt made the first steam-engine.* He discovered the power of steam by observing the movement of the lid of a tea-kettle filled with boiling water. There is the value of thinking.

Now, little ones, I must not tell you any more, or you will be bewildered with thinking how everything is made.

To-morrow we shall play at a new game for Cheshire, Staffordshire, and Birmingham, and if you like to include Lancashire, and Yorkshire too, you may do so.

SUPPLIES FOR THE EMIGRANT.

One person, *e.g.*, Charles, goes out of the room. The rest are seated round. Each child takes the name of a town. Thus Charles returns, and addresses No. I, saying—The emigrant is preparing to go to Australia, with what will you supply him :—

No. 1 With nails to hammer up his wooden house.
Charles—Birmingham.

No. 1 No; try again.
Charles—Sedgeley.

No. 1 Right—pass on.
Charles next inquires of No. 2.

No. 2 A handkerchief for his neck.
Charles—Macclesfield.   He passes on.

No. 3 A store of salt.
Charles—One of the " Wiches," I dare say—Northwich.

* Page 21.

No. 4 Cups and saucers.
Charles—Oh! from the Potteries.

No. 5 A tea-tray.
Charles—Birmingham.

No. 6 A pair of boots.
Charles—Dudley.

No. 6 No, no ; Dudley is an iron town.   You must pay a forfeit.

No. 7 A lot of buttons.
Charles—Birmingham again.

After going all round, another child might go out.   If any one mentions a wrong article for the town he personates, he must pay a forfeit ; as also the one who guesses a wrong town.

———

In the school-room division of the lessons, the towns of Cheshire and Stafford might be classified on the slate. The commercial towns, the agricultural towns, the cathedral towns, the manufacturing towns.   The three rivers of Cheshire might be traced, and the three divisions of Staffordshire described.

WARWICKSHIRE.—Part II.

WARWICKSHIRE may be reckoned the most central county in England.   If you look on the map, you will see it is the furthest from the sea on all sides, and, if you look again, you may observe that its rivers run in three directions. In the north, there is the Tame, running towards the Trent, which, as you know, is hastening to the Humber. Through the middle of the county, from east to west, runs the Avon, which empties itself into the Severn ; whilst, in the south, is a small river, which runs off in the direction of the great Thames.

The greater part of Warwickshire is very beautiful. The banks of the Avon are green and well wooded, and the scene of much interest. The soil is generally good; and the pastures, and large trees, the fields of corn, flax, and turnips, tell how fertile the country is. Dear old England! Don't you think every county has its interest and its beauty?

The only town of consequence on the Tame is Tamworth. Tape and paper are made here. Near it is Drayton Manor, where the celebrated Sir Robert Peel lived.*

Following the Avon, you will very soon see Rugby, famous for its railway station, where so many different lines meet, and still more famous for its school, where good Dr Arnold taught. It is the scene of "Tom Brown's School-days." Amongst the many good men educated at Rugby was Henry Fox, the missionary. He worked hard for Jesus in Southern India, and when, on account of his health, he could remain there no longer, he came back to England, and did all he could to interest people about mission-work. Soon his work was over, for the Saviour he loved sent His messenger, Death, and took him to his heavenly home.

North of the Avon is the old city of Coventry. Parts of it are very ancient; the gable ends of the houses nearly meet across the street, and are formed of old wooden beams placed crosswise, filled up with brick and plaster.† There are some fine old churches with high spires. The cathedral was destroyed at the Reformation. Coventry is very famous for the manufacture of ribbons, and there are more watches made there than in London. When no one will speak to some unfortunate person, he is said to be " sent to Coventry." I suppose you would not like in this way to go to Coventry.

* Pages 86, 92. † Page 102.

South of Coventry is Kenilworth, a small town, celebrated for the ivy-covered ruins of its once magnificent
castle. Knights have often ridden across its courts in
gorgeous dress. The first time silk was worn in England was here, at a grand tournament in the reign of
Edward I. Queen Elizabeth visited her favourite, the
Earl of Leicester, at this castle. She remained nineteen
days, enjoying every sort of festivity. I think our good
Queen Victoria would not like some of the amusements
they had in those days. One was bear-baiting, that is, a
poor bear was tormented by a great many dogs, endeavouring to tear it in pieces. On Sundays, too, there was, in the
evening, dancing or play-acting. Now all the grandeur is
passed away, and the walls are moss-grown.*

Between Kenilworth and the beautiful Avon is Stone-
leigh ; in the park are very large and old oak-trees.

On the little river Leam, before it joins the Avon, is
Leamington, a famous watering-place. Invalids go there
to drink the waters, which became celebrated owing to a
very clever man, Dr Jephson.† Early rising, good exercise, and healthy air, are the principal causes of the
benefit gained.

About two miles from Leamington is Warwick, where
there is a beautiful old castle, not a ruin, but a splendid
residence.‡ It was re-built by Ethelfreda, the daughter
of Alfred the Great. Here lived Warwick, the king-maker,
who helped to dethrone Henry VI., and afterwards fought
against Edward IV., and, for a short time, made Henry
king again. About a mile from Warwick is Guy's Cliff,
where the celebrated Guy of Warwick lived as a hermit.
There are many strange stories told of him ; but he lived
so long since—in the time of Athelstan—that we do not
know how far they are true. It is said that the Danes

* Pages 9, 14, 17, 32, 105. † Pages 48, 57. ‡ Page 15.

were advancing far into England, and that Athelstan feared
he should lose his throne.   They had a great champion,
an African giant, called Colebrand, whom no Englishman
could be found to fight.   At length, Guy of Warwick
appeared.   No one knew his name.   He seemed a poor
pilgrim, just landed at Portsmouth.   The giant looked
scornfully at him, but soon they met in single combat.
What anxiety is there !   Athelstan dares not watch.   He
turns aside to pray.   Colebrand staggers—he falls—a cry
of joy rings through the English army.   The victor tells
his name to no one but the king.   He hides from the
people, and retires to this cliff on the Avon, where he hews
out for himself the cave, and lives and dies, unknown even
to his wife, who was living at the neighbouring castle of
Warwick, anxiously expecting the return of her pilgrim-
husband.*

Further down the Avon is Stratford, the birthplace of
the celebrated Shakespeare.   Here the house still stands
in which he is said to have been born ; and, in the parish
church, is the marble slab beneath which he is buried.   I
will write out for you a few verses in which he described
the beautiful Avon, whose banks we have been following.

> " The current, that with gentle murmur glides,
>   Thou know'st being stopp'd impatiently doth rage;
>   But, when his fair course is not hindered,
>   He makes sweet music with th' enamell'd stones,
>   Giving a gentle kiss to every sedge
>   He overtaketh in his pilgrimage :
>   And so, by many winding nooks he strays,
>   With willing sport to the wild ocean."

On the borders of the county is Edgehill, the scene of
one of those dreadful battles, when Englishmen fought
against Englishmen, in the reign of Charles I.†   It is at

* Page 17.   † Pages 45, 105.

the west end of the valley of the Red Horse, a pretty fertile vale, full of corn-fields and green meadows. Some day I shall tell you about the valley of the White Horse; but now good-bye to Warwickshire.

DERBYSHIRE.—PART I.

WE now reach another of the central counties of England —one famous for manufactories, especially as regards their history—famous for the valuable mineral treasures it possesses, and famous for its very beautiful scenery and splendid caverns.* I think, when I have told you all I can about Derbyshire, it will be quite one of your favourite counties.

Now, look on the map and see what counties touch it. North, south, east, and west? Look again, and see what rivers flow through it. The Derwent and the Dove are the principal, both falling into the Trent. They are beautiful rivers, and full of trout. The Derwent, moreover, is a very busy one, helping, as it rolls along, all sorts of manufactories. Again, look at the map, and besides the towns, do you see anything else marked? A mountain range. Yes, the backbone of Old England divides and forms the Staffordshire hills of which I told you, and the Peak of Derbyshire. You can now trace it all the way from the Cheviots in Northumberland.† The Peak is a range of mountains without any great height, but with very fine scenery. The most northern part is called the High Peak. Here are deep dells and towering rocks, and caverns as wonderful as those in Yorkshire. The dales are full of bright green meadows, and look beautiful, contrasted with the bare and rugged mountains. The south of the county is very fertile, and there much wheat and barley

* Page 35.　　　† Pages 15, 35, 65, 102, 109.

are grown; but in the north, oats, which do not require so rich a soil, are cultivated. On the hills small mountain sheep feed, and light and slender horses, which, though drawing loads of stone, with great agility ascend and descend the mountain sides.

The stone in Derbyshire was considered the best for building to be found in England, and was therefore chosen in preference to any other for the erection of the new Houses of Parliament.

The chief riches of Derbyshire are underground : * coal, lead, iron, gypsum, and marble are all found there. Gypsum is a beautiful glassy-looking sort of spar; sometimes precious stones, such as chalcedony and onyx, are discovered, and there is also a beautiful spar called "Blue John." It is of various colours, violet, yellow, or rose colour, and is made into all kinds of pretty ornaments. In the mountainous districts, there are several warm salt-springs, where the water tastes of soda, or of magnesia ; † and also lime-water, as at Knaresborough, which encrusts everything placed in it with stone.‡

Besides natural products, Derbyshire is noted for many manufactures, especially silks, cottons, muslins, tape, and candle-wicks; silk stockings and silk gloves are, I believe, made only in this county. At Derby, there is a manufactory for very fine china. There are, also, iron works, coal and lead mines, paper mills, etc.

In the extreme north-west of the county, not far from Stockport, in Cheshire, is Glossop. Here again we meet with cotton manufactories : but these are nearly the last of which I shall tell you, as we shall then have gone through what we may call the cotton country, viz., Lancashire, Cheshire, and this town in Derby.§

* Pages 4, 26.   † Pages 48, 57, 123.
‡ Pages 44, 46.   § Pages 94, 103.

And now you must hear of some of the wonders of the High Peak. I must tell you of a castle on one of its summits; of a cavern which runs through its centre; and of a hole far deeper than its foot.

First, the castle. It was built by a son of William the Conqueror, called Peverill, and because he built his castle here he was always known as Peverill of the Peak.* Very little of it now remains; but you have a beautiful view from its ruins.

Second, the cavern, called the Peak Cavern.† To visit

Peak Cavern.

it you must approach through a narrow ravine, with steep towering rocks on each side. This ravine is closed at the further end by a high cliff, at the bottom of which is the mouth of the cave.

Here are met many noisy, wild-looking men, women, and children, who have taken possession of this strange

* Page 20.   † Page 46.

place as a sort of workshop for spinning twine. At first, everything seems dark; but as your eye grows accustomed to the feeble light in the centre, you begin to discover the cavern walls. Then you reach the first water. Here the roof and water seem almost to meet; and to proceed, you must get into a little boat, and lie flat till you cross the stream. Then you walk through a number of chambers, some so high that even with a blue light let off, you cannot see the roof, and others so low, that only very little people can pass without stooping. One of these is called Roger Rain's House, because water is always dropping through the roof; another, Great Tom of Lincoln, with beautiful stalactites, like icicles hanging from the roof; sometimes there are natural arches; in one part is a sort of musical gallery, where singers are sometimes placed, whose voices echo beautifully. A gunpowder explosion there is very awful; it is like a loud crashing peal of thunder, echoing again and again, more and more softly, till at last it dies away in the gentlest whispers.

Now I have to tell you, thirdly, of the deep hole. It is "Eldon Hole," in what is called the "Peak Forest." It is about thirty yards long and ten yards wide. How much larger than this room? Its depth is not known. It is very awful to stand beside it and look down its yawning gulf, so deep, so dark.

Another curious place is Mam Tor, or the Shivering Mountain. This is formed of a kind of broken stone, which slides down under any additional weight. Frosts often loosen the stones above, which, slipping down, set the whole face of the hill in motion.

These and the mine for the Blue John, and Wingats, a pass, with rocks about 1000 feet high on either side,* are

* Pages 35, 72.

near Castleton and Buxton, which you will see on the map.

In the Lower Peak are Dove Dale and the valley of the Derwent, where the scenery is both grand and beautiful; the rivers flowing between limestone rocks of the oddest and most grotesque shapes. At Buxton, Bakewell, and Matlock, all in these districts are warm springs of mineral water. It seems strange that hot water should come out of the ground; but very likely the interior of our earthly ball is fire, and as it is known that in mines the further you are from the surface, the hotter the air becomes, we imagine that the sources of these springs are very deep. Sometimes close to a hot spring is a cold one, which shows that though they may be very near each other at their surface, they are very far off at their source.

I must tell you of a little village, Eyam. About 200 years ago, a box of woollen clothes had been sent there from London, where the plague was raging dreadfully. It was incautiously opened, and the plague broke out in the district. The good vicar immediately did what he could to stay its progress to surrounding villages; he made a boundary line, beyond which his people were not to pass, and to which the neighbouring villagers brought the necessaries required. Here may still be seen troughs, which were then filled with water, to purify the money given in payment. In order to prevent any crowded meetings, he had service in a lonely little valley at the end of the village; and making a rock his pulpit, the vicar told his sorrowing people of the love of their chastening Father. The plague did not extend beyond the line; but for seven long months it lingered amongst the inhabitants of that quiet parish. Out of 330 people, only 80 survived. The good vicar lived; but his noble wife, who shared her husband's labours, died, and her tomb may still be seen in Eyam church-yard.*

Now think of all the interesting things you have heard to-day, and to-morrow I hope to tell you of old castles and new castles, and of two or three more busy towns.

DERBYSHIRE—PART II.

BEFORE we leave the neighbourhood of Matlock and the Peak, I must tell you of a large old house where you may see how English people lived a hundred years ago, and of a grand modern house, where you may see how the very rich English nobility can live in the present day. I will first, however, mention Hardwick Hall, also a large old house. In the ruined mansion standing close beside it, the unfortunate Mary, Queen of Scots, lived a prisoner for some time.†

Old things before new, like old people before little children; so I will talk first about Haddon Hall, and then about Chatsworth. Haddon Hall is not in ruins, like many old castles, nor has it been made suitable to live in at the present day, like Windsor and Alnwick and War-wick.‡ It was built about 400 years ago. The Duke of Rutland, to whom it belongs, prefers living in another of his beautiful castles; so he keeps this one as it was to show the manners of our forefathers. In one room, called "the chaplain's," there are immense pewter dishes and platters, on which dinners used to be served; very different from the elegant silver services and porcelain plates of the present day. There are curious old jack-boots, clumsy match-locks, and an antique baby's cradle.

Then there is the great hall, where the lord of the castle used to dine with his servants and dependents. He and

* Page 80. 　　　 † Page 42. 　　　 ‡ Pages 15, 123.

his friends sat at the upper end, the servants at the lower. Here is a curious relic of the barbarous customs of those days—an iron handcuff fastened against the screen, as high as the hand can reach above the head. If any guest refused to drink what was offered him, his hand was fastened tight in this, and the contents of the cup poured down his sleeve. The hinges of the doors are very old, and, *we* should say, clumsy. The walls are hung with tapestry, a sort of worsted work, very fine, representing beautiful pictures, which the ladies and their maids spent many hours in stitching; for women cared little then for reading and writing. The garden looks as strange as the house; the trees clipped to odd patterns, and the hedges tall, straight, and even, with narrow walks between them.

Now, you shall hear about Chatsworth. It belongs to the Duke of Devonshire, and is reckoned by many, the most splendid residence in England. It is on the river Derwent, not three miles from Haddon Hall, to which it is a great contrast. It is almost a new house, the greater part of it having been built within the last forty years. The front of the house, the pillars, the statues, the ornaments, are very beautiful, whilst inside are paintings, carved wood-work, and statuary of the finest kind. The conservatory is full of the rarest flowers, and so large that a carriage and four can drive into it. The Duke of Devonshire had a very clever gardener called Paxton. He planned this conservatory; afterwards he planned the building of the Great Exhibition in Hyde Park; and then the still greater Crystal Palace at Sydenham. He was knighted, and became the celebrated Sir Joseph Paxton.

The gardens at Chatsworth are very famous. There is a fountain which throws the water up 300 feet. How beautifully it glitters, like streams of silver! Again, there is a grand cascade. The waters seem to flow from beneath a stone temple, and descend over numberless steps. Again there is a tree, beneath which you stand, and, all at once, water pours from every branch. You rush away from this unexpected shower-bath, and, behold! serpents are around you, from whose mouths issue streams of water. The rock-work, too, is very wonderful; massive rocks are brought there to resemble nature as much as possible. At one part, the rocks are placed similar to the Strid at Bolton Abbey, and the water rushes wildly between. From the little I have told you, do you not think that Chatsworth deserves the name of the Palace of the Peak? But remember, earthly greatness will not make earthly happiness, and that, though your home on earth be but a cottage, you are invited by God to an eternal mansion in heaven.

Now we must leave the picturesque scenes and mansions of the Peak, and talk a little about the towns of Derbyshire. In the north-east, on the borders of Yorkshire, is Chesterfield. It is a busy manufacturing town, in the neighbourhood of coal pits and iron furnaces.* The church has a very curious crooked spire, made of wood, and covered with lead. Near Chesterfield a great deal of camomile is grown, a daisy-like flower used in medicine.

Below Matlock, on the Derwent, is Bromford, where the first cotton factory ever built was erected by Sir R. Arkwright, who greatly improved, as I told you, the spinning machinery.† The building still stands, the river Derwent still turning its great wheels. East of Cromford is an iron district, where iron is not only dug and smelted and formed into pigs and bars, but is also wrought into many useful things. Vauxhall Bridge, in London, over the Thames, was cast in this district.

Further down the Derwent is Belper. Here nails and

* Pages 20, 40, 51, 109, 114–116.   † Pages 86, 94.

earthenware are made; but its largest manufactories are for silk and cotton stockings and gloves.

About seven miles from Belper stands Derby, the chief town of the county. In Derby are several large churches, one of which has a very high spire, and another a handsome tower. There are also many schools and hospitals; but what particularly marks Derby is a beautiful public park, called an Arboretum; the noble gift of Mr Strutt, a very wealthy and excellent manufacturer. The day of its opening was one of great joy. In the evening a large crowd of people assembled in front of his door, and sang, with warm hearts, "The fine old English gentleman." How pleasant it must be for the Derby workman to walk on a holiday with his wife and little children amongst these beautiful trees, and to sit in the summer-houses, or on the benches placed for his comfort!

And now you shall hear of the employments of Derby workmen. Many of them are making all sorts of ornamental things of "Blue John," the beautiful spar of which I have before told you. Others are working in iron, others making lead pipes, or sheet lead, for the tops of houses, and others at the sadly unhealthy white and red lead works.* Many are making lace and bobbin-net; and others are engaged manufacturing the beautiful cups, saucers, and plates which are used for breakfast and dinner.† Many also are making stockings, particularly the ribbed kind, which, perhaps, mamma buys for her little boy or girl; but the greater number are manufacturing silks.‡ The first mill for spinning silk erected in England was built here by a person called Lombe, about 150 years ago. Till this time the Italians only knew how to convert raw silk into thread, but a young brother of the Lombes went over to Italy, to

* Page 21.　　　　　　　　† Page 110.
‡ Pages 94, 103, 104, 113.

find out the secret; this was very difficult, for whenever he
went into the manufactory, the wheels were kept on purpose so hard at work, that it was impossible to discover it.
At last, he pretended to be a poor youth wanting employment, and was engaged to work in the mill. He slept
there also, and during the night took drawings of the
wheels and other parts of the machinery. The Italians
were very jealous of any one finding out their manufacturing secrets, and, had they known, they would have put
him to death. He sent the drawings home, and then escaped. It is, however, said that when the Italians heard
of it, they were so angry, that they sent a woman over to
England, commissioned to poison him, and that poor John
Lombe died when only twenty-nine, from the effects of a
deadly slow poison. We feel very sorry for his death;
yet we wish he had found out the secret by thinking,
as Arkwright and Stephenson made their discoveries,
rather than by taking what was not fairly his own.*

There are no remarkable towns south of Derby, excepting Burton-upon Trent, noted for its ale, which is sent not
only to all parts of England, but to India, China, and other
hot countries. The country in this district is fertile,
without any hills. Many cows and horses feed on the
rich green grass; and cheeses are made there as in Cheshire.†

It would be well to review Warwickshire and Derby
together. Any of the former plans suggested might be
repeated; or, as a variety, an evening might be spent in
the following manner :—

The teacher personates a traveller, and describes the different scenes of which the children have heard, leaving it
for them to supply the name. Thus :

* Pages 9, 86.   † Page 100.

Teacher.—The railway whistle sounds. I approach a large station. Many boys jump from the train. They are going to school. She looks to Willie for an answer; who says Rugby, or pays a forfeit.

Teacher.—I walk between high rocks. I enter a passage below a mountain. I lie down in a boat. I am pushéd across. I wander long in beautiful halls beneath the ground.

Amy replies : The High Peak Cavern, near Castleton.

Teacher.—I stand before a noble mansion. I wander in the most lovely gardens. I rest beneath a tree. Away ! away ! it is a shower-bath !

Cave will not be long in exclaiming Chatsworth.

Teacher.—On the banks of a beautifully-wooded stream, I wander beneath the walls of a fine old castle. I think of many scenes of history it has witnessed, and I remark with pleasure, that it is not hastening to decay.

Charlotte.—You must mean Warwick Castle.

Teacher.—I stand alone in a wild and quiet district. I enter the churchyard and read the name of the worthy vicar's worthy wife, who died during a dreadful pestilence.

We hope that Laura does not forget Eyam.

NOTTINGHAMSHIRE.

Now, dear children, we have come to the egg-shaped county. You already know its name? Try to name the four counties which lie around it.

Nottinghamshire is like many of the other counties of dear old England—a very beautiful one, full of green fields and broad fertile valleys. There are no mountains. It is on the east side of the line that we once drew between the Exe and Tees.* Still, it is not a flat county, and

* Pages 4, 36.

there are a good many rocks, many of them formed of red sandstone.*

On the borders of Derbyshire, coal is found; but Nottingham is not generally a county for minerals. It used to be famous for Sherwood Forest, twenty-five miles long, and nine or ten broad; where, probably in the reign of Edward I., lived Robin Hood, and his knight, "Little John."† The poor people liked Robin Hood, for he took their part against the proud barons; but he was the dread of all travellers that passed that way. Little John was only seven feet high! There are still remains of the forest, and some of its venerable trees ornament the parks of different noblemen, who have beautiful seats around a little town, Worksop, which you will see on the map. This district is called the Dukeries—Worksop Manor, belonging to the Duke of Norfolk; Clumber Park, to the Duke of Newcastle; Welbeck Abbey, to the Duke of Portland.

It is very pleasant to take long drives under the high trees and along the grassy roads of these beautiful parks. Not very distant is Newstead Abbey, where the talented but unhappy and unfortunate Lord Byron lived. I say talented, for he wrote poetry that was wonderfully beautiful; I say unhappy, for he never learned to conquer his passions, nor knew how to make God his friend; and I say unfortunate, for his mother showed no thoughtful love in bringing him up. Poor Lord Byron! God gave him great talents; but he never used them to the glory of that God.

All kinds of grain grow in Nottinghamshire; and also hops, used in brewing, of which I shall tell you more when we arrive in Kent, or Worcestershire. The Trent enters the country in the south-west, and runs north-east all through it, on its way to join our old friend the Humber.

* Page 60.   † Pages 51, 102.

If you find out why the Trent is like a ravelled skein of silk, you will never forget that it runs into Notts. Now we will trace its banks, and, as we visit its towns, you will discover in what, besides farming, Nottinghamshire people are employed.

The first town about which you shall hear is Nottingham, built on the river Leam, not far from the Trent. It had a castle erected on a high rock. This rock is full of holes and passages, called Mortimer's holes; for here it was that Mortimer, the guilty favourite of poor Edward II.'s queen, Isabella, was seized and made prisoner. Here Charles I. first raised his unfortunate standard. About 200 years ago, the old castle was destroyed, and a new one built. It was, however, burnt down by a rabble during riots in 1831, and nothing now stands but blackened ruins.

In Nottingham are many churches and chapels; the largest and handsomest is St Mary's, where about 2000 people may be seated. The town is badly built; the houses crowding much upon each other. This is owing to Nottingham having been encircled with some hundred acres of common. This being public property, no one could encroach on it; so, instead of houses spreading outward, they were built closer and closer together. Now, however, the townsmen have leave from Parliament to build upon the ground; so I hope the poor stocking and bobbin-net weavers will have more room to live in than formerly.

Almost all the stockings made in Nottingham are of cotton.* As we have yet to come to the county for worsted stockings, I will not tell you, till then, how hosiery is made. Now you must hear about the bobbin-net machines, the peculiar characteristic of Nottingham.

* Page 126.

They are beautifully constructed, and many Nottingham people are employed in making them. Some are worked by steam, others by the hand; some make the narrow quillings that trim a cap, and others, net five yards wide. I cannot describe to you the making; but; when made, it has to pass through gas flames, which are so managed as to singe the little hairs without hurting the net. The machines worked by steam are large, and placed in factories; but the hand machines are small, and often kept at the poor people's houses. They make both the stockings

Stockinger at Work.

and the net in their own cottages, the women helping in the work, sewing up the stockings and embroidering the lace. They are, however, badly paid;* and at the Nottingham

* Contrast pages 7, 38, 85.

market, which is a very large one, farthings are much more used than in many places. At a stocking-frame, in Nottingham, once sat a poor boy, Henry Kirke White, who was very clever, whose thoughts were very beautiful, and who wrote sweet poetry. His poetry was so good, that some kind, rich people sent him to Cambridge, where he studied too hard, and died very young. One of the beautiful hymns he wrote, was about the Star of Bethlehem.

We must now leave Nottingham, and visit Newark. Here are the ruins of an old castle, built in the time of Stephen, and then called "New Work," from which the town takes its name.* In this castle King John died. The fine parish church has a beautiful spire. There is a very large trade in corn here, and in stage-coach days there used to be fifty inns, Newark lying on the direct road from London to the north. Near Newark is found plaster of Paris, so much employed in statuary. To the south-east lies a lovely valley, called the Vale of Belvoir.

Leaving the Trent, we will look near the source of the Idle, a river that joins it in the north of the county. There is Mansfield, in the neighbourhood of Sherwood Forest, with stocking and other manufactories similar to Nottingham. A story is told about King Henry II., which will, I think, amuse you. The king had been out hunting all day in Sherwood Forest, and had been separated from his attendants. He reached the house of a worthy miller, who received him as a wandering stranger, in a blunt but kind manner, asking him if he could not eat something, which the hungry king was very glad to do. He then begged him to remain all night, and the tired king consented. The next morning, some of the attendants, much alarmed at the loss of their king, called to inquire about him, and the miller and his wife were, as you may ima-

* Page 20.

gine, astonished to hear these gentlemen address the stranger as their sovereign.

Near the part where the Idle joins the Trent is East Retford.   Here there is an important railway-station. Nottinghamshire is well supplied with canals and rivers and railways, which help much in carrying merchandise through the county.*   Now you have heard enough for one day; to-morrow we will travel a little southward into Leicestershire, to complete, what may be termed, the hosiery, that is, the stocking and glove district of England.

LEICESTERSHIRE.

Now, little ones, what is our new county?   Leicestershire.   Not a very large one; but I think we shall find plenty in it to interest us for one day.   First, find out all the counties that surround it, not forgetting little Rutland in the corner.   It is chiefly watered by the river Soar and its branches.   The Welland separates it in the south from Northampton.   These are not clear, quick-running streams, passing between high banks and rocky chasms, like many of which I have told you, but quiet rivers wandering amongst corn-fields and green meadows, and full of reeds and water-plants.†   Leicestershire is not, however, a very flat county.   That you will guess, when I tell you that in one part, towards the west, coal, slate, sandstone, and limestone are found.   Near Ashby-de-la-Zouch, is Charnwood Forest, not a forest now, but surmounted with craggy steeps.   Bardon Hill, the highest point, is not very lofty, but as the country all around is low, the view is most extensive.‡   Northwards, you may see Lincoln Cathedral,

* Pages 50, 86, 116.   † Pages 4, 17, 32, 36, 47, 49, 61.
‡ Pages 40, 64, 69.

sixty miles off, and the Derbyshire Peak; south-east, the Dunstable Downs, in Bedfordshire; westward, the hills of Worcester and Shropshire; and sometimes, with a good glass, on a very clear day, the heights of some of the Welsh mountains.

In the west of Leicestershire, the ground is a good deal cultivated for corn, but in the east, principally for pasture. Here are fed the cows from whose milk the famous Stilton cheeses are made;* and, also, the celebrated Leicestershire sheep, large and fat, with long wool, very useful in the making of the woollen hosiery, the peculiar manufacture of the county. Leicestershire pigs and horses are also reckoned very good.†

Besides stockings, there is made here a good deal of lace and silk plush for hats; and, in the clay districts, fire bricks are manufactured. Leicestershire is, also, a famous county for hunting, Melton Mowbray, in the north of the county, being the head-quarters of the huntsmen and their horses. Eight hundred horses are sometimes collected together at Melton. It is famous, too, for pork pies.

But before speaking of other places, I must try to explain a little how stockings and gloves are woven. They are called hosiery, and are the chief manufacture of Derby, Nottingham, and Leicester; those of Derby being principally silk; Nottingham, cotton, and Leicester, woollen. I suppose the long wool of the Leicester sheep has been the original cause of this becoming the hosiery district of England.

Stockings are not like calico, woven in large mills, with hundreds of frames working at once, but are rather manufactured, one by one, in the separate stocking-frames, which are at each separate cottage. The manufacturer

* Pages 40, 100.　　　　　　　　† Pages 37, 77.

buys the cotton or the silk probably at Manchester, and the worsted, either from the neighbouring worsted-spinners, or, perhaps, at Bradford. He gives out to each stockinger, as the workmen are called, a certain quantity of yarn, which he takes home to the stocking-frame, for the use of which he pays a weekly rent; he weaves a certain number of stockings; his wife and children sew them up; he takes them back, either to the manufacturer or to the middleman, whom the master appoints, and receives payment for what he has done. This payment is very low, and, perhaps, that is the reason why stockings are still made by hand-power and not by steam. The stocking-frame is a very puzzling looking loom. It stands upright, and a number of little steel hooks are placed in it, so as to twist the new thread through the loops of that thread which just before crossed the loom. The stockingers have very curious names for different kinds of work, such as "bothering-up," and "bothering-on." One kind of stocking they call "cut-ups," and another "drop-offs."

Stocking-frames were invented in the reign of Queen Elizabeth, by a clergyman. The lady whom he loved seemed to think more of her knitting than of him, so he determined to try and discover how to make a machine knit, imagining that then the lady would have more time to care for him. He succeeded, and gave up his ministry for his loom. Queen Elizabeth once went herself to see his wonderful new machine, but she would not reward his invention till he had made it fit to weave silk stockings.* Before that, the queen wore stockings cut out of a piece of silk and sewn up. There are now about 50,000 stocking-looms employed in the three hosiery counties. Which are they?

Now, I will tell you about the Leicestershire towns,

* Page 126.

where the stockingers live and work. We will begin with Leicester, in the centre, and then draw a circle all round.

Leicester is a large and very ancient town, with nearly 100,000 people. It has wide streets, open squares, and a great many gardens. Over the river Soar, on which it stands, are several bridges. There is plenty of spring water, every large house having a well. It seems as if built in the middle of a saucer; the plain surrounding it, and beyond that a rim of hills. Leicester was a town in the time of the Romans; but there are now few remains of its ancient buildings, excepting the churches, some of which are very beautiful.* In the Blue Boar Inn of Leicester slept Richard III., the night before the battle of Bosworth. He brought his own bedstead with him. It had two bottoms, like a floor and its underceiling; and between these, he had hidden a quantity of gold. His dreams that night were wretched. He imagined himself in the midst of torturing demons, and when he arose in the morning he looked piteous. Wretched man! Can you wonder that his conscience gave him no rest.

Not far from Leicester is Thurcaston, the birth-place of good Bishop Latimer.

Now, beginning our circle round Leicester, as the sun does, in the east, we shall start from Melton Mowbray, of which I have already told you. Going northwards, we reach Market Harborough. Here is a handsome church, built by John of Gaunt, the brother of the Black Prince, and the friend of Wycliffe.

Then turning west, we come to Lutterworth, good old Wycliffe's parish.† Here is still the pulpit in which he used to preach, and his gown, the table at which he wrote, and the chair in which he died. He lived to give England the blessing of an English bible. Forty-four years after he died, his grave was opened, his body burnt by his unhappy enemies, and its ashes thrown into the little brook, Swift, that runs beside Lutterworth Church. The Swift conveyed them to the Avon, the Avon to the Severn,

Lutterworth Church.

the Severn to the narrow seas, they to the wide ocean; an emblem of the blessed Bible doctrines that he preached, which are now spreading from pole to pole.

Hinckley is a busy stocking-making town; where, from relics that have been found, the Romans must have lived long long ago.

Going north is Market Bosworth. At the Grammar School here, Simpson, who wrote on mathematics, and Dr Johnson, who made the big dictionary, used to teach. Near this town is the battle-field, where the cruel Richard, who ordered his little nephews to be smothered in the Tower, was met by Henry VII., conquered and killed.

A little out of the circle, is Ashby-de-la-Zouch, a prettily-situated small town, near which are the ruins of a curious old castle. Here was born good Bishop Hall, who wrote beautiful contemplations on the history of the Bible.

Our last town is Loughborough, next to Leicester, the largest in the county. The kind of stockings principally made here, is the Angola, as thin as fine cotton, though made of wool. Here, too, a good deal of bobbin-net is made; and near it, is a famous foundry for something that young ones like, because it is of no use unless it makes a noise. It is a bell-foundry.

In the north, near Lincolnshire, is Belvoir Castle, a beautiful place belonging to the Duke of Rutland. It is said to be the oldest house in the county, having been originally built in the time of William I.* It was in a great measure destroyed by fire, in 1816. The duke rebuilt it more beautiful than before, expressing his thankfulness to God, who had preserved the lives of his wife and five children. The picture gallery is full of very valuable paintings. There is a golden key for the castle gate; and, if any of the royal family visit Belvoir, it is presented by the chief of the Stauntons, who inhabit the outwork of the castle.

This has been a long chapter; but to-morrow you shall have a very short one, about the least of all the counties in dear old England.

RUTLAND.

Now for a short account of England's little county, Rutland. And a pretty little county it is, with gently rising hills, and green sloping valleys, and cattle and sheep feeding pleasantly, and shady woodlands, where the graceful

* Pages 20, 127.

K

deer are still preserved wild. The soil of Rutland is rich for growing grass and corn. In some parts, there is a good deal of limestone, and several sandstone quarries, out of which are built many very good houses. The farmers take particular care of their sheep and cows, and therefore the sheep are very good; and the cows give excellent milk, from which is made the same kind of cheese as that in Leicestershire, called Stilton.*

The largest town in Rutland is Oakham; but there are not 3000 people living in it. Here was born a very little man, a dwarf, called Geoffery Hudson. He lived in the time of Charles I. Once, to the amazement of the queen, a pie was served up with Geoffery inside. So I suppose

> " When the pie was opened,
> Geoffery began to sing,
> Oh ! was not that a dainty dish
> To set before the king."

Oakham has a castle, now used as a court-house. All round its gate, and even on the judge's bench, are stuck horse-shoes of all shapes, of all sizes, and of all metals. Some are as large as a breakfast table, and some so small, they would only fit little Charles's play-horse. What can this mean ? It was a very old and strange custom, that if a nobleman went through Oakham, he must give to the owner of the castle, one of his horse-shoes. This is sometimes rather inconvenient; so the bailiff of the town keeps all kinds of horse-shoes, which are purchased and presented according to the visitors' generosity.

I have heard the following story of sad interest, regarding the last man that was hung at Oakham. It shows the danger of going into temptation; and it also shows how cruel justice may be when there is no mercy.

* Page 141.

A very poor man lived with his wife in a little cottage, surrounded by several starving children. There had been nothing in that cottage to eat all day, no work could be procured, and the miserable father wandered out. As he wandered near his house, a bad man, a sheep-stealer, accosted him. "Neighbour, how fares it with you?" He told him of having no employment, and of his starving family. Poor man! we wish that he had told this to God instead. The sheep-stealer said, "Why starve, when so many fat sheep are feeding round. I am going to take one to-night. Come with me and you shall have half." Conscience said "No;" but hunger said "Yes." He went. There were watchers there. They saw the booty divided; they followed the man home. He opened the door. His good, gentle wife saw the meat. "O father! where be ye to get that," she said in alarm; for she guessed it was stolen. "Don't ask me," he said, "or you will drive me mad;" he was very wretched. The poor starving children rushed forward, and began to eat the flesh raw. The watchers entered, and the man was taken to prison, tried, found guilty, and, according to the law, hanged. Oakham people say that the town has never prospered since. Surely that beautiful text was forgotten, "Blessed are the merciful, for they shall obtain mercy."

The only other town of any consequence is Uppingham, in the south-west of the county. These are quite agricultural towns; for we have left, for a time, the manufacturing districts of England. To-morrow, we must again go north, and hear about a large county, which has the German Ocean washing its eastern shores.

LINCOLNSHIRE.—Part I.

We now come to a part of England which, excepting Holderness, in the south-east of Yorkshire, is very different to all of which I have been telling you. What kind of a district was Holderness?

Lincolnshire is a county, the surface of which is very flat and low; a great part of it lower than the level of the sea. Broad and strong embankments are raised to prevent the sea from breaking in upon this portion. There is very little rising ground above; no metals below, and it is a county thoroughly free from manufactories. It is both very ancient and very modern, for there are found there many Roman remains, Roman embankments, and Roman roads, and the town of Lincoln was one of the largest Roman military stations; * and yet there are thousands of acres of land that have never been anything but watery marshes or lakes, till the last fifty years.† I think the best adjective to put before Lincolnshire would be watery. It is, however, a very fertile region. The soil is rich, and corn and grass grow there luxuriantly; there are immense numbers of very large sheep and cattle; and many of the fine dray horses that are brought to the London market come from this county.‡ There are also great numbers of ducks and geese, wild water-birds, rabbits, and hares; so Lincolnshire is a county for farming, and supplying the necessities of the larder, as much as Lancashire is for manufactories, and supplying the wants of the wardrobe. The farm-buildings in Lincolnshire are good; and most of the landlords, farmers, and labourers do all they can to make the ground as productive as possible. Some thousands of years ago, this county must have been covered with

* Pages 19, 44, 90, 106, 143.   † Page 54.

‡ Pages 37, 141.

forests, where the elk, and the wild boar, and other animals roamed; and then the forest land must have sunk, and the swamps spread themselves over their surface.* Down the middle of the county, runs a chain of low green hills; these hills break, as it were, where the Witham passes; and on the river's northern bank, the town of Lincoln is built.

After the Romans, the Danes built a good many towns in this county. Most of the towns which they founded end with "by," and this termination you will often find in Lincolnshire.

Here have been born many famous men. Woolsthorpe, near Grantham, was the native place of Sir Isaac Newton. He was a wonderful thinker, and from seeing an apple fall, discovered the law by which God makes the earth, the moon, and all the planets, revolve round the sun. I daresay you have wondered why we do not tumble off the earth, which you know is round. It is all through this law, called the law of gravitation. Ask some one to explain it to you. The apple-tree was blown down some years ago, but a chair is shown made of its wood. Sir Isaac Newton was not a passionate nor impatient man. Once he left his study; on the table was a lighted candle, and several papers, on which he had written the calculations which had occupied him for many years. He had a little dog, called Diamond, which, on this occasion, did terrible mischief. It jumped on the table, knocked down the light, which set fire to the papers and destroyed them. When Sir Isaac returned, he saw the mischief, but instead of angrily beating the poor dog, he only said, "Di, Di, thou little knowest the mischief thou hast done." Not far from Isaac Newton's house was a windmill, which the boy very carefully watched. At length, he

* Pages 53, 54.

himself made a model mill, with neat linen sails, and all the internal machinery so complete that, if a handful of wheat grains were put into the little hopper, it would be ground into flour. His schoolfellows were delighted with his cleverness. "But," said one, "you have forgotten something." "What?" inquired Isaac. "Why, where is the miller?" Isaac determined he would look for one. No man was small enough, and with all his ingenuity he could not model a man. What could be done? He found a mouse — appointed him miller; he, however, did not prove very trustworthy, being suspected of frequently helping himself to the grains of corn.

At Spilsby, another town in Lincolnshire, Sir John Franklin was born. He made many discoveries in the polar regions. He was a brave man, and one that feared God. He wished to find out a passage round the north of North America; but the last time he went, he and all his brave companions perished. No one lived to tell the sorrowful tale; and it was many years before his sad fate was known. Near Spilsby was also born Thomas Scott, the celebrated Bible commentator. Tennyson, the Poet Laureate of the present day, was also born in this country.

This county, like Yorkshire, is divided into three parts; the most southern is called "Holland," or Hollow Land, and like Holderness in Yorkshire, resembles very much Holland on the other side of the sea. It forms part of what is called "The Fens," which consist of a low plain surrounding the Wash. The Fens also extend over parts of Norfolk, Northampton, Cambridge, and Huntingdon. The scenery is generally wearisome; but on a bright summer's day, there is the same freedom about its apparently boundless expanse, as about the wild prairies of America. It seems like a sea of rich golden corn, or of beautiful green meadows. There are broad rivers, and drains almost as broad, and wide ditches, instead of hedges, dividing the fields, and rushy swamps; here and there a few pollard-willow trees, scattered farmsteads, or

The Fens.

a village spire, and there is the bright blue sky, seeming to meet far, far away, the outspread earth. When the people wish to pass from one place to another, they often do so by steeple-walking. They mark the village steeple in the distance, and for it they start, across the fields and the watery dykes. Over these they swing themselves by means of the long poles that they carry with them.

Lincolnshire is not a healthy county, being very low and damp; but it is greatly improved, owing to the drainage works and the water machines forcing the water to run off more quickly towards the sea.

Having mentioned the Wash, I must tell you a story about King John. The Wash is an arm of the sea where, when the tide is out, a great deal of sand is left, along which carriages can drive. This resembles, what inlet on the western coast?

Louis, the eldest son of the King of France, had been offered by the English barons the crown of England, for John was so wicked and base in his conduct that his people detested him. He had been retreating before Louis, but having got possession of Lincoln, was regaining a little courage, when he determined to cross the Wash from Lynn, in Norfolk. The army had passed safely over; but before the king reached the other side the waves rolled quickly forward, and though he escaped, his baggage, together with his crown and sceptre, was lost in the water. John had been so alarmed, and was now so vexed, that he became very ill, was carried to Newark on a litter, and there he died. Had he lived, he probably would have made the freemen of Lynn ride across the Wash as he made those of Alnwick plunge through the bog.*

To-morrow I hope to tell you of the principal towns in watery Lincolnshire.

LINCOLNSHIRE.—PART II.

TO-DAY we will first of all talk of the towns on rivers that fall into the Humber, and then of those on or near the rivers going to the Wash. First, then, we will follow the Trent. The only town of consequence on it is Gainsborough. It may be called a river port, for canals or rivers connect it with Manchester, Liverpool, London, and Gloucester.† It lies low, and sometimes, after rain, the river rises, and the streets of the town are under water. Not far from the Trent is Epworth, the village in which the great and good John Wesley was born.

On the Humber, opposite Hull, is Barton, a seaport which

* Pages 16, 139.   † Page 53.

is not a great favourite with ship-captains. They generally prefer Great Grimsby, a rapidly increasing town, farther down the coast, where large docks have been made from the waste mud banks formed at low water.* Is it not good, by industry, to turn an evil into a blessing? Most of the houses in this part of England are built of red brick, with red tiles.

A few miles inland from Grimsby is Caistor. Its castle was built by the Saxon Hengist, on a piece of ground which he could encircle with an ox-hide cut into strips, according to a grant from a British king. Here Rowena, a Saxon queen, taking a goblet of wine, dropped down on one knee, and drank the king's health. This is said to have been the first time that a health was drunk in England.†

Now let us follow the course of the other rivers, about which I will give you a riddle: "Why may we suppose that they are very dirty?"‡ First, there is the Witham; and, as it at first flows north, we must track its course from the south of the county. The first town of any consequence is Grantham. It has a very high church steeple.§ At its grammar-school the great Sir Isaac Newton used to study when a boy. In this town a quantity of malt is prepared, to be sent to the breweries.

Our next town is Lincoln, the most important in the county. It has a splendid cathedral, with the second highest tower in England, and with the famous bell called Great Tom of Lincoln. The cathedral was commenced in the time of William the Conqueror. The bishop by whom it was built is said to have been very small in body, but very large in mind. For three months of each year he fed a thousand people every day, and clothed those amongst them who were blind and lame. Another bishop who en-

---

* Pages 95, 105.   † These stories are also told of Tong Castle, in Kent.
‡ Because they are always going to the Wash.   § Page 151.

larged the cathedral, was buried in a large coffin of pure gold. This was turned into money in the reign of Henry VIII.

The approach to Lincoln gives a beautiful view of the city, built on a hill above the Witham, and crowned by the grand cathedral.* It is a very ancient town, having been, in William the First's and other reigns, a much more important place than it is now. The first stone church built in England was erected in this town. Many of the houses are very old and curious. One is called John of Gaunt's stables; but it probably formed part of his palace.† The Guildhall is built on an arch that spans the street; and there is an old Roman gateway, reckoned the most perfect in England.‡ What a long time that must have been built ! Can you find out how many years ?

Following the Witham, you will see a small river joins it from the north. Near its source is Market Rasen, a busy little town in selling cattle and corn; farther down is Horncastle, where every August there is one of the largest horse fairs in all England; § and near the point where it joins the Witham is Tattershall, where there is an old castle, with a curiously-carved chimney-piece.

The Witham continues to flow through the flat fenny country. Boston, at its mouth, has a beautiful church spire or lantern, which may be seen at a distance of forty miles, and is a landmark for travellers both by sea and land. Once Boston was, next to London, the greatest sea-port in England. Then the Witham became choked up, and Boston lost its consequence ; but now, through drainage, it is becoming much more thriving.|| A great deal of corn is exported. John Fox, who wrote the history of

* Pages 30, 45.   † Page 143.   ‡ Page 45.
§ Pages 37, 148. || Pages 105, 106.

the martyrs of Queen Mary's reign, was born in this town.

Between the Witham and the Welland are several small towns. They generally have high church steeples, very useful to the people in walking. One village is called Threckingham, because three Danish kings were slain and buried there. On the Welland, in the south-west corner of Lincolnshire, is Stamford, a large town, with railway trains and canal or river boats constantly passing. There was here a strange custom.* Exactly three weeks before Christmas-day, a bull was turned loose into the streets, the gates being stopped with waggons. The people ran after it till it was killed, and then it was cut up and given to the poor. The butchers were obliged to furnish the bull, as the condition of having the right of feeding their cattle in some meadows near the town. Further down the river is Spalding, another town where a great deal of wool and corn is sold, and coal and timber bought. It is thought to be very like a Dutch town.†

Now I will only tell you of one more place, Croyland, which is remarkable for its bridge, built exactly where the Wyse and the Welland join. Its centre is over the middle of the waters, and its three bases or ends are on the three shores. It is said that one base is in Lincolnshire, another in Cambridge, and another in Northampton. On one of the wings is a very old figure of a Saxon king; who, a thousand years ago, built here an abbey now in ruins. It was to please a very foolish monk, St Guthlac, who wished to live in the Fens, only because it was disagreeable.‡ How little he could have known that beautiful text, "God is love," or he would never have thought that to torment himself was pleasing to God.

Now enough for to-day; but before we cross the Wash

* Pages 16, 103, 146.   † Pages 38, 150.   ‡ Page 31.

I should like to know what you remember of Nottingham, Leicester, Rutland, and Lincolnshire.

In this review, the scenery painting might be reversed, and put into the mouths of the children. If many of them, they might endeavour to puzzle one another; or, if few, their effort might be to puzzle the teacher. Persons as well as places might be described.

Thus, let Cave commence: "Amy, I am walking through a forest. It is nicely shaded; the trees are very high and beautiful; but hark! Oh I am so frightened; I hear a bugle. There are robbers here. Shall I hide? They march towards me. One is a very fine-looking man, not very savage; and a great tall man stands behind him."

Amy replies: "O Cave, it is Robin Hood, with Little John, in Sherwood forest."

"Now I am thinking of somebody. It is a very good man, who preached in a little church beside a river, and translated the Bible into English, and died quietly; but a great many years afterwards, wicked people dug up his grave and threw his bones into that little river."

Cave answers: "Wycliffe—good John Wycliffe."

Then Charlotte: "Harriet, I see a beautiful cathedral, with such a high tower, built on a hill, and looking over all the flat country round about."

Harriet replies: "And that is Lincoln. And I am think-ng of a young man, who sits busily weaving stockings, but he is making poetry all the time."

Charlotte: "Yes, I know, and he went to Cambridge and died soon, but I can't remember his name."

Harriet tells: "Henry Kirke White."

Such is a sample of the lesson or game that might be played. Each answer might be written down on a slate, and a good mark given for each question asked or answered correctly. If preferred, the old plan of the manufacturer, tourist, antiquarian, in their various capacities, passing through the counties, might be followed advantageously.

NORTHAMPTONSHIRE.

NORTHAMPTONSHIRE is a pretty, quiet-looking county, with gently sloping hills and beautiful valleys, and soft-flowing streams, but it has no peculiar feature to distinguish it from the other counties we have mentioned. I cannot find an adjective for Northamptonshire. It is, however, surrounded by more counties than any other. Try and name them all.

The farmers are chiefly employed in rearing sheep, 100,000 of which are sent every year to London, as well as 15,000 fat cattle.* Besides the fields there are pretty woodlands, for the county was once covered with forests. In Salsey Forest is an oak, supposed to be 1000 or 1500 years old. It is nearly sixteen yards round the stem. Northampton is not a county for minerals, and so we do not expect to find many manufactories.† Its chief trade is in boots and shoes, great numbers being made here to supply the army. We must not look in the map for mountains, but we will for rivers. The one on the north, which separates it from Leicester, Rutland, and Lincoln, is the Welland, and the one flowing through the centre is the Nene, whilst, in the south of the county, rises the Great Ouse, which, at first, flows southward into Buckinghamshire, and then north-east, till it also reaches the Wash.

This county is one of the fertile ones of old England,

* Pages 23, 37, 141, 148.   † Pages 85, 109, 114, 132.

with plenty of grass and good wheat, and numbers of sheep and cattle grazing.* In the north-east, we find again the fenny country, as in Lincolnshire. Here hemp is grown, the fibres of which make ropes and canvas. These fen-lands have been greatly improved by the cutting of a deep canal at the mouth of the Nene. It was a great surprise to the inhabitants, when they found the waters of their sluggish rivers running off so fast, and great good it did them, draining the land and preventing so much of the damp air rising, which caused ague, rheumatism, and many other complaints.†

There is no particular town on the Northampton side of the Welland river. Not far from Stamford, however, is Burleigh House, so large, that it looks almost like a little town. It was built by the Lord Burleigh of whom we read in Queen Elizabeth's reign.

Naseby is a small village, very near to which rises the Nene, flowing to the German Ocean, and the Avon, flowing westward to the Severn, and thence to the Atlantic; so you see it stands on the line of watershed between the German and the Atlantic Oceans.‡ Near it was fought the last desperate battle in the civil war in Charles the First's reign. Charles was completely defeated, and soon afterwards gave himself up a prisoner to the Scotch army. One of Cromwell's army has been supposed, by a great writer, Lord Macaulay, to describe this battle, as follows:

" It was about the noon of a glorious day in June,
    That we saw their banners dance, and their cuirasses shine,
    And the man of blood was there with his long essencèd hair,
    And Astley and Sir Marmaduke and Rupert of the Rhine.
    The furious German comes, with his clarion and his drums,
    His heroes of Alsatia and pages of Whitehall;

---

* Page 4.   † Pages 54, 151.   ‡ Page 121.

They are bursting on our flanks; grasp your pikes, close your ranks,
For Rupert never comes but to conquer or to fall.
Stout Skipton has a wound—the centre hath given ground.
Hark! Hark! What means the trampling of horsemen on the rear?
Whose banner do I see, boys? 'Tis he! Oh yes, 'tis he, boys!
Bear up another minute, brave Oliver is here!"

And then is described the triumph of Cromwell's soldiers.

"Like a whirlwind on the trees, like a deluge on the dykes."

Several skirmishes were also fought in Charles's reign near Daventry, pronounced Dayntree. Here many whips are made; and, as in most of the Northamptonshire towns, a great many of the workpeople are shoemakers. Near Daventry is Weedon, a famous station for soldiers and military works. Following the Nene, you will see Northampton, the county town. It is built of reddish stone. The woods, meadows, and villas around look bright and pretty. There are some fine old churches, but the castle is quite in ruins. Here, about 10,000 people are busy working at the boot and shoe trade.

The next town is Wellingborough, also well built. In this place, besides the boots and shoes, a quantity of patent leather is made, the kind that shines without being blackened.

On a northern branch of the Nene, is Rothwell. Its old castle was a favourite home of William the Conqueror.

Between Northampton and Peterborough are many villages, with their inhabitants industriously employed either in making shoes or bobbin net. Near a small village, Oundle, are the ruins of Fotheringay Castle, where the poor, unfortunate Mary Queen of Scots was beheaded. Her history is a most sorrowful one; her crimes, her misfortunes, and her beauty were all so great. Queen Elizabeth ordered her execution, and a sad, sad blot it is on the character of a queen who did otherwise so many good and noble things for dear old England. For nineteen years, poor Mary was a prisoner in England. Do you remember any of the castles we have mentioned in which she was confined?*

Nearer Peterborough is " Wandsford in England." Why has it this name? Long ago, on a summer's day, a lad went to sleep on a haycock, in a field near the river Nene. A flood came suddenly down the river, surrounded the haycock, which quietly and noiselessly commenced its voyage towards the sea. The lad slept on. The haycock reached Wisbeach, and was almost in the open sea, when some fishermen, sailing near, espied the boy, and rescued him. They then asked, Where are you from? And the boy, as if he imagined that he had floated across the sea to Holland or Belgium, answered, " Wandsford in England; " and thus the little village got its name.

Peterborough is a small, but well-built city. Remember that all towns which have cathedrals are called cities. The Saxon king, Edgar, who rebuilt Peterborough cathedral, after it had been destroyed by the Danes, gave the abbey so much land, that it was called for some time " Gilderburgh," or the Golden City. Here are the tombs of Catherine of Arragon, the first wife of that cruel king, Henry VIII., and also of the unfortunate Mary, of whom I have just told you. Peterborough is a busy town for traffic, both by the river and the many railways that now pass through it.

Several celebrated men have been born in Northamptonshire; amongst others, Dryden, the poet, and Dr Carey, the first missionary to Bengal. The last, like Morrison, was once a shoemaker, but God gave him the

* Pages 42, 130.

needed talent and the willing mind, and prepared him, as his messenger, to advance the gospel of his dear Son in that mighty empire.*

Earthly crowns made neither Charles I., nor poor Mary, nor Catherine of Arragon happy. Rather strive, like Dr Carey, for a better glory, for " they that turn many to righteousness shall shine as the stars for ever and ever."

BEDFORDSHIRE.

BEDFORDSHIRE, of which I have to tell you to-day, is a neat and pretty little county. Can you guess why I have chosen it first, though farther south than Huntingdon? My reason has something to do with the course of its principal river, the Great Ouse, which enters it from Buckinghamshire. Now tell the counties that surround it. North? South? East? West?

Bedfordshire has pretty low hills, and valleys full of trees, grass, and corn. The sheep and cattle are not so famous as in Leicester, Northampton, and Lincoln; but there are many vegetables grown, such as turnips, cabbages, pease, and beans. The onions here are nearly equal to those of Portugal, and a great many cucumbers are raised in the open air. We have now reached counties where the climate is much warmer than in the north of England, where the country-people's voices are much softer, and their manners more gentle; but I do not think their hearts are warmer, and their minds are not generally so intelligent. The dress of the countrymen is different. Instead of corduroy coats, they wear white or blue blouses, on which patterns are often worked. It is a very pleasant sight to see the men come to church on Sunday, with their clean white blouses and red neckerchiefs.

* Page 9.

L

The most noted manufacture of the county is straw plait for bonnets, which is only excelled by the Tuscans in Italy. Straw is not yet plaited by steam. It is generally done by women. The straw is split, bleached, and moistened with water, before it is fit for plaiting. Lace is also made in this county, but not nearly so much as before steam was employed in weaving it.*

The Great Ouse, which is the chief river, flows very slowly and has a very winding course. From Turvey to St Neot's, the distance, in a straight line, is nineteen miles; but following the borders of the stream it is seventy. In wet weather it overflows its banks, making the pastures on each side rich and fertile.

The chief town upon its banks is Bedford. About 300 years ago a gentleman left some ground in Holborn, London, for the support of a school in Bedford, to teach the children grammar and good manners. London grew large, and this ground was wanted for houses, and let for a great deal of money. It is now worth £16,000 per annum. This money maintains a grammar school for boys, who hope to be learned men; a commercial school for those who expect to be business men; a national school for boys and girls, and also an infant school. Then £20 is given as a marriage portion to each poor maiden; £20 or £15 to good boys or girls going out as apprentices; and £10 when the years of their apprenticeship are over. Besides this, there are fifty-six almshouses for the aged and needy, and about £500 given away every year to the poor. How little did the gentleman, who left this piece of land, imagine that 300 years afterwards it would be of such good to the town.

But the most interesting thing I can tell you about Bedford is, that it is the place where the good John Bunyan

* Page 138.

lived, who wrote the "Pilgrim's Progress." He was a poor man, the son of a brazier or tinker. By God's grace, his heart was changed, and he became very anxious to do good. He was made the pastor of a little chapel in Bedford; but was persecuted for his religion, partly for preaching out of doors, and was thrown into prison. Here he wrote that wonderful book, which, next to the Bible, has, I believe, been more read than any other.

I will tell you a short story about John Bunyan's imprisonment. His conduct was so good, that his jailer often allowed him to go and see his friends. His persecutors hearing of this, sent an officer to search the prison in the middle of the night. That night, John Bunyan was at home; but he could not sleep, so he got up, telling his wife, that though the jailer said he might remain till morning, he could not. The jailer blamed him for coming in the middle of the night; but very early in the morning the officer arrived.

" Are all the prisoners safe?" he inquired.

" Yes."

" Is John Bunyan safe?"

" Yes."

" Let me see him."

He was called and appeared. When the officer was gone, the jailer said to Bunyan, "Well, you may go in and out again just when you think proper, for you know when to return better than I can tell you."

Bunyan's own pilgrimage was a very long one. He was more than ninety years old when the messenger was sent to summon him across death's cold river to the heavenly city. In the chapel vestry are shown his chair, and Fox's "Book of Martyrs," which he used to read. Do you remember where Fox was born?*

* Page 154.

Another excellent man was born near Bedford, John Howard, called the Philanthropist, because he loved his fellow-men so much, that he spent all his life and fortune in doing them good. He particularly visited prisoners in jails, who were at that time very badly treated, and sought to relieve them. For this purpose, he travelled through most of the countries of Europe, and at length died, in the South of Russia, away from all earthly friends, but we cannot doubt that God was with him.

In the west of Bedfordshire is Woburn, and near to it stands Woburn Abbey, the beautiful seat of the Duke of Bedford. Here is a model farm, and everything is done to improve the tenantry, their houses, and the land. In the Park grows the largest oak tree in England.* It is ninety feet high. In the south of the county, are Dunstable and Luton; towns famous for straw-plaiting and lace-making. †

On the river Ivel is Biggleswade. Here a ploughman once dug up a yellow pot, in which were 300 gold coins, of the reign of Henry VI., and at another time, some labourers, striking upon something hard, found it was a large helmet, farther down they discovered arms, then a shield, then the skeleton and armour of a horse. Afterwards several other skeletons were found, all standing upright, so it is supposed that in some war, soldiers had been thus buried in a horrible pitfall. ‡

There are many beautiful parks in Bedfordshire;§ but these we must leave, as it would not do for us to linger like the slow and winding Ouse, in this pretty little county.

* Page 157.   + Page 137.
‡ Page 63.   § Pages 19, 136.

HUNTINGDONSHIRE.

On leaving Bedfordshire, the Ouse flows through a still smaller county—Huntingdonshire. Formerly, there were a great many forests here, in which was much hunting; and from this the little county derived its name. There are hardly any woods now; but the land is ploughed and sown, or used as meadows. The corn is not very good; but the meadows along the banks of the Ouse are amongst the richest in old England. Mustard-seed and hemp are also grown.* In the north of the county we find ourselves among watery fens once more. In one part there is quite a lake, called Whittle-sea-mere. It is much smaller since the land was drained but still it abounds with wild water-fowl.† Sailing there is very pleasant; though the scenery cannot be compared with that of the beautiful lakes of Westmoreland and Cumberland. Huntingdonshire, besides being noted for its wild birds, is famous for its numerous tame pigeons. Though there is much water—ponds, drains, rivers—there are very few wells; and thus it is difficult to procure good clear drinking water. On the banks of the Ouse, where it enters Huntingdon from Bedford, is St Neot's, named after a brother of King Alfred. Here a quantity of paper is made. Paper is made from all kinds of cotton and linen rags. They are boiled in strong acids, to take out all the dirt or dye. A powerful wheel then tears them to shreds, and reduces them to a pulp. This pulp, passing through many waters, at last becomes so thin, that it resembles milk or cream more than anything else. It then passes along a sieve, through which the watery part falls. After this the more solid particles are pressed between hot rollers, and in a very short time, a roll of

* Pages 37, 158.   † Page 148.

paper as long as a web of calico is thrown out, or more probably paper cut by machinery, the required length. Writing paper is made in smaller moulds. There are not enough rags to supply the need of paper; and much of the commoner kind is made from straw. Bank notes are made of new linen. Brown paper is made of old ropes. In the west of the county, is Kimbolton, near which

Kimbolton Castle.

stands the castle belonging to the Duke of Manchester. Here lived the unfortunate Catherine of Arragon, the first wife of Henry VIII. Where was she buried?

Further down the Ouse, is Huntingdon; and opposite to it is Godmanchester. The farmers here have a custom, which is, if the sovereign passes by, to attend him with ploughs, ornamented with the smaller implements of husbandry, and drawn by their best horses. They cannot, however, keep up this old custom, when the royal train rushes onward, conveying, at a rapid rate, our dear Queen Victoria to her northern home.

Huntingdon was the birthplace of Oliver Cromwell. When his mother became a widow, he helped her in taking charge of a brewery; and is therefore sometimes called "The Brewer of Huntingdon." He became Protector of England, when Charles I. was dethroned.

Passing farther down the Ouse, you will see St Ives, a small town, where there is a very large sheep and cattle-market.* Perhaps you have heard the old-fashioned riddle about St Ives. If not, guess it :—

> "As I was going to St Ives,
> I met a man and seven wives;
> Each wife had seven sacks;
> Each sack had seven cats;
> Each cat had seven kits.
> Kits, cats, sacks, and wives.
> How many were there going to St Ives ?"

In the north of the county, is Stilton; where the famous cheeses were first sold, which are made from the milk of the cows, that feed in the beautiful pastures of—what counties ?†

Now you have to remember about the paper-making, and Oliver Cromwell, and all the towns on the Great Ouse, and to find out the riddle concerning St Ives.

> So now away;
> Enough for to-day.

CAMBRIDGESHIRE.

I HAVE a great deal to tell you to-day about Cambridge-shire, so I must have quick eyes and listening ears for at least half an hour.

* Pages 115, 154.   † Pages 141, 146.

First, through the eyes, find the names of all its surrounding counties.. There is a much greater diversity in the appearance of Cambridgeshire than in that of the counties of which I have lately told you. You observe the Ouse flows across its centre. The land between it and the Nene, in the north, is called the Isle of Ely. This is quite a fen country.* Towns and villages are built on the few elevated spots, and look like islands rising from the low marshes. As in Lincolnshire, the church-steeples are seen from a great distance. In the north-east of the county, where the marshes are partly salt from the sea-water of the Wash, wheat grows luxuriantly; the only drawback is, that a flood frequently rises, and washes it all away.† I suppose the farmers there must learn both to cut corn and "make hay when the sun shines."

There are beautiful meadows along the banks of the Ouse and the Cam, so this district is quite a dairy one. At one place, remarkably good cream-cheeses are made, and much of the butter there churned is sold in London, the dairymaids often make it in long rolls, and instead of being sold by the pound it is sold by the inch or the yard. In the Isle of Ely, and near Wisbeach, a great deal of mustard is grown.‡ In the south of the county the land is much higher than in the north, and not so fertile. Here is the low range of the Gog-Magog Hills. Standing on them, you may see thirty-three churches, the principal one being Ely Cathedral.

How pleasant to see, in a country which God has made so fair, so many houses for our heavenly Father's worship.§

"Behold yon spires, which upwards rear
　　Their venerable head;

---

* Pages 148, 150, 153, 165..　　† Pages 152, 158, 160.
‡ Pages 37, 165.　　§ Pages 73, 89.

The point aspiring to the stars,
The base among the dead.

" This indicates the life of those
Whom grace divine inflames;
In earth old Adam seeks repose,
At heaven the New Man aims."

In these high and chalky districts are large heaths and commons, where numbers of sheep feed.* The chief and most celebrated town in the county is Cambridge, built on each side of the River Cam, with several bridges spanning the river. It is situated low, and when people first arrive they are disappointed with the appearance of the town; but as they go from place to place, and see the churches, halls, colleges, and the number of students, in their gowns and caps, then they are able to suppose that Cambridge may be one of the chief universities in the world. The professors, or lecturers, at the universities, are generally very clever men. The students call them " dons." The Cambridge men excel in mathematics. Every year there is a great examination. The young men who give the best answers are called " Wranglers," and he who excels all the rest is the Senior Wrangler. The devoted missionary, Henry Martyn, who worked so hard for Christ in India, was Senior Wrangler in the year of his examination. Many celebrated men have studied hard at Cambridge. In the garden of one college, is the mulberry tree said to have been planted by Milton, one of England's greatest poets. Sir Isaac Newton and Lord Bacon, two of her greatest philosophers; Pitt, one of her greatest statesmen ; Wilberforce, one of her greatest philanthropists,† were students here. So also were Bilney, Cranmer, Latimer, and Ridley,‡ of the noble band of reformers ; George Herbert, who, long ago, wrote sweet sacred poems ;

* Pages 15, 37, 77.   † Page 54.   ‡ Page 19.

John Elliot, Noble, and Ragland, missionaries ; Bishop Hall ; * the Milners ; † and many others, wise in winning souls to Christ, and learned in human wisdom.·

In St Mary's Church, Charles Simeon preached for many years, and was the means of sending many faithful pastors through the length and breadth of dear old England.

There are seventeen colleges and halls in Cambridge, the largest of which are Trinity and St John's.   Many of

Trinity College.

the buildings are very beautiful, especially King's College Chapel.   The windows and turrets outside are very much admired.   The great wonder, however, is the beautiful and lofty stone ceiling, the breadth of which is fifteen yards, the length about one hundred, and the height about twenty-six,

* Page 145.   † Page 68.

You can hardly fancy an apartment so high. Yet the stone ceiling covered with beautiful tracery is thrown across, and there is not one pillar to support it. It cannot be copied, for no architect has discovered the way in which it was built.

Cambridge has been visited by two of our English queens, Queen Elizabeth and Queen Victoria. When Elizabeth was there, she made a Latin speech to all the clever men, which pleased them very much.* Our own Queen went when her husband, the Prince Consort, was installed as Chancellor, a position in the college of the highest honour, and to which he was elected or chosen by the members of the university.

In the market-place at Cambridge is a conduit, which was made, in the reign of Charles II., at the expense of Hobson, the celebrated carrier. He was the first person who let horses, and whoever hired them was obliged to take that which was nearest the door, so that each animal might have its turn of labour and of rest. From this circumstance arose the phrase of "taking Hobson's choice," which means that we must either take a thing or do without it.

Before we leave Cambridge, I must tell you a very curious story of a woman buried in the snow whilst travelling between Cambridge and Trumpington.† She had been riding, but her horse ran away from her, and in vain she tried to catch it. Weary and exhausted, she at length sat down to rest on the ground. The snow falling thickly, and drifting also, gathered round, so that it soon buried her. The next morning she observed a hole covered with thin ice, and through this she thrust, as a signal of distress, a stick, at the end of which was her handkerchief. This, however, made her very cold, because it let in the outer air. Being Sunday she could hear the church‑bells

* Page 123.   † Pages 15, 31, 78.

ringing, and even the conversation of the people who were passing. She had enough light in the middle of the day to read an almanack that had been in her pocket. She was not hungry, only thirsty, and she satisfied her thirst by sucking the snow. At last the snow began to melt, and the hole in her prison grew larger. She tried to get out, but was too weak. Another Sunday came, the eighth day of her imprisonment. Then she was discovered; but when taken out of the snow, she fainted. Her feet were dreadfully frost-bitten, and she lost all her toes. For some time she seemed gradually to get better; but again she grew worse, and died the following September.

East of Cambridge, and principally in Suffolk, in a flat uninteresting country, is Newmarket, where noted horse-races are held, and horses trained. In its neighbourhood are the seats of many gentlemen.

On the Ouse is Ely, with its grand old cathedral, and three towers, seen from afar. It was, probably, begun in the reign of the Plantagenet kings. In the neighbourhood of Ely are curious water-plants and water-birds.* The rivers are very full of fish, especially eels, from which the town has, probably, received its name. King Canute having heard, on the mainland, the monks at Ely chant, visited them, crossing the morass in a little boat. This morass is now solid ground, over which the railroad passes.† This district is called, by the people, the rough country. As in Lincolnshire, a great deal of the waste land is reclaimed; but before the ground can be tilled, the peat surface must be pared off. The peat, after being cut, is stacked and used as fuel.

A few years ago, the Little Ouse, which, coming from Norfolk, joins the Great Ouse, burst its banks, a little to the north of Ely. The flood did not entirely subside till

* Pages 148, 165.   † Page 88.

the end of the following year; but it left behind it, instead of desolation, so rich a soil that the farmers were able to sow wheat over the whole land, and the following autumn the 30,000 acres waved like one vast sheet of golden corn.

Before the drainage-works, floods used to be very frequent. The people call the Ouse the "Bailiff of Bedford," and in wet weather there was frequently a seizure of corn and cattle.

Wisbeach, in the north of the county, is a well-built town. It stands on the River Nene, which you remember flows through—what county? Vessels of a considerable size can now ascend the river to Wisbeach, so there is here a good deal of trade. Clarkson, who laboured with Wilberforce to set free every slave under British dominion, was born here.

Is there not a great deal to think about in Cambridgeshire? Another day, I hope there will be a review of the four last counties. They are almost entirely agricultural, that is, the people are employed in the culture of their fields, not in manufactures.

———

Northampton, Bedford, Huntingdon, and Cambridge, might be reviewed, by tracing the courses of the rivers on a slate, or writing in an exercise-book all the places of interest on the Nene and its branches, and on the Ouse, and its branches. Then might be written a list of all the noticeable objects, such as shoemakers making strong shoes; women plaiting bonnet straw; dairy-maids churning butter; students walking in caps and gowns, &c., Another column might contain a list of all the celebrated men, connected in any way with these counties, which, as they include Cambridge, would be considerable.

NORFOLK.—Part I.

If you look at the map, and find Norfolk, you will observe that we reach again the wide, wide sea; that we to-day shall talk about a county which is washed, both on the north and east by its ever restless waves. Don't you love the beautiful blue sea? And when you try to measure how wide are its waters and how countless are its sands, do they not remind us, "God's love is a sea, immensely wide," and that His mercies are as numerous as the sand on the sea-shore.

Norfolk is the fourth largest county in England. Which counties are larger? It is not a pretty county; for it is generally plain, without hills and valleys, and wanting the richness which woodlands always give to a landscape.* Still, we should find some pretty spots, and the coast scenery on the north-east, where the sea washes chalky and crumbling cliffs, cannot fail to be interesting.

Another pleasing thing to see, is the capital and good farming practised.† In the north-east of the county the soil is light and sandy; some years ago it was covered only with sheep-walks. It was found, however, that beneath it lay a richer kind of earth, called marl; this was dug up and spread out, and now there are fields full of golden grain. All kinds of grain are grown, but that which grows best is barley. This is generally made into malt for brewing. Do you know how malt is made?

The barley is first steeped in water till it begins to sprout, then it is put on a kiln-stove, heated with coke or wood, and left there till dry. This is malt. When brewing commences, the malt is mashed, and warm water poured over it. After standing a few hours, the liquor

* Page 4.   † Pages 146, 148.

called wort is drawn off. This is afterwards boiled with hops.

Rape-seed is also grown in this county, as well as in Cambridgeshire. From this an oil is extracted, used in manufacturing woollen goods.

A great many sheep and cattle are fed and fattened.* The poultry-yards are very famous. I daresay you have heard of Norfolk turkeys, amongst which there is much slaughter at Christmas time. They are the largest turkeys in England, and sometimes weigh between 30 lbs. and 40 lbs. A great deal of game is also shot in Norfolk, not black-cock and grouse (where are they found?) but beautiful pheasants and partridges.† Off its coast, the waters of the sea supply plenty of fish, especially mackerel and herring. These are small fish that come in large shoals, hundreds of thousands of them being caught in one night.

Though there are no metals, clay for bricks, sand for glass, and potters' earth for pottery, are found in different parts. Several things are manufactured, chiefly woollen fabrics, such as poplins, barèges, mousseline-de-laine, soft and thin black dresses and crapes; also, mohair yarn, which, after being spun, is sent to France, and there woven into the plush that is generally used in liveries. There are, also, cotton factories, but, still, we cannot say that the manufactories of Norfolk at all rival those of Yorkshire and Lancashire. In this county is the little village of Worsted, which gave its name to the yarn so well known. Norfolk is indebted for its worsted factories to the Flemings, who came over in the reign of Edward III. Many more arrived in the time of Queen Elizabeth, who were poor persecuted Protestants, glad to find, in dear old England, a land to shelter them from their enemies; to this

* Pages 8, 23, 37, 148, 167. † Page 8.

day, Norfolk and Suffolk are reckoned the most Protestant parts of England.

Do you remember what part of Yorkshire suffers from the constant encroachments of the sea? In the same way Norfolk is losing a portion of its coast; ships now sailing over ground where villages once stood; but, as in Yorkshire so in Norfolk, what is lost is recovered. There formerly was a considerable arm of the sea, extending to Norwich, and now there is only a narrow river, whilst from the Wash, many acres have been saved for agriculture.*

The lakes and pools and expanses of water in Norfolk are called "Broads." Here, as in Lincolnshire, quantities of wild geese and other fowl are caught, principally by "decoys."† From the swamps, ditches are cut, called pipes; they have hoops over them, covered with netting. To entice the wild fowl up these pipes, tame ones are educated. They know the way, and, as they have always been kindly treated, are not afraid to go. They seem to persuade their visitors, who quickened, perhaps, by the barking of a little dog behind them, readily follow, and fall into the draw-net at the end. The tame duck is soon set free, whilst the rest are kept prisoners, speedily executed, and sent up as dainties to the London market. Take care, lest you sometimes meet decoys of another kind to lead you astray.

I will now tell you two stories about Norfolk sailor-boys, the one to amuse and the other to instruct you. Copy the one, and you will do well; do not copy the other, or you will surely fall.

* Pages 36, 55.   † Pages 148, 165, 172.

TWO STORIES, OF TWO NORFOLK SAILOR-BOYS.

STORY I.

In the city of Norwich is a beautiful cathedral with a spire 315 feet (how many yards?) high. One Sunday in July, many years ago, a sailor-boy, about thirteen years old, obtained leave to go into the tower. From the tower he clambered to the spire, and ascended inside of it till he reached the highest window. Here he crept outside. Upwards, upwards he went, scrambling from crocket to crocket, though each of these was more than a yard distant from the other. At length he gained the summit, and having walked twice round a narrow ledge, he amused himself with twirling the weather-cock. Crowds of people watched from below, trembling lest his foot should slip, and he should be dashed to pieces. Foolish child! thus to imperil his life. At length he begins to descend; from crocket to crocket he lowers himself in safety. Again he enters the little window, and reaches the ground without any injury. How kind was God's care over that thoughtless youth, but what aching hearts his conduct must have caused. I hope his poor mother was not standing in the crowd.

STORY II.

John's father was dead, and his mother was a poor widow, who found it difficult to support him; so John set off to Yarmouth, to seek for a situation as cabin boy. He went to several captains. "You are too small, young 'un," said one. "Enough without you," said another. "I do want one," said a third; "but I never take boy or man without a character." John looked sad. How could he prove that he was a good boy? A wise thought struck

M

him. He pulled out his pocket Bible; on the first leaf of which was written, "John M——, given as a reward for diligence and good conduct at his Sabbath-school." The captain looked pleased, "Yes, my boy, this will do," he said; "I would rather have this character than any other."

The ship was bound for St Petersburgh; but on the way a terrible storm arose. The sailors all thought they should be lost. John took out his Bible; knelt down and read the 60th and 61st Psalms, the captain and men kneeling around him.

The storm ceased, and at last the ship reached St Petersburgh. One day, John went on shore; he saw many smart ladies and gentlemen in sledges, which are carriages without wheels, that slide over the snow and ice. A bracelet fell from a lady's arm; he picked it up, but the lady was out of sight.

He brought it to the captain, who said, "Why, Jack, your fortune is made; these are diamonds. I will sell them for you when we get home."

"No," said John; "they belong to the lady; and if we should have a storm at sea, captain, what would become of us."

The captain then said he would try and find out the lady; this he did, and she gave John a large sum of money.

With this, the captain bought furs for the honest boy, which he sold in England for twice as much; and John with his money and a happy heart went home.

The cottage was shut up; the mother gone. John trembled, lest she should be dead; but a neighbour said, "She is in the workhouse."

Was not her good son happy to bring his mother out, to take her again to her dear cottage home, to make her once more comfortable, and to leave her money, that she might not be again hungry?

John was afterwards mate of the ship in which he had been once the little cabin-boy.

NORFOLK.—Part II.

To-day for the towns and remarkable places of Norfolk.

First, we will follow the Little Ouse. Thetford is a very ancient town, having been a British city before the time of the Romans. Not far from it, is Kenninghall, where the British Queen Boadicea held her court. Farther on, is Downham, called Sandy Downham; because, about 200 years ago, there was a great flood of sand covering a quantity of the ground.*

Now we must stop, for the last time, on the shores of the Wash, and describe the last place of interest in the great fen country. This is Lynn Regis, or King's Lynn, situated on the Ouse, about twelve miles from the sea. Three hundred ships could ride in its harbour; but the tide rises so rapidly and so high—twenty feet—that it is not reckoned a very pleasant anchorage. It is, however, a considerable place of commerce, being connected with the centre of England by canals and rivers. Corn, fine sand for glass, and great quantities of shrimps, are sent from this town. The inhabitants continued very faithful to King John; so he gave the mayor a large silver cup and sword.† It received its regal name from King Henry VIII., who took possession of it, instead of the bishop of Norwich.

North-east of Lynn, is the village of Castle Rising. It was a seaport, when Lynn was only a marsh. It is a very ancient place, and has a fine old church and castle. Near

* Pages 152, 158, 160, 168, 173.   † Page 151.

this is Sandringham Hall, the seat of the Prince and Princess of Wales.

Following the northern coast, is Wells, a small sea-port, near which is Holkham Hall, the princely seat of the Earl of Leicester. It is built of a curious light-coloured brick. There is a central building, with an open court, and four wings, each having an open court likewise in its centre. Here lived the gentleman, Mr Coke, who thought of the plan of converting the barren parts of Norfolk into fruitful land.* He was afterwards made Earl of Leicester.

Farther along the coast, is Cromer, a very pleasant sea-bathing place. The inhabitants are chiefly fishermen. The bay is very dangerous, and life-boats are always at hand, to help in case of shipwreck. A seaman from this village, called Bacon, discovered, in the reign of King Henry IV., the icy and yet fiery island of Iceland.

Almost all the Norfolk rivers, excepting those going to the Wash, flow towards the Yare, which enters the sea between Norfolk and Suffolk; so we will follow their separate courses, till we reach Yarmouth.

First, we will follow the Wensum, which flows from the north, in a south-east direction. Fakenham, on its banks, is a flourishing market-town, which has this peculiar privilege, that none of its inhabitants need serve on juries. If you do not know what juries are, ask some one to tell you. Near this town are some very handsome seats belonging to different noblemen. One, Houghton Hall, was built by Sir Robert Walpole, and belonged to him and his celebrated son Horace. These were famous statesmen, in the reigns of George I. and II.

On a branch of the Wensum, is East Dereham, where Cowper, the poet of sweet Christian spirit, is buried.

* Page 174.

Following the course of the Wensum, at its junction with the Yare, stands Norwich, a large cathedral town, or city. An old writer has described it, "a city in an orchard, or an orchard in a city; so equally are houses and trees blended in it." Notwithstanding this pretty description, which is still appropriate, there are narrow and dirty streets in Norwich. The great beauty of the town is its handsome cathedral. Do you remember how high

Norwich.

the spire is?* The view is taken from Household Hill, not a high one, but almost the only one in the county. In the reign of Edward VI. it became the scene of a great rebellion, headed by Kett, a tanner. For seven weeks the rebels encamped on this hill, breaking down

* Pages 153, 154.

all the surrounding fences, and laying hands on such numbers of deer, and sheep, and cattle, that in their camp a fat sheep was sold for 4d. There was, at last, a battle with the king's troops, in which the rebels were quite defeated. The ringleaders were all hung; Kett, on the top of Norwich Castle; and his brother at the top of the church steeple at Wymondham, at which place they had lived. Norwich has suffered much from fightings and quarrellings. At one time, there was a terrible warfare between the monks and the townspeople. The cathedral was commenced in the reign of William Rufus. The interior is even more beautiful than the exterior. There is a very handsome stone roof, containing more than 300 figures from Bible history.* Besides the cathedral, there are forty churches; one of them has almost the best chime of bells in England, twelve in number. In the picture, you will see in the distance Norwich Castle. This was built in the time of the Saxons. The more modern buildings are chapels, and infirmaries, and hospitals. Do you observe that castles for warfare are almost all ancient buildings; and infirmaries for the sick, modern? How much better is it to save life than to destroy it!

Amongst good and famous people born at Norwich, was Archbishop Parker, a very learned and pious man, who lived in the reign of Elizabeth; also, Dr Samuel Clarke, a dissenter, of whom the same character may be given.

At Norwich, there are about 14,000 looms employed in weaving all kinds of fabric——silk, cotton, but chiefly woollen.† Much of it is sent abroad.

There is no remarkable place along the higher part of the Yare, and though there are many large villages south

* Page 170.   † Pages 49, 91-93, 141.

of Norwich, I will not tell their names, for I am sure you would forget them. The country is so beautifully cultivated, that it is quite like a large garden, whilst the cottages look very pretty with woodbine and roses. You would also be struck by the number of windmills. In this neighbourhood is the little village, Aslacton, where the great reformer, Archbishop Cranmer, was born. He was cruelly burned alive at Oxford, in Queen Mary's reign.*

We now reach the borders of Suffolk, and will follow the northern bank of the Waveney. The first town of note is Diss, built on a small lake, abounding with eels, † and in which is found a curious fish called the chafer, which has only three scales. The people here are employed in breweries, or in making coarse cloth or stockings. Then we pass Harleston, where waterproof cloth is made, and at the mouth of the river, we find Yarmouth, the largest seaport in the county. Here Lord Nelson, the victor of the great sea-battle at Trafalgar, and Sir Astley Cooper, a very celebrated surgeon, were born. Yarmouth is built on a narrow strip of land between the river and the sea, which 900 years ago was under water.‡ It has been likened to a gridiron; five long streets going from north to south, and 156 narrow alleys crossing it from east to west. Some are so narrow that if your arms are stretched out, you would touch each side with the tips of your fingers, whilst in others the projecting houses meet above, and form a sort of tunnel below. There is a good harbour at Yarmouth, the best quay in England, and two good piers. Yarmouth is very celebrated for its herring fisheries. Yarmouth bloaters, as the salted fish are called, are sent to all parts of England, and also abroad. At this one port, during the season, one hundred ton weight

* Pages 9, 27, 106, 169.   † Page 172.   ‡ Pages 36, 176.

are caught nightly.   In the charter of the town, it is required that 100 herrings be sent every year to the sheriffs of Norwich, who are to make them into twenty-four pies, for presentation to the king.

There is a high column erected to the memory of Lord Nelson, who was born in Norfolk.   Besides other hospitals and asylums, there is one for lunatic soldiers.   The old parish church is a very handsome building—commenced in the reign of Henry I.   In it is a painted window to the memory of Sarah Martin.   This excellent woman, though a humble dressmaker, was able to do much for her Saviour's sake.   She was born at Caistor, near Yarmouth, once a Roman encampment.   Though she had to earn her own livelihood, yet for thirty-two years she constantly visited the workhouse and jail, cheering the poor by telling of Him, who for their sakes had nowhere to lay His head, and endeavouring to lead the criminal to Him, who came to seek and save the lost.

The Yare, before it reaches Yarmouth, expands into a wide sheet of water, which, at high tide, looks quite like a lake.   It is here that it receives the Bure from the north. Close to Yarmouth, running along the shore, are the "Deres," great sand-banks, on which are built "Lookouts."   These are square wooden rooms on the top of poles, to which you ascend by a staircase, and where you have a good view of the Roads and all the ships.   These sandbanks are constantly changing their shape.   The sand, as well as the sea, helps to destroy places on the coast.   A village called Eccles has thus disappeared; all that now remains of it being the church tower, whose body is completely buried in the sand.

Yarmouth Roads consist of a passage of deep water between the shore and a ridge of sand-banks, which do not rise to a level with the water. Moored on the sand-banks are light-ships, that is, ships with lights, to warn off mariners. The great rolling waves break upon these banks, and thus, the water nearer the shore is sufficiently smooth for ships to ride at anchor even in stormy weather.

Now enough about Norfolk, where farms, and factories, and fisheries all flourish.

SUFFOLK.—Part I.

To-day we reach another maritime, or sea-shore county. It lies south of Norfolk. This part of England was once called East Anglia; then the people, who lived on the northern division, were called North-folk, and those in the south, South-folk; and so the counties received their names. Suffolk is not quite so flat as Norfolk. There are many rivers in this county, with sufficient water for boats to pass, which near their mouths generally widen to form little arms of the sea. Off the coast, a great many fish are found, mackerel and sprats being more abundant than they are farther north.* Fresh-water fish are also numerous; such as tench, pike, carp.†

As an agricultural county, Suffolk stands very high. The land is well and carefully farmed, and the people are very willing to try new improvements for reaping, plough-ing, or threshing.‡

It has been said, "that it is cultivated the best, most ably, most carefully, most skilfully, of any piece of land in the whole world." Neither you nor I know if this be true, as we have not been over the world. It is also said to be a county of very industrious and virtuous people, and "its towns are all cleanliness, neatness, and good order." The parishes in Suffolk are small, and there are many good

* Pages 8, 175.   † Pages 63, 172, 183.   ‡ Page 174.

pastors to teach the people the fear of God, which we know is the beginning of all wisdom and happiness.

On most of the Suffolk farms all kinds of very good grain, turnips, and hemp are grown. There are also dairy farms, where both butter and cheese are made. The cheese has the name of "Suffolk thump," and is said to be the worst in England. Suffolk cows, horses, and pigs, are all famous, and there are plenty of rabbits, turkeys, and pigeons, so, like most of the eastern counties, it supplies the wants of the larder.*

There are few manufactories; the most interesting are those for making machines and tools to assist the agriculturist. Ipswich is famous for its stay-making, and at a few of the other towns silks and stuffs are woven. There are no valuable metals, but there are large beds of shell-marl, or petrified shells. Many fossils are found in Suffolk. The formation of the eastern shore of England is not nearly so old as that of the western parts, so the fossils are of a much more recent date than those found west of the line we once drew between Devon and Durham.†

Two rivers flow north-west through Suffolk, and join the Little Ouse. These are the Linnet and the Larke, the names of two of our sweetest song-birds. On the Larke stands Bury-St-Edmunds. This is a very old town, with fine old churches; here still stands the gateway of what was once a famous abbey. Very long ago, when the Saxons and Danes used to fight, Edmund, King of East Anglia, was killed. The legend says, that the body was beheaded, and the head thrown into a wood, where a wolf guarded it. This wonderfully good animal gave it up to some monks, who, having found the body, were searching for the head. They soon placed the two together, when to their great astonishment they re-united.

* Pages 8, 23, 37, 141, 148, 157, 175.   † Pages 58, 69.

Wonderful things continually happening at the grave, they removed the coffin to this place, where was built a large church, and the town received the name of Bury-St-Edmunds, being more commonly called Bury. Bury has excellent schools, and is reckoned one of the healthiest towns in England. Near it are some handsome country seats.

In the extreme north-west of the county is Fakenham, the birthplace of Robert Bloomfield, who wrote a very pretty poem, "The Farmer's Boy." He was once a plough-boy himself.

Following the Waveney on the Suffolk or southern bank, we find Palgrave, where "Honest Tom Martin," the anti-quary, was buried, and where Mrs Barbauld had a school. Perhaps you may have learnt some of Mrs Barbauld's pretty prose hymns. There is one which says, "God made the elephant and the great whale, and the little worm that crawleth on the ground." The country near this is very pretty. In a rich district, full of large farm-houses and beautifully tidy cottages, lies Eye, a neat town, with a good church and the ruins of an old abbey.

Farther down is Bungay, with an old castle and nunnery, and at last the Waveney reaches—what estuary, or the wide mouth, of what river?

A few miles along its coast, is a very curious old Roman castle, called Burgh. The walls, which are partly stand-ing, are very strong. It is supposed to have been built A.D. 49, which was at the very time that the Apostles Paul, Peter, and John, were alive. Now we come to Lowestoft, a pleasant town, situated on the most eastern point of all England. It is older than Yarmouth, and there has always been a rivalry between these towns. It is an excellent bathing-place, with a hard sandy beach.

Following the coast, and passing several fishing villages,

we reach Dunwich, now a small village of only twenty houses, but once a very important place, and a bishopric. At that time there was a wood standing, which extended a mile and a half between the town and the sea; but its trees have long been laid beneath the ocean. Onward, onward came the waves, piece by piece the cliffs fell, and churches, monasteries, houses, and fields have all been swept away.*

Farther south, between the river Ald and the sea, is Aldborough. Here, likewise, the sea has been stealing houses and streets. Sandbanks have, however, been thrown up to prevent further inroads, and many new houses have been built, as it has become quite a favourite place for bathing.† Crabbe the poet was born here.

Farther inland, near the source of the Ore, is Framlingham. Here are the remains of what has been a magnificent castle, where the Dukes of Norfolk used to live. When good Edward VI. died, Queen Mary remained here till it was safe for her to go to London to be crowned. At the month of the Ore is Orford, and here, also, there are the ruins of an old castle, which is a landmark for the sailors and fishermen skirting this coast.

The next river with a broad mouth is the Deben. At the point where it widens, is Woodbridge, a small commercial town, prettily situated. Here, as in several other neighbouring places, the churches are built of dark flint interspersed with light freestone.

The next river is the Gipping, flowing through rather pretty scenery, and passing many gentlemen's seats. On it is Stow-Market, near to which hops are cultivated, and where several acres of land are used for growing roses and dahlias. Passing Needham, once famous for manufacturing coarse woollen cloths, now a mere village, you find, in

---

* Pages 55, 176.   † Pages 21, 55, 57, 58, 98, 180.

the neighbourhood, Helmingham, with its fine old hall, surrounded by a wide moat full of water, and two draw-bridges, which are still raised every night.*

To-morrow, dear children, we must have a short chapter about Ipswich, and, I hope, an interesting story about Hadleigh, and then, leaving the coast of England, we will follow a large river in the west.

SUFFOLK.—Part II.

Do you remember the name of the river we last followed? At Ipswich it widens much, forming one of the Broads, and is then called the Orwell. Ipswich is an ancient town; many of the houses are built of wood and plaster. Much of the wood is curiously carved, and the gable ends of the houses face the street, which makes them look, in a drawing at least, much prettier than a straight frontage.†

Ipswich is a good-sized town, about half the size of Norwich. It is both manufacturing and commercial. Formerly, broad cloth was made here. We still have the names of Linsey and Kerseymere, from two villages in Suffolk. Most of these manufactures have, however, travelled into Yorkshire.‡ Stays and silk, malt and artificial stone, and manure from the coprolite, a kind of fossil, in which there is much lime, are made here; and also there is what seems strange in a county where there is neither coal nor iron, a great iron foundry to make agricultural implements.§ What do these hard words mean? Ploughs, harrows, rakes, spades, and machines for thrashing or cutting corn and other things. There are 1000 people employed at this foundry. Ipswich used to have a great many churches; now there are thirteen.

---

* Pages 9, 15.   † Pages 74, 106.
‡ Page 38.   § Pages 114, 185.

Cardinal Wolsey, a proud and ambitious man, who lived in the time of Henry VIII., was born here. When he came to die, he said, "Had I served my God as faithfully as I have served my king, He would not have forsaken me now." How miserable to discover this too late!

On the Stour, which separates Suffolk from Essex, stands Sudbury, a neat, clean place. Here the Flemish weavers, whom Edward III. brought over, were received very kindly, and it was long famous for woollen cloth.* Now, the chief manufacture is silk or crape. You must remember, however, that, compared with the great manufacturing towns of Yorkshire and Lancashire, this, and many other places I have mentioned, are merely villages.

On the Brett, a branch of the Stour, is Hadleigh, with many curious old houses, ornamented with carved wood, and rude figures. At the time of the Reformation, Hadleigh was one of the first towns in England that received the Word of God.

At that time, there lived here a worthy rector, Dr Rowland Taylor. In Queen Mary's time he was condemned to be burned, because of his love for the Bible. He had been tried in London, and sentenced to be executed on Aldham Common. He was obliged to pass through Hadleigh as a prisoner, escorted by the sheriff and queen's officers. The people all stood sorrowful and dismayed watching him, and crying, "There goes our good shepherd; what shall we scattered lambs do? O merciful God, strengthen him and comfort him." At the bridge, a poor man with five little children met him. They fell down upon their knees, and said, "O dear father and good shepherd, Dr Taylor, God help and succour thee as thou hast many a time succoured me and my poor children."

Coming to the almshouses, he gave money to the poor

* Page 175.

people who stood there, and, at the last cottage, not seeing the inhabitants, he said, "Are the blind man and blind woman that dwelt here alive?" "Yes, they are within," was the answer; and then he threw in at the window his glove filled with money.

When he reached the common, and uncovered his head, the people, seeing his dear face and long white beard, wept again and prayed, "God save thee, good Dr Taylor; Jesus Christ strengthen thee and help thee; the Holy Ghost

Dr Taylor's Martyrdom.

comfort thee!" When the good man tried to speak, the guard thrust a staff into his mouth. At last, with a loud voice, he said, "Good people, I have taught you nothing but God's holy word; and those lessons that I have taken out of God's blessed book, the Holy Bible, and I have come hither this day to seal it with my blood." Then one of the guard gave his head a great blow with a cudgel.

Afterwards he went to the stake and kissed it, and stepped into the tar-barrel in which he was to stand. His hands were folded, his eyes looked towards heaven, and he seemed to pray. He was then fastened with chains, and the sheriff said to a butcher, "Set up the fagots." The butcher answered, "I am lame, sir, I cannot." The sheriff threatened, "Do, or I send you to prison." But he would not. Others, however, did so; and soon the flames burnt. One man most cruelly cast a fagot at him, which broke his face, so that the blood ran down. Good Dr Taylor meekly said, "O friend, I have harm enough. What needed that?" His last words were, "Merciful Father of heaven, for Jesus Christ my Saviour's sake, receive my soul into Thy hands!"

On Aldham Common is a stone on which is roughly engraved, "1555, Dr Taylor, in defending that was good, at this plas left his blude." When you thus hear of one of the noble army of martyrs, thank God for the faith they had, and determine—

> "We won't give up the Bible,
> We'll shout it far and wide,
> Until the echo shall be heard
> Beyond the rolling tide;
> Till all shall know that we, though young,
> Withstand Rome's treacherous art,
> And that from God's own sacred Word,
> We'll *never, never* part."

I need not tell you of any other remarkable place on the Suffolk side of the Stour; though, another day, you shall hear of a large fort on the Essex shore of the river.

In reviewing Norfolk and Suffolk, each child might have

apportioned to him a particular river, a little narrative of
the course of which he must either write or give verbally.
Or the teacher might draw a diagram of the two counties
with their rivers, leaving the children to give the names of
the streams, and of the different towns on their banks.
This might be made very interesting, by imagining that
they are all setting out on an excursion, and marking, by
a dotted line, their progress from one place to another.
Elder children might afterwards write the description of
their imaginary tour.

SHROPSHIRE.

TO-DAY we shall commence quite another district in England.   We will follow the course of the Severn, and the
rivers that flow into it.   The Severn is the largest river in
England.   It rises in Wales, and the first English county
through which it passes, is Shropshire, or Salop.   What
counties border Salop ?   You see, we are not far from our
old friends, Cheshire and Staffordshire.   Two other English counties, Hereford and Worcester, touch it ; and on
the west there are three counties of Wales.   The north
of the county is generally flat; but in other parts, there
are considerable hills, the principal being the Wrekin.
There are many dingles, deep hollows between hills.   The
soil of the county is generally of a reddish cast, as the old
and new red sandstone prevail.*   There is also another
kind of rock, the Silurian, very full of the fossils of shellfish, but without those of any creature that has a backbone.   In the east of the county, coal and iron are found
as they are in Staffordshire ; and there are great iron-
works in a beautiful valley called Coalbrook Dale.   It is
curious to see iron manufactories in the midst of the beauties

* Pages 60, 65, 136.

N

of nature ; to hear the noise of the hammer, with the soft murmuring of the brook; and to see the grimy chimney rise above the luxuriant foliage. Across the Severn, in this neighbourhood, was built the first iron bridge that was made in England. Do you remember what river, in the north of England, the second iron bridge spanned ? This, too, was the first place in our land, where coke, (burnt coal,) instead of charcoal, (burnt wood,) was used for smelting iron. This discovery was of great consequence, as coke answers much better, and England is much richer in coal than in wood. Also in the neighbourhood of Coalbrook Dale, the first wooden railway was made, about 200 years ago.*

The people in Shropshire are variously employed ; some in mining; some in manufactures, especially in iron works; and a great many in agriculture. In this county was born and lived Old Parr, the oldest man that we read of in England. He was born in the reign of Edward IV., and died in that of Charles I., aged nearly 153 years. The names of Jones, Williams, and Davis become very common here, as they are all over Wales.

Some of the old Roman roads, or streets as they are called, remain very visible in Shropshire,† and lately there have been found, not far from Shrewsbury, at Wroxeter, considerable remains of an ancient Roman city, called Uriconium. The houses, the bath-rooms, the roads, the market-place, have all been traced ; and even the worn-out stone that led to the latter, and the gutters on the sides of the road. Hidden amongst the flues, under a bath-room, was found the skeleton of an old man, who must have taken refuge there, when the city was destroyed ; and beside him lay a quantity of Roman coins. In a dust-heap, the sweepings of ancient drawing-rooms were found, hairpins, buckles,

* Pages 33, 87.   † Pages 83, 148.

needles, and coins, probably handled once by Roman dames. An inscription discovered on a stamp shows how, ages ago, people pretended, as they do now, to cure all diseases. The translation is " The dialebarium of Tiberius Claudius, the physician, for all complaints of the eyes, to be used with egg." This city was inhabited nearly 2000 years ago by people, then full of life and spirits as we are, but now passed away. Does not this fact teach us all the lesson, that here " we have no abiding city," therefore seek a home without foundations, whose builder and maker is God !

In the north of the county are several small lakes, called meres, full of fish.* The Severn was formerly famous for salmon; but there are not nearly so many now.† On one of these meres is the thriving little town of Ellesmere. In a park near it, are some of the finest elm trees in England. Not far distant, and very near the borders of Wales, is Oswestry, a place noted in early English history. Here, in the time of the Saxon heptarchy, more than 1200 years ago, was fought a great battle between Oswald, the Christian king of Northumbria, and Perda, the Pagan king of Mercia. The Pagans gained the victory, and poor Oswald lost his life.‡ In Shropshire are many border fortresses, similar to those we heard of in Northumberland. Can you think why we might expect to find them here ?

The first place of consequence, on the banks of the Severn, is Shrewsbury, the chief and county town of Shropshire. It has a great trade in Welsh flannels and cloths, brought from the neighbouring counties of Wales. Shrewsbury is also famous for its cakes, and for brawn.

Many of the houses of Shrewsbury look pretty in a picture. Being very old, beams of timber cross the plaster-

* Pages 63, 183.   † Page 8.   ‡ Page 10.

work, and gables point the streets.* There are several churches, covered with ivy, and the ruins of an old abbey, the stone pulpit of which is now in the midst of a garden. The old castle was built in the time of William I., who gave the men of Shrewsbury certain privileges, on condition that twelve of them should watch around the chamber of the king when he slept in that city, and attend him armed when he hunted in the neighbourhood.

Near Shrewsbury is Battlefield. Can any one remember between whom a battle was there fought? If not, look back to the county of Northumberland. On the road to Battlefield is a very old oak, which it is said Glendower climbed to see the battle. It is quite hollow now; six people can stand inside of it. At the bottom, it is nearly fifteen yards round.†

Instead of following the Severn, let us follow the Shrewsbury and Birmingham railway, and we soon reach Wellington. This is almost like one of the "Black country" towns, so full is it of iron-works and nailers.‡ Near it is the Wrekin, a pleasant hill, with a beautiful view. Large pleasure parties often come here, out of the busy crowded towns, to enjoy the clear fresh air. In a due east direction, passing Shiffnall, and other small but busy towns, there stands, on the borders of Staffordshire, Boscobel Wood, celebrated as the hiding-place of King Charles II. I dare say you have heard of

The 29th of May,
The Royal-Oak day,

which commemorates the young King Charles' escape from his enemies, after the battle of Worcester. He was hidden in one of the oak trees, whilst some of Cromwell's soldiers passed below. The king had been placed by his faithful friend, the owner of Boscobel House, under the

---

* Pages 106, 189.   † Page 157.   ‡ Page 114.

charge of three brothers, who lived at a farm, called the White Ladies. They promised to take care of him; and that he might not be discovered, they cut off his long hair, smeared his face with soot from the chimney, and changed his smart buff-coat and royal ornaments, for a countryman's coarse garments. This, however, was not enough. When the rebels were near, the king took refuge in the wood. In the famous oak, he and three of his friends stayed for a night and day; and so tired was the poor king, that he laid his head on the knee of one of his companions, and slept soundly. The brothers afterwards ventured to hide him in a secret room in the cottage. There were often rooms without any visible entry built in the massive walls of old houses.

Returning again to the Severn, and following its course, we reach Coalbrook Dale, with its iron-works and iron bridge. The towns belonging to it are called Madeley Market, and Iron Bridge. On the opposite side of the river, on a hill, is Broseley, noted for its glazed tobacco-pipes and fire-bricks.

Further down on both sides of the river is Bridgnorth, built on steep hills. The higher part of the town is reached by steps, cut out of the rock, and guarded by an iron rail.* Once, the town had rows like Chester, and there are still the ruins of castles where kings have often lodged. The chief manufacture is that of carpets. Here is the church where good Richard Baxter began his ministry.

In the west of the county are, Church Stretton, where flannel is made;† Bishop's Castle and Clun, on the little river Cluno, and several other small towns. In these places, on market days especially, you would meet numbers of Welsh people, talking quite a different language to

* Pages 43, 92.　　　　　† Page 92.

ours.   Near the meeting of the Cluno and Teine is a hill
fort, called Caer Caradoc, or the castle of Caractacus,
where that brave Briton long resisted the power of the
Romans.

In the south of the county, at the junction of the Corve
and the Teme, stands Ludlow, a town of some trade, and
famous for its old castle, now in ruins.   It was formerly
inhabited by the princes of Wales.   The unfortunate young
Edward V. was proclaimed here, and Henry VII. prepared
it for the residence of his son Arthur, the elder brother of
Henry VIII., who died here quite young.   The great poet
Milton wrote a play, which was first acted in this castle;
and, could its now deserted walls speak, no doubt they
might tell many a story of feasting and of fighting.   The
town of Ludlow is still surrounded by walls, through
which are seven gate-ways.

Now I think I have told you enough of Shropshire.   It
is a pleasant county, though not remarkable for its scenery;
and it is a useful county, though not full of manufactories
like Staffordshire or Lancashire.   Historically it is an interesting county from the time of the Romans, and their
great station of Uriconium, down to that of King Charles
and the oak at Boscobel.

To-morrow we must, with the Severn, pass southwards
through the pretty county of Worcester.

WORCESTERSHIRE.—Part I.

WE shall read to-day about a pretty fertile county of dear
old England, with beautiful rivers wandering through its
valleys, and green hills in the south-west, with fine fresh
air and very lovely views.

How many counties touch Worcester?   From what

county does the Severn pass into it? From which does the Avon? From which would you enter it, if travelling from the north, the south, the east, the west?

The Severn has not in Worcester the hilly banks that it has in many parts of Shropshire. It runs for thirty miles through a valley, sometimes a quarter of a mile and sometimes a mile wide. All kinds of pleasant things grow in this county, not only golden-eared corn and bright green grass, but hops, twisted prettily round tall poles, and covered with elegant green flowers,* and apple and pear trees, laden in spring with their pink and white blossoms, and in autumn with their glowing fruits. There are, also, fields of pease and vetches, and sweet-scented beans and excellent carrots. The mistletoe grows on the apple-boughs, looking green when everything else is brown. Most of the apples and pears are made into cider and perry. Worcestershire is particularly famous for its perry, which is probably the reason why three pears are borne in the arms of the city of Worcester.

In the extreme north of the county, Worcester touches the black country, Dudley being partly in Worcestershire. What two minerals do you expect to find here?

Nearer the centre are some famous salt-springs. The Malvern Hills extend about ten miles from north to south, between Worcester and Herefordshire. The highest of them is about 1400 feet high. How many yards is that in a perpendicular line?

Carpets, needles, porcelain, gloves, and many other things, are manufactured in this county, of which I hope to tell you more as we reach the various towns.

Formerly there used to be so many salmon in the Severn, that the apprentices bargained not to have it for their dinners more than twice a week. I suppose, however,

* Pages 136, 188.

salmon do not like manufactories; for they have, in a
great measure, disappeared.

And now, having given you an idea of the county, we
must begin to find out all its busy or pleasant towns, following the Severn and its various branches.   As the river
leaves Shropshire, it passes Bewdley, which means Beau-
Lieu, or Fine Place; it is very prettily situated.   Here

Augustine and the British Bishops under the Tree.

as at Ludlow, Henry VII. built a palace for his son Arthur.
In this neighbourhood stood a famous tree, called Augustine's Oak.   Augustine was the missionary Pope Gregory
sent to England; but long before his time there had been
many Christians among the ancient British.*   Augustine
and his friends were very proud, and wished to rule the
good British bishops.   The British, not liking their pro-
posals, delayed to give the Italian missionaries an answer

* Pages 10, 57.

till their next meeting, which was fixed to be under the oak tree. On their way the British bishops consulted a very wise and pious hermit.

He answered, "If Augustine be a man of God, follow him."

"How shall we know that?" they inquired.

The Hermit answered, "Our Lord was meek and lowly of heart. If Augustine be so, he has learned of him; but if he be stern and proud, he is not of God."

"How shall we prove this?" they again asked.

"Let him arrive first at the meeting," said the hermit. "If he rise to greet you, receive him as meek and lowly; but if he despise you, who are so many more in number, his counsel must be rejected."

Augustine remained seated, his manner was very haughty, and the British bishops did not yield to him. It is sad to think that these good men were all slain shortly after; and the Romish bishops introduced many superstitious practices.

Now look on the borders of Warwickshire, and you will see, on the Stour, Stourbridge. It is a busy, smoky town, with glass and fire-brick works.* Its fire-clay is in great request, as it is well suited for glass-house pots and crucibles, which must bear very strong heat.

Further down the Stour is Kidderminster, famous for its Brussels carpets.† The carpets called Kidderminster are made in Scotland, whilst most of those sold in England, under the name of Brussels, are made here, and very good carpets they are.

Three miles below Kidderminster, where the Stour joins the Severn, is Stourport, a small manufacturing town. Numbers of canal or river boats come up the Severn to this port, with pig iron from South Wales, or china clay from Cornwall, or other materials for the many manufactur-

* Pages 20, 29, 96, 118, 197.　　　　† Pages 33, 50, 197.

ing towns around.* Many of the boatmen make the boats
their houses, and live month after month in them, with
their wives and children. How would you like to have
your house on the water, continually moving from place to
place, up and down the Severn and the canals adjoining?
The Severn is not a clear river. It looks sandy, owing to
much of its course being through soft sandstone.

On the Salwarp, a branch of the Severn, is Bromsgrove,
a town where you may see some of the curious old wooden
houses, ornamented with black and white stripes. Here
the workmen are engaged, making buttons, nails, and
hooks.† A little to the east of this, is Redditch, a small
place, but the produce of which, it is likely that almost
every little girl has used. About 70,000,000 of needles
are made every week at or near Redditch.

Needles pass through many hands and many processes
before they are fit for use. The square bit of steel has to
be heated and beaten into a cylindrical form, and then
that must be pulled out, until the wire is as fine as necessary. This is cut into proper lengths, and each length is
flattened at one end to make the head and eye. The
needles are again put into the fire to soften, and then the
eyes are pierced with a little punch, another punch taking
away the tiny crumb of steel left in the eye. The corners
have then to be rounded off, the point of the needle
made by means of a file, and the whole smoothed. "It is
surely done now," you think. No, it has to be made red
hot, and then thrown into cold water to harden it. Again
it is heated and straightened, as it is frequently twisted by
the cold water. All that now remains is the polishing;
12,000 or 15,000 needles are placed on buckram in a heap.
Emery and olive oil are sprinkled over them. The needles,
emery, and oil are rolled up in the buckram, over which is

---

* Pages 54, 152.   † Pages 117, 119.

placed a thick plank, laden with stones, which two men work constantly backwards and forwards for one or two days. Then they are washed with soap and water, wiped with hot bran, and swung about in a box till dry. Afterwards they are sorted, their points polished with an emery stone, and at last they are packed up in papers.

Below Bromsgrove, on the Salwarp, is Droitwich. What, from the name, would you expect to find here? If you say salt, you are right, as a great deal of very good salt is procured from salt springs. If you remember what I told you in Cheshire, you will now be able to tell me, by what means?* Droitwich is a very old town, where several coins and pieces of Roman pavement have been found.† Besides churches and schools, there is an hospital for thirty-six old men and women.

Still following the course of the Severn, we reach Worcester, the chief town of the county; but I think, for one day, you have plenty to think about. Augustine's oak and the Severn, canal boats, Redditch needles, Droitwich salt, and,—what else? To-morrow for Worcester and its pretty porcelain.

WORCESTERSHIRE.—Part II.

WE will commence where we left off, at Worcester, an ancient and well-built town on the Severn. The Cathedral is the most important object. The walls are externally plain, but it is large, and there is a handsome tower 200 feet high. In it are the tombs of King John,‡ and Prince Arthur, Henry VII.'s son.§ King John begged to be buried between two bishops, whom he regarded as very holy, thinking that if he were in such good company, the

---

* Page 101.   † Page 194.
‡ Pages 16, 139, 151, 179.   § Pages 198, 200.

evil spirits would not seize him.   I dare say you can think
of a verse of Scripture which shows how foolish was the
thought of this wicked king.   St Andrew's church in Worcester has a very beautiful spire, which is almost more admired than the tower of the Cathedral.   I must tell you
about a boat made into a church floating on the Severn.   A
very good clergyman, observing the numbers of river boatmen
who never went to a place of worship, had a boat-church
made, where he preached every Sunday, and was the
means of doing much good.   The old boat-church is worn
out now ; but an iron church near the river is built instead.
Worcester is much celebrated for its very fine china or
porcelain, which is not excelled in any country.*   A few
years since a beautiful dessert service was made for the
Queen, costing between £3000 and £4000.   Each plate
cost ten guineas, and the dishes for grapes, bon-bons,
cakes, &c., were far more expensive.   Several women and
some children are employed.   At Worcester, Dent's kid
gloves are made, and the town is likewise famous for the
manufacture of hair-cloth, vinegar, pickles and British
wines.   Close to this town was fought the famous battle
in which Charles II. was beaten by the Parliamentary
forces, and obliged to fly.   Then it was that he took
shelter, as I have told you, in Boscobel oak tree.

A little below Worcester, the Teme from the west joins
the Severn.   Of what town on the Teme have you already
heard ?   The only town in Worcestershire that it passes is
Tenbury, a small place.   Here there are mineral springs,
and also a good deal of trade in cider and perry.   These
are much taken by the labouring people instead of beer and
spirits, and are less intoxicating.

Further down the Severn, but at a little distance to the
west, are the Malvern Hills, on both sides very beautiful,

* Pages 110, 133.

but sloping more gently to the west than to the east. The air here is so fresh, and the water so exceedingly pure, that a village on the hills, Great Malvern, has become a favourite watering-place, and grown into a very picturesque town, where many invalids seek to recover strength. There the little children greatly enjoy riding on donkeys amongst the fresh green hills. There is an excellent college for boys, and a beautiful old church. On the Severn is Upton, whence a great deal of cider is shipped for various places.

The Severn, on reaching Gloucestershire, is joined by the Avon, which, if you remember, rises in Northamptonshire, very near a river (name it) that runs north-east to the Wash. In following the Avon through Warwickshire, we passed the old town where Shakespeare lived, and now I must tell you something of the beautiful valley through which it runs in Worcestershire. It is a very fertile district of old England. The chief town in it is Evesham, standing on a little hill, which the winding Avon nearly surrounds. Most of the inhabitants are gardeners, supplying the markets of the neighbouring towns with all kinds of fruit and vegetables.* Others make stockings; and, formerly, a great many women used to sew the Worcester gloves, which, however, are now generally made by machinery. Parchment is also made here. This is a material for writing upon much stronger than paper, and used for documents required to be kept a long time. It is made from the skins of animals.

There are some fine old churches, and the ruins of an abbey, which was once one of the greatest in England; very little besides the tower now remains.† Near Evesham was fought, in the reign of Henry III., a very bloody battle. The barons, headed by Simon de Montford, Earl of Leicester, fought on one side; and Prince Edward,

* Page 161.   † Page 43.

his father, the king, being a prisoner in Montford's hands, fought on the other.   The barons fought for their liberties, because Henry was not only a very foolish king, but he refused to keep the promises that both he and King John had made.   During the battle, this weak king was in danger of being slain by his son's soldiers; but he cried out, " Hold your hand, I am Harry of Winchester."   When the brave Prince Edward heard that, he fought his way to his father and rescued him.   De Montford and his son, both of whom were brave and noble, were killed.   The royalists, who gained the victory, gave no quarter.   The barons' party fled about a mile and a half, where hundreds were slain. Some took refuge in woods, and lived but lawless lives.* There is still a puddle at the bottom of an orchard called Battlewell, which, it is said, was choked with dead bodies. How many places in dear fair England are stained with the remembrance of civil wars ! †   We should pray that God may never allow another; but that He will keep our good Queen Victoria reigning righteously all her days, and preserve our dear fellow-countrymen from disobeying her just laws.

Another gardening town on the Avon is Pershore.   It has this name, on account of the many pear-trees that grow here.

I have nothing more, particularly interesting, to tell you about Worcestershire; but I should like you to draw me a little map, of the course of the Severn, as it passes through Shropshire and Worcester, putting in the branches of the Stour, the Salwarp, the Teme, and the Avon.   Then try and mark the towns on or near these streams, putting a red dot for those where battles have been fought; a black one for towns, where there are manufactories ; and a green one where the chief business is in garden produce, or apples and pears.   When this has been nicely done, we

* Pages 102, 136.   † Pages 9, 45, 124, 158, 181.

will follow farther still the Severn, and find in Gloucestershire old castles and busy towns, about which, I think, you will like to hear.

GLOUCESTERSHIRE.—PART I.

AGAIN I must tell you about a county, beautiful and pleasant, full of green pastures and fruit-bearing trees.* Look on the map, and tell me all the seven counties that touch Gloucester. Though chiefly inland, it may be classed among the maritime counties of England, as the mouth of the Severn forms quite an arm of the sea ; and Gloucester, a few miles up the river, is a port with considerable trade.

The county is generally divided into three parts; first, the hill, or Cotswold, district ; secondly, the valley district ; and thirdly, the forest district. Wold is an old English word for mountain; and cote is from the sheepcotes ; so the word shows that sheep used to graze on these hills ; great numbers do so still; I believe about 600,000.† Amongst the mountains are many beautiful valleys, with clear streams running through them. The great Thames rises on the side of a hill, near Cheltenham. Below a rock, covered with bright green trees, are seen seven little springs, clear as crystal, never failing in summer, and never frozen in winter. Their waters soon unite, and start brightly and merrily on their onward course— destined to carry on their bosom the greatest ships of the world. I always think the source of a river is very like a little child ; and perhaps you will find out why. The hill district of Gloucester extends from Chippen-Campden in the north-east, to Bath, in Somersetshire.

Between the hills and the Severn lies the valley district, comprising the south side of the beautiful valley of Eves-

* Page 199. † Pages 15, 42, 77, 157, 169.

ham; the vale of Gloucester, one of the largest in England; and the valley of Berkeley.* The last is very beautiful, with its rich green grass, on which many cattle feed; its wide river, and rising and falling tide; and the beautiful beech woods clothing the sides of the hills. In this district, the famous Gloucester cheeses are made, which are reckoned almost as good as those of Cheshire.

The forest district is on the western bank of the Severn. It receives this name from the Forest of Dean, which was a royal forest twenty miles long. Its oaks were so famous for shipping, that the officers of the Spanish Armada had special orders to burn the forest. It is much smaller now, as the country has become more cultivated. Here, however, the stag is still found wild. Some of the trees are very fine; one chestnut had in the hollow of it a pretty wainscoted room, furnished with seats, and lighted with little windows. Would you not like to have a tea-drinking there? Another chestnut was said to have been planted in the days of the Saxon Egbert, and measured seventeen yards round. There was an elm eighty feet high.† Beneath the Forest of Dean, are extensive coal-mines. Iron is also found. When the Romans lived in Britain, they obtained most of their iron from this district; and, in the time of the Saxons, Gloucester was the chief town in England for iron manufactures. It is curious that manufacturing districts, as well as persons and goods, should move from place to place.‡

Now, the manufacturers of Gloucestershire are chiefly engaged in making broadcloth. § In a beautiful valley, in the east of Gloucester, called the Vale of Stroud, most of their manufactories are erected. Here, too, is a famous place for making pins, of which I shall hereafter tell you.

* Page 36.   † Pages 136, 157, 164, 196.
‡ Pages 19, 38, 109, 141, 175, 189.   § Page 49.

There have been celebrated people born in this county, and, I am sorry to say, fierce battles fought, and kings and princes cruelly murdered. As we mark the different places, I must tell you some of these sad tales.

On the borders of Gloucester and Worcester, near to the confluence of the Avon and Severn, is Tewkesbury. It has one of the largest abbey churches in all England.* Part of its beautiful carving has been copied in the new and splendid Victoria Tower of the Parliament Houses in London. Outside the town is a green smiling meadow, where the wild flowers now hide themselves amongst the grass. It bears, however, the horrible name of the " Bloody Meadow," because about 400 years ago, it was dyed red with the blood of Englishmen. It was the last of those grievous battles that the Lancastrians fought against the Yorkists. Queen Margaret and her son, the brave young Prince Edward, were taken prisoners.† When brought before Edward IV., the latter was asked how he durst so presumptuously enter the realm with banner displayed? He boldly answered : " To recover my father's kingdom and heritage, from his father and grandfather to him, and from him, after him, to me, lineally descended." Though in his mother's presence the coward king struck him on the face with his gauntlet, and his cruel uncles and two other men stabbed the defenceless prince to death. Prince Edward and many nobles who fought in that battle are buried in Tewkesbury church.

To the west of Tewkesbury, at the foot of the Cotswold Hills, is Winchcombe. Near it is Sudeley castle, where Catherine Parr, the queen who lived to be the widow of Henry VIII., dwelt with her second husband.‡

To the south-west of this, on the Chelt, a very small stream running towards the Severn, is Cheltenham, a fa-

* Pages 19, 54, 82, 205.   † Page 19.   ‡ Page 83.

O

mous watering-place.* It is a large and beautifully built town, with very elegant villas, terraces, and crescents. Amongst these buildings, trees and gardens are continually mingled, the trees almost embowering the streets, and shading the passengers on the hot summer days. It is not a hundred and fifty years since the springs which have made it famous were discovered. It is said that a flock of pigeons first found out their virtues. Good King George III. came to visit it with his court. This brought it into so much notice, that out of little more than a village, the beautiful modern town sprang up. There are now several churches, a college for educating boys, many schools, libraries, and charitable institutions. There is no trade in the town, so the people have not the busy appearance of those in London and other large places. Cheltenham is on a plain, nearly surrounded by hills; and many pretty villages, with their old church towers or spires, stud the country. Amongst the prettiest of these is Leckhampton. Its church stands at the foot of the hill, on the other side of which the mighty Thames has its source. At Witcomb, a short distance from Cheltenham, were found, some years since, the remains of a Roman villa, with large bath-rooms and other remnants of the past.† Throughout Gloucestershire, there are frequent remains of the Romans, for it was one of the frontier parts of England, where they defended themselves against the inhabitants of South Wales.‡ To-morrow, I hope to tell you more of this pretty, fertile county.

GLOUCESTERSHIRE.—PART II.

RETURNING to the banks of the Severn, you will see Gloucester, the county town, marked on the map.

* Pages 123, 205.   † Page 194, 203.   ‡ Pages 19, 68, 106, 198.

A mile above this city the Severn divides, and forms an island, where in the time of the Danes and Saxons, there was a famous single combat between Edmund Ironside and Canute the Great. They both fought very hard, but, as neither gained the victory, they agreed to divide the kingdom between them.*

Gloucester is a very ancient city; the four principal streets, forming a cross, are called Northgate, Southgate, Eastgate, Westgate. There are many curious old houses with strange carvings. In the reign of Charles I., the city was besieged by the king's party, but, after a steady defence, was preserved by the arrival of some London soldiers, who had marched through great danger to its rescue. When they arrived, there was but one barrel of powder left. On the Southgate, there is carved, in remembrance of this deliverance, these words, "A city assaulted by man, but saved by God." The cathedral is a very handsome building, but you shall hear the account of it from a little boy, who, when seven years old, was taken to see it.

" I went one day on a little tour to see a grand cathedral in Gloucester. It had hardly any walls, for it was covered with windows. I went in, I saw a beautiful monument in a large kind of hall, (the nave,) supported by pillars. It was the monument of the man who thought of the vaccination. I saw a great many monuments, of which I shall tell you all about. There was a pretty one; it was a lady rising out of the water of the sea, who had been buried in the sea with her baby in her arms. The text that was written below was, 'The sea shall give up her dead.' There was one monument of a large family, the father and mother, and nine sons and seven daughters. There was the tomb of Robert Duke of Normandy, and

* Page 155.

his figure, which was laid at the top, cut out of bog oak. He had spurs on his feet. Then I saw the tomb of Edward II., who was so cruelly murdered in a castle. Then we went up-stairs to a gallery, called the Whispering Gallery. A man went through a long passage into another gallery, where he whispered to us. After I answered him, I went through this long dark passage, for it was very dark; then I whispered to my aunt, and she came through. We went down and saw more curious things. Then, outside of the cathedral, there was a gentleman called Bishop Hooper, burnt for loving Jesus, and he would not give up the Bible. It was in the Roman Catholic time. I think it was a very wicked thing of them to burn him."

And so will you think, dear children, especially when you know that he was a most pious excellent man, and, by God's grace, was able to meet death with joy, though the manner of it was so cruel. He suffered much from the slowness with which the flame burned, as the fagots were green, and the high wind kept it from rising. During three-quarters of an hour, the flames slowly consumed his limbs; but amidst all his agony his prayers were simply "Lord Jesus, have mercy on me," several times repeated; and his last words were those of the martyr Stephen of old, "Lord Jesus, receive my spirit." *

I must now write for you a verse written on the Whispering Gallery that the little boy mentioned :—

"Doubt not but God, who sits on high,
    Thy secret prayers can hear,
When a dead wall thus cunningly
    Conveys soft whispers to the ear."

In Gloucester was born George Whitfield, who, about one hundred years ago, was a very famous preacher. He

* Page 190.

was the means of leading many people to care for their souls, and to seek salvation through Jesus.

There are not now many manufactories of consequence in Gloucester. It was once famous for its pins, but these are now made at Stroud. It is, however, a busy commercial town; a great deal of corn and timber being brought from America, and iron, salt, and coal being exported.* The coal comes from the Forest of Dean on the western bank of the Severn, and the salt,—from what town in Worcestershire? The timber-yards are amongst the most extensive in England. Here were made the huts for our weather-beaten soldiers in the Crimea. Ships do not reach Gloucester by the river Severn, as they reach London by the Thames, but by a broad and deep canal; for the Severn, though the longest, is not the most useful river of England, having near its mouth many shoals and windings. The tide rises in it very suddenly,† and making a loud noise, rolls onward four or five feet above the level of the river. This is called the Bore, and is dangerous when there are floods.

Some miles below Gloucester, the Severn receives the Stroud water. It flows through the beautiful valley I have mentioned, where there are many factories for making cloth. The water of the Stroud is reckoned particularly good for fixing the dye of scarlet. Here, also, solid headed pins are made entirely by machinery; one machine making forty or fifty pins a minute. Where pins are not made in this manner, each passes through the hands of about eight persons. First, there is the drawing out of the wire; then the straightening of it, then the cutting of it in proper lengths, then the grinding of the points, then the making of the heads, then the whitening of the wire, and, lastly, the polishing of it in bran. Pins are

* Pages 54, 96, 105. † Page 179.

made of brass, and whitened by being boiled in a mixture of tinfoil and port wine lees. Black pins are made of iron wire.

The Valley of Stroud.

Still descending the Severn, which is now become a very wide river, we reach the town and castle of Berkeley. You have, no doubt, heard of Berkeley Castle, the place where the unfortunate but weak-minded Edward II. was most horribly murdered.* It is said, the Bishop of Hereford, at the desire of Queen Isabella, wrote to the keeper of the castle the following words:

"Edward the king kill not to fear is good."

He purposely put no stop, so that he might *say* he meant it to be read either way, though he knew the keeper would understand what he meant. The poor unhappy Edward's screams were heard in the town, so that an old

* Pages 51, 137.

historian writes, " Divers in the castle and town of Berkeley being awakened thereby, as they themselves confessed, prayed heartily to God, to receive his soul." How frightful are the sins which quarrelling causes. The castle still stands almost as it stood then, and, like Warwick * or Alnwick, is a fine specimen of the ancient castles of England. In Berkeley vicarage was born the famous Dr Jenner, " the man who thought of the vaccination." Perhaps you have on your arm a mark made by the doctor when you were a very little baby, to put in some matter, which gave you a complaint which will probably prevent you from taking the small-pox. That this matter should have such an effect was discovered by Dr Jenner, who was thus permitted by God to confer an immense benefit on the human race, as small-pox, without vaccination, is one of the worst and most fatal diseases. Still further down the Severn is Thornbury, an ancient town with a castle; and in the very south of the county is the large city of Bristol. As it is situated partly in Somersetshire, I shall tell you of it when we reach that county. In the Forest of Dean, there are few towns, but several scattered villages inhabited by miners.

On the other side of the Cotswold Hills, in the basin of the Thames, that is, on the slope whose waters all find their way to the Thames, is Cirencester, called Cicester. It has a very beautiful church, a college for teaching farming, and near it have been found several ancient remains—of what people? Guess, from the name of the place. Here are made woollen cloths and carpets, and it is famous for curriers' knives. We must now leave Gloucester, for want of space, though I could tell many more legends and tales of its old castles and towns. To-morrow we will follow the banks of the ·Wye in beautiful Herefordshire.

* A disastrous fire in December 1871, has destroyed a great portion of Warwick Castle.

This county might be reviewed by making a list of the towns, and telling the children to put before their names all the characteristic adjectives of which they can think. Thus, "Tewkesbury," "ancient, historical, picturesque, most northern." Or, they might write under the name of a place whatever they could see on visiting it. Thus, "Gloucester," "cathedral, Severn, Dr Jenner's monument, whispering gallery, ships, canal, timber yards," &c. Or, the map proposed for Shropshire and Worcester might be continued, and the green, red, and black dots again respectively marked.

HEREFORDSHIRE.

You will see a small county in the west of England, lying between Worcester and Wales, called Herefordshire. The adjective we may well put before it, is fruitful, for it is almost like a large garden, full of apple and pear trees. Here are, as in Worcestershire, large hop-gardens; and where pasture land is seen, you would be delighted with the beautiful sheep and cattle that are grazing. The banks of the rivers are celebrated for their beauty; hill and dale are mingled, and the woodlands contain fine trees; so that Hereford might claim another adjective?—picturesque, or what I daresay the little ones have already guessed—beautiful. There is an old country rhyme, saying—

> "Blessed is the eye
> Between Severn and Wye."

Now, the chief produce for which this little county is famous is cider from the orchards,* hops from the gardens,† and wool from the sheeps' backs;‡ and some people say, that Herefordshire cider, hops, and wool are the best that can be procured in England. So, surely, it is a county little and good. The sweetest apples are not chosen for cider-mak-

* Page 199.   † Pages 136, 188, 199.   ‡ Page 141.

ing, but those that for eating we should think the worst, the hardest and the most sour. When gathered, they are laid in a heap, to ripen more fully. As soon as ripe, they are broken in a mill, a large stone being rolled over them. Then they are put into hair bags, and strongly pressed. The juice that runs from them soon ferments, is bottled, and reckoned a pleasant draught to take in hot weather.

Hops grow up tall poles, which they clasp with their tendrils. Their leaves and green flowers are very pretty,

Hop Picking.

and form one of the most beautiful climbing plants we have. They ripen in September, and the farmers know when they should be gathered by their strong scent. The value of the crops varies very much, according to the year. You know that they are used in brewing beer.

The sheep in Herefordshire are quite white, with fine wool growing close round their eyes.

I have read of some curious customs among the people in this county, which will, I think, amuse you. One is wassailing the ox. For this purpose, a large cake is baked, through which a stick has been thrust. When enough baked, the stick is removed, and the hole left to fix the cake on the ox's horns. The ox tosses its horn, feeling the weight, and men and boys sing to its health. The boys often tickle the animal behind. And why? Because if the ox throws the cake forward, it belongs to the men; if backward, to the boys. Another custom is observed, in three of the parishes, on Palm Sunday. Some money was, long ago, left to be spent in cake, and also to promote peace and good neighbourhood among the people. After afternoon service, the churchwarden gives the minister a cake, saying, "Peace and good neighbourhood." The minister breaks off a piece, and the cake is passed to another, and so onwards. Afterwards, ale is poured into a silver cup, and passed round in like manner. Once a farmer and an old lady quarrelled about some badly-behaved pigs, and they did not like to speak to each other. On Palm Sunday, however, they met at church. After service, the farmer feeling rather uncomfortable, offered cake to his angry neighbour, saying, "Peace and good neighbourhood." She looked very pleased, and her eyes got quite bright; and she said, "Do *you* say so?" And then she took the cake, broke off a piece, ate it heartily, and was a good friend of the worthy farmer ever after. Now, when you quarrel, get something nice and offer it to your angry little companion; and say, like the Herefordshire people, "Peace and good neighbourhood;" and I fancy the angry eyes will laugh, and the sulky mouth will smile.

For a long time, Hereford and Monmouth were btoh regarded as belonging to Wales; and these counties formed a portion of the district, belonging to the Silures—an old British tribe, whom the Romans could never altogether overcome. Abounding in this part of England, and in the south of Wales, is a kind of stone—which I mentioned in Shropshire—not so old as the granite and slate of—what district ?* Nor nearly so new as the coal or chalk found in—what parts of England ?† This stone, from the district in which it lies, has received the name of Silurian. In it are found the remains of very many fossil shellfish, supposed to be the first animals that were made. The Wye is the principal river of Herefordshire; so we will follow its course, and those of its tributaries. It is reckoned the most beautiful of English rivers. Near the borders of Wales, is an old castle, Clifford; where, it is said, Fair Rosamond, who lived in Henry II.'s reign, was born; and further down the river, is Mocca's court, where Owen Glendower, who fought with Harry Hotspur against Henry IV., died.‡ The first large town we meet is Hereford, the chief in the county. It is beautifully situated, with dark hills rising to the north and west, and the lovely Wye flowing quietly past its cathedral and other ancient buildings. The cathedral was built here, because it was the spot where a young Saxon king, Ethelbert, who had been murdered, was buried. It was pretended that many miracles were worked at his tomb; and in the north aisle is the tomb of Cantilupe, a man supposed to cure miraculously. All round are hooks, on which banners, lamps, and other gifts were hung up by the devotees. Near the town were found Roman remains, a Mosaic floor, a large bath-room, and on the frowning hill, to the north, are the vestiges of a very large camp. There is an ancient

* Page 69.　　† Pages 8, 23, 58, 186.　　‡ Pages 16, 196.

grammar school in Hereford, with valuable scholarships; a blue-coat and many other schools.   There are a few small manufactories, and trade is carried on by the river in cider, hops, oak-bark, wool, and corn.*

A little below Hereford, the Wye is joined by the Lugg. Let us trace its waters from their source, and hear what tales they have to tell.   After passing ancient castles, and running through a very fertile country, they reach Leominster, pronounced Lemster.   It has old-fashioned looking houses of timber and brick.   Here, as in many other English towns, there is a ducking-stool, which used in former days to be for the punishment of quarrelsome, scolding women.   The culprit, when judged guilty, was seated on this stool, a kind of arm-chair, with wheels and shafts.   It was brought to a pond or well.   Then the shafts being taken away, the chair was lowered by ropes, and the ducking was administered to the unfortunate occupant. We must hope it sometimes had the effect of cooling her temper.

Leominster is noted for its fine wool and good wheat. Lemster bread is quite famous in the county.   Further down the river is Sutton, where Ethelbert was murdered, when on a visit to King Offa.†   There are curious stories of stones and hills moving very strangely in this neighbourhood.   One is, that about 200 years ago, two great stones in a meadow, that were water-marks, were removed 250 paces, no one knows how; although to set one of them in its place again required nine yoke of óxen.   Another is, that in the reign of Queen Elizabeth, a hill, called Maley Hill, rose, as it were, from sleep, lifted itself up, and making a great bellowing noise, began to travel, overthrowing a chapel, moving trees, and driving everything before it. The old writer finishes by saying, " Having walked · in

* Page 205.   † Pages 51, 214.

this sort from Saturday evening till Monday noon, it then stood still." Probably some hidden opening had undermined the ground above, causing this great landslip.*

An interesting place in this neighbourhood is Hampton Court, built originally by Henry IV., who was called, after his birthplace, Henry of Hereford. Before the Lugg reaches the Wye, it is joined by the Frome, on which stands Bromyard, a town diminishing instead of increasing.

On the Wye, in the south of the county, and beautifully situated, is Ross, chiefly famous for an excellent citizen, called John Kyrle, who lived and died here. He is generally known as the " Man of Ross.'" He was not very rich, but he loved to do all the good in his power, and was wonderfully free from selfishness. Amongst other benefits to the town he planted a great many trees, especially elms. Some of these were placed round the churchyard ; but those nearest the church were afterwards cut down. The roots sent up fresh shoots. These spread underground, and strangely appeared in Kyrle's old pew. The people would not have them cut down; and now they grow inside the windows as high as the roof, no one molesting them—an emblem of the saved Christian—a living tree within the temple above.

Below Ross, the Wye receives the Dore, which flows through a valley so rich, and covered with so many yellow flowers, that it is named the Golden Valley. Near this part of the Wye is Goodrich Castle, quite a ruin now, and very picturesquely situated. It is terrible to hear of the deep underground dungeons, still existing there ; in which unhappy prisoners were formerly confined.† Dear as England has always been, it is, I think, far dearer in the present day, than ever it was before. Ledbury, famous for its cheese and cider, is the only other place in fruitful and beautiful Herefordshire, of which I will tell you. It is

* Pages 62, 128.　　　　　　† Pages 15, 45.

situated at the southern base of the Malvern Hills.   The
church has a beautiful tower standing a few feet apart
from the building.   Now, tell me in what county the Malvern Hills chiefly lie ; and then we must cease to look at the
map, and talk no more of Herefordshire, till you relate to
me, to-morrow, all that you remember of to-day's lesson.

MONMOUTHSHIRE.

I MUST take you to-day through the last of the English
counties bordering on Wales.   It contains even more beautiful scenery than Herefordshire, though it is not quite equal
to it in fertility.   The Wye separates this county from
Gloucestershire.   The beauty of its borders increases as
it approaches the Severn, and on its banks are the ruins
of fine old castles, and of the most beautiful abbey in
England.   In the west of the county the scenery is wild
and mountainous, and there is found a quantity of coal,
iron, building stone, and of a kind of mill-stone, especially
used in crushing apples for cider.*   The Usk, which is a
very pretty river, flowing through Monmouthshire, divides
the part of the county where coal is found, from the part
where the rock is red sandstone.

Monmouth, as well as Hereford, was long considered a
Welsh county, and the people have many of the manners
and customs of Wales.   Do you remember which brave
King Henry was known by the name of Henry of Monmouth ?   The Monmouthshire sheep are like those of
Hereford ; the cattle, too, are very good, and it is particularly famous for its mules.   There are many orchards,
and woods full of oaks and ash-trees ; but it is not so
noted for cider as Herefordshire.

What is particularly remarkable about Monmouthshire
are the old ruins,† so perhaps the best adjective for this
county is, "interesting;" and now you will expect to

---

* Pages 8, 26, 37, 85, 100, 109, 193, 208.   † Pages 19, 53.

learn something interesting, so we will at once begin with its towns and castles.

Very soon after the Wye enters the county from Herefordshire, it reaches Monmouth, passing through the most lovely scenery. Monmouth has its name because at that place the Munnow joins the Wye. It is an ancient town, the birthplace of a famous old historian, who lived in the reign of Henry I., and went by the name of Jeffery of Monmouth.

Hardly anything is now left of the old castle. Many of the houses of the town are pleasantly built, standing in gardens and orchards. It is not a large town; but there is a little trade in the iron found in the neighbourhood. Near Monmouth, on another small river that joins the Wye, is Troy House, where you see the cradle in which Henry of Monmouth was rocked, and the armour which he wore when fighting in the battle of Agincourt. About a mile below Monmouth, on the Wye, is Penalt, with a beautifully situated church. On its common, there is a very ancient stone, where all passing funerals stop, and the coffin being placed upon it, the assembled friends sing mournful psalms.

In this neighbourhood is an extraordinary rock called Buckstone. It is a sort of plum-pudding stone. At the bottom it is only eleven feet round, whilst on the summit it is fifty - three. How many yards? No doubt the earth has gradually worn away, leaving it thus wonderfully balanced.

Some miles to the west of Monmouth is Ragland Castle, once a magnificent and important place, but laid in ruins during the civil wars in Charles I.'s reign.

On the Wye, you would be surprised to see the curious boats or coracles used by the fishermen. They are very small and light, only weighing about 12 lbs., as much as a good-sized joint of beef. They are the shape of half a walnut-shell, and are made of tarred canvas, stretched over a wicker frame-work. The boatman sits on a seat placed across, and whilst he paddles with his left hand, he either fishes or steers the boat with his right. They go very quickly, but are easily upset.

The Wye is a difficult river for ships to ascend, owing to the many rapids, or weirs, in its course.* These increase the beauty of the river, but decrease its usefulness in commerce. The boats that pass from Monmouth to Chepstow are large barges, called "trows." They partly advance by sails; but when they reach the long rocky shallows, they have to be dragged by main force, the men landing and using all their united strength. It is painful to see them exert themselves so much, and they often injure their health by it.

Between Monmouth and Chepstow stand the ruins of Tintern Abbey, which was founded more than 700 years ago. There is no roof left, but the arches are very perfect, and some of the windows have the fine old stone tracery preserved. Ivy and creeping plants clothe the ancient gray walls; and ash trees grow here and there from between the crevices. Its situation and its size cause it to be reckoned one of the finest ruins in Europe.†

On the Wye, about two miles and a half from its junction with the Severn, is Chepstow, a beautifully situated small commercial town. Many ships are built here, and several carry on a trade, bringing wine from Portugal, or wood, hemp, and pitch from Norway and Russia, and taking away bark, cider, iron, coals, and mill-stones. There is no place in Europe where the tide rises so high as at Chepstow. Sometimes sixty feet higher than at low-water mark. Just fancy the ground that was dry six hours

* Page 213.　　　　　　† Pages 42, 48, 52.

before, covered with water twenty yards deep.* Chepstow is chiefly celebrated for its fine old castle. It looks
very beautiful, nestled amongst trees, overhanging the fine
craggy steeps. It was commenced, like most of our castles,
during the time of the Norman kings. In Charles I.'s
reign, it was taken by Cromwell's forces; then suddenly
retaken by a brave and loyal Welshman, Sir Nicholas
Keneys. He and his little garrison of 160 men defended
it so bravely, that it was long before the Parliamentarians
could again take it; not, indeed, until the brave Sir
Nicholas, and forty of his men, were killed, and the rest

Chepstow Castle.

nearly starved. Chepstow Castle is well fortified, the
entrance being through a gateway between two round
towers, with a double portcullis, and iron gates.†
Near Chepstow are Piercefield and Windcliff, two beau-

* Pages 179, 213.   † Pages 9, 15, 72, 105, 123, 145.

P

tiful seats, whence are some of the most lovely views in England—hills, water, woodland, meadow, ships, mouldering walls, uniting in a manner not often seen. From Windcliff you can see nine counties. Look on the map, and find what they are.

The other river which flows through Monmouth is the Usk, which comes from Brecknockshire in Wales. The scenery, through which it passes, is also very beautiful, though not so cultivated as that through which the Wye flows. The first town about which I shall tell you, is Abergavenny. Here the river Gavenny flows into the Usk. Wherever there is a town commencing with Aber, you may know that there a river either falls into another river or into the sea. Here assemble every year the members of a society for encouraging everything Welsh,—manufactures, music, history ; and many prizes are given. Abergavenny is beautifully situated at the head of a valley, surrounded by mountains. It used to be famous for periwigs, made of extremely white goats' hair, for many goats feed on these mountains. But as gentlemen do not wear periwigs now, the people in Abergavenny find employment either in wool and iron trading, or in tanning.

Further down the Usk is Usk, a small town, with the ruins of an old castle. Here a great many salmon are caught.* To the west of Usk, is Pontypool, where the art of polishing iron, so as to be like Japan varnish, was discovered. Here most of the people are employed in iron-works.

Still further down the Usk, is Caerleon, now a very small place, but once the capital of Wales ; and hundreds of years before Manchester, or Liverpool, or Birmingham existed, it was reckoned the third largest town in Great Britain.† Round it are found large pieces of stone, which

* Pages 10, 195, 199.   † Page 44. Contrast page 97.

probably formed its walls. Here King Arthur held his court; and because he had so many brave knights, none of whom he wished to place before the other, he had his table made round, without either top or bottom, and called his friends the Knights of the Round Table.*

Five miles from the mouth of the Usk is Newport, the largest town in Monmouthshire, a place both for commerce and manufactures. It has good docks for shipping. A great deal of wood from America is brought here, and coal and tin plate are exported.† Many ships are built, and there are manufactories for anchors, chain cables, and masts.‡ It is Newport, and so we must not expect the old castles here, that so many other towns in Monmouthshire possess.

Now, do you not think you would like a real journey in interesting Monmouthshire better than a paper one? To-morrow, however, we shall find out a pencil way of reviewing Hereford and Monmouthshire.

On the following day, the children might arrange, in different columns, the towns, the places of interest, and the productions of Herefordshire and Monmouth; or they might make a double column of the streams, the Wye and Usk, and mark whatever they would observe on them.

SOMERSETSHIRE.—Part I.

AT length we have reached the county which, if you remember, we thought like a baby's sock in shape. It is the last of the counties which can be said to lie in the basin of the Severn. When we have talked of its scenery, its manufactures, and its large towns, then I mean to tell you of the game of the Severn; but we must have lessons first, and play afterwards.

* Page 41.   † Page 213.   ‡ Pages 29, 33.

Somersetshire is a large and important county. The climate is warm, and the scenery varies much. In the north-east, near Bath, are several hills; and the banks of the Avon, the river which runs through that part of Somersetshire, are very beautiful, passing between great chasms of limestone. South of these, the Mendip Hills extend from near Frome to the Bristol channel. They are about four miles broad and twenty-five long, and are chiefly covered with short turf and heath, where sheep feed. More to the west are still higher hills, called the Quantock, the highest of which is " Willie's Neck; " whilst in the extreme west, is part of the wild, desolate region of Exmoor, the highest point of which is Dursberry Beacon, where the hearths of four large beacon-fires may still be traced. The meadow land in Somersetshire is very luxuriant, and the cattle fed in this county are reckoned very valuable, both by the butcher for beef, and the dairyman for milk. The eastern part of the coast and some of the central parts of the county are swampy; but towards the west, lofty, stately cliffs skirt the shore. The two principal rivers are the Avon, running north-west, and the Parret, running north-east. There are also several smaller streams, which I shall mention when we talk of the towns upon their banks. Somersetshire has specimens of all kinds of towns. There is Bath, a cathedral town and fashionable wateringplace; and Bristol, a very busy, commercial city. Frome and Taunton are manufacturing towns, where a great deal of fine broadcloth is made; and Chedder, an agricultural one, is famous for its cheeses. In Somersetshire, the people have almost as strange a way of speaking as they have in the north of England.* One of their peculiarities is sounding Z for S; so they would talk of the " zoomer zoon," instead of " summer sun." Another is, that they throw their words

* Pages 8, 38, 61.

together, such as saying, "cham," for "I am," and "chil," for "I will," and "pont," for "put it on." In these western counties, the custom is still continued of dressing up the May-pole on the 1st of May; and many of the young people of the villages assemble and dance round it.

Now look at the map, and you will observe that just as the Avon enters the county from Wiltshire, it receives a small river called the Frome. On its banks is Frome, a town where broadcloths, kerseymeres, and carriage-linings are manufactured. It has three churches, and the neighbouring country is extremely pretty, but it is not nearly so large as the manufacturing towns in Yorkshire and Lancashire.* A little farther down the Avon is the city of Bath. This is one of the most ancient cities in Britain, famous in the time of the Romans, who built their beautiful houses and ornamental temples with pillars and statues, and made great baths, and called the city Aquæ Solis, or Waters of the Sun. There is a curious story about the discovery of the waters, by which pigs get the same credit that pigeons do for the Cheltenham waters, only the Bath pigs are of a much more ancient date.† Long, long ago, in the time of the Britons, a young British prince became a leper, and was, in consequence, banished from his father's court. The only comfort he possessed was a ring from his mother, so that she might know him, if ever he returned cured. The poor prince hired himself to feed swine; and the swine seemed infected with his leprosy. He was afraid his master would be very angry; but the swine wandered to a marsh on the Lansdown Hills, where Bath now stands, and there wallowed until their disease was cured. The prince, observing this, tried the same remedy, and was cured also. He soon returned to his father's court, and on a day that the king and queen

* Pages 49, 91.   † Page 210.

banqueted in public, he dropped into his mother's cup the ring that she had given him.* When the queen drank the wine, she beheld at the bottom the well-remembered ring. He was welcomed back, and afterwards became king, and rewarded his old swine-master by granting him land, and building him a palace near the hot springs.

When the Romans left Britain, Bath lost its consequence, and did not rank as a large place till about a hundred years ago, when, through the cleverness of a very gay and singular man, called Beau Nash, it became very fashionable. The situation of the town, on the sides of the hills, overlooking the Avon, is very beautiful, and the houses are considered better built than those of any other town in England; for not only are they very handsome in their architecture, but they are built of a remarkably good kind of stone found near Bath. There are bath-rooms, and hospitals, schools, and several churches, but the handsomest are the old abbey church and St Michael's. Bishop Ken, who wrote the beautiful morning and evening hymns, was bishop here. In James II.'s time, the king brought to the abbey church his confessor, who showed off all the fine things the Romanists use at their worship, and then denounced all Protestant heretics. Bishop Ken was present, and loving his own faith, he, without fearing the king, begged the people to remain, ascended the stone pulpit, and answered Huddlestone, the confessor, out of the Bible, with great power.

Farther down the Avon, eight miles above its mouth, is the great city of Bristol, with its beautiful suburb, Clifton. This ranked formerly, as Liverpool does now, next to London, the largest port in England.† But whilst Liverpool has made rapid advances, Bristol has comparatively stood still. It has, however, in the last few years, again increased; and

* Page 153. † Page 154.

when you hear of all the things made in Bristol, and of the various articles of commerce, you will think that it must be one of the busiest towns of England.

Bristol has many glass-works, similar to those on the banks of the Tyne, for plate-glass, and to those at Birmingham, for cut-glass, and others for common glass bottles.* There are also works in nearly all the metal produce of Great Britain; great steam-engine works,† smith houses for forging anchors and chains and roperies for cables. Bristol is also famous for its sugar refineries; these are places where coarse sugar becomes, by boiling and other processes, finer and finer, until it is the white loaf-sugar, used at the tea-table. There are also chemical works, and tobacco manufactories, and a large cotton factory, employing about 2000 people.‡ Most of the cotton here made is sent to the Levant. Where is that? A good deal of ship-building likewise goes forward. Here was built the *Great Britain*, the largest steamboat known, before the monster *Great Eastern* was completed.

Bristol has been, for many hundred years, a place of great commerce. From this port sailed, in Henry VII.'s reign, Sebastian Cabot, the first European who discovered the mainland of North America. He took possession of Newfoundland, and of the shore of North America, for the English king. The trade of Bristol is principally with the West Indies; but ships also go to India, China, the United States, and many other places. When you look again at the list of manufactories, you will be able to fancy with what things these are laden. A great many ships are in the coasting trade and many sail for Ireland. Bristol is famous for its churches, hospitals, and schools. One of its schools is called the Red Maids School. The little girls are all dressed in scarlet frocks

* Pages 20, 28, 29, 118. † Pages 21, 118. ‡ Pages 90–93, 132, 175.

and white tippets.   The old cathedral church is very
handsome, and St Mary's Redcliffe, on one of the hills of
the city, is much admired.   Though Bristol has a cathedral,
it has not a bishop of its own, the see having been united
with that of Gloucester.   I am sure, there were enough
towns, and parishes, and people, to give two bishops plenty
of work.   In 1831, there were frightful riots.   They continued for three days; the bishop's palace, several public
buildings, and about forty private houses were burnt down,
and many people were killed.*   How sad is the havoc
that stormy passions make!   I could tell you many interesting stories about Bristol; but, after giving you a list
of famous people born in this town, I will tell one, and
no more.   There were Sebastian Cabot, the navigator;
Sir Thomas Blanket, who in Richard III.'s reign invented blankets; William of Worcester, a famous describer
of places in olden time; and Chatterton, who, whilst a
poor charity boy, wrote very good poetry.   Instead of
saying that it was his own, he pretended it was found in
a room above the porch of St Mary's Redcliffe.   Poor
Chatterton had no friend to give him good advice, no religion to stay him.   Disappointed, miserable, and starving,
he, when only seventeen, put an end to his own life.
Bowdich, a famous African traveller; and Southey, who
lived among the beautiful lakes, and was for a time the
royal poet, or poet-laureate, of England, were also born in
Bristol.†

Remember these names; and now for the story.   Amongst
the richest merchants of Bristol, and the greatest bene-
factors of the city, was Edward Colston.‡   He founded a
school for maintaining and afterwards apprenticing one
hundred boys, who all wear, in their caps, the figure of a
dolphin; and for this reason;—a ship of Colston's, laden

* Page 137.   † Pages 70, 81.   ‡ Pages 133, 162.

with a very valuable cargo, was expected from India. It sprung a leak; and, notwithstanding all the efforts of the ship's crew, the water rushed in so rapidly, that it seemed impossible to save the vessel. Suddenly, and mysteriously, the leak was stopped; and without further danger, the ship reached Bristol. Then it was discovered, that a dolphin had wedged itself into the hole, and thus had been God's unconscious instrument in saving the ship, her crew, and cargo. According to a curious bequest, a fresh nosegay is, every week, placed in the hands of the statue of Edward Colston, which stands in All Saints' Church.

The story is now finished; the chapter is at an end; and to-morrow I hope you will like to hear more of Somersetshire and its towns.

SOMERSETSHIRE.—Part II.

When I told you about Bristol, I mentioned that it had a beautiful suburb, called Clifton. Clifton may, however, rather be considered as a separate town; it contains about 20,000 inhabitants. It is situated in Gloucestershire, but its connexion with Bristol leads me to speak of it now. From its name, you will guess that it is near grand cliffs; and so it is, for the rocks, on the banks of the Avon, are very stupendous. A beautiful suspension bridge of great height unites them. In the rocks pretty crystals are found, called Bristol diamonds. The Clifton Downs, high moorland hills, where the air comes fresh from the Bristol Channel, are reckoned very healthy, and the waters, at what are called the Hot Wells, are so useful for invalids, that many sick people go there to live. The houses are well built, and the situation very beautiful. Opposite Clifton, are the Leigh Woods, whose varied trees clothe the dark valleys, and crown the rocky heights.

I must now tell you of a very interesting village, with
a beautiful church tower, to the south-west of Bristol.   It
is Wrington, where lived Hannah More, an excellent lady,
who wrote wise books for the educated, and interesting
tracts for the poor; and led a great many to care more
for serving God than they had done before.   She and her
sisters loved the poor, and spent almost all their time in
helping them.   They would often walk for miles over the

Clifton Hot-Wells.

hills, to teach the little ones in a Sunday-school, or the
bigger people in a cottage; for in those days there were
very few schools or lectures, or earnest clergymen.   At
Wrington, John Locke also was born and lived—he was a
great philosopher, which means a lover of wisdom.   He
said that philosophers are often great readers, often great
writers ; but always great thinkers.   He attributed a great
deal of his knowledge to the fact of never being ashamed
to ask a question, when he did not know a thing ; and to a

rule he made, always to talk to any man he met on the subject of his trade or profession.

In this part of Somersetshire, near the coast, are pleasant watering-places, such as Clevedon and Weston-super-Mare. Near Weston, amongst the Mendip Hills, are two very remarkable places—Banwell Caves, and the Chedder Cliffs. The caverns were discovered by workmen searching for ochre. The first was called the stalactite cavern, from a beautiful stalactite found hanging from the ceiling, and nearly meeting another that rose from the ground. Amongst a quantity of sand and ochre, which covered the floor, were many white bones, found to be those of deer, including the elk; of horses, oxen, wolves, and of a very large bear. Do you remember a place in Yorkshire where similar bones were found?[*] The Chedder Cliffs, more than four hundred feet in perpendicular height, are very grand. Here, too, is a curious cavern, full of stalactites, that take very extraordinary shapes, sometimes of pillars with curtains, sometimes of plants or animals. One is called a loaf of bread, another a piece of bacon. Others are like fine turkeys hung up by their legs, with an ox tongue suspended below them. I wonder if there is one called a Chedder cheese.[†]

Farther inland, on the southern side of the Mendip Hills, is Wells, a small cathedral city, the chief manufacture of which is knitted stockings. The cathedral is exceedingly beautiful. There is not a Bishop of Wells now, that see having been united with that of Bath.[‡] In olden days, the Wells bishops were great hunters.[§] One of them is said to have killed all the wild beasts of the Mendip forests. However noble this sport might be for the knights, it was certainly not the

[*] Page 53.　　　　[†] Pages 46, 127.
[‡] Page 232.　　　　[§] Page 41.

work with which God intrusted bishops. About two miles from Wells is another very curious cavern, full of all sorts of oddly-shaped things, called "Wookey Hole."

Near Wells is Shepton Mallet, where about two thousand people are employed in making silk into various textures, and where there is a beautiful cross, built three hundred years ago.

Another interesting town in this neighbourhood is Glastonbury, where are still the ruins of what was once the richest abbey in England. More interesting than this is the story, that here was built of twigs and mud the first house in Britain for the worship of the real God.* It is said that Joseph of Arimathea was the missionary. Can you fancy him and his friends among our savage forefathers, telling of the Saviour whom he had seen laid in his new sepulchre, and who had risen again? They must have gone forth with their message as our missionaries have done among the savage New Zealanders, or among the tribes of Borneo. A curious thorn-tree grows at Glastonbury, which always blossoms at Christmas, instead of in the month of May. The renowned King Arthur was buried in this abbey.† On the Yeo, near the borders of Dorsetshire, is Yeovil, where many thousands of leather gloves are made weekly. In most of the small towns of this neighbourhood, such as Ilminster, Ilchester, and Somerton, the chief employment of the people is the making of gloves.‡ Ilchester was a large town in the time of the Romans, and is noted as being the birthplace of Roger Bacon. He was a monk, who lived in the time of Henry III., and was fond of mathematics, and made discoveries in chemistry. Amongst other things, he found out how to make gunpowder. He also invented reading-glasses, and a kind of telescope and microscope. Somerton,

---

* Pages 10, 154.   † Pages 41, 227.   ‡ Pages 204, 205.

perhaps, gives its name to Somersetshire, which means
the pleasant land. Here, in a strong castle, John, king of
France, was kept prisoner, after he had been taken captive
by the Black Prince.

Near the Parret river is Sedgmoor, the scene of the
defeat of the unfortunate Duke of Monmouth, in the
reign of James II. Those were sad days for the country
people who joined him, as numbers were tried and hung;
the tyrannical Judge Jeffreys delighting, apparently, in
condemning them to death.

On a small branch of the Tone, itself a branch of the
Parret, stands Wellington, a town where druggets and
other woollen goods are made. From this place, the great
conqueror of Waterloo took his title.

On the Tone is Taunton, situated in the midst of orchards, gardens, and rich pastures. Here is an old castle,
built by William the Conqueror, which withstood a long
siege from the Royalists.* The besieged had so nearly
consumed all their food that nothing but a half-starved
pig was left in the town. This was whipped round the
walls, that it might squeak in different places, and thus
make the king's army believe that there was plenty of
provisions. The Duke of Monmouth was here proclaimed
king, and fearful were the assizes that followed, still
known as the "bloody assizes." Judge Jeffreys, the execrable, as he has been fitly called, presided. Taunton was
long famous for woollen manufactures, now silk ones have
taken their place. Lace is also woven here. This manufacture travelled very suddenly from Nottinghamshire to
Somersetshire, on account of the violent attacks of the
frame-makers in the county of its birth. †

At the meeting of the Parret and the Tone, we find
the Isle of Athelney, which used to be separated from

* Pages 211, 225.   † Page 137.

the land by the marshes, especially when the rivers were flooded. This is the place where Alfred and his friends found a refuge from the Danes. Whilst here, he wished to know something of the Danish army, which was in the neighbourhood; so he put on the dress of a harper, and went to their camp. The Danes liked the sweet music of the poor minstrel, and bade him stay with them, but he remained only for a short time. He summoned his faithful friends around him, unexpectedly attacked the Danes, and gained over them a great victory.

Near Bridgwater, on the Parret, is found the peculiar mixture of clay and sand, of which the celebrated Bath brick is made. About 20,000 tons of them are sent away every year to all parts of the world. They are chiefly used in cleaning knives and forks for the table. Bridgwater is a small trading port, principally importing timber, and exporting bricks and field produce. Its old name was Burgh Walter, the town of Walter, one of William the Conqueror's followers. It was the birthplace of Admiral Blake, who gained many victories in Oliver Cromwell's time.

On the coast are two small but very pretty bathing-places, Minehead and Portlock.

You have, no doubt, found out that Somersetshire is a county having a great many places of interest, connected with which are a great many remarkable people. Think well over to-day's chapter, and to-morrow I hope you will all be ready for the " Game of the Severn."

THE GAME OF THE SEVERN.

The teacher, having provided himself with a bag of ginger-nuts, or marbles, or a basket of apples, pictures, or small books, seats himself in the midst of the children, and commences somewhat seriously,—

"The Severn rolls,—the Severn rolls,—and enters—Shropshire." A pause, for one of the children to mention some feature connected with the county; thus, perhaps, little Lucy says :

" The county where lived the oldest Englishman." That is enough; she gets her reward. Harry's hand is up, to show that he, too, knows something, and proclaims :

" A county where there are ironworks, and that in the middle of pretty scenery."

Harry, too, gets a reward.

Teacher.—" The Severn rolls, the Severn rolls, and passes Shrewsbury."

Charlie.—" There Shrewsbury cakes are made."

Cave.—" And there Harry Hotspur was killed."

Robin.—" And there all the Welsh flannels are sold."

Each gets a reward.

Teacher.—" The Severn rolls. It reaches Coalbrook Dale."

Septima.—" And goes under the first iron bridge."

Teacher.—" The Severn rolls. It reaches Bridgnorth."

Perhaps of Bridgnorth none can answer correctly; and if so, all have to return one of their rewards. Whenever a mistake is made, one of the nuts, or whatever they have earned, should be given back.

So the teacher continues, till the children have had *nearly* enough. Another evening, the lower part of the Severn's course may be described, or the course of its tributaries, looking back to Warwick for that of the Avon. The pleasure of gaining much will be increased by dividing the treasures with the smaller ones who have not been so fortunate.

OXFORDSHIRE.—PART I.

HAVING completed the counties forming the basin of the Severn, we will now try to follow the course of the Thames. You remember, I hope, the county in which it rises.* That little stream called the Churn runs onward for about twenty miles, and at Cricklade, in the north of Wiltshire, it meets the Isis, from that county. Below that place, it is very frequently called the Thames, though it is properly the Isis till it is joined by the Thame, some miles below Oxford. I shall not tell you about Wiltshire just now, for the rivers through the principal part of the county flow southward to the English Channel; so look on the map, and find what county lies on the north of the Thames after it leaves Gloucestershire. Tell me now the names of all the counties that touch Oxfordshire. I am sure you have heard of Oxford before this; and so have all the little English boys and girls who have had teachers to instruct them from the time of Alfred the Great. But it is the town rather than the county that is so famous. You will, however, like to know in what kind of county the learned town of Oxford is placed.

The northern part of Oxfordshire is not very picturesque; but, though the centre is somewhat level, there are in it a great many trees and woods, and the south-eastern portion is very pretty, being varied with hills and dales, with soft-flowing rivers, and rich beech woods. The hills in this part are called the Chilterns; they form part of the same range which, in Cambridgeshire, are called the Gogmagog Hills.† They are chiefly formed of chalk, and the soil is not of the kind in which

* Page 207.   † Page 168.

mineral treasures, such as iron and coal, are imbedded. You will, therefore, not expect to hear of many manufactories in Oxfordshire; but, as there are plenty of rivers, we expect rich grass, and so we look, and not in vain, for plenty of dairies, where good butter is made.

Now look again at the Isis, or Thames, and you will see that it receives, on the left, the Windrush. On its banks stands Burford, with the ruins of an old abbey, and Witney, a town famous for its nice warm blankets.* Soon another river joins it, the Evenlode, from a forest, the remains of what formerly covered the whole county. Near this river is Woodstock, where there is a large manufactory of gloves.† Here was the palace in which Queen Elizabeth was confined, during part of the reign of her sister Mary; and here, if Chaucer was not born, he, at any rate, wrote some of his poems. Chaucer was the first famous English poet, and has been therefore called the father of English poetry. He lived in the reign of Edward III. Near Woodstock is Blenheim, a magnificent palace built for the Duke of Marlborough, who, in Queen Anne's reign, gained several famous victories over the French. Blenheim is not only a very splendid building, but it is very famous for its collection of pictures. The great Duke of Marlborough's wife is nearly as celebrated as himself. She was a great friend of Queen Anne's, and for years they wrote to each other under feigned names—the one being Mrs Morley, and the other Mrs Freeman. At last, however, the duchess became so insolent that the queen was angry with her and banished her from the court.

Following the Thames to its union with the Charwell, we find Oxford, one of the most beautiful, interesting,

* Pages 92, 232.   † Pages 204, 205, 236.

and celebrated cities of dear old England. 1 will first tell you a little about the town, and then about the university.

The town is very pleasantly situated on a hill between two rivers. Part of the walls that once surrounded it remain, and also the keep of the castle. I have a story to tell you concerning this castle, which, I think, will amuse you. In the time of Stephen, the Empress Matilda fled thither from London. The king besieged her. It was a very cold winter; no food could be procured by the garrison, and they were nearly starved to death. At

High Street.

length they resolved to submit; but the night before they did so, one of the gates opened gently, and four figures, clothed in white, issued forth. The snow lay deep upon the ground; the rivers were thickly frozen; the figures glided softly past, only casting their shadows on the driven snow. The besiegers did not stay them, probably fearing their ghost-like appearance. Onward the party went. It consisted of Matilda, and three of her most trusty knights. At Abingdon, in Berkshire, they procured horses, and at length reached a friendly castle in safety.

The High Street of Oxford is one of the handsomest streets in England ; it shows the fronts of some of the beautiful ancient churches, the gable ends of some of the picturesque old houses, and very elegant modern shops.

You could not, I fear, remember the description of all the churches in Oxford. There is the cathedral, not so handsome as most English cathedrals, and badly situated. There is the university church, called St Mary's, with a very fine tower; close to another, St Mary Magdalene, is the Martyrs' Memorial, a beautiful monument, in honour of the noble martyrs, Latimer, Cranmer, and Ridley, who, near this spot, perished in the flames, rather than deny the Lord they loved.* You have probably heard how cheerfully good old Bishop Latimer encouraged his friend Bishop Ridley to meet the terrible death. Good old man ! his heart's blood was poured out for the cause of truth ; but his prophetic words have been fulfilled. The candle was lighted in England, which, by God's grace, has never been put out; and we trust that it never will be ; for, lighted from the Word of God, it is heavenly fire that shall burn for evermore.

Oxford appears to have been a place for learning from a very early time. Alfred the Great lived here, and probably founded the first classes, which afterwards grew into the famous university. There are now nineteen colleges and five halls. Christ Church College is the largest and grandest. The building was commenced by Cardinal Wolsey, who wished it to be called Cardinal College. The entrance is through a very handsome gateway,

* Pages 9, 144, 183, 190, 212.

over which is hung the great bell, Tom of Oxford.* Every
night, at ten minutes past nine, it tolls 101 times, being
the number of the students on the foundation, and before
it has ceased to strike, most of the college gates are shut.
The kitchen was the first part erected by Wolsey. There
you may see an enormous gridiron of olden times. It
moves on wheels, and is large enough to cook a whole
animal. I could tell you something interesting about
nearly every college in Oxford, but I have not time, and
your little heads have not space for storing it all. Merton College can prove itself the oldest by deeds and
writings, whilst University College claims the greatest
age from tradition. Find out what that means. Queen's
College was founded by Queen Philippa, the good
queen of Edward III.† New College, by William of
Wykeham, a Bishop, a Lord Chancellor, and the architect
of Windsor Castle, of this college, and of other celebrated
buildings. Balliol College was built by the father of
John Balliol, of whom we read in the history of Scotland.
Brazennose received its name from a brazen knocker like
a nose, which was on a gateway at Stamford, in Lincolnshire, to which place the students once retreated, after
being worsted in a fight with the townspeople. ‡

Some of the old customs of the colleges are very curious. At Queen's College, the blowing of a trumpet summons the members to dinner ; and on New Year's Day,
the bursar presents each member with a needle and
thread, saying, "Take this, and be thrifty." At University College, on Easter-day, a large branch is dressed up
with flowers and evergreens. As each member leaves the
hall, he chops at the tree, and gives the cook, who stands
by, a present. At Magdalene College, there still stands
the old stone pulpit, where formerly, on St John Baptist's

* Page 153.   † Page 30.   ‡ Page 155.

day, a sermon was preached to the members of the University, who stood round the quadrangle, which was fenced and strewed with green boughs, to give the effect of preaching in the wilderness.

To-morrow I hope to tell you of the libraries, and of some of the celebrated men of Oxford, and what I can of the rest of the county. To-day you have heard a great deal, and as I have told you of the Martyrs' Memorial, try and find out, in another book, more about these holy men ; and pray, like the good young King Edward VI., who, as he was dying, said these words :—

"O Lord God, save Thy chosen people of England. O my Lord God, defend this realm from Papistry, and maintain the true religion, that I and my people may praise Thy holy name, for Thy Son Jesus Christ's sake."

OXFORDSHIRE.—Part II.

I said you should hear to-day about the libraries at Oxford. Perhaps your father has a library, or you have seen some gentleman's library—a room the walls of which are covered with book shelves, filled with books of all kinds and sizes. Now, a large book-case holds a great many books, the four sides of a room more ; but how many must there be in a number of rooms, and those of very large size, very long and very high, with books up to the ceiling. The largest library in Oxford is the Bodleian, which takes its name from Sir Thomas Bodley, who, nearly three hundred years ago, spent both his life and fortune in collecting rare books. Even before this, the library had been commenced by Humphrey, the good Duke of Gloucester; but only one book of his library remains, and that must be nearly five hundred years old. The Bodleian library has a right to a copy of every book published in England.

Besides books, there are many portraits and beautiful models and some curiosities. One is a chair made out of the ship in which Admiral Drake sailed round the world; and another is the real old lantern which Guy Fawkes held in his hand when he was discovered. Another library is the Radcliffe, founded by a celebrated doctor in Queen Anne's reign. Here, besides books, is very fine ancient statuary. The money Dr Radcliffe left built also an infirmary and an observatory. This latter is a building for watching and making observations on the heavenly bodies through telescopes. Another interesting place is the Ashmolean Museum, founded by a very strange man, Dr Elias Ashmole. He had many ingenious thoughts; but one of the strange ideas that filled his mind was the search for what is called the " Philosopher's Stone; " that is, a stone which can turn all it touches into gold. The only stone of that kind I know of is contentment. Have you ever found this stone, dear children ?

It would fill a book were I to write of all the celebrated men who have studied in Oxford. I can only mention a few. There was John Wycliffe,* the morning star of the Reformation, and the famous Thomas Linacre, who taught such good Greek in Henry the Seventh's reign, that Erasmus and many noted foreigners came over to Oxford to study under him. Then there were some of the good and noble martyrs, of whom I have already told you; Fox, who wrote their lives;† Tindal, who first had the Bible printed in English; and Jewell, Jeremy Taylor, Hooker, Butler, Arnold,‡ Daniel Wilson, and very many good and learned clergymen. There were also Sir Thomas More, Raleigh, Canning, Pitt, C. J. Fox, Sir R. Peel, Gladstone, Lords Eldon and Stowell, and most of England's celebrated statesmen; Locke the philosopher;§ Samuel Johnson the Dic-

* Pages 39, 143. † Page 154. ‡ Page 122. § Page 234.

tionary man ;* and the poets, Ben Jonson, Dryden, Cowley, Heber, and Keble.†

I have heard that Dryden had once to write a prize poem on the miracle at Cana in Galilee. He neglected it till very nearly the time that it should have been presented. Then, suddenly seizing his pen, he wrote in Latin a beautiful line, which gained the prize. The translation is—,

> " The modest water saw its God and blush'd."

I cannot tell the names of *many* Oxford men employed in the noblest work of heart and head, the mission field; but there are some now working, and others preparing for this blessed cause.

We must leave Oxford now, with its many spires and pinnacles, its hoary towers, its groined windows, its museums, its libraries, its great printing-office, its caps and gowns, its light skiffs, its lovely gardens, its learned professors, and look if, in the north of the county, near the source of the Charwell, we cannot find any town of interest. Yes ; here is Banbury, very interesting to little folks. Few babies have not heard of

> " Ride a cock horse
> To Banbury Cross."

And many children have tasted Banbury cakes, which have been famous for more than two hundred years. Near to the borders of Buckinghamshire is Bicester, a very old town, where a great many Roman coins have been found. Here was the well of a Romish saint, the waters of which were once thought to be very holy, and to possess the power of curing diseases. Below Oxford, on the Thames, or Isis, is Iffley, an old straggling village with one of the prettiest of village churches. Below this is Nuneham Park, the beautiful grounds of which are often visited by persons

---

* Pages 114, 144.   † Page 102.

from Oxford. A few miles onward, and the Isis joins the Thame. From this point it takes their united names, and becomes the world-renowned Thames. Not far from its banks is Cuddesden, where there is a new college. In this part of Oxfordshire are several pretty villages and small towns, the male inhabitants of which are chiefly labourers, and the females are makers of pillow lace, in which you often see them busily engaged on summer evenings at their cottage doors.*

The course of the Thames is very beautiful. There are often little islets, which the people call aits, covered with trees such as the alder and willow, or the still smaller ones with osiers. Pretty water-flowers, crimson and yellow and purple, edge these little islands, forming a rich border against the blue waters.

As the Thames leaves Oxfordshire, it passes Henley, a small town, but on account of its river trade, the most business-like in the county; timber, corn, and malt being taken away in barges.† Malt and beer are made here, and a silk mill is worked. With the soft-flowing Thames, we must now leave the county of Oxford; and to-morrow we hope to enter Buckinghamshire.

BUCKINGHAMSHIRE.

WE must still look on the north side of the Thames; and adjoining Oxford we find Buckinghamshire. You may remember it by its odd shape. In the first chapter, I told you what I thought it resembled. A riddle, which I once heard, may help you in remembering its position. Why is Buckinghamshire like a goad?‡

Tell me all the counties touching Buckingham.

* Page 162.   † Pages 152, 201, 207, 224, 238.
‡ Because it runs into Oxon and Herts (oxen and hurts.)

Buckinghamshire is not a manufacturing county, nor one noted for mineral productions.* The soil is fertile, especially in the vale of Aylesbury, which runs through the middle of the county. The ground is, however, very badly cultivated, the landlords not caring much about improving the land, and the farmers, who only take their farms from year to year, not caring to spend much money on what they may leave so soon. The labourers have only nine or ten shillings a week, and many of them cannot read. Their houses, too, are very poor, frequently of rough timber and badly thatched. Very little of the land is ploughed, and in some parts, an old-fashioned wooden plough is used, instead of the modern iron one.† The dairy farms are rich. There are nearly thirty thousand cows in the county, which give their milk "so pure and white." A great deal of this is churned for butter. The butter is packed in neat little baskets called flats, and sent to London for sale.‡ A great many pigs are fed on the butter-milk, and on the ponds numbers of ducks are swimming, not wild ones, as in Lincolnshire, but the common and useful farm-yard duck.§ Some of the species, especially those called Aylesbury ducks, are very famous, and about fifteen thousand pounds are received for them every year.

Looking at the map, you will observe that Buckingham rivers run two ways, those in the south winding their course towards the Thames, whilst in the north we meet our old friend the Great Ouse. Do you remember anything about it? Between these two water-courses, you may rightly expect high ground; the Chilterns you found in Oxfordshire, cross the county into Hertford.

The first town on the Ouse is Buckingham. The river

* Pages 148, 157, 186, 241.   † Contrast pages 174, 185.
‡ Page 168.   § Pages 148, 176.

almost surrounds it. The people here used to be much
engaged in making lace.* The trade is now chiefly in
malt for making beer, and in wool. Even in Edward
III.'s reign, Buckingham was a great place for selling
wool. Near it is Stowe, belonging to the Duke of Buckingham, which was very famous for its gardens. In them
were a number of buildings to represent the old Greek
temples and statues, and the ground was arranged by art
to make the view as beautiful as possible.† Now people
think, and justly, that nature is more beautiful than art,
and that what is natural is more pleasing than what is
studied. Remember that, young ones, and let there be no
pretence about you, but *be* what you *seem* to be.

Further down the Ouse is Stony Stratford, a town remarkable for its rough and dangerous streets. Still further
down is Wolverton, one of England's railway towns, it
being a station where locomotives are repaired, and where
good provision is provided for hungry travellers. Neat
houses are built for the railway men, as well as a church,
and schools for their children.

Then we reach Newport Pagnell, where you would still
see many people making lace. On a little stream that
here joins the Ouse, is Fenny Stratford, so called because
it is situated amongst fens, just as the other Stratford is
amongst stones. Do you remember anything of a still
more famous Stratford? ‡

Following the Ouse, we reach Olney, neither a flourishing nor a pretty village, but one about which we like to
hear, for here lived William Cowper, the Christian poet,
and John Newton, a good clergyman, whose letters and
sermons are full of beautiful thoughts about our Father
in heaven. These two friends wrote the Olney Hymns.
Perhaps you know some of them. One by Cowper begins,

* Pages 162, 248.   † Page 131.   ‡ Page 124.

"God moves in a mysterious way." One by Newton is called, "Thoughts on the sea-shore," and show how ocean, sands, rocks, and tide, each convey a lesson about the goodness of God, and the sinfulness of man. Poor Cowper was sorely tried in his mind; he was very melancholy, and low-spirited. A lady, who was a great friend of his, told him, one day, the story of a citizen of London going to Edmonton on his wedding-day, and all the troubles that befell him. Cowper laughed much at this, and then throwing the tale into verse, wrote the diverting history of Johnny Gilpin, a story which has probably made your eyes sparkle, as you laughed merrily over it.

And now leaving the Ouse, we must think of the rivers which flow towards the Thames, and the towns near to them. As an intermediate town, I will mention Leighton Buzzard, on the Grand Junction Canal, and also on the North-Western Railway. There is some trade here, and many of the women are busy lace-making and straw-plaiting. The men also make lace, when they have no field-work. There are here a fine old cross, and church.

Aylesbury, famous for ducks and tame rabbits, is in the midst of a very fertile valley, through which the Thame flows towards the Thames. Not far from it is Wendover, which for many years sent to Parliament the famous John Hampden, who, in Charles I.'s reign, refused to pay an unjust tax. It was also the parish of a faithful servant of God, Spencer Thornton.

We must now turn quite to the south of Buckingham, and mark the towns on or near the continually-widening Thames. First, there is Great Marlow, and not very far to the north is High Wycombe, both small, quiet, agricultural towns.

As we proceed down the Thames, we meet many little islands, of which I have before told you. One of these is called Monkey Island, on which the Duke of Marlborough built a pleasure-house, which is said to have cost £10,000. In the dining-room he had monkeys drawn, sitting, or riding, or walking, eating, or sleeping, exactly like human beings. Was not this a strange ducal fancy?

A little below, on the Thames, is a place well known to many boys, Eton, famous for its school or college, which ranks, as the highest public school in England. It was founded by the unfortunate King Henry VI. There are usually about 600 boys—the leader of whom, viz., the first boy in the sixth form, is called the Captain of the School. Till within the last few years, there was observed a curious custom on the Whit-Tuesday of every third year. The scholars, dressed in fancy costume, marched like soldiers, under a marshal, colonel, &c., to a mound called Salt Hill. There were numbers of spectators, amongst whom two salt-bearers (so called, because formerly they offered salt) collected money, sometimes upwards of £1000. Much of this went in feasting, and paying for damages; but the remainder was given to the Captain to help him on entering college. This gathering led often to much harm; and therefore, though a pretty sight, and an old custom, it was wisely abolished.

In the college library, is a service book, full of pictures, which belonged to Mary Queen of England, a very curious old history of the world, containing pictures of Adam, Methuselah, Noah, and others, not only dressed in full attire, but each wearing a coat of arms! There is an album, too, for autographs. Here is written Victoria, and Albert, and Wellington, and many others. The Eton boys, also, have a library, and in it are some treasured manuscripts, such as a French translation, in the poet Gray's own handwriting, of one of his poems; and there are also many volumes, the gifts of kings, queens, and noblemen.

Eton boys are extremely fond of rowing, and are often seen pulling their narrow skiffs on the sunny waters of the Thames.

Not far from Eton is Slough, famous as containing the house in which Sir William Herschel and his family lived, and where he made celebrated discoveries among the stars. The old telescope, through which the planet Uranus was discovered, is now taken down. From the first records of astronomy till the timé of Herschel, it was thought that only six planets moved round the sun, therefore his was a great discovery. He thought a great deal, and observed very patiently. He was often much assisted by a dear useful sister. Whilst he gazed through the great telescope, she sat in a room below, marking in a book his observations, which he made known to her by a peculiar manner of pulling certain strings. Thus they worked together, gazing at the starry heavens, and wondering at the stupendous works of the mighty Jehovah. Is it not an encouragement for you, dear children, to think that He who made those immeasurable worlds, said also, " Suffer little children to come unto me ? "

I must just tell you of one more pretty and interesting village in Buckinghamshire. It is Stoke, where Gray lived, who wrote the "Elegy in a Country Churchyard." Probably he thought of the Stoke churchyard, where his aunt and mother were buried, and where he, too, is laid to rest. I dare say you have the poem in some "Readings of Poetry." Search for it, as I think you will understand some of its pretty verses. In this neighbourhood, are some very famous trees, called the Burnham beeches. They have very curiously twisted roots, which, covered with dark green mosses, contrast beautifully with the smooth bark above. If you live in the country, I hope you know the smooth stem of the beech, so different from the rough ones of the oak and elm.　If not, try and find it out in your walk to-day.

Enough !　To-morrow I hope to hear from you a great deal about the county you have so long known, as like the old woman with a pack on her back.

BERKSHIRE.

TO-DAY we must go across the Thames, follow its progress on the south side, and listen to all the tales that I can tell you of the fair county of Berkshire, the county containing the great castle of our English kings—Windsor.　Now let the map tell you all it can about Berkshire.　What counties touch it ?　Any rivers flowing through it ?　Any hills in it ?　Yes ; there are pretty streams flowing northeast, hastening to join the Thames in their way to the sea ; and there is a range of " Downs," as the chalky hills, gently sloping, rounded at their summit, and covered with short-wooled sheep, are usually called in the south of England.　North of these Downs, the soil is remarkably fertile—the valley of the White Horse growing some of the finest wheat and barley in England.*　Another beautiful and productive valley lies along the course of the Kennet.　Quite in the west of the country are rich green pastures, and there the kind of cheese called " Double Gloucester," is made.　In the east of Berkshire the country is much wooded, for there the ancient royal forest of Windsor still remains, with its fine old trees.

Berkshire used to be famous for its woollen manufactories ; but it is not so now.†　It is more celebrated for its live stock, its cows and its sheep, whilst its pigs are reckoned the best in England.

I have mentioned the valley of the " White Horse," and

* Pages 36, 99, 125, 208.　　　　　† Pages 189, 237.

I can tell you a story about its name. Almost a thousand years ago, in the time of King Alfred, there was fought here a great battle between the English and the Danes. Alfred gained the victory, and to commemorate it the White Horse, the Standard of the Saxons, was displayed on the side of the hill.* It was made 125 yards long, from head to tail, and can be seen to this day. How could such an enormous thing be made? The hill is of white chalk, covered with green turf—the turf was removed in the shape of this great horse, and every year from that time to this, the people in the district have a great holiday for " scouring the horse," which, when the sun shines upon it, can be seen from a great distance, as far as fifteen miles.

Now look at the map, and we will try and search out the towns of Berkshire, beginning at the west. In this valley of the White Horse is Farringdon, the most famous place for pork in England; and very near the horse, is Wantage, the birthplace of our celebrated king, Alfred the Great. Where the Ock joins the Thames, is Abingdon, an old Saxon town.† Here there are several almshouses, and some coarse canvas manufactories. In the old monastery Henry I., called Beauclerc, or the fine scholar, was educated. There is an important railway junction at Didcot, and a little further east, on the Thames, is Wallingford. This, too, is a very old town, which was once defended by a strong castle.

Leaving the north of Berkshire, we will follow, for a little while, the Kennet,

"The Kennet swift, for silver eels renown'd."

The first town on its banks is Hungerford. The town is governed by a constable. When he is to be chosen, the

* Page 41. † Page 243.

inhabitants are called together by the sound of a brass
horn. The original horn, preserved as a curiosity, was
given to the town by John of Gaunt. Who was John of
Gaunt ?* The next town is Newbury, once very noted for
woollen manufactories. Here there lived, in Henry VIII.'s
time, John Winchcomb, called "Jack of Newbury." He
was a famous clothier, and when Henry wanted soldiers
for his war with Scotland, he brought 100 men to the king,
clothed in uniform, and with them marched to Flodden
Field, where he helped to gain the victory over the Scots.†
This worthy man also rebuilt the greater part of the church
at Newbury. Near this town were fought, in King
Charles' time, two bloody battles. Almost the same
spot of ground was, in each case, dyed with the blood of
fellow-countrymen.‡ At the junction of the Kennet
and the Thames is Reading, so called from an old word
"Rhedin," which means a "fern;" ferns having once
grown here very plentifully. Reading is a large town,
with spacious streets, and is very pleasantly situated.
Few things are manufactured here ; but it is a great place
for trade, all the products of Berkshire being forwarded
from this place, either by the river or rail, to London.
What will these be ? Timber, cheese, malt, corn, bark,
and many other things. At Reading, there are still the
remains of a famous abbey, founded by Henry I. He, his
queen, and his daughter, the Empress Maud, were all
buried here. In this town, Archbishop Laud, who was
beheaded during the reign of Charles I., was born. His
father was a clothier.

A few miles from Reading, on the Great Western Railway, is Twyford, where was fought a battle between the followers of William of Orange, afterwards William III., and
those of James II. This is almost the last battle fought in

* Pages 143, 154.   † Page 15.   ‡ Pages 45, 124, 158, 204.

civil warfare in the south of England. In the south of
the county is Sandhurst, where there is a famous military
college; a place where young men are taught how to become good officers, to conduct a war, not only bravely,
but with wisdom.

Again, following the Thames, we find Maidenhead a
quiet little market town; and further down is the village
of Bray, famed for its vicar, who lived in the reigns of
Henry VIII., Edward VI., Mary and Elizabeth, and always changed his religion to that of the reigning sovereign. Unwise man! to think more of his earthly than of
his heavenly King.

And now I have only to tell you of one more place, and
that is the most interesting in all Berkshire,—Windsor, the
grand old residence of our beloved Queen Victoria. The
town is pleasantly situated on the Thames, and the magnificent castle rising above it, is visible for a great distance
round. The king, who laid the foundation of Windsor
Castle, and planted its extensive forest, was William the
Conqueror. So long as wars were frequent in England, it
was regarded as a place of defence, and the chief consider-
ation was to build towers and to make it strong. But
now, our kings and queens live in happier days, and
have only thought of increasing its beauty and comfort.
Almost all our English sovereigns have lived here.
Edward III. altered it very much; Queen Elizabeth
raised a fine terrace, which was continued by Charles
II. round three sides of the castle; George III. repaired
the beautiful St George's Chapel; and all the sovereigns
since have greatly increased its splendour. Would you
like to hear of some of the rooms? One is called St
George's Hall, where the royal banquets are held. Another
is the Waterloo Room, adorned with portraits of the Duke
of Wellington and other celebrated persons who were

R

living at the time of the battle. Another is the Vandyke
Room, hung with portraits by that celebrated painter. He
lived in Charles I.'s time; and the pictures are principally
portraits of that unfortunate king, his wife, and pretty children. His face looks sad, and reminds one that he was

Wind or Castle.

a prisoner at Windsor before he was taken to Whitehall to
be beheaded. Some of the state rooms are hung with very
beautiful tapestry, on which is worked the story of Queen
Esther and Mordecai. The private rooms for the use of
visitors are in suites, consisting of three or four chambers,
each suite having a private staircase. St George's Chapel
is considered one of the most beautiful chapels in England.
Here the Knights of the Garter are installed; each has his
appropriated seat, over which waves, in crimson and gold,
his special banner. Within this chapel, many who once
wore earthly crowns, now lie buried. The rival kings of

York and Lancaster; the cruel Henry VIII.; the unfortunate Charles I.; good old George III.; and the sailor king, William IV.* The contrast between the pomp of the living and the vaults of the dead is very great, and seems to speak to us in the words of Jesus, " Lay not up for yourselves treasures on earth, where rust and moth doth corrupt, and thieves break through and steal, but lay up for yourselves treasures in heaven, where neither rust nor moth doth corrupt, and where thieves do not break through nor steal." There is a beautiful monument to the Princess Charlotte, George IV.'s only child. Everybody loved her, and she loved God; and all England mourned when she died. On the base of the monument, the sculpture represents the princess lying powerless and dead; whilst above, it shows her rising heavenwards, two angels beside her, one holding her new-born baby, and the other leading her to glory. Here, too, died in 1861, the good Prince Albert, Queen Victoria's beloved husband. Then England kept a sad Christmas holiday, for a good and wise prince was dead, and our Queen's heart was well-nigh broken. He is buried in a beautiful mausoleum.

Everything about Windsor is interesting; the fine old trees of its wide forest, the beauty of Virginia Water, the elms of the long walk, and even the stables, with their beautiful horses, from the splendid Arabian charger to the tiny Shetland pony.

The view from the Round Tower, where the royal banner waves, is very extensive. From it twelve counties may be seen. Try to count them on the map.

I should like to tell you of some of the old oak and beech trees of Windsor Forest and Park, of the oak called Queen Victoria's Own, which before a branch is thrown out is fifty feet, or nearly seventeen yards high;† of the

* Pages 160, 203, 209, 256. † Pages 157, 164, 196.

beautiful deer, of the white Cashmere goats; of the lovely views; of the late Prince Consort's model farm, and of Queen Victoria's school, where I have heard she and the princesses often teach the little children. But I fancy you will like still better to hear a story—a story of our good old king George III. and a little shepherd boy.

A little shepherd boy was sitting on a wall under a tree, with a book in his hand, when an old gentleman came up and asked him, "What book have you there?"

"The A B C Book," said the boy, fearlessly.

"Can you read, then?"

"A little."

"Let me hear," said the gentleman and kind king, for it was he who stood beside the little fellow and heard him read.

"Can you spell words of two syllables?"

"Yes, I think so."

"Abbot, then."

"A b, ab, b o t, bot."

"Right, now crimson."

This, the child also spelt; and the king said, "Do you go to school, and do you read the Bible?"

The lad's face fell, and he answered sadly, "Mother is too poor to send me to school, and she has only a part of the Bible, and that is so torn and dirty, that it is quite useless."

"Ah, that is bad, very bad, indeed. What is her name? Where does she live?"

The boy replied, and the king left him. The child felt disappointed because he did not get a penny from the gentleman for spelling so well.

The king went home, and taking a Bible, wrote on its title page, "From George III. to M." He then put into it a £5 note, told his secretary to take the parcel as directed, desired that the little boy should be sent to school, adding, " Let it be sent forthwith ; for it is our will and pleasure that every one in our kingdom shall have the opportunity of reading the Bible."

HERTFORDSHIRE.

As the Thames leaves Buckingham, it receives a little river from the north, called the Colne. Its source will take us into Hertfordshire. We will hear all we can of this small but cheerful county, before I tell you of the still smaller, but much more important one, Middlesex. I call it a cheerful county, because there are no large towns, with close streets, neither are there extensive commons, nor morasses, nor barren lands, and the whole county is dotted over with gentlemen's seats, and smiling little cottages, and pretty straggling villages, with their spires looking upwards to the sky, or church towers, which seem to tell us that God is our refuge and our strength.* Hertford is, also, very full of trees; its lanes being overhung with their branches. The oak is so plentiful, that it is called the weed of Hertfordshire. If you look on the map, you will see that here the rivers run south, whilst, in Bedfordshire, they all run north. Would you, therefore, expect to find the north of the county hilly or flat ? The chalk hills, of which we have heard in Oxford and Buckingham, extend across the north of Hertford, continuing the name of Chilterns, until they enter Cambridge,—under what very strange name ? †

Most of the land is arable; its wheat and barley are very good. In the south-west there are many orchards, where, in June, you may gather bright red cherries, and in August, golden apples.‡ The hay is excellent; and the

* Pages 72, 89, 168.   † Pages 168, 240, 249.   ‡ Pages 199, 207, 216.

straw being of good quality, as in Bedfordshire, many cottagers are employed in plaiting it.* Much paper is made in this county.†

The principal rivers are, the Colne, in the west; the Lea, which crosses the centre, and then forms a part of the eastern boundary. In Hertfordshire is also the New River, a sort of canal, or artificial stream, cut in King James I.'s time, in order to supply London with water. It was principally made at the expense of Sir Hugh Myddelton, a wealthy and energetic citizen. He accomplished the undertaking; and, to this day, the citizens of London feel the benefit of his work; but, I am sorry to say, it cost him all his own large fortune, and he died a poor man, yet happier, I think, than if he had died rich, and had made no one better or healthier.

Now let us begin Hertfordshire on the west side, following the rivers and their tributaries. In the very west is Tring, on the North-Western Railway. The chief part of the town is new. It has a manufactory for silk. Further east, following the little river Gade, and also the railway, we reach Berkhampstead, the birthplace of Cowper, the poet.‡ Here are the remains of an ancient castle, belonging to the Princes of Wales. When William I. marched to London, after the Battle of Hastings, the Abbot of St Alban's met him here, and made him promise to keep all the good old Saxon laws. William made the promise, but very soon, as you know, broke it. Berkhampstead was a royal nursery in James I.'s time. Here lived, when little boys, Prince Henry, who died early, and Prince Charles, afterwards the unfortunate king, who was beheaded. Hemel Hempstead is east of this, where are some of the largest paper-mills in

* Page 162. † Page 165. ‡ Pages 180, 250.

England. Following the little Gade, we reach King's Langley, where Henry III. built a palace, and where Richard II. is buried, and very near it is Abbot's Langley, where Nicolas Brakespeare, the only Englishman ever made a Pope, was born. Though he allowed the Emperor Frederic to hold the stirrup of his horse, he was so hard-hearted and selfish, that he suffered his own mother to receive alms from the Church at Canterbury. The Gade joins the Colne at Rickmansworth, near which are flour, silk, and paper mills.

Now, we must trace the Colne, and I shall tell you of two principal towns on its banks. The first is St Alban's, built on the site of the ancient Roman city, Verulam. St Albans is one of those towns, very important in bygone days, but not so now. We, however, often love old things, and so we like to think of the ruins and buildings of old towns, and wonder what has happened in former times. Thus you may fancy the Romans mustering their legions at Verulam, and the cohorts marching off, headed by a Severus or a Constantine; or you may imagine Queen Boadicea and her brave but savage Britons, suddenly descending on the city and massacring thousands of the Romans.*

The town was called St Alban's, after the first British martyr. The story of his death is very interesting. He was a citizen of Verulam, and had given shelter to a Christian, who fled thither from Wales, during the persecution in the reign of the Emperor Diocletian. Alban, having heard that the Christian's retreat was discovered, sent him away secretly, before the arrival of the soldiers, whom the judge had sent to arrest him. Then he put on his clothes, and surrendered himself to the soldiers instead of giving up the man whom they sought. Standing before

* Pages 3, 179, 198.

the judge, he boldly threw off the cloak, declared how he had let the persecuted Christian escape; and likewise made known his belief in the crucified Saviour. The anger of the judge was great. Alban was first very severely scourged, and then, as he would not deny Christ, he was led away to a neighbouring hill and beheaded. The great town of Verulam has perished; but from its ruins has been built the town which bears the name of the once despised martyr. God, you know, has said, "Them that honour me, I will honour." The Abbey church is a very large one, built in various styles, and of all sorts of stones, probably old stones of Verulam. The monastery, the abbot of which was once reckoned the first in England, was destroyed in Henry the Eighth's time. Here is buried Humphrey, the good Duke of Gloucester, uncle and guardian to Henry VI., who was only one year old when he became king.*   Two great battles were fought during this reign at St Alban's, in one of which Henry was taken prisoner, and in the other he, or rather his wife, Margaret of Anjou, was successful.†   The next town on the Colne is Watford, a long straggling town, with several silk mills.

Before we follow the Lea, try and find in the north of the county, amongst the chalky hills of which I have told you, Royston, Baldock, and Hitchin, all market towns, with large breweries, and inhabitants engaged in straw-plaiting. These towns are built on the old Roman roads, which pass through this county, leading northward from London.‡

The first town on the Lea is Hatfield. Near it is Hatfield House, once a royal residence, where both Edward VI. and Queen Elizabeth were living when they heard of their succession to the throne. It now belongs to the

* Page 245.   † Pages 19, 209.   ‡ Pages 82, 148, 194.

Marquis of Salisbury. Some years ago, a great part of the old house was burnt down, and the Marchioness burnt to death.*

Further down the Lea is Hertford, where was also a royal castle. Here John of France and David of Scotland were confined as prisoners in Edward the Third's reign.†

At Hertford, the Lea is joined by the Beane. Not very far from the upper part of its course, with the church standing on a pretty height, is Stevenage. Here was erected, in the reign of Henry VII., the first paper-mill of which we have authentic information; but Shakespeare informs us that one had been erected about forty years before, by Lord Saye, and the worst charge that the ignorant and insolent Jack Cade and his mob could bring against that nobleman was, that he had employed printing, and had built a paper-mill. Further down the Beane is Watton, for many years the parish where good Edward Bickersteth laboured. His name you will learn to love, for he loved God very much.

At Amwell, near Hertford, is the river-head where commences the cutting of the New River. Near this is Ware, with its seventy malting houses for the London breweries.‡ It was to Ware that John Gilpin's horse would go; for there its master, the calender, lived. Perhaps you remember how he refused his friend's hospitality, because

> "Said John, ' It is my wedding day,
> And all the world would stare,
> If wife should dine at Edmonton
> And I should dine at Ware.' "

Further down the Lea is Cheshunt, where is still seen the house in which Richard Cromwell, who might have succeeded his father, spent his quiet life, and died, aged

* Page 145.   † Pages 30, 237.   ‡ Pages 153, 250.

eighty.   Near the borders of Middlesex, is Waltham
Cross.   It is one of the places where good Queen Eleanor's
body rested, on its way to Westminster from Grantham
in Lincolnshire, where she died.   Her husband, Edward I.,
built a cross at each of the fifteen places where the sad
procession halted.   The cross at Waltham is the best preserved of any of these beautiful erections.*

And now, I think we have found a great deal of interest
in so small a county as Hertfordshire.   How much more,
though, will there be in the yet smaller Middlesex, which
I hope we shall reach to-morrow.

MIDDLESEX.—Part I.

To-day we reach the most important county of all
England, and yet almost the smallest, the county of
great London, which is not only the capital of England,
but also the largest city of the civilised world.   Great
London is, therefore, of far more consequence than little
Middlesex; but, as I do not like little things to be forgotten when great things come, I will tell you of Middlesex first, and of London afterwards.   There is a good but
very long adjective for Middlesex, which distinguishes it
from all the other counties in England, me-tro-pol-i-tan,
because of London the metropolis, or great town.

Middlesex has the Thames bounding it on the south,
and the map must tell you what counties touch it north,
south, east, and west.   Our old Hertfordshire friends, the
Colne, the New River, and the Lea, run through it.   There
are no mountains, but in the north are some pretty rising
grounds.   The only kind of farming produce for which
Middlesex is famed is hay, the making of which is well
understood.†   About 8000 cows are kept in the county,

to help to supply the immense demand for milk in London. To meet this demand, many dairymen mix the milk with water, and then thicken it with chalk, so that it is very difficult in London to get wholesome milk. There are no minerals in Middlesex, and I do not think a rock could be found in the whole county. The soil is either clay or gravel. These rest on chalk, and form what is called the basin of London. Many interesting fossils are found in it, not nearly so ancient as those in the marble rocks of Derbyshire, in the alum cliffs of Yorkshire, or in the coal beds of Durham. Of the clay a great many bricks are made, and gravelly soil is particularly healthy for a town, as the wet easily sinks through it. Along the banks of the Thames there are many gardens, whose apple trees, in spring, form a mass of white blossom.

The first town of any consequence on the Colne is Uxbridge, where a great quantity of bricks are made. Further down is Horton, where Milton lived for some years.* In the church is the slab which marks the burial-place of his mother. That great poet studied very hard when living here, for he felt that if he wished to write anything more than ordinarily good, he must take more than ordinary pains. Staines, very near Magna Charta Island, of which more hereafter, stands at the junction of the Thames and Colne.

Now, following the Thames a short distance, we reach Hampton, about a mile from which is the magnificent palace of Hampton Court. It was originally built by the proud Wolsey, who always seemed unusually proud when he stayed there.† Discovering, however, that his master, Henry VIII., was jealous that he should live in a grander palace than himself, he presented it to the king, and here was born that good young prince Edward VI. There are

* Pages 169, 198.　　　　　　† Pages 190, 243.

three large and very fine courts, one built by Wolsey, another by Henry, and the third in the time of William III. The last king who lived here was George II. There is a splendid banqueting hall, and twenty-six other rooms, with 1000 pictures, some very fine, others curious, and others inferior. The gardens were laid out in the Dutch fashion by William III. They look very formal, but curious. The trees are magnificent. The largest vine in Europe grows here; its grapes in one season weighed about a ton. The fruit is reserved for the Queen's table. At Hampton Court, in James I.'s time, the bishops and clergy consulted about the best translation of the Scriptures, and gave us the precious English Bible as we now read it. Learned men are again consulting to make, if possible, a still more exact translation.

Close to Hampton Court is another royal residence, Bushy Park, where good Queen Adelaide lived. It receives its name from its very pretty old thorn-trees.

The Thames next passes Teddington, so called because the ebb and flow of the tide ceases there. The largest manufactory in England of wax candles is at this village. A little further on, the river reaches Twickenham. Here lived the poet Pope. Perhaps you know a beautiful piece of his poetry, beginning,

"Vital spark of heavenly flame."

At Isleworth, a little rivulet joins the Thames. If we follow this to its source, we shall reach almost the north of Middlesex; and on one of the highest hills of the county, we should see Harrow, with its old church and lofty spire. Harrow has a school for boys, which is as celebrated as that of Eton.* It was founded nearly 300 years

* Page 252.

ago, by John Lyon, a farmer of the parish, for the free instruction of the boys of Harrow; but strangers were to be allowed to go on the payment of certain sums of money. It would not now be a suitable school for the poor; but a good English school has been provided for them.

Near the Thames, on a branch of this little tributary, is Hounslow. Here are great gunpowder mills. An explosion in one of these is very terrific, and may be heard for many miles around. Near this is Hounslow Heath, once noted for highway robberies; but now famed for military reviews. Below Isleworth, the banks of the Thames are very pretty,—Kew Gardens on the one side, and Sion House, belonging to the Duke of Northumberland, on the other. Further on, at Brentford, the little Brent runs into the widening Thames. Here a great quantity of soap is made. If we track the Brent, we almost reach Hertfordshire. I will tell you, therefore, of Barnet, a town partly in Middlesex and partly in Hertfordshire. In stage-coach days the common was noted for robberies, and Barnet was the first stage in travelling north from London. Here four horses could be harnessed in less than a minute.* The railways have taken from it this celebrity; but you will like to think that the most famous inn for supplying horses for coaches and beds for travellers is now an orphan house for soldiers' children. Near Barnet was fought one of the bloody battles of the Roses, in which the Earl of Warwick, who then supported Margaret of Anjou, was defeated and slain.† Adjoining is Hadley, with an ancient church, on the top of whose tower is an old iron basin, for holding the fire that was to give warning, in the days of beacon-telegraphs.‡

Some of the little rills the Brent receives flow from the pretty hills to the north of London, the hills on which

* Page 139.   † Pages 19, 45, 51, 123, 209, 264.   ‡ Pages 16, 228.

Hampstead and Highgate stand. In former days this was a very dangerous country, infested with highwaymen, who stopped noblemen's or gentlemen's carriages, and demanded either money or life. There is a story of one, called Claude Duval, who stopped a lady's coach, in which were four hundred pounds. He agreed to take only one hundred, if she would alight and dance with him upon the heath. I think it must have been a sorry dance, with failing heart and trembling limbs.*

The next interesting place on the Thames is Chiswick, where magnificent flower shows used to be held; roses, geraniums, dahlias, and verbenas, arranged in beautiful order, and specimens exhibited of the finest kinds. Here, too, is Devonshire House, where two great statesmen, Fox and Canning, died. Next on the Thames is Hammersmith, with a beautiful iron bridge. This town, with others, such as Hampstead and Highgate, are still called villages. So they were a few years ago; but now they each contain from 20,000 to 40,000 inhabitants. People wonder, as they draw near London, from north or south, or east or west, to see the numbers of new houses springing up; and they say, " To what will London grow at last ?" A little below Hammersmith is Fulham, where has been the palace of the Bishops of London from the time of Henry VII.

MIDDLESEX.—PART II.

LONDON.

BEFORE we travel through London, from west to east, I must try and give you some idea of this vast metropolis of Great Britain. If you live a long way from London,

* Page 186.

you will like to know what great London is like, and, if
you live in London, you will like to find out whether your
eyes tell the same tale, when you look at this book and
when you walk through the streets. First, then, I will tell
you something about its people; secondly, about its size;
thirdly, its history; and, fourthly, its manufactures and
commerce. This will do for chapters for two days, and
then you shall have others describing the parks and palaces, the gardens and bridges, the churches and public
buildings, the museums and charities, for which London is
so famous.

First, the population. London is the most populous
city in Europe. It is reckoned that three million and
a quarter of people live in it. You know a million is a
thousand thousand. Were you ever in a large church
with one thousand people present. Well, try and fancy
three thousand of such churches all put together and
crowded with people, and you may get an idea of the
population of great London. Now do you ask, and what
are so many people doing? A great variety of work; and,
if you walked through the streets, you would think that
every person looked busy about something. London is
quite a city for work, it is no idle place. When people
want to rest, they always try to leave London. It is a
place for the richest and for the poorest people. There our
queen has her palaces; the grand nobility have their
splendid mansions; the merchant princes have their lux-
urious houses; and there is to be found the garret, with
its piteous inmates lying amongst heaps of rags; the
cellar, where, amidst a horrible stench, and filthy vermin
and cold damp, poor neglected children are living, and
perhaps dying. The contrasts in London, between ex-
ceeding splendour and dire poverty, are most sad. But in
this great city are many good people, who give their

money and their time to help the poor; and I trust that these are more cared for now than formerly. In every parish there are schools, where a great many boys and girls are clothed and educated. Once a year there is a gathering of about 10,000 of these children beneath the high dome in St Paul's Cathedral. They sing most sweetly, and have a sermon preached to them. It is a beautiful sight; each school arriving with its banners and devices waving, and the children looking clean and neat in their different costumes. Thousands of visitors likewise assemble, all within that grand cathedral, and the children's voices ascend, like the sound of many waters. It seems a whisper of that time, when, from all lands and kindreds, the young and the old shall be gathered together to sing their glad hallelujahs. Notwithstanding all these schools, there are many thousand children, whose parents are too poor or too wicked to send them to school at all; but ragged schools have been established for them, and many that would have been beggars or thieves are now taught to earn their bread honestly. Some have been formed into brigades for standing in the corners of the streets to blacken shoes. They are dressed in uniform, from the colours of which the brigades are named, red, yellow, brown, &c. Many boys have thus earned enough money to pay their passage to Australia.

Has it entered into your young thoughts—no food grows in London. How are all these thousand thousands of people fed? I hardly know how to tell you the manner in which, every day, fish and flesh, vegetables and groceries, are brought into London. There is enough to supply every man's wants, and yet no human being directs the provisioning. It is truly arranged by God's providence, who gives to all living things their meat in due season. It has been calculated that every week-day, there are slaughtered, on an average, 5000 sheep, 800 oxen and 100 calves, 11,000 fowls, between 2000 and 3000 hares and rabbits, and about 100 pigs, without reckoning the bacon and ham sent up cured. The quantity of fish is enormous; and of eggs, the foreign ones alone number 75,000,000 every year.

To give a still better idea of the quantity of food consumed in London during the year, I will mention some calculations made in the *Quarterly Review*, a few years ago. Supposing we could pile together in Hyde Park all the barrels of beer consumed in London, we should have about one thousand columns, not far short of a mile in perpendicular height. Now, if you stood on their summit, and looked along the northern road for all the oxen consumed in London in one year, they would reach, travelling ten abreast, the whole way to Peterborough. If you looked westward for the sheep, the shepherd at the end of the flock, also marching ten abreast, would be just leaving Bristol, one hundred and twenty miles distant. For seven and a half miles eastward the road might be crowded with calves; and for the same distance, another road might be filled with slowly-pacing, deeply-grunting pigs. Then you might imagine the air become suddenly dark with birds, both game and poultry; and they would form a square of nearly fifty-one acres, as large as St James's Park. Again, Hyde Park might become suddenly filled with hares and rabbits; and if they were feeding, two thousand abreast, they would extend at least a mile. To get an idea of the bread consumed, imagine a pyramid of loaves, sixty-seven yards square, and piled up to be four hundred and thirty-one yards high. Regarding vegetables, all I shall tell you is, that 40,000 people are continually employed in preparing, or selling, or carrying them. The supply of water fit for drinking is astonishing; and also of gas for lighting.   There are thousands of miles of pipes below the streets of London.

London is reckoned more healthy than any other large city in Europe.   Less rain falls here than in most places in England.   During November there are often very thick fogs, of a dull, deep yellow colour.   It becomes so dark, that lights are needed in the middle of the day; sometimes neither carriage nor steamboat can move, and passengers pass along with link-boys running beside them, holding lighted torches.

Secondly, the size of London.   It altogether covers twenty-one square miles, and its complete circuit, including the suburbs, is about sixty miles.   If you live in the north of England, you must remember it is about as large as twenty-seven Newcastles, or fifty Yorks.   It would take more than five Manchesters to make one London. If you live in the middle of England, remember it is as large as forty Leicesters, or ten Birminghams; if in the east, thirty-five Norwiches, or one hundred and thirty-eight Lincolns; if in the south, nearly sixty Exeters or fifty Southamptons.   It comprises a very great part of the county of Middlesex, and stretches into Essex and Kent, besides having a large portion lying in Surrey.   Railways encircle it, and an underground railway passes under its midst, by which thousands of persons travel every day. The *city* of London forms a small, but a very important part, of the London metropolis—the part of commerce and merchandise.   During the day, it is densely populated. The streets are crowded with people hurrying to and fro; and cabs, and carriages, and carts, and omnibuses are so numerous, that these vehicles are frequently blocked up, and for some time cannot move forward.   It is wonderful that accidents are not more numerous; but perhaps in no town is driving so perfect as in London.   There are upwards of ten thousand streets and lanes and squares. Owing to its great size, you might a long time walk or drive about London without seeing green fields, or breathing country air. I remember once meeting the boys of the shoe-black brigades in the country. As they were marching through a park, a flight of crows passed overhead. The boys halted, and saluted the crows with a shout of pleasure, because the sight was so new to them.

With a beautiful story, showing how the poor have sometimes helped the poor, I will finish this chapter.

A lady called one day in March, at a room in Bloomsbury. There, crouching over a little bit of fire, and only half clothed, were several starving children. They had had no breakfast that day; but a neighbour had just sent them a loaf of bread. Soon the lady went into the kind neighbour's room, and found her a poor, pale, destitute-looking woman. Her husband had had no work for six months; but she had been able to earn something for her little ones. Her dress was neat and tidy; but when she rose to open the door, the lady saw that her feet were bare. "Can it be," she inquired, "that you have no boots?" "Well, ma'am," she answered, looking ashamed, "I have, and I haven't; and that's the truth; for I have good ones, but I was obliged to put them away last night, to get bread for my children." Yet, this was she who had sent the welcome loaf to the poor starving ones next door.

> My little ones be this your prayer,
> Great God, for ragged children care;
> And think if you can't something do
> To save from cold and hunger too
>   Children starving, starving, starving.

MIDDLESEX.—PART III.

LONDON, (*continued.*)

LONDON is supposed to have been originally a British town. It was not at first the Roman capital, but in time, finding it admirably suited for commerce, ships being able to sail up the deep waters of the Thames, the Romans made it a chief town for their merchants. In the reign of Constantine the Great, a strong wall was built all round. Little of this now remains but the names of the gates, such as Moorgate, Aldersgate, Ludgate, and a street called London Wall.* In Cannon Street, there was formerly the central milestone, from which the great Roman roads started.† A fragment of it is still preserved. There is a tributary of the Thames called the Fleet, up which ships could formerly sail; but as years passed, it became smaller, till at length it was known as the Fleet Ditch. It is still a very rapid stream, and flows under Farringdon Street. Although it cannot now be seen, its name is kept up in that of Fleet Street.‡

The city of London has often been nearly burnt down; the most terrible fire occurred in the reign of Charles II. Then, street after street caught the flame, and building after building fell crashing down. The old cathedral of St Paul's was totally destroyed; the lead, becoming molten, poured off its roof. Evelyn, who lived at that time, describes the frightful sight thus:—" God grant that my eyes may never behold the like, now seeing above 10,000 houses all in one flame; the noise, and cracking, and thunder of the impetuous flames; the shrieking of women and children; the hurry of people; the fall of towers, houses, and churches, was like a hideous storm; and the air all about so hot and inflamed, that

* Pages 44, 106, 154, 229, 263.   † Pages 82, 148, 194, 264.
‡ Pages 36, 176.

at last one was not able to approach it; so that they were forced to stand still, and let the flames burn on, which they did for nearly two miles in length, and one in breadth." Frightful as this fire was, London gained real good from it. The year before, the city had been desolated by the plague; but now the air was purified, and new and broader streets were built. Yet, I do not doubt that those two dreadful calamities were God's punishments, for the wickedness of man was indeed great upon the earth. There have frequently been severe pestilences in London; one, in Edward III.'s reign, was frightfully fatal. London has always suffered much, when the cholera has raged in England.[*] It is, however, much more healthy than formerly—indeed, it is the healthiest of large towns.

The city had no regular lights till the reign of Henry V., who ordered cords to be placed across the streets, on which lanterns were to be hung. Paving was unknown till the time of Henry VIII. Can you fancy the mud and mire before that time? Side flags, for foot passengers, were not placed till James I.'s reign.

It is only within comparatively few years that London has grown very rapidly. Islington, Kensington, and Chelsea, not long ago, were villages in the country. In the reign of Queen Elizabeth, even St Giles' and St Martin's and Spitalfields were literally "in the fields;" whereas now, they are in the very heart of the metropolis; and the Strand, for many ages, was a high road, having on one side a row of noblemen's houses, connecting the separate cities of London and Westminster. Not much more than 100 years since Oxford Street was an uneven road, at the side of which stood here and there a cottage. At the present time, it is reckoned that the population of London increases at the rate of 1000 people every week.[†]

I am glad to tell you that the charities in London are

---

* Pages 29, 80, 108, 129.   † Pages 92, 97, 162.

very numerous. Some hospitals are for diseases of all kinds; others for particular complaints, such as consumption, fever, small-pox. There are two hospitals for children—poor little sick children! The rooms are large and airy; the matrons are kind, and the children look as happy as sick little children, without a dear mother, can look. I once went to one to see a little boy almost blind. There were many pretty toys in the rooms; and nice children's books for those that could read. In the convalescent room there was a rocking-horse and other pleasant amusements. One dear little girl had been there for a very long time, and was not likely ever to leave her bed again. As we walked through the rooms, several little boys were going to bed, and we listened as they repeated their prayers. How pleasant was the thought, that Jesus cared for these weary little lambs. There are also in London many reformatories, for boys or girls who have early learnt bad ways; and there are asylums for the aged and the maimed; for the orphan and the helpless; for the idiot and the lunatic. There are houses to provide nightly shelter for the destitute; and institutions for teaching the blind, and the deaf and dumb.*

The employments of London people are most varied, from the Queen opening Parliament, to the crossing-sweeper, who stands all day sweeping away the mud, in hopes of a passing penny. There live the great statesmen who help the Queen to govern her mighty dominions; and the gentlemen who are sent to Parliament to talk about new laws and taxes.† There live numerous clergymen; some working very hard in their immense parishes, and some earnest, eloquent preachers. There meet the cleverest lawyers, and the most celebrated doctors. There are the wealthiest merchants, and tradespeople of every grade. There, too, is the poor over-worked sempstress.

* Pages 182, 231.   † Page 5.

"Stitch, stitch, stitch,
    In poverty, hunger, and dirt,
    And weave with a double thread
    A shroud as well as a shirt."

The manufactures of London are numerous. The breweries, the distilleries, and the houses for refining raw sugar—that is, making coarse sugar white—are the largest in England.* In one district called Clerkenwell, great numbers of people are employed in clock and watch-making.† Spitalfields is the district for silk-weavers.‡ There are many men employed in plate and jewellery; and 14,000 workmen are engaged in printing and book-binding. Millinery occupies about 40,000 people. London is likewise noted for its cabinet-making, and coach-building. Besides these things, there are great engineering works, and soap and candle manufactories, and large chemical and dye-works; many ships, also, are built, and cables made, and houses unceasingly erected. It would be difficult to say in what man is not occupied, or what earthly production there is, which may not be purchased in this great city. Amongst all these things I shall only tell you, particularly, of two printing establishments—the one is great, but the other is far, far greater. The one is of the *Times;* the other, of the British and Foreign Bible Society. The rapidity with which copies of the *Times* are struck off is astonishing. One of the machines prints 12,000 copies in an hour; and another, an American invention, can even print 18,000. It is wonderful to see in how short a time the blank paper, winding round the cylinder, is thrown out, covered with so much important news. By the British and Foreign Bible Society, God's blessed book is printed in nearly 200 different languages, and from it about 2,000,000 copies of His Word are sent forth yearly,§ Who shall measure the good of those efforts, when we

* Page 231.   † Page 122.   ‡ Page 118.   § Page 261.

have God's own promise, "My word shall not return unto me void?"

Now I must tell you a little about the Lord Mayor of London, and then to-day's chapter will be done. You have heard of him, no doubt, ever since you sang—

> "Turn again, Whittington,
> Lord Mayor of London."

This worthy citizen is chosen every year on Michaelmas-day. Whilst his office lasts, he is, within the city, second only to the king. Excepting one regiment, called the "Old Buffs," no troops can, without the Lord Mayor's leave, pass through the city with drums beating or with colours flying. On the 9th of November, called Lord Mayor's day, he is installed; he and his retinue proceeding to and returning from Westminster, in gaudy carriages, with very smart footmen.

The first Lord Mayor was made in the reign of Edward III. When the sovereign visits the city of London, the gates of Temple Bar are shut, that the Lord Mayor may go in form, and present the keys which open them. When the sovereign dies, the Lord Mayor sits at the Privy Council, and signs before any subject.

MIDDLESEX.—PART IV.

LONDON, (continued.)

YOU shall now hear of interesting places in London, travelling very gradually from the west to the east. Just below Battersea Bridge is Chelsea. Here is a hospital, commenced in the reign of Charles II., for old soldiers who have served long in the British army. A great many flags and ensigns taken in battle, are hung in the hall and chapel. Between four and five hundred old pensioners live here, and are provided with all they need; and from the funds of the hospital seventy-six thousand soldiers receive a pension. We are glad that England cares for those in old age, who have fought for her in youth. A very old soldier lies buried at Chelsea, who was married, when above one hundred years old, and died aged one hundred and twelve. The inscription on his tombstone concludes with these words, "Read, fellow-soldiers, and reflect, that there is a spiritual warfare, as well as a warfare temporal." Nor do you forget that, at baptism, the promise was made to God that you would "fight manfully under Christ's banner, against sin, the world, and the devil." Serve Him now, and He will *never* forget you.

Between Chelsea and Kensington is the warmest part of London. Here we find one of the consumption hospitals, where the poor have proper food and all these comforts which sometimes, for a little while, stay that sad disease. In South Kensington is a very interesting museum. The object of it is to lead people to see and copy the beauties of art, and to give them wise thoughts about common things, such as food, fuel, clothing. One part is full of beautiful drawings, paintings, and mosaics, specimens of china, armour, clock-work, musical instruments, and other works of art. Here are the famous cartoons of Raphael, a great Italian painter. They are large Bible pictures, beautifully drawn, intended to be copied in tapestry, the fine wool-work of olden days. Another is filled with books, maps, and models suitable for schools; and others, with models of inventions that have been made during eighty years, thus showing how gradually art has reached its present condition; with models of building, and specimens from all countries of the materials of which our houses, food, and clothes are made. You would like to see the museum lighted. Little cars seem to run along the ceiling, lighting hundreds of gas jets, and then run

back, lighting those that may have at first been missed.
Near Kensington Museum are the Horticultural Gardens,
or gardens for making experiments in the cultivation of
plants. Here there are very lovely flower shows. Adjoining the Gardens is the Royal Albert Hall, a splendid place
for music ; and the buildings for the International Exhibitions, where pictures and specimens of manufactured
goods from all nations may be occasionally seen.

Kensington Palace was bought by William III. He
and his wife, Queen Mary, Queen Anne, and George II.,
all died here. But what will interest you most is to know
that it is the birthplace of Queen Victoria, and her home
when a baby and a little girl. There she was residing when,
on June the 20th, 1837, the Archbishop of Canterbury
arrived, in the early morning, to announce the death of her
uncle, William IV., and her own accession to the throne.
At first she wept, and then she begged the Archbishop to
unite with her in prayer, that God would strengthen her
for her many high duties. Kensington Gardens are now
freely opened, and thousands of people continually enjoy
the pleasant shade of its fine old trees, and the smell of
its sweet flowers. Through these gardens and Hyde Park,
which is adjoining, the Serpentine, an artificial river, flows,
where thousands of Londoners bathe in summer and skate
in winter. Hyde Park is the fashionable place for driving
and fishing. Eight hundred carriages have been known
to assemble there at one time. A military review there
is a grand spectacle. Here Queen Victoria reviewed the
Rifle Corps, when they assembled in such great numbers
in 1860, and showed how ready they were to defend their
sovereign ; and here the Crystal Palace for the Great
Exhibition of 1851 was erected. A magnificent monument
has been built here to the memory of the good Prince
Albert, who originated these exhibitions, and many other
useful schemes. The horse-road is called Rotten Row,

supposed to have been originally "Route du Roi." What does that mean? One of the entrances is under a very fine marble arch, that once stood in front of Buckingham Palace. Near it is Tyburn, where, in former days, many criminals were hung. Under this place lie the bones of Oliver Cromwell. He had been buried in Westminster Abbey; but when Charles II. succeeded, his body was shamefully disinterred, and meanly deposited here.

North of this lies Tyburnia, a district of many well-built streets and squares, and then passing over Paddington, we reach another beautiful park, laid out when George IV. ruled in his afflicted father's stead, and after him called the Regent's Park. You will like to hear of Regent's Park: because the Botanical and the Zoological Gardens are both enclosed within it.

Here is also St Dunstan's Villa, in the garden of which stands the curious old clock which once adorned St Dunstan's, in Fleet Street. There are figures of giants, who do duty in striking the hours and quarter-hours.

The Botanical Gardens are very beautiful. Not many years ago, they were a piece of level nursery garden ground. Now they are hollows and hills, lakes, bridges, caverns, and streams. There are said to be 10,000 specimens of hardy plants, from all parts of England, arranged in proper order; also medicinal plants, regularly placed, and beautiful flowers in parterres. Here, too, there is a most delightful winter house. Entering it from the frosty air, one seems transported into a fairy land; one walks amongst the gayest flowers, and the sweetest perfumes. The flowers are not growing as in a hot-house, but are as placed in a garden; plants that we are accustomed to look upon as shrubs, grow as trees, and the space is so large that 2000 people may stand inside.

Then there are the gardens which, of all others, children like the best—the Zoological. I think my little friend, who wrote about Gloucester Cathedral, shall also describe these to you. The only interesting animals he has omitted to mention are the pelicans, with pouches under their bills in which they keep the fish that they have caught for food, and the birds of paradise with their splendid feathered tails. He writes:—" I saw the salamander; it lived in water instead of fire. I saw some green frogs; they were so pretty, that auntie said she could have made pets of them; and we saw an enormous ugly frog, called a bull-frog. I saw a seal, it is between a fish and an otter; it sometimes was out and sometimes in the water. The otters are something like the seals; they did eat fish. I saw the rhinoceros; its skin was so very thick, it would laugh at the shake of a spear. There were such beautiful deer, with horns like the branches of a tree. I saw boa constrictors; they were very enormous, and they could crush leopards, or almost an elephant, to death. I saw the rattlesnake; but did not hear him rattle with his tail. I saw the puff-adder; it puffed out its cheeks in such a dreadful way. There were a great many vipers, and different kinds of snakes. I saw magnificent Poll parrots, and all kinds of pretty little birds, and beautiful pigeons, and cranes, and storks; and I saw some vultures and eagles, and the bush turkey, which makes a hill for its nest. The civet cat was something like my kitten, only a great deal larger, and had a very nasty smell, which, after you passed, smelt like musk. I saw the lion, and it did kick up a noise at one time, after the man had given it a little morsel of meat. The man put his hand into the tiger's mouth. Though it is the fiercest animal, it was quite gentle with him, and was such a beautiful creature. We saw the nasty wolves, which had a worse smell than the civet cats. The polar bears were messing about in water; they were quite white, that they might hide themselves in the snow. I did not like the monkeys; I could not bear them, for they did nothing but fight. A little one almost cried with the way in which they hunted him about. One monkey was beautiful; it was white, with a striped tail. We saw a great many guinea-pigs, all eating, on a heap of grass. We went into the fish-house, and saw crocodiles and tortoises. I thought the crocodiles very small. The king-fisher sat on a bough, and watched for a long time the fish; but I did not see it eat any. We saw fish alive in their shells, paddling about the water, and sea-anemones, and white newts. The clouded tiger was fast asleep on the bough of a tree. It was very beautiful indeed. I saw the hippopotamus in the water; it drinks quantities. We saw the elephant; it took up biscuits in its trunk, and then popped them into its mouth. Its feet were immense, and its toes enormous. The giraffe was eating leaves off a tree, with a neck higher than our drawing-room. It was a very happy day, and I should like to go there very, very often."

The panoramas and dioramas are also great favourites with the young, giving views of places and scenes large as life, and very like reality. One of the best was the earthquake of Lisbon, with the houses falling, the water rising, and the ground opening. Another was Albert Smith's famous ascent of Mont Blanc. The Voyage down the Mississippi, Battles in India, Paris in flames, and all the most interesting subjects of the passing day, were shown on these moving pictures. Madame Tussaud's wax figures are also among the sights of London, where famous characters are so modelled and dressed, that they are often mistaken for living people. One of the best and most improving sights in London is the Polytechnic, where all kinds of model machinery are in motion; little steam-engines running, and boats sailing; where you may get into a diving-bell, and go down below the water; where you may see dissolving views and wonderful ghosts, and hear very interesting lectures, about air, light, or chemistry.

Regent and Oxford Streets are the two principal ones
for shops and bazaars. The bazaars are collections of stalls
in spacious buildings, where nearly every kind of pretty
thing is to be bought. The oldest of these is the Soho, in
an old-fashioned square, where the unfortunate Duke of
Monmouth once lived. To-morrow we must go back to
the west, and, starting from Belgravia, talk of Buckingham Palace, and of many interesting places.

MIDDLESEX.—Part V.

LONDON, (*continued.*)

BELGRAVIA is reckoned one of the most fashionable parts
of London; but very near it are some of the poorest and
worst districts of the metropolis. I do wish that every
person in Belgravia would remember there is work for
him to do in Westminster. Buckingham Palace lies
close to this district. Here Queen Victoria lives when in
London; here all her sons and daughters have been born;
and here, England's fair young Princess Royal was married
to the Prince of Prussia. Other parks adjoin Buckingham
Palace. In St James' Park Charles II. spent hours every
day in feeding the ducks.

Between the Palace and the Thames lies Westminster,
with its beautiful ancient abbey, and splendid new Houses
of Parliament. Westminster Abbey is interesting, as a
beautiful building, with its many arches and rich tracery;
but more, it is especially interesting as the last resting-
place of many great ones of the earth. Here lie kings and
queens, and princes; those who have fought against one
another in life, sleep quietly side by side in death. Queen
Elizabeth and her sister Mary are close together; and in
the same chapel is Mary Queen of Scots. Here lie
statesmen and poets; the literary and the scientific. To

be buried in Westminster Abbey, or to have a monument there, is one of fame's highest distinctions. Before the battle of the Nile, Nelson's words were, "Victory or Westminster Abbey." One portion is especially filled with monuments to English poets, and is called the "Poets' Corner." The beauty of the chapel, in the east end, called Henry VII.'s, is very great;* and so is the interest of another, called Edward the Confessor's; for here is the coronation chair, used when our kings and queens have been crowned ever since the time of Edward I. Beneath it is the stone that Edward brought from Scotland, and on which it seems very probable the Scotch kings have really been crowned since the time of Fergus, 330 years before Christ. The old tradition says, it is the stone on which Jacob's head rested when he dreamed; but this, of course, is only a fable. Close to the abbey is Westminster School, where many celebrated men have been educated, especially poets; such as Herbert, Cowley, Dryden, Prior, Cowper, and Southey. Before Cowley left school, he published a volume of poems. Westminster Hall is, excepting the hall at Padua, the largest room in Europe, unsupported by pillars. It was first built in William Rufus' time, and rebuilt by Richard II. Here took place the trials of Sir Thomas More, Guy Fawkes, the Earl of Strafford, Archbishop Laud, Charles I., the seven bishops, and Warren Hastings. Can you find out, from English history, in whose reigns these famous people were tried? Adjoining Westminster Hall are the new Houses of Parliament, the most splendid building erected in the present age. Do you remember whence the stone was brought? † Unfortunately the stone is not so good as was expected, and is already beginning to decay, The old houses were destroyed by fire; and these have been commenced and finished during Queen Victoria's reign. The grand Victoria tower is the highest, and per-

* Pages 170, 258.   † Page 126.

haps the most beautiful that has been raised by man.* The clock tower, too, is of great height. Here is hung Big Ben, weighing eight tons, the largest striking bell in the world. Unfortunately, however, there was a crack in the metal, and Big Ben's tongue had to be silenced, and the bell taken down to be recast. The clock has four faces; and you may imagine its size when I tell you that the hour numbers are distant from each other, the height of a man, and that the minute hand is more than five yards long. There are gilt ornaments on the tower, which look like toy crowns, but each of which weighs a ton. The flag is twenty yards long, and fifteen broad.

The Queen generally opens Parliament in the month of February. Gorgeously attired in her state robes, she enters the House of Lords, passing through corridors painted with beautiful frescoes;† when she is seated on her magnificent throne, her faithful Commoners are summoned from the other house to hear her speech, which she delivers in a clear silvery tone. Then follows what is called the parliamentary session. Day after day, and week after week, the Lords and Commons meet to discuss the affairs of the nation : and there are made the brilliant speeches of the statesmen of England; speeches, which the next day, are inserted in the London daily newspapers, and are read with interest in all parts of the civilised world. The importance of these debates is very great; and we should, indeed, pray that God will so rule the hearts of our senators, that "peace and happiness, truth and justice, religion and piety, may be established among us for all generations."

Not far distant is Whitehall, where are the offices of Government. There is the Admiralty, whence orders are sent to the British navy in all parts of the world; the

---

* Pages 153, 209.
† A fresco is a painting not on canvas, but on the wall.

Horse Guards, whence orders are sent to the army; the Treasury buildings, where the Prime Minister lives, and where the Ministers, who have the ordering of home, or colonial, or foreign affairs, have their offices; the Exchequer, where everything about the revenue or taxes is fixed; and the house where India business is transacted. Here also are two interesting museums. One is that of the United Service, which contains military and naval trophies and relics, such as the swords of Cromwell, Wolfe, or Nelson, and those few things found by the Esquimaux, which told of poor Sir John Franklin's sad fate. The other is the India Museum, full of Hindoo idols, carved Chinese work, Indian gauntlets, and beautifully wrought necklaces. Among other curiosities is an organ that was intended to amuse Tippoo Sultan, who cordially hated the English. It represents a tiger tearing an English soldier to pieces. As the handle turns, the music plays, the man shrieks loudly, and after every fourth shriek, the beast growls fiercely. Travelling north, we reach Trafalgar Square, where is the National Gallery. Here are exhibited beautiful pictures, by painters, who lived in different parts of Europe a long time ago. Many of them painted very lovely pictures of our Saviour as a little baby, watched over by his mother; but others are disfigured by superstitious fancies. A picture which you would like to see is John the Baptist, as a boy, in the wilderness of Judea, with a little lamb placing its foot on his arm. At Burlington House in Piccadilly, there is an annual exhibition of paintings, by living artists; and this is the neighbourhood of picture galleries, and there are several very good ones.

Crossing from the National Gallery, one of the worst parts of London, St Giles—the scene of many a frightful crime; but which, I trust, is even now improving, through the labours of clergymen, of missionaries, and of Bible women—we reach a building which, next to the Zoologi-

T

cal Gardens, is, I think, the place in all London you would most like to see. I mean the British Museum.

If you have read ancient and Bible history, you would be delighted to see the enormous sphinxes, the colossal heads, the ancient tombs, the preserved mummies, the old lamps, the drinking utensils; the figures of sacred animals from the land of Egypt; or to look at the stone tablets, telling of the huntings, of the fightings, and of the victories of the kings of Assyria; or to see the great figures which stood at their temple-gates, with the face of a man, the wings of the eagle, and the feet, in some cases, of the lion, in some, of the bull. As you look on them, it is interesting to think, that at those self-same Egyptian figures, Abraham, and Joseph, and Moses, and Aaron, have probably gazed; and at these Nineveh sculptures, Jonah, and Ezekiel, and others of whom we read in the Bible, have looked; and that there are the portraits of the very Pharaoh who ordered the infants to be drowned, and of the very Sennacherib who wrote so insolently to the good king Hezekiah. If you have read Greek history, you will be interested in seeing some of the most beautiful sculpture that art has ever produced, from the Parthenon in Athens, and tales told in marble of combats of Amazons and Greek warriors, of the battle between the Trojans and Greeks for the body of Patroclus. There are also elegantly shaped and painted vases from Etruria, the modern Tuscany, of more ancient date than the foundation of Rome. There are also some of the playthings of the little Etruscans, small, jointed dolls, just like those you use, but made of baked earth, called terra cotta, instead of wood. The Rosetta Stone is one of the most valuable things in the Museum. This contains the same inscription in three languages; one, the Greek, was well known; another, the hieroglyphic, had not been understood in modern times, but, by comparing the two, clever men discovered how to read what had always seemed incomprehensible riddles on the Egytian tombs. The third is the demotic. In another part of the Museum, are all kinds of stuffed beasts, birds, and fishes; in another, all kinds of shells, and the most lovely corallines and pieces of coral; in another, are stones and minerals, excellently arranged; in another, are fossil plants and animals, those great animals with very long names, that are now unknown, but which sported in the waters when God said, " Let the waters bring forth abundantly living creatures after their kind; " and there are pieces of stone which bear the footprints of enormous birds, that stood on the stone, when once it was sand, tens of thousands of years ago.* The medal-room is filled with coins of every date; and in the adjoining room are gold ornaments and jewels of the Greeks and Romans, Oliver Cromwell's watch, and many other things; and the library, I fancy, would almost bewilder you. Imagine, if you can, more than a million of books.† Many of them are very rare; amongst others is the earliest printed book known, a copy of the precious Bible, in Latin, on vellum; and there is the first printed book with a date, " 1457." Here, too, is the original but partially burnt Magna Charta; the prayer-books of the unfortunate Mary Queen of Scots, Lady Jane Grey, and Queen Elizabeth; and interesting letters and MSS., as Oliver Cromwell's letter, describing the battle of Naseby,‡ the Duke of Wellington's, written on the field of Waterloo; Milton's agreement to give to his bookseller his splendid poem, Paradise Lost, for £15,§ a piece of music composed and written out by Mozart when only eight years old, the signature of William Shakspere, and, altogether, more things than ever I can tell you, which you will believe, when I say, that the catalogue of the library is so large, that it alone would load a cart.

Not far from the British Museum is the London Uni-

* Page 53.   † Page 245.   ‡ Page 158.   § Page 267.

versity College, which is particularly celebrated for its School of Medicine.

In the Strand is Exeter Hall, a very large building, which holds more than 3000 people. Here, in May, many clergymen and others meet, to hear of the progress of missions at home and abroad; and it is delightful to listen to the thrilling speeches, to receive glad tidings of fresh work done for Christ, and to hear the thundering applause which testifies to the rejoicing of those who listen.

Somerset House, also in the Strand, is devoted to various purposes; there is King's College for education, and there are apartments for several learned societies; there are offices for stamps and taxes, registrars, &c., in all of which about 900 clerks are employed. There are 3600 windows in Somerset House. It was the palace built in Edward VI.'s time by the Protector Somerset, who suddenly rose to power, and, as suddenly, lost both power and life.

In the next chapter you will, I hope, hear of the city of London, for remember, we have not yet passed the city gates. Is not London a wonderful place? and is not everything in it, of which we talk, large, first-rate, and well worth seeing?

MIDDLESEX.—Part VI.

LONDON, (continued.)

On the western border of the City of London is, what may be termed, the lawyers' quarter. Here are the Inns of Court and the Courts of Chancery. These were once colleges for studying law, but are now principally residences for members of the bar or barristers, with halls, chapels, and libraries. There are four, the Inner and Middle Temple, Gray's Inn and Lincoln's Inn. The Inner and Middle Temple are close to Temple Bar. What have I already told you about that? The Temple is so-called because the Knights Templars, of whom we read at the time of the Crusades, formerly lived here. The Temple church, where the knights are entombed, beneath cross-legged effigies, is a very beautiful place. In the Temple Gardens two noblemen were once walking, and talking of the different rights of the houses of York and Lancaster. The one that defended the House of York plucked a white rose, proposing that all who thought with him should do so; the other plucked a red rose, making it the badge of the House of Lancaster. Shakspere represents these noblemen addressing each other thus:—

> "Hath not thy rose a canker, Somerset?
> Hath not thy rose a thorn, Plantagenet?"

A canker that for many dreary years ate into the peace of England—a thorn which caused life-blood to flow from many a gallant heart. Along the Thames for some miles is now raised a broad embankment. It is planted with trees, and forms a very pleasant drive.

St Paul's Cathedral is the largest Protestant church in the world. It was built, after the Great Fire, by Sir Christopher Wren. Over the entrance of the choir is an inscription to him in Latin, meaning, "If a monument is required, look around." A short lesson for us. Wherever we are, let us live to do good, and we shall have a better monument than a carved one. In St Paul's crypt are the graves of some of the men who have fought and conquered for dear old England, Lord Nelson,* Lord Collingwood,† and the great Duke of Wellington. There are the graves of great painters, Reynolds, Lawrence, West, and Turner; of great engineers, Mylne and Rennie, and of the great architect, Sir Christopher Wren. The first monument erected in St Paul's was to the memory of Howard the philanthropist.‡ A monument in the crypt is to Dean Collet, who founded St Paul's school, close to

* Page 184.   † Page 9.   ‡ Page 164.

the cathedral. Amongst the celebrated men educated at this school are Milton, the great poet; Halley, the astronomer; and Churchill, the famous Duke of Marlborough.* The ascent to the ball is very fatiguing, 616 steps; but the view early on a clear morning from the Golden Gallery below it is well worth seeing; the vast metropolis, its streets, its squares, its public buildings, its many-arched bridges, its crowded river, and the distant sound of its busy din. Above the golden ball, which can hold eight people, is the golden cross. There are several galleries in the ascent; one is called the Whispering Gallery, the slightest whisper being conveyed very plainly and rapidly to the opposite point of the circumference.† At the north-east corner of St Paul's Churchyard stood the old St Paul's Cross, where bishops and others used, in former days, to preach out-of-door sermons to crowds of listeners.

Very near St Paul's is Paternoster Row, famous for book-publishing. Then passing Newgate Street, a great market for butcher's-meat, we find Christ's Hospital, or the Blue Coat School, a famous place for education, founded in the time of Edward VI. The dress is a blue coat, yellow petticoat, and red leather belt round the waist, yellow stockings, a clergyman's band round the neck, and a flat black woollen cap, which is hardly ever worn.

Near this is Smithfield, till lately a great cattle market. It is very interesting to us, as the place where so many of the noble army of martyrs were content to suffer cruel death rather than to deny the faith they loved.

A little further north is the Charter House, a celebrated public school.‡ Here Wesley was educated;§ and the famous writers, Addison and Steele; and Blackstone, noted for his books on law.

An extremely busy and important part of London lies

* Page 241.　　　　† Page 212.
‡ Page 252, 268.　　§ Page 152.

between Newgate Street and London Bridge. Just at the corner of Cheapside, in St Martin's-le-Grand, is the General Post Office. Wherever you live you have seen letters that have passed through there, as it is reckoned that these number about 200,000,000 every year. The rapidity of sorting is wonderful, almost too great for the strength of the clerks. Every one is anxious to receive letters quickly; and the Government is anxious to do all it can to help them. Then, in Cheapside, is St Mary-le-Bow Church; its bells are called the Bow Bells. All born within their sound are styled Cockneys. In Milk Street, on one side of Cheapside, Sir Thomas More was born, and opposite, in Bread Street, the great Milton. In St Giles, Cripplegate, Milton was

Bank and Royal Exchange.

buried, and also Fox, who wrote of the martyrs, whilst in the parish burial-ground were laid good old Bunyan and Defoe,

the author of Robinson Crusoe.*   Near Cheapside is the
Guildhall, where, on the Lord Mayor's Day, a great dinner
is given in the olden style.   One item is 250 tureens of real
turtle soup.   At the upper end of the room, all the dishes
are hot; at the lower, all are cold, except the turtle.   The
giant figures in this hall are called Gog and Magog.
From Cheapside you enter the Poultry, where is the
Mansion House, the residence of the Lord Mayor during
the year of his office.   Near this in Threadneedle Street,
(a strange name,) is the Bank of England, where 9,000,000
bank notes are issued yearly, and where a great deal of
gold is kept, partly in coin and partly in bars.   These
are small slabs of gold, each worth about £800.   Nearer
Cheapside stands the Royal Exchange, where merchants
meet and transact business.   What exchanges are there
made in one day, of one kind of riches for another!   The
old Exchange shared, more than thirty years ago, the fate of
so many London buildings.   It was burned by fire.†   As
it burnt, the bells of the tower played one of the Lon-
doner's favourite airs, and they played on, one by one,
till they fell into the burning flames.   A new building
was soon erected, and, on the portico, over the entrance,
was carved a beautifully appropriate text, chosen by the
good Prince Albert, "The earth is the Lord's, and the
fulness thereof."   This is the bankers' quarter, and, consequently, a very wealthy part of London.

Not far distant was the old East India House, where
sat the council of the East India Company, which, from
Queen Elizabeth's time to the year 1859, transacted the
business of that distant and important empire.

In this neighbourhood is what we may call the Jews'
quarter; and here, too, is the synagogue, where the Jews
of London have their religious worship every Sabbath,

* Pages 267, 154, 163, 54.   † Pages 276, 287.

that is from 6 P.M. Friday to 6 P.M. Saturday, and special services at the time of their Passover, which is our Easter.

Near London Bridge is the Monument, marking the place where the dreadful fire commenced. Immediately below it is Billingsgate, the great fishmarket, once very notorious for the coarse scolding language there heard. East of this is the Custom House, where millions of money are received by Government every year in taxes on articles brought from foreign countries. Thus, a certain sum of money is paid on every chest of tea, on every hogshead of wine, and on many other things, and this helps, like other taxes, to pay our soldiers, sailors, &c.

Further on is the Tower, that Tower of which you have so often read in the History of England, where many great men, and some that were good, moreover, were beheaded or murdered. Here were smothered, by cruel Richard's order,* the fair little princes, Edward V. and the Duke of York, and here the Duke of Clarence was, by his brother, Edward IV., drowned in Malmsey wine. Women also suffered. Anne Boleyn, clasping her little neck laid it down beneath the executioner's axe; and the pious Lady Jane Grey committed her spirit to the God who gave it.† If walls could speak, there are none in England that could tell of such varied scenes as those of the Tower, of kingly feasts, of quartered troops, of captive prisoners. Some inscriptions, written in Queen Mary's reign, on the walls of the prison cells, can still be traced. One is " He that endureth to the end shall be saved." Another, " Be faithful unto the death, and I will give thee a crown of life; " and another, " As virtue causeth life, so sin causeth death."

In the tower is now kept the regalia of England; the beautifully gemmed crown, which our Queen wore at her coronation, and four other crowns; the orb, an emblem of universal sovereignty, the golden eagle, from which the

* Pages 143, 144.   † Page 291.

anointing oil is poured ; the sword of mercy; the royal sceptres, and other kingly symbols. Here, also, is an armoury, the oldest in the kingdom, and containing many curious relics of ancient days. One part is called the Horse Armoury, and contains twenty-two figures on horse-back, the size of life. They are dressed in the armour worn in different reigns, from the time of Edward I. to that of James II., and give an admirable idea of the appearance of ancient knights, mounted on their chargers, ready for battle. There are also ancient halls filled with modern weapons ; some are very beautifully arranged in the shape of leaves and flowers, and a bayonet plume of the Prince of Wales' feather. Before we leave the Tower, with all its dark and mournful memories, I will tell you one story, somewhat brighter and very curious, about a prisoner, in Richard II.'s time. He was thrown into one of the Tower dungeons, and would have been starved to death, had not a cat daily visited him, laden with provision. This was a pigeon, which pussy stole each night from a neighbour-ing dove-cot. When the knight was liberated, he always showed particular fondness for cats, and whenever his picture was drawn, a cat was represented beside him.

Near the Tower is the Mint, where every piece of money used in England is coined, and marked with the sovereign's image. The steam power with which this is done is so great, and the arrangements so complete, that £50,000 of bullion (the term for the metal before stamped) can be, in twenty-four hours, changed into coin. The great Sir Isaac Newton* was once Master of the Mint, and lately Sir John Herschel the astronomer, of whose father I have told you.†

Further east lie the docks. What particularly distin-guishes them from those of other large towns, are the im-mense warehouses and cellars for storing away goods. Those for tobacco cover five acres. At one part called the

---

* Page 149.   † Page 253.

Kiln bad tobacco is burned, and the long chimney that carries away its smoke is called the " Queen's pipe." The vaults for the wine are far larger, one alone covering twelve acres. Ask the size of some square or field you know of to get an idea of this extent. It is very strange to go for miles through the dimly-lighted passages with great hogsheads of wine on either side. Rats swarm in the warehouses; it is said that the cats kept there to clear the rats cost £100 a year.

The West India Docks, where immense quantities of rosewood or mahogany may be seen, are cut across the isthmus connecting the Isle of Dogs with Middlesex. Here the land is very low and unhealthy ; but the work done in ship-building, ship-loading, &c., is immense. Here the Great Eastern was built.*

At this point the River Lea enters the Thames, and separates Middlesex from Essex. Its short course will lead me to speak of one or two small towns, and then we shall cross the River Thames, and enter Surrey. Enfield, Edmonton, and Tottenham, are small towns on or near the Lea. At Enfield are the remains of a royal palace. Its grounds, no longer forest land, are still known by their ancient name—the Chase. At Edmonton is the Bell, the famous inn where Johnny Gilpin wished to dine ; and at Tottenham is another place where Queen Eleanor's body rested.† The last of those resting-places was at Charing Cross, in London, and in its name Charing, you may trace that of Chère Reine. Here a new cross, copied from the old one, has been recently built.

I should like you to imagine a few walks in London, or to make lists of palaces, churches, exhibitions, Government offices, famous men, or employments, connected with this great metropolis.

* Pages 29, 33, 97, 231.   † Page 266.

SURREY.—PART I.

LONDON, (*continued.*)

BEFORE I tell you of the county of Surrey, you shall hear about London on the south side, and of the famous bridges which connect Middlesex and Surrey. We will begin with Battersea, where there are two bridges—one for the railway. This was once a famous place for wild flowers, and here the first asparagus was grown; but now it is chiefly remarkable for the quick growth of villas. Battersea Park has been recently made, and its fresh air is very valuable to the inhabitants of the neighbourhood. Further down the Thames is Lambeth, the palace of the Archbishops of Canterbury, in the chapel of which they have all been consecrated since the reign of Henry III. One part is called the Lollards' Tower, for here it was supposed that the persecuted followers of Wycliffe were confined.* There are large iron rings in the wall, probably for the purpose of chaining prisoners.

Below Lambeth Palace is Westminster Bridge, quite a new building. From it there is a beautiful view of the new Houses of Parliament. East of this is Bethlehem Hospital, generally called Bedlam, for unfortunate lunatics. Not far from this is a central point, to which the various roads passing along the different bridges converge. Here is built an obelisk, which gives its name to the spot. In this neighbourhood is Spurgeon's immense chapel, where this celebrated preacher addresses many thousands of people at once. Further down the river, beyond large candle and other manufactories, is Charing Cross Railway Bridge, very long and traversed by four lines of railway. Then comes Waterloo Bridge, thought by many to be the finest

* Page 144.

in the world! Then Blackfriars' Bridge, from which is the best view of St Paul's Cathedral. Close to this is another railway bridge. Then Southwark Bridge, a very handsome iron one; and, lastly, London Bridge, built of the finest granite, and having the greatest traffic of any bridge whatever. The old London Bridge, which had houses built along its walls, was once the only one to span the Thames, and when it was proposed to build a new one at Westminster, the bargemen of the Thames most violently opposed it. Now, no city in Europe has bridges at all equal to those of London. Two miles below London Bridge is a more wonderful structure still—not a bridge over the river, but a tunnel beneath it. It cost a great deal of money, but is nearly useless, as no carriages nor carts can pass.

The south side of London is very inferior to the north. St Saviour's Church is reckoned one of the most beautiful ancient buildings of the metropolis, and very interesting, as being the scene where the cruel Bishop Gardiner arraigned the Protestants, in Queen Mary's reign. Near this were two very large hospitals, St Thomas's and Guy's, for the sick and lame, where the poor patients are carefully attended, and everything done to relieve their sufferings. St Thomas's has, however, been removed to where the air is fresher and sounds gentler, for this is the neighbourhood of the South-Eastern Railway Terminus, one of the busiest in England. I have not told you of the railway termini in London, and yet they are amongst the most remarkable features of the present century. The buildings are excellent, and the arrangements most careful. The bustle and stir of them must often greatly surprise people coming, for the first time, from the country.

We must leave London now, and I will endeavour to tell you what I can about the county of Surrey. But first

tell me what you can—relative size?—counties bordering
on it?—any rivers?—any hills?

Surrey is very varied in its surface and in its inhabitants:
some extensive districts being barren heaths, and others
fertile gardens; some parts being wild and almost mountainous, others the evident suburbs of a metropolitan city.
In some parts, the inhabitants are simple countrymen; in
others, adepts in London thieving.   In parts, the parishes
have a few hamlets sprinkled on the mountain side, a few
cottages on the heath; in others, they consist of crowded
thoroughfares, and the close alleys of the most populous
city of the world.

The hills that stretch across the county from west to
east are the North Downs,* and further south is a range
of sandstone hills, called the Hog's Back.   The highest of
them is Leith Hill, from which, on a clear day, ten counties
may be seen.   Which are they?   These hills are chiefly
covered with heather and furze, numbers of adders leaving
their hiding places, on a hot summer's day, to bask in the
sunshine.

There are no mines at present worked in this county;
though, in the time of the Tudors and Plantagenets, the
most famous district for iron was in Surrey, Kent, and
Sussex.†   Now, however, it bears no resemblance to the
black country of Staffordshire!   In one district, "fuller's
earth" is found in greater quantities than in any other part
of England.   This is used for cleaning woollen and other
cloths.   Dorking fowls are the most famous animal produce in Surrey; they are as large as small turkeys, and
of delicate taste.‡   They have five claws on each foot.
How many have birds generally?   In vegetable produce,
besides ordinary grain, grass, &c., Surrey contains hop
plantations; and what is peculiar to this county, fields

---

* Page 254.   † Page 208.   ‡ Compare 148, 165, 175, 249.

and gardens of medicinal plants, such as horehound, marsh mallows, rhubarb, poppies, camomile, peppermint, lavender, rosemary, and damask and red roses. The perfume of these flower farms is smelt for some distance around.*

The manufactories of Surrey are chiefly in London. There is some calico bleaching and printing on the Wandle, and in other parts there are brick-fields, glassworks, and potteries. There is one historical incident connected with this county which makes it, so far as history is concerned, the most important county in all England — that is, the signing of the Magna Charta, either in a meadow at Runnimede, or in a little island in the Thames, close beside it.† To this charter, signed, it is true, by one of the most unworthy kings of England, our dear country owes, through God's blessing, much of its precious freedom. John, for himself and his successors, put his name to the plainest promises, that the sovereign should no more oppress the people, and neither make laws, nor gather taxes, without their consent; and this great charter is to this day "the keystone of English liberty," converting a despotic into a free monarchy.

The west of Surrey is marked by many extensive heaths, which are now in many parts planted with beech trees. Near Chobham, the parish where the excellent Mr Cecil, and his curate, Daniel Wilson, afterwards the good Bishop of Calcutta, laboured, is the site of the Chobham Camp, where many regiments spent the summer of the year 1853, and learned something of the discipline and ways of camp life.

Part of Windsor Forest extends into Surrey, and that a very pretty portion, including Virginia Water, an artificial

* Page 188.　　　　　† Page 267, 291.

lake a mile and a half long.   When the camp was at
Chobham, there was a mock fight, and the engineers of
the army threw, very rapidly, a bridge a hundred and
eight yards long, across this water, over which the soldiers,
horses, and artillery marched.   Below Runnimede, of which
I have already told you, is Anningsley, where lived Mr
Day, who wrote "Sandford and Merton."   He thought
that no horse would continue unruly if it were kindly
treated ; but trying to break in a foal himself, it threw
him and kicked him on the head, so that he died.   Mr
Rarey has, however, since then succeeded in training by
kindness and firmness the most vicious horses.   Further
down the Thames is Chertsey, the village where the poet
Cowley died.*   On a little hill near this village is the
gigantic Crouch Oak, under which, it is said, Wycliffe
preached and Queen Elizabeth dined.   Close to some
beautiful old cedars, the Wey reaches the Thames.   To-
morrow, we will find out many an interesting spot on
this pretty little river.

SURREY.—Part II.

THE Wey rises amid wild and picturesque scenery, amongst
the North Downs.   In the neighbourhood of this river,
Creswick, a famous landscape painter, has often strolled,
and painted the wooded lanes, hills, and farms.   In one
place are the most ancient chestnut trees in England ; in
another are sandy mounds, which interest geologists ; in
another, hollows and commons, of which strange and
dreary legends are related.   The first town is Farnham,
where sail-cloth, oil-cloth, and hemp carpeting are made,
and which is famous for its hops.†   The hop gardens
extend for some distance between the town and the castle.

* Page 287.   † Pages 136, 188, 199, 217.

This castle is a very fine old structure, where the bishops of Winchester live. It was built by a certain bishop, Henry de Blois, the brother of King Stephen. In the garden is a tea-tree, growing in the open air. At Farnham an excellent clergyman, Toplady, was born, who wrote several books, and the beautiful hymn which begins, "Rock of Ages, cleft for me." Here also was born Cobbett, who wrote on politics, that is, on the art of governing the state. Below Farnham, close to the river, are the ruins of Waverley Abbey, from which place Sir Walter Scott took the name for his famous novels. There are strange wild stories about treasures in the ruins, and witches in the caverns; and at Farnham church is shown a huge copper caldron, said to have been borrowed from the white witch in the cave; but not having been returned at the proper time, the witch has never been seen since. Once people believed these stories; but now they only laugh at them. The next town on the Wey is Godalming, a royal hunting seat in Charles II.'s time. On a little branch of the Wey is Shere, close to which is Albury Park. The gardens are very beautiful. Here is a very curious yew hedge, a quarter of a mile long, with bare trunks for eight or ten feet, and then solid heads of foliage, making a continuous umbrella.*

Farther down the Wey is Guildford, the county town of Surrey, where some of the kings of England have occasionally lived. Formerly it was a town famous for its cloth;† and Queen Elizabeth passed a law, ordering every public-house to have the sign of a woolsack. Now it is a famous market town, with an iron foundry, where the celebrated Guildford plough is made,‡ and an ancient castle rising high above the other buildings. Here is Archbishop Abbot's Hospital, and also his tomb; his

* Page 131.   † Pages 189, 237, 256.   ‡ Page 189.

U

brothers were Bishop of Salisbury and Lord Mayor of London; their father, simply a cloth-worker.   In the Valley of Chilworth, amidst very lovely scenery, were probably erected the first gunpowder mills in England.*

Another interesting little town is Woking, where also was once a royal palace.   Here Wolsey was staying with Henry VIII. when he received the news that he was made Cardinal. Yet farther down the Wey is Weybridge; the scenery is flat, but pretty.   In the little Roman Catholic chapel here, Louis Philippe, King of the French, the good queen Marie Amalie, and their two daughters-in-law, are buried.

Descending the Thames, we find Walton, where Bradshaw, one of the chief men in the time of Oliver Cromwell, lived.   Near the pulpit are written these verses, said to have been composed by Queen Elizabeth :

> " Christ was the word and spake it,
>   He took the bread and brake it;
>   And what the word doth make it,
>   That I believe and take it."

Here is preserved the gossip's bridle, intended to be fastened on gossiping women.   It is a thin iron plate, fitting closely round the head and fastening with a padlock; a piece of thin iron projects in front, so as to go into the mouth and hold down the tongue.   Was not that a strange punishment for gossips and tell-tales ? †

Near Walton, is the place where Cæsar is supposed to have crossed the Thames, when, on his second invasion, he pursued the brave British chief, Cassivelaunus. ‡

The Mole next enters the Thames, whither it finds its way from the hills in the north of Sussex.   One curious circumstance about its course is, that at certain places called Swallows, the Mole, in dry seasons, disappears, continues underground, in natural tunnels, among the chalk

---

* Pages 236, 269.   † Page 220.   ‡ Pages 198, 263.

hills, and after a few miles re-appears.* Whether it is called the Mole on this account, I cannot tell; but it seems a very appropriate name. A great many sand-martins, generally a rare kind of bird, are found in the heaths, bordering its early course. These heaths are covered with beautiful wild flowers.† In this part of the county is Reigate, prettily situated on a hill, in former days famous for its castle; now, for its railway station. Beneath the castle, are very large vaults or caverns; but whether used as cellars, hiding-places, or dungeons, must ever remain a mystery.‡ Along the ridge of hills, approaching Reigate, is an ancient track, called the Pilgrims' Way, frequently bordered with yew-trees, said to have been traversed by pilgrims from the west of England to the great shrine of Thomas-à-Becket, at Canterbury. One of these hills, on account of the native boxwood growing on the west side, is called Box Hill.

Near the Mole, on its opposite side, is Dorking. I have already told you of its fowls. In the neighbourhood is Deepdene, a beautiful residence, in which is some very fine sculpture. Two pieces are by Thorwaldsen. He had been studying sculpture earnestly at Rome; but receiving neither notice nor orders, was on the point of leaving that city, heart-sick and discouraged. Then Mr Hope, apparently by accident, entered his studio, saw a design, and ordered it to be executed in marble. It was beautifully done, and the artist soon became very celebrated. Remember this when you are disappointed after trying hard, and try again. Through a rich country and through beautiful parks, with splendid trees, beeches, chestnuts, cedars, and yews, and where the nightingale sings most sweetly, the Mole flows onward towards the Thames. Before it reaches that river, it passes near Claremont, where the good Princess Charlotte, George IV.'s

* Page 46.　　　† Page 7.　　　‡ Page 137.

daughter, died, and all England wept.*   Once the Princess
met a gardener, and, talking to him, discovered he had no
Bible.   She went home, procured a copy, and gave it him,
having written his name on the fly-leaf, with these words :
" From his friend, Charlotte."   Louis Philippe and his
Queen lived here from the time of the French Revolution
in 1848, until their death.   Near the Mole is Esher, where
Cardinal Wolsey was sent when in disgrace with King
Henry.†   Listen to what he might have said—

> " I have ventured,
> Like little wanton boys that swim on bladders,
> This many summers in a sea of glory ;
> But far beyond my depth : my high-blown pride
> At length broke under me ; and now has left me
> Weary, and old with service, to the mercy
> Of a rude stream, that must for ever hide me."

Kingston is the next town of consequence on the
Thames.   It became early of importance, as the lowest
ford on the course of the river.   Many of the Saxon kings
were crowned here ; and in this neighbourhood were fought
the first and last battles between Charles I.'s party, and
that of the Parliament.‡   Kingston is now celebrated chiefly
for its great fair of cattle, sheep, and horses.

A little river here enters the Thames, flowing from the
neighbourhood of Epsom, once very famous for its mineral
waters, which give the name to Epsom salts ; this town is
also noted for horse-races.

Following the Thames, the banks of which as it approaches London become studded with villas, we reach
Ham House and Ham Common.   Here the Cabal ministry
—for which look at Charles II.'s reign in your English
History—held its meetings.   In the library are many

* Page 259.   † Pages 190, 267, 306.   ‡ Pages 45, 124, 137, 158, 256.

curious books, several printed by William Caxton, who first printed the Bible in English.*

Now we reach a town, from the hill above which is one of the richest and most beautiful views in England; I mean Richmond. The silvery Thames, covered with barges and skiffs, gives brightness to the scene already enriched with hills and valleys, woods and fields, English homes and English spires. Richmond used to be called Shene, but its name was changed by Henry VII., whose title had been Earl of Richmond. It was long a royal residence. Here died Edward III., deserted by all; and here died Queen Elizabeth. Very little of the old palace remains; but the park, which is enclosed, is very beautiful; deer sporting on the grass, and blackbirds, thrushes, and nightingales warbling amongst the trees. The ponds in the park are full of fish, and here numbers of heron assemble at one period of the year. At Richmond the poet Thomson lived and was buried.

Leaving Richmond, the Thames passes Kew Gardens, as celebrated for plants as the Zoological Gardens are for animals.† Immense conservatories contain palms of all kinds; those from which cocoa-nuts, dates, vegetable ivory, and sago are gathered. Sago, however, is the pith, not the fruit of the tree. At Kew you also see sugar-canes, from the burning West Indies; cotton-trees from America; poison-trees from Madagascar and Java; bread, mahogany, coffee, cinnamon, chocolate trees; the papyrus, from which paper was formerly made; the gutta-percha plant; the rice-paper plant; the india-rubber, or caoutchouc tree; nutmeg, clove, and ginger-trees; besides curious serpent-gourds; pitcher plants, with their neat little lids; the lace plant, with its leaf veins beautifully interlaced; curious water plants, and the splendid water-lily, called the Vic-

* Pages 39, 42, 279, 291.   † Page 283.

toria Regia; beautiful cacti, and many extraordinarily formed succulent plants; ferns, most lovely and varied; plants whose roots grow in the air; and azalias, rhododendrons, camellias, and nearly every sort of plant which is rare and beautiful. Kew is a pretty old-fashioned village, and adjoining the gardens there is another royal palace.

The Thames winds on, passing Mortlake and Barnes, where, about two hundred years ago, a horrible duel was fought between two noblemen; the wife of one, dressed as a page, holding her husband's horse. A duel is a meeting of two people, who have determined to settle a quarrel by coming coolly together to shoot or stab one another. Once, this was called "*honour;*" but now, I rejoice to say, Englishmen call it, what the Bible shows it to be, "*murder.*" Villas are very numerous, till a little below Putney, where the historian Gibbon was born, and where the great statesman, Pitt, died, we find Wandsworth, a town whose inhabitants are busily engaged dyeing or printing calico, or working in oil-silks. Wandsworth takes its name from the little river Wandle, which we will now track from its source. Near its head is Croydon. This place used to be famous for charcoal-burning, before coke took the place of charcoal; * now it is chiefly famed for basket-carriages and walnuts. The old palace was formerly the residence of the Archbishop of Canterbury, who now lives at Addington, five miles off. Though old, Croydon is a place of rapid modern growth.† Near it is Addiscombe, where cadets used to be prepared for going out to India; those who did best, gaining good appointments in the Engineers or Artillery.‡ The Wandle passes Mitcham, with its fragrant fields of flowers; Merton, with a noisy copper-mill, and silk-printing works; and Wimbledon, with its beautiful park and common, on which are

* Page 194.   † Page 300.   ‡ Page 304.

the remains of ancient camps that remind us of battles, said to have been fought in the times of the Saxons. Here every year the great trial of skill between the volunteer rifle corps takes place, when the best marksmen shoot for prizes.*

Wandsworth, Clapham, and Brixton may all be reckoned suburbs of London. They are thickly peopled, and possess many churches, large orphan institutions, and other charities.

Beyond, there is Dulwich, a college founded by Edward Alleyne, containing a famous gallery of pictures. The master and warden must always be of the founder's name. Near this is Norwood, the once famous resort of gipsies. Now, however, London villas are quickly springing up, and the gipsies are removing, as well as the oak-trees which they regard as sacred.

Enough of Surrey. To-morrow we must cross the Thames into Essex.

ESSEX.

THE county of Essex will bring us to the mouth of the Thames, on its northern shore. It is a large county, resembling, in many ways, Norfolk and Suffolk, though not so level. In the north-west, there are gentle hills and dales ; but in the south-east not only is it very level, but there are such extensive marshes that the country is very unhealthy, especially in the spring and autumn, when the inhabitants suffer much from fever and ague. Otherwise the climate is good, and it has been remarked that less rain falls here than elsewhere in England. As in most of the eastern counties, farming is very good, and Essex is particularly noted for its excellent wheat, peas, beans, and large crops of potatoes.† Hops are also very

* Page 282.   † Pages 148, 174, 185.

much grown, and, what is almost peculiar to the county, carraway, coriander, teasel, and saffron.* Carraway and coriander are plants with white umbrella-shaped flowers, chiefly valuable for their seeds. Teasel, I hope you remember, is useful in combing broad-cloth, whilst saffron, though sometimes used as a medicine, is chiefly employed as a yellow dye. The flower is a kind of purple crocus, blossoming in autumn. The only valuable part is the yellow stigma; this is the tiny three-parted ball, growing on the fine thread in the centre of the flower. Early in the morning, before the flowers expand, they are gathered, the stigmas taken out, dried, and then pressed between sheets of white paper. The saffron harvest lasts for several weeks.

Essex is not particularly famed for cattle or sheep; there are, however, a great number of calves, which are fattened for about three months, and then slaughtered for London. On the coast many fish are caught, and some parts are very famous for oysters. There are not many manufactories, only a few silk mills; but many of the poor are employed in straw-plaiting.

Essex is well watered, and ships can sail a considerable way up its rivers.† There are a number of salt-water creeks, which in several places cut off the land, forming islands similar to what you see in the map of Holland. Foulness and Canvey, at the mouth of the Thames, are the two largest of these. Chalk, lime, flint, gravel, and good clay for brick-making, are found in Essex.

Now let all the eyes be on the map, and let us follow the course of the various rivers. First the Stour, our old Suffolk friend. The only place to note on it, is the seaport of Harwich at its mouth.‡ Sometimes this haven is

---

* Pages 37, 132, 188, 303.   † Pages 162, 262.   ‡ Page 185.

very full of ships, as, when a strong easterly wind blows, it is the only place between the mouth of the Thames and Yarmouth Roads which affords them shelter. There is also a great deal of fishing here, sprats particularly abounding on this coast.* These are chiefly caught during gloomy nights in November and December. They are not only sold very cheap for food, but thousands of tons are every year used by the farmers of the Eastern counties as manure.

Our next river is the Colne, on which stands Halstead, a town where crape and silk are made, and where many women and children plait straw; and farther down is Colchester, the chief town of Essex. It is a very ancient place, supposed to have been the residence of an old British king, many of whose coins have been dug up there.† The castle, which still stands, was probably built in the time of the Normans. It was besieged in the reign of Charles I. After six weeks' hard defence, it was surrounded by the parliamentary army, and the three brave leaders of the defence were tried and shot.‡ In Queen Mary's time, seventeen of God's faithful martyrs were burned in this town.§ There are now several churches, good schools, and the ruins of an old abbey. The oyster fishery is the chief business. A silver oyster is kept to measure the size of the oysters that are permitted to be sold. The beds, or layers, in the river are guarded with great care. Oysters may only be taken in the months that have an "r" in their names. Which months are these? Near Colchester lived, a long time since, a lady called Honeywood, and when she died, at ninety years of age, she had no less than 267 children, grandchildren, great grandchildren, and great great grand-children.

On the river Brain is Braintree, a thriving little town, where people are employed in making silk and crape.

Now let us follow the Chelmer. On it is a little village, Dunmow, noted for a singular custom of giving a flitch of bacon to any married couple, who, after being married for a year and a day, could positively declare that they had never quarrelled, nor once repented of their marriage. The flitch is said to have been claimed only six times since the reign of Henry VI. Since the year 1837, however, the flitch has been given to those who brought up their children without parish relief.

Farther down is Chelmsford, in the neighbourhood of which are hop grounds.* The town is quite an agricultural one, without manufactories; but with well supplied markets and fairs. Large corn mills are built on the banks of the Chelmer. Where the river joins the Blackwater is Maldon, an old Roman station, where there are now salt-works, a fishery, and a good deal of commerce. This is one of the places where the younger, instead of the elder son succeeds to the father's property. In this neighbourhood the Danes made many ravages. Near Chelmsford is Danebury, or Danesbury Hill, and there is a plant growing there, which still goes by the name of Dane's-blood.

Now, looking quite to the north-west of the county, on the side of a hill, we shall find Saffron Walden, which takes its name from the saffron of which I have already told you. It has a very beautifully finished church. Near it is Audley Park. The house was built by the High Treasurer to James I. James wished to purchase it; but when he heard that the building had cost £190,000, he said, "It is too much for a king, but it may do for a Lord High Treasurer."†

* Pages 136, 199, 217, 304.   † Pages 267, 292.

On the banks of the Lea is Waltham Abbey, where King Harold founded a college, and where he and his two brothers were buried, by the arrangement of their distressed mother Gitta.* The abbey was begun in Henry II.'s time; its remains now form a portion of the parish church. Farther down the Lea is Walthamstow. This is close to the borders of Epping Forest, formerly a royal hunting ground, now one of the most celebrated places in the neighbourhood of London for pic-nics. Many a van load of people go there on a summer morning, and enjoy under the green-wood, may be, the only holiday that they have for all the year round. The south-west corner of Essex, between the Lea and the Thames, may be said to form part of the outskirts of mighty London. Here, on the north side of the Thames are the new Victoria Docks. The first river the Thames receives from Essex is the Roding, which gives its name to several villages on its banks. In the village of Greenstead is a very ancient wooden church, nearly 1000 years old, supposed to have been built as a resting-place for the body of the Saxon Edmund, who was buried at Bury St Edmunds.† The Roding passes between Epping and Hainault Forests, where Henry III. gave the citizens of London leave to hunt. In former days, the Lord Mayor and Aldermen of London, with a great many citizens, used, on Easter Monday, to ride out here, and hunt a beautiful stag, which, with its long antlers, bounded through the forest, till, perhaps, caught in a thicket, the hounds sprang on it, and it was killed. Farther down the Roding is Wanstead, where a number of dear little orphans are educated, and thus they know the truth of the orphan's verse, "When my father and mother forsake me, then the Lord will take me up."

* Page 45.   † Page 186.

Nearer the Thames is Barking, famous for its fishing smacks. On the Bourne, the next stream that enters the Thames is Romford, a very old place, which has possessed a market for more than 600 years. Near it is an old palace of the Saxon kings, Havering, whence there is a fine view, which embraces five counties. Which are they?

The Essex bank of the Thames is very marshy. Once it was covered with water, but was rescued by immense embankments. About fifty years ago there was a great breach made by a very high tide, covering 1000 acres of the cultivated land.*

The next little creek that enters the Thames is the filthiest in the county; for much of the London drainage enters it, and when the tide is high, it is covered with barges for manure, and when low, it is a "mere muddy sewer." Farther on is Purfleet, where Queen Elizabeth reviewed her troops when the Spanish Armada was preparing to descend on England. She told them that though she had the body of a weak and feeble woman, she had the heart and stomach of a king. When she saw her few ships, it is said she exclaimed, "Oh! my poor fleet!" and so the town was called Purfleet. You know how God preserved England from the proud Armada, scattering it by the storms and winds of heaven. In this neighbourhood are limestone rocks, full, as usual, of caverns.† It is said the Britons used them for granaries, and also, that they were hiding-places from the fierce Northmen's fury, and so are called Dane's Holes. At the bottom of one of the limestone pits a chapel is now built. Farther on is Tilbury fort, built in the reign of Charles II. It is very strong, and intended to defend London, in time of invasion, from any enemies' ships ascending the Thames. Its

* Pages 148, 172.   † Pages 35, 46, 115, 127, 235.

guns have hitherto only fired salutes; let us pray God to give us such continued peace, that the great strength of Tilbury Fort may never be tried by the foes of dear old England.

To-morrow we shall once more cross the Thames, and visit Kent, which has been called the Garden of England.

KENT.—Part I.

KENT is a county in England, to which all these adjectives may be prefixed—maritime, agricultural, undulating, picturesque, fertile, important, historical.   Look at it on the map ; see its position, rivers, sea-shore, neighbouring counties.   It has been divided into three distinct parts, which I think you will remember.   First, health without wealth; this is the hilly district of the North Downs.*   Second, wealth without health ; these are the rich but sickly pastures of Romney Marsh, and those in the north of the county, between the Medway and the Swale.†   Third, health and wealth together ; and this is the character of all the rest of the county.   Kent is very famous for its cherry trees and its hops.   The former look beautiful in spring, with their snowy blossoms, and the latter in autumn, with their bright green foliage.   In James I.'s time, it was a favourite amusement to try who could eat the most cherries, and a tombstone in Plumstead churchyard has a curious inscription, in memory of a child who died from eating too much of this fruit.

The scene of hop-picking is very curious.   All kinds of people engage in it.   Thousands of the poor inhabitants of St Giles, and other unhealthy parts of London,‡ find their way into Kent, earning good wages and breathing fresh country air.   They sleep. at night in huts or stables, at

* Pages 254, 302.   † Pages 54, 150, 311.   ‡ Page 289.

the side of the road, or in little tents, and there they
light their fires and cook their food. Besides cherries and
hops, all kinds of fruit are grown; canary, radish, and
spinach seed raised; remarkably fine wheat, and other
kinds of corn, cultivated. Kent is also famous for
meadows and pastures, which will lead you to expect
that the cattle and sheep are good too.* So they are,
especially one breed of sheep, the Romney Marsh, which
has long combing wool. There is also plenty of poultry
and game. The pheasants in Kent are the largest and
best in England. Excepting the large military works, the
only manufacture for which Kent is famous is paper. The
paper mills in this county are generally on the banks of
rivers, worked by water, and look picturesque.† All
kinds of paper are made; but the writing paper is
especially good.

The history of Kent is very interesting; for, being the
county that lies nearest to the Continent, the various invaders and visitors of England have usually landed here,
from the time of Julius Cæsar onward. William the Conqueror landed in Sussex, but when he entered Kent from
Sussex, the inhabitants are said to have met him in a very
formidable manner, looking like a moving forest, for they
all carried immense boughs of trees. They compelled William to grant them the continuance of several privileges,
such as that of selling their lands when they liked, without
obtaining the permission of their lords, and of dividing them
equally among their children, instead of giving all to
the first-born.‡ This custom is called gavel-kind. The
hills in Kent are principally chalk. They extend in a
belt to the sea-shore, and there form the famous white
cliffs of Dover, which extend all the way from Folkestone to Walmer. These originated the name of Albion

* Pages 23, 141, 146, 148, 150.   † Pages 165, 262, 265.   ‡ Page 314.

for our dear Old England.* It is supposed that long ago
England was connected with the mainland of Europe by
an isthmus, between Romney Marsh and Boulogne, which
is now the shallowest part of the Channel. Had this continued, Great Britain would never have been our island
home, but only a peninsula adjoining France. God had,
however, other things in store for us. He has shown that
His intention was that England should be the land of
freedom, the land of the Bible, the land of Christian missions; and for this blessed purpose, I believe He separated us from other countries, and made the deep blue
waters of the sea to encircle us. I want all English children to remember this; for on Englishmen a special duty
lies—to make evident by their high moral character and
earnest missionary effort, that national freedom and the
Christian religion are the blessed gifts from Heaven which
exalt a nation.

There have been many changes on the coast of Kent.
There are old traditions that the Goodwin Sands, dangerous sand-banks off the coast, were once part of the mainland, the property of the Earl Goodwin, who was the father
of King Harold, and that the sea came in upon it, and
" buried towns and men very many, and oxen and sheep
innumerable." If this be true, the sea has made some
amends. Rye, once overflowed, is now two miles inland;
Dover is probably built on the ground over which Cæsar
sailed; and the passage between the Isle of Thanet and
Kent, through which the Roman ships passed, consists
now of fruitful fields and luxuriant meadows.†

Let us now look on the map, and trace the rivers of
Kent, following the Thames for the last time, and those
few lower branches that it receives from this county.

The first tiny rivulet that flows into it from Kent is the

* Pages 3, 36.   † Pages 36, 176.

Ravensbourne. One of its sources is close below some curious Roman remains of a large military station. It passes Hayes, where Lord Chatham died, and his famous son, William Pitt, was born.* Afterwards, it flows past Bromley, where there is a house and annuity provided for forty widows of clergymen. Not far distant, on a pretty brook, is Beckenham, with its pointed white spire rising above the old clipped yews. Captain Hedley Vicars, the brave soldier, who, whilst he served his Queen, likewise served his God, often stayed here; and in the church a tablet bears his name. In this parish have been many meetings with the navvies, when English hearts have been warmed, and English hands strengthened, in the warfare we all must maintain against sin and Satan. In Beckenham churchyard there was buried a queen of the gipsies, a hundred and nine years of age.† The next interesting place is Sydenham, which has become so famous for its wonderful Crystal Place, built by Sir J. Paxton, of whom we heard at Chatsworth.‡ The building, covered with its crystal roof, extends for nearly three-quarters of a mile. If the iron pillars used were placed in a straight line, they would extend more than sixteen miles. A visit to the Crystal Palace seems like one to fairyland, did such a land exist. The beauty of the plants, the glittering of the fountains, the lovely works of art, the variety of designs, the distant places to which one seems transported, and the remote ages, the forms of which appear around you,—all combine to make one inquire where one really is. It is difficult to say which is the most beautiful portion of the palace and its gardens. In one part, you seem to wander among the halls of the gorgeous Moorish palace, the Alhambra, in Spain; in another, you pass through rooms modelled after Roman dwelling-houses, according to the remains of Pompeii;

* Page 310.   † Pages 194, 281, 311.   ‡ Pages 131, 282.

here you see mammoth figures from Egypt, and imitations of Nineveh sculptures, whilst there is a magnificent tent from India. In one part are grouped representations of people, animals, and plants, from different parts of the world, such as Hindoos, elephants, tigers, and palm-trees from the East; and Red Indians, Esquimaux, polar bears and snow from the North. In the galleries there is quite a bazaar, all kinds of pretty things being exposed for sale. There are often concerts, flower-shows, and various kinds of exhibitions. At one time a terrific wind blew down part of the building, and more recently a large portion of it was consumed by fire. The fountains in the gardens far surpass any others in England. The water can be thrown up two hundred and fifty feet. When the sun shines, the *jets d'eau* are like a shower of precious stones, with sometimes bright rainbows on their rising spray. Near a pond or lake in the gardens are the figures of strange monster animals, such as those whose skeletons were found—in what part of Yorkshire?—or are now exhibited in what great museum?*

Now, leaving this fairy land, we must return again to the little Ravensbourne, which at Lewisham, a long straggling town, receives the Lee. Not far from this is Eltham, an old royal palace, where Edward III. grandly entertained his prisoner, John of France; where other kings feasted daintily; and where Queen Elizabeth, when a baby, was often sent for change of air.† The Ravensbourne joins the Thames at Deptford. This is one of our naval dockyards, where, since the time of Henry VIII., ships have been built or repaired. Peter the Great of Russia stayed here when he visited England, himself working as a shipwright. He lived at the house of a very worthy gentleman, John Evelyn, who has given us very interesting accounts of the doings and manners of the time of Charles II.‡

* Pages 58, 291. † Pages 241, 264. ‡ Page 276.

Deptford is also noted as a victualling place for the navy;
that is, it furnishes stores of meat for the ships' crews. It is
very curious to see how rapidly the biscuit-making goes on.
Here Queen Elizabeth visited the ships in which Admiral
Drake had completed his first voyage round the world, and
knighted the bold sailor.*   Below Deptford, is the *Dread-
nought*, an old ship engaged at Trafalgar, but which is
now used as a hospital.   The next town is Greenwich,

Greenwich Hospital.

with its fine palace, now changed into a hospital for aged
seamen of the royal navy.†   At this palace, Henry VIII.,
Queen Mary, and Queen Elizabeth were born; and here,
good King Edward VI. died.   Queen Mary, the wife of
William III., proposed that it should be converted into
a hospital; and great additions were made for this purpose, under the direction of Sir Christopher Wren.‡   It is

* Pages 40, 231.   † Page 280.   ‡ Page 293.

a larger building than any of Queen Victoria's palaces, except Windsor. There are between 2000 and 3000 pensioners. Each man who lives in the hospital has what he terms his cabin; that is, a little partition to himself, in a very long dormitory. Many little pictures are hung on its walls, and by the side of each .bed is a shelf for books. There is a beautiful terrace fronting the river, on which the old pensioners can walk, and see the ships passing and repassing. Yet it is said that they are grumblers; but, certainly, not all. It seems a pleasant home for the old weather-beaten sailor, and one from which, if he could trust his Saviour, he might peacefully look out for the summons to take him across that sea, whence he shall not return. Behind the hospital is the park, whence there is a beautiful view over London, and up the Thames. Here Greenwich Fair used to be held during Whitsun-week. It was attended by thousands of Londoners. In this park is the Royal Observatory, a very important place, which has been called the astronomical capital of the kingdom.* It is not a place for making discoveries in the heavens so much as for noting down the exact position of the sun, moon, and planets, as they reach their highest point in the sky. From these observations is formed the "Nautical Almanack," which greatly assists seamen to find how far they are to the east or west of Greenwich; for the imaginary line which passes through Greenwich, reaching upwards to the north, and downwards to the south pole, is called by Englishmen the first meridian. Here, too, the direction of the wind, the weight, the temperature of the air, and the quantity of rain, are all exactly measured. As ship captains go down the rivers, they set their timepieces, called chronometers, by Greenwich time, which is made known by the sliding, every day at one o'clock, of a

* Pages 246, 253.

large ball down the mast which is at the top of the Observatory.   If the captains have good chronometers, they will
find them right on returning from their voyage.   At Greenwich, there is an excellent naval school, where boys are
especially taught nautical science, that is, how to manage
their ships.   The Painted Hall at Greenwich is very fine.
The artist was nineteen years at work ; in order to complete the ceilings, he was obliged to paint week after week,
lying on his back.

In the Thames, off the town, white-bait is caught between the months of April and August.   It is a very de-
licious fish ; and just before Parliament closes, the Queen's
ministers go down to Greenwich, to eat the white-bait
dinner.

To-morrow we must visit other places nearly as important as Greenwich, on and near the Thames.

KENT.—PART II.

On some high ground near Greenwich, is Blackheath, distinguished for its pleasant bracing air.   Here it was that
Wat Tyler encamped with 100,000 followers, and that
Charles II. met the ranks of that army which had restored
to him his crown.   Many pretty houses are built in this
neighbourhood, and it is famed for its schools.   According
to an old agreement, the master of the grammar-school may
be displaced if he wears long, curled, or ruffian-like hair.

The next town of consequence on the Thames is Woolwich, possessing a Royal Dockyard, an Arsenal, Military
Repository, and a Royal Military Academy.*   The dockyard is reckoned the oldest in England.   In Henry VII.'s
reign, the *Great Harry* was built here, then the largest
ship that England possessed.   Here blocks of wood are

* Pages 257, 310.

sawn by steam, and cold iron cut asunder. Nasmyth's hammer is here employed. Look back to Birmingham, the birth-place of this mighty engine.* Woolwich Dockyard is the chief place for making the great iron steamships for the navy. Here gangs of prisoners may be seen working hard in chains. How different their forced labour to the free cheerful exertion of the honest smith, taking to his happy home the earnings of his work! It is God's righteous law, that has ever linked sin and sorrow together.

The arsenal is a very large establishment for manufacturing great guns, shells, and rockets, and everything by which gunpowder can destroy human life.† In the present state of the world these things are necessary; and though we long for the day, when none shall hurt nor destroy in all the earth, we hope that English guns may be so good, and English cannon so celebrated, that it may be a means of preventing other nations from declaring war against us. Do you know what we mean, when we say, "Prevention is better than cure"? The Repository is a large piece of ground given up to the exercise of the artillery corps—the soldiers who fire cannons. Through it canals are cut, across which the engineers exercise themselves in throwing pontoons—a sort of portable bridge; and they draw out cannons, which have been sunk on purpose.‡ The artillery are taught to move and serve the large guns. Here is the tent in which George IV., as Prince Regent, gave a grand banquet to the sovereigns of Russia, Austria, and Prussia, after Napoleon's downfall, in 1814. In it are strange old guns, and modern ones taken in battle. Here is also the funeral car, which conveyed Napoleon Bonaparte's body to his grave at St Helena; and, under

* Page 118. † Page 21. ‡ Page 304.

a glass case, the ashes of 56,000,000 of £1 bank-notes; an emblem, it is said, of the results of the expenditure on war.

The Royal Military Academy is for instructing the cadets, who are to become artillery and engineer officers. They must study a great deal before they know how to build fortresses for defence, or to cast up batteries for offence.

Farther down the river is Erith, where there are large public gardens. All along the Thames, on each side, are strong embankments, which are necessary, as the level of the land is lower than that of the water.* We cannot tell when these were made, probably in the time of the Romans, but whenever done, they were a great and noble work.

Below Erith, we reach the mouth of the Darent. The little river Cray, which flows into it, gives its name to many pretty villages on its banks, and turns the wheels of many paper-mills. In this neighbourhood are curious chalk caves, such as those I mentioned in Essex.† On a breezy common near the Cray, is Chiselhurst, where the ex-Emperor Napoleon III. resides.

> "The still Darent, in whose waters clear,
>   Ten thousand fishes play, and deck his pleasant stream,"

rises near Westerham, the birth-place of Frith, a martyr and reformer, and friend of Tyndale, who translated the Bible.‡ It is also the birth-place of General Wolfe, who died before the walls of Quebec as the cry of victory was shouted in his ear. Not far distant is Sevenoaks, which takes its name from Sir William Sevenoaks, Lord Mayor of London, and he is said to have received his name from being discovered a poor, helpless, deserted baby in the hollow of an oak tree. He became very industrious and good, grew rich, gave his money in charity, and founded schools and alms-houses at the place where he had lived. Near Sevenoaks is a beautiful baronial hall, Knole. Here

* Pages 148, 316.   † Page 316.   ‡ Pages 27, 39, 42, 268.

several rooms are still furnished as they were in the time of Elizabeth, of James, and of Charles I.* There is a bedroom furnished for King James I. The bedstead, chairs, and stools are covered with gold and silver tissue; and the tables, mirror-frames, and other ornaments are of silver. The park is very beautiful, and Lady Amherst, to whom it belongs, kindly lets people walk in it whenever they like. The only town of consequence on the Darent, is Dartford, where there are large paper and powder-mills. The paper-mills have been established since the reign of Queen Elizabeth.† Here began the insurrection of Wat Tyler the blacksmith, of which you read in English history. It happened in the reign of Richard II.

Following the Thames, we reach Greenhithe, where the chief business is making chalk into lime, and shipping it for London. From this little town, Sir John Franklin sailed on his last voyage to the polar regions, whence, you know, he never returned.‡ The next important town is Gravesend, where, in former days, the Lord Mayor used to receive all important strangers approaching London by water. Vessels leaving England stop here to complete their cargoes, or take up a pilot; and those arriving from foreign countries, deliver up their papers and take on board the officers, who fix the amount of duty. Many Londoners come here for bathing, as the Thames, which at this place is more than half a mile wide, contains a great mixture of salt water. Opposite Gravesend is Tilbury Fort, of which I told you in Essex. A little inland is Swanscombe, where the men of Kent are said to have met William the Conqueror, with their green boughs. Southend is the next town, with the longest pier in England, a mile and a quarter in length. Near it is the Nore Sand, on which is

* Page 130.　　　† Page 265.　　　‡ Pages 150, 289.

moored the well-known " light vessel," that guides every vessel sailing by night, in and out of the great river.* Here we reach the mouth of the Medway, which we must now try to follow to its source. The Medway has been called the Bride of the Thames. It rises in Sussex, and enters Kent, receiving a little streamlet from the hills where stand Tunbridge Wells. In this range of hills a great deal of ironstone is found. This has given to the springs that rise in the valley a taste of steel, and these are the iron-waters which have so long caused people to resort to Tunbridge Wells. In the time of Charles I. and II., and in that of Queen Anne, it was frequently visited by the royal family. The walks are numerous and very pleasant. On the wild commons, many mountain plants are found; one, a rare kind of fern, being almost confined to this neighbourhood. On these hills are curious rocks, such as the "Toad Rock," and the " Chiding Stone," which, it is said, was used as a sort of judgment-seat. A very pretty kind of inlaid woodwork called Tunbridge ware is made here. The woods chiefly used are cherry, plum, holly and sycamore.

The Medway is now joined by a small river, the Eden, from the west. On it stands the remains of Hever Castle, once the property of Anne Boleyn's father. Here she was probably born and brought up. Here Henry often visited her, and wrote her letters. The roads were very bad, and it is said, that when he stuck fast in the mud he blew a horn, upon which the castle-servants, holding torches, came to his assistance. Poor Anne Boleyn! Her life and happiness were both sacrificed to that wicked king. High life, and virtues, and happiness do not always go together.† At Hever Castle Anne of Cleves also lived and died.

* Page 185.   † Pages 161, 308.

The next place of interest, past which the Medway flows, is Penshurst. Here lived, in the days of Queen Elizabeth, the accomplished scholar and good man, Sir Philip Sidney. He was beloved by all. One nobleman dying desired no other epitaph on his tomb but this, "The friend of Sir Philip Sidney;" and Queen Elizabeth would not let him go in her expedition against the Spaniards, lest, as she said, "she should lose the jewel of her dominions." The story of his death is very interesting. He was wounded at a battle in Holland, and, thirsty from the quantity of blood he had lost, he asked for water. As he put the bottle to his mouth, he observed the anxious and ghastly look of a poor dying soldier. He would not drink it then, but gave it to the poor man, saying, "Thy necessity is yet greater than mine." The first time there was a public mourning in England was on the death of this brave, good, and learned man.* An oak is shown at Penshurst, said to have been planted on the day of his birth, in the year 1544 A.D. Algernon Sidney also lived here. He was a virtuous and noble-minded Englishman, unjustly accused of sharing in a plot in Charles II.'s reign, and, without any proof of guilt, beheaded. The furniture of Penshurst is very curious and old. One drawing-room, called Queen Elizabeth's, was furnished by her majesty, the embroidery being, it is said, the work of the queen and her maidens.

Farther down on the Medway is Tunbridge, where are the remains of an old Norman castle. Here is a grammar school, where eleven boys may each gain a hundred pounds per annum to assist them at college.† A great deal of Tunbridge ware is made in this town, and there is also a manufactory of gunpowder. The Medway runs hence through a district so beautiful, so rich in meadows,

* Pages 259, 308.   † Page 162.

corn-fields, hop-gardens, and orchards, that it is called "the garden of Eden;" and perhaps for fertility it is the finest piece of land in England.* Formerly, this part of Kent was much wooded; and even in Queen Elizabeth's time, wild swine and other animals were found in it. We next meet Maidstone, a pleasant town, and the principal one in West Kent. There are curious old houses in the town, and the remains of the palace where the Archbishops of Canterbury formerly dwelt. Maidstone is a great place for trade in hops, apples, cherries, and other produce of this fertile district. Near Maidstone is Penenden Heath, where all the great county meetings have been held since the time of the Saxons.

With a story about an old castle, Allington, which stands a little below Maidstone, and an account of Kit's Coty house, I must finish this chapter.

At Allington there lived Sir Henry Wyatt, the gentleman saved by a cat in the Tower.† His boy, Sir Thomas, afterwards a poet, made playfellows of a lion's whelp and an Irish greyhound. They used to wait for him at the hall door, and leap, and roar, and bark for joy when he returned. As the lion grew older, he grew dangerous, and at length he ran roaring at his master, flying fiercely at his bosom. The faithful greyhound rescued the boy, by leaping on the lion's back and pulling him down. Then young Wyatt very coolly drew out his knife, and killed the lion on the spot.

Kit's Coty house, an ancient British building, is a small room composed of four large stones, three of them forming the sides, and the fourth the roof, leaving the front open, built very much as a little child would build a house with bricks. Not far distant is a large group of stones, called

* Pages 99, 205, 221, 254.   † Page 298.

the Countless Stones; and for many miles others may be traced, which has led people to think that this was a great burial-place of the Britons.* They died in heathen darkness, having no hope. How happy should we be, who have the Bible to teach us of the resurrection of the body and of the life everlasting.

KENT.—PART III.

IN former days, the banks of the Medway must have been thickly studded with Roman villas. I must, however, leave both ancient and modern villas, and only tell you of Cobham Castle, a few miles west of it. This, for many ages, belonged to the Lords Cobham, one of whom was the famous Sir John Oldcastle, the follower of Wycliffe, who was very barbarously put to death in Henry V.'s reign.† There is now at Cobham a beautiful collection of pictures, and in the park splendid giant trees. One is a chestnut, nearly eleven yards round, and called the four sisters, because it divides into four great arms.‡

On the Medway is Rochester, an ancient town, where there is a cathedral, with a very old crypt, probably built in the time of the Saxons. There is also a fine old ruined castle, with walls of great thickness, very necessary in olden days, when they had to stand many a siege. Now such castles are no longer needed, for we live in happier times; and instead of cannon on the walls, we find the pretty little pink and other wild flowers growing abundantly.§ The chief trade of Rochester is in oysters, and excepting ship-building, there are no manufactures. In this neighbourhood is Gadshill, where, in a brick house under spreading cedars, lived and died Charles Dickens, the noted writer. Adjoining Rochester is Chatham, quite a naval and

* Page 65.
† Pages 144, 300.
‡ Pages 208, 259, 304.
§ Page 10.

military town, not nearly so ancient, but more populous than its neighbour. The Medway is here so deep that the largest ships can ascend it, and thus Chatham was thought a fit place for a naval dockyard.* Very large ships are built here; the machinery for making them being very good. There is a rope-house, 1100 feet long, for twisting the enormous cables, and a smith's shop, with forty forges, for making immense anchors. In the reign of Charles II., the Dutch, with whom we were then at war, sailed up the Medway, and burnt several English ships. If you were to see the strength of the fortifications here, you would think him a bold man who would venture to attempt such a thing in Queen Victoria's reign. There are many regiments quartered at Chatham, and military hospitals, which our Queen and her young sons and daughters visited, when the brave soldiers lay there who had been wounded in the Crimea.

After leaving Chatham, the Medway soon enters marshy land, abounding in wild geese. The river becomes choked with mud, and instead of a broad expanse, there are little channels, forming a "wilderness of islands," of little use, as a flood or high tide almost covers them.† Soon it is joined by a little strait, the river Swale, which separates the Isle of Sheppey from the mainland. At Sheerness, where 10,000 Saxons were baptized the Christmas day after Ethelbert's conversion, the Swale joins the Thames.‡

Sheppey, or the Isle of Sheep, is being rapidly destroyed, the cliffs continually crumbling away. Anciently it must have been a land of spicy breezes, for amongst its fossils, quantities of palm-like and other tropical plants have been discovered, and the remains of crabs, turtles, sharks, and animals of the crocodile species.§ Here are found many

---

* Pages 321, 324.
‡ Page 54.
+ Page 11.
§ Pages 53, 54, 235.

pyrites, a stone whence copperas is obtained, used in making ink and black dye. Sheerness is the most important town in the island, being another great naval station. Because the ground is so swampy, the buildings are all on piles; 100,000, it is said, have been driven into the ground. Formerly fresh water could not be procured; but lately wells, 500 feet deep, have been sunk. In order to do this, men bored through a subterranean forest, burning its wood. What strange discoveries are made under ground!

Adjoining the Swale is the marshy district of wealth without health, where ague and fever prevail. Here is Sittingbourne, where Henry V. had a grand dinner, costing 9s. 9d., and the town of Milton, where the best oysters in England are found. The largest town is Faversham, in the abbey church of which King Stephen is buried. Here James II. was brought after the fishermen had discovered him, when he sought to escape from Sheerness. He was very frightened, and resolved to punish their rough handling of him should he ever be king again. Faversham is now most famed for gunpowder and oysters. *

Farther along the coast is Herne Bay, a bathing-place, and near it the little village of Herne, of which good Bishop Ridley was vicar.† Farther on, are the ruins of Reculver, once a strong Roman fortress. The sea, which is here gaining on the land, has washed away its north walls; but portions of the others are still standing. There are also the west towers of the old church, still a landmark to sailors, who, in former years, lowered their top-sails as they passed.‡ Here Ethelbert lived, when he gave up his own palace at Canterbury to the missionary, Augustine. A little east of this is Pudding-pan-rock, whence the oyster fishers often drag pieces of

* Page 313. † Pages 9, 243. ‡ Page 188.

ancient pottery, whether from a wrecked Roman vessel or an old pottery, which the waves have covered, we cannot tell.

The north-east corner of Kent is called the Isle of Thanet, though no longer an island. The largest towns here are Margate and Ramsgate, and its most famous cape is the North Foreland, with a lighthouse. Off this was fought, in 1666, a great sea-fight between the English and Dutch. The English were beaten; but they fought so well, that the Dutch admiral said, "They may be killed, but they will not be conquered."

Margate may also be called a sea-bathing suburb of London; about 100,000 visitors, principally tradespeople, going there during the season. Here is a sea-bathing infirmary, so that the sick poor may gain benefit from the sea-side. Ramsgate is another large watering-place, with good houses, having a beautiful sea-view, and two stone piers. An enormous quantity of eggs is landed here from France every year. A very pleasant and quiet bathing-place in Thanet is Broadstairs. South of Ramsgate is Pegwell Bay, said to be the spot where Hengist and Horsa disembarked when invited by the British king, and afterwards where Augustine landed, when sent by Gregory on his mission to convert the Anglo-Saxons.*

The Stour forms the southern boundary of Thanet. We will follow it from its source, and find some interesting places along its banks. It rises on the south side of the chalk hills, health without wealth, and at first flows north-east. The first town it passes is Ashford, said to be the birth-place of the Kentish man John Cade, who raised an insurrection in the reign of Henry VI.† A little to the east of this, in a village churchyard, stands a yew tree, thought

* Pages 10, 57, 200.   † Page 265.

to be three thousand years old ; so perhaps it grew in the time that Gideon, or Samson, or Ruth lived.* Farther down the Stour is Wye, with a grammar-school, held in a very ancient college.

Some miles below this is Canterbury, one of the most interesting cities of Dear Old England. Here it was that after the Anglo-Saxons had possessed the land, Christianity again took root in Britain, and spread rapidly over the whole island. A church in this city, called St Martin's, is supposed to have been the first English Christian church, that is, the first amongst the Saxons ; for amongst the ancient Britons, there had no doubt been many.† Indeed, this church is itself thought to have been built by Roman Christians, and used as a house of prayer by Ethelbert's Christian wife, before Augustine's arrival. Here Ethelbert, King of Kent, was baptized. One looks on the spot with peculiar interest, as one remembers the importance to the rest of the world of English Christianity. From England it has gone forth to North America, and now the English and Americans are together carrying it, I trust, to all parts of the earth. St Martin's church is like the spot where the acorn is planted that becomes afterwards a great oak, or like the rock whence the water issues that afterwards swells into a mighty river. Where an ancient abbey stood is now a college for missionaries, called St Augustine's, which, I hope, may send far and wide many faithful messengers of Christ's gospel.‡ Augustine was not, however, like the early apostolic missionaries. His manner was very haughty. Do you remember the meeting with the British bishops under the oak-tree, in Worcestershire? Much also of his teaching is not according to the Bible; for already many Romish errors

* Pages 157, 305. † Page 154. ‡ Page 105.

were creeping into the Christian Church. I must now tell you of Canterbury Cathedral, a very beautiful building, and famous during the history of many centuries. It is the burial-place of Edward the Black Prince, of Henry IV. and his queen, of all the archbishops down to the Reformation, and of several persons called saints by the Church of Rome. Here the proud Thomas-à-Becket was barbarously murdered by four of Henry II.'s knights; and here at his shrine, Henry II. wrapped in a sheet, barefooted and carrying a taper, did penance; here, too, the king was scourged, receiving five strokes from each bishop or abbot, and three from each of the eighty monks. For very many years this shrine or altar was one of the most revered in Europe, and the steps leading up to its chapel have been worn away by the treading of pilgrims' feet. In several parts of Kent are remains of the road called the Pilgrims' Way.* The shrine was covered with jewels presented by kings and great people. Edward I. offered there the golden crown of Scotland. Henry VIII. of England, and Charles V. of Germany knelt together before it; yet this was the Henry that afterwards despoiled Becket, and took for himself all the jewels. The pilgrims used devoutly to bow before or kiss not only the bones of Becket, Dunstan, and other supposed saints, but a bit of stick called Aaron's rod, and some clay, out of which, the monks told them, Adam was made. In St Dunstan's church, in Canterbury, is the burial-place of the Ropers; and here was found, in the coffin of his loving daughter, Margaret Roper, the head of Sir Thomas More, which she had preserved in an oak chest that it might be buried beside her.†

Outside the walls of Canterbury is the Martyrs' Field; and here, as at Oxford, Smithfield, Gloucester, and Col-

* Page 307.   † Pages 246, 287.

chester, were burned, in Queen Mary's reign, those who, for Christ's sake, counted not their lives dear to them. With thoughts of this hallowed spot, sacred with the blood of the martyrs, we will close to-day's chapter.*

KENT.—PART IV.

LOOK on the map for the name of the strait separating Kent from France. I told you about the Goodwin Sands, eight miles long and six broad. Between them and the shore lie the Downs, very safe roads for ships to anchor. The sands and the shore shelter them from the north, east, and west; so only a southerly gale can endanger them.† Along the coast are three capes, the North and South Forelands and Dungeness; the two former are great chalky cliffs, and the latter is a low tongue of land, where the yellow poppy grows, and where the guillemot lays its single egg, amongst swamps, shingles, and sands. These capes have all lighthouses. The shingle round Dungeness increases rapidly. Old people who are living can remember when the sea was a mile farther inland than it is now.‡

The ports of the south-eastern shore of England have, since the time of the Romans, been under an appointed governor, who, from the reign of William I., has been called the Warden of the Cinque (or five) Ports. These ports were originally Sandwich, Dover, Hythe, Romney, Hastings, to which, in Henry III.'s time, Winchelsea, Rye, and Seaford were added. There were also many smaller ones, called Subs. As I tell you of them, you will see what changes have taken place on the coast since those days. These Cinque Ports were to furnish fifty-seven ships when the king required them; and the freemen had in return many privileges, such as not being obliged to

* Pages 190, 212, 243, 294, 313. † Page 184. ‡ Pages 36, 176.

Y

serve as soldiers, ranking as barons, holding the canopy at the coronation, sitting at the king's right hand. Sandwich, the most northern, is now distant two miles from the sea. It used to be a frequent landing-place, even for kings; but about three hundred years ago, the harbour began to fill with sand. Many French and Flemish Protestants settled here in Queen Elizabeth's time, and they cultivated the first market gardens ever seen in England.* Sandwich is still noted for its celery.

Near this, on the Stour, is Richborough, a famous Roman station.† It was not a large walled city, like London, but a strong military fortress. Here the Romans generally landed when they crossed from Gaul, and here they used to feast on oysters, which they reckoned most delicate. Many Roman remains have been found here, amongst others, not fewer than one hundred thousand coins.

Farther south, the sea is gaining on Sandown Castle, built in Henry VIII.'s reign, to defend our shores. Beyond this is Deal, with a castle built at the same time. Deal is famous for its boat-building; and the hardy pilots and fishermen of the town are noted for their brave and successful attempts to save the lives of those shipwrecked on the Goodwin Sands. ‡ Here lived, about one hundred years ago, a very learned lady, Mrs Carter, who translated a Greek work, and understood ten languages; but she could make a pudding as well as translate, and embroider a handkerchief as well as compose a poem. I would advise all little girls to know something of sewing and cooking, as well as of languages, music, and drawing. Very near Deal stands Walmer Castle, where the Warden of the Cinque Ports lives. The great Duke of Wellington held this office, and, whilst residing at Walmer, he died,

* Page 175.   † Pages 19, 69, 187, 219, 333.   ‡ Pages 6, 12, 22.

deeply mourned for by every true Briton.* Here there grow two young trees from shoots taken from a weeping willow which shadowed Napoleon's grave at St Helena.

The next town along the coast is Dover, from which the distance to Calais in France is only twenty-one miles.† The town is built in a hollow caused by the outlet of the Dore between chalky cliffs. The white cliffs from Deal to Dover were those that, when Julius Cæsar appeared, he

Dover Castle.

saw covered with fierce and warlike Britons. The castle is a very large and strong fortress, and contains the remains of a lighthouse built by the Romans, of a church built by the Saxons, and of walls and towers built in many successive reigns. In King John's time it endured a long siege from Louis of France,‡ and its brave defender, Hubert

* Pages 237, 293.　　† Pages 3, 10.　　‡ Page 152.

de Burgh, not only resisted him, but, knowing that his own castle was safe, went out with about forty ships, provided by the Cinque Ports, met eighty French sail, and destroyed nearly all of them. The view *from* the castle is very fine, and so is that *of* the castle from the water. The cliff is honeycombed, with long galleries for provisions and powder, and chambers for lodging two thousand men. On the other side of the town is Shakespeare's Cliff, which the poet describes in magnificent language. Part of its overhanging chalk has fallen away in large masses. At one time, forty-eight thousand tons fell at once. Through this cliff there is now a railway tunnel, to make which an enormous quantity of chalk was removed by gunpowder. After it was discharged, the rock glided like a stream into the sea. Dover is the only one of the Cinque Ports which has a harbour; and this has with difficulty been preserved from accumulated shingle. Now, a very fine harbour of refuge is being built; the stone piers are eighty feet wide at the bottom, which is forty-five feet below water. Here the diving-bell is very useful. From Dover, the first telegraphic wires under the sea, called the Submarine Telegraph, were laid. These are encased in gutta-percha, round which is wrapped a strong iron cable. For several years the attempt to lay it across the mighty ocean failed; but God at length gave success to man's efforts, and now it reaches the shores of India and America, so that it takes but a short time for messages to speed round three quarters of the world. Dover is a favourite bathing-place, and the chief port for crossing to France.

South of Dover stands Folkestone, where Harvey was born, who discovered the circulation of the blood : that is, that our blood is ever, during life, leaving the heart, passing through arteries and veins, and returning to it again. Folkestone is built on hills; and with its crooked streets, and steep flights of steps, leading from one to the other, is very picturesque. Its harbour has been much improved; and steamers continually sail hence to Boulogne in France.

A short way from Folkestone, is Sandgate, another bathing-place, with a castle, built like Sandown and Deal in Henry VIII.'s time. All along this coast are martello towers, which were built about 1807, when England was in danger of an invasion from France.

The next town is Hythe, which once had a famous harbour; it is now deserted by the sea. Beneath the chancel of its beautiful church, is a crypt with an immense number of human bones, very carefully arranged. They must be more than 1000 years old; and many show, by holes in the skulls, that whoever possessed them had probably been killed in battle.*

Hythe stands on the borders of Romney Marsh, which is protected from the overflowing of the sea by a strong wall three miles long.† The divisions are made as in Lincolnshire, by watercourses, instead of hedges. Owing to its unhealthiness, few people, that can help it, live here; and so, in former days, it was much infested by smugglers. Smugglers are people who secretly bring on shore goods from foreign countries, on which duty—that is a tax to the Queen—has not been paid. There are few smugglers now; not, I fear, because people are better; but because, owing to free-trade, there is no longer so much duty to be paid; and so, there is no longer the same temptation. Lydd, in the Marsh, was the chief town for these men. New Romney, *only* 800 years old, lost its river, the Rother, by a great storm in Edward I.'s time, when the stream chose for itself a new channel. Its harbour was soon filled

* Pages 42, 63, 164. † Pages 148, 316.

up with sand, and now it is some distance from the sea. Here there is an annual fair for the beautiful sheep of Romney Marsh.

West of the Marsh lies the Weald of Kent, a wooded district with a clay soil, in which the oak especially grows.* The principal village in it is Cranbrook, where cloth was woven by the Flemings, long before it was thought of in Yorkshire, and where it is said to have carpeted a mile of the road along which Queen Elizabeth walked.† Most of the villages in the Weald end with "den," which means an enclosed pasture in a forest, principally used for feeding swine. Many are the curious customs still existing. At one church, when there is a wedding, the ground is strewed with the emblems of the husband's trade; so the carpenter and his bride walk on shavings; the butcher and his, on sheepskins; and the blacksmith and his, on bits of old iron. At another church, on Easter-day, a quantity of cakes, made the shape of two women, are, with bread and cheese, given away to the poor. William Caxton, the first English printer, was born in this district.‡

Now we must finish beautiful, interesting Kent; thankful that so rich and pleasant a county has been given to dear old England.

It is suggested that there should be a school-room revision of the Thames, after every two or three counties, according to the teacher's discretion. After which, the following game may be introduced among children who can write easily.

CONGLOMERATION CONCERNING THE THAMES.

Let all be seated round a table; each furnished with a

* Page 261.　　† Pages 175, 190, 237, 256.　　‡ Page 309.

slate, or paper and pencil. Each child mentions a noun, the name of a place, or of something connected with the history or custom of one of the counties bordering on the Thames. Thus, the following words are given successively:—"London," "Folkestone," "Oak-tree," "Wedding," "Oxford," "William the Conqueror," "New River," "Caxton." Each person then writes, according to his fancy, a letter, a journal, a story, or rhyme, bringing in the words in order, and telling something concerning them that they have learnt from "Dear Old England." Thus one writes :—

London, July, —

DEAREST MOTHER.

I have just returned from France, *viâ* Boulogne and *Folkestone.* Folkestone is a curious town, with such steep narrow little streets! From Folkestone, we went along the coast to Hythe; then crossing Romney Marsh, we entered the Weald of Kent, where the *oak-tree* seemed abundant. As we passed a country church, we observed the ground strewed with small pieces of glass; soon the bells chimed, and we heard it was the *wedding* of a glazier. Had the bridegroom been a blacksmith, old iron would have taken the place of glass. To-morrow, I hope to be at *Oxford,* and see the Bodleian Library, and the place where Cranmer, Ridley, and Latimer suffered. There is a curious story in Kent, about the people meeting *William the Conqueror,* under cover of boughs, and seeming like a moving forest, which so frightened him, he gave them what they asked. My cousin Frank has just been here. He has had a few days' fishing in the *New River,* in Hertfordshire. I forgot to tell you, in the Weald of Kent, that famous old fellow, *William Caxton,* the first English printer, was born.

Ever, dearest mother,
Your own boy,
CHARLES.

Another writes :—

Little Henry lived in *London* and seldom saw green-fields, but only the great squares and many streets of that enormous town. One day, he went with his aunt to *Folkestone,* that he might bathe. He was very fond of going up and down the steps of the steep streets, and watching the steamers going over to France. His aunt often told him nice stories. One was about a little baby-boy, left in the hollow of an *oak-tree,* who afterwards became very rich and was Lord Mayor of London ; and what was very kind, he then gave money to help the poor people in the village, where the old oak-tree stood. And that village is now called after him. It is Sevenoaks, in Kent. Once, Henry went with his aunt into the Weald of Kent, and there saw a *wedding ;* the bride and bridegroom walking over shavings, because the husband was a carpenter. Another time, Henry visited *Oxford*, famous for learning even before the time of *William the Conqueror*. Henry went to some of its famous libraries, and there he read in a book all that Sir Hugh Middleton did, to make the *New River* in Hertfordshire. Another trip he took was to Ham House, and there he saw some books, printed by *William Caxton*, the first English printer, who was born in the Weald of Kent.

A younger child might write as follows :—

London is on the Thames ; and *Folkestone* on the sea-side. I should like to see Queen Victoria's *oak-tree*, in Windsor Forest, and Hever Castle, where poor Anne Boleyn lived before her *wedding*. When I am a man, I hope to go to *Oxford* and study. I don't like *William the Conqueror*, for breaking his promise to the Abbot of St Albans. I suppose there was no *New River* in Hertfordshire then. One of the most celebrated men born in Kent was *William Caxton* the printer.

A grown-up person might write in rhyme, such as follows :—

> Children, list to an old man's tale,
>   Of wonders he has seen
> In mighty *London's* famous town,
>   Wonders they are, I ween.
>
> From *Folkestone*, I travelled, they say, per rail ;
>   'Twas mighty quick, I know.
> Different to when I travelled once,
>   To see the *oak-tree* grow.
>
> The tree that marked the olden date
>   Of Philip Sidney's birth ;
> And saw old Hever's castle walls,
>   Scene of Anne Boleyn's mirth ;—
>
> Scene of her mirth, before the day—
>   Her fatal *wedding* day ;
> When to the king, she plighted troth,
>   And promised to obey.

In London, I walked through *Oxford* Street,
  And gazed at beauties rare,
So new—so wonderful—so great.
  I thought, Where am I?—Where?

How changed, since *William Conqueror*,
  So proudly came through Kent.
Until at Swanscombe, forest men
  His stubborn will had bent.

How changed, since good Hugh Middleton,
  A mighty wonder wrought;
When he the clear *New River*
  To thirsty London brought.

How changed, since *William Caxton* saw
  His printing press succeed
And gave to happy Englishmen,
  The Book of books to read.

Great was thy work, Hugh Middleton!
  Th' assuaging spring to find;
But greater thine, good Caxton!
  Thou fedst the thirsty mind.

SUSSEX.—Part L

Sussex is decidedly an agricultural county, for, though there is much ironstone, there is no coal, and, consequently, there are no manufactures; and, though there is a great deal of sea-shore, there is hardly any commerce. Do you remember a town in Suffolk an exception to this general rule, of coal and manufactures being linked together?* Sussex, like a part of Surrey, formed, in early times, what might be termed the "Black Country" of England; but when coke was used to smelt iron instead of charcoal, the iron-works emigrated, and took up their abode—in what counties?† Where was coke first used?

From Hampshire, two chains of chalk hills branch off

* Page 189.   † Pages 21, 40, 51, 114, 116.

eastward to the sea. These are the North Downs, of which you have already heard in Surrey and Kent,* and the South Downs, which extend to a fine rocky headland in Sussex, called Beachy Head. The country between these ridges is called the Valley of the Weald, and is rich and cultivated.† The rivers do not, however, run through this valley eastward towards Romney Marsh, but find their way either in tunnels through the hills, flowing north, like the Mole, or south in a passage between them, like the Ouse. In the east of the county is a beautiful district, called Forest Ridge. There are remains of the deep forests that in former days covered the whole of Sussex, excepting the South Downs.

Sussex is not famous for tillage, though some hops are raised on the borders of Kent; good hay is cut on the marsh-lands, and along the coast there are heavy crops of corn. The South Downs are mostly noted for their excellent sheep. Here, also, the wheat-ear, a bird good for eating, is caught in great numbers, as was formerly the bustard, or wild turkey. In this district, oxen are often employed in ploughing, and sometimes in drawing carts. The shepherds used to be quite a peculiar race, living in caves or huts, which were covered with earth, on the side of the hills. One of them, writing about himself, says, " It was in *my* cave that I first read about Moses and his shepherding life, and about David's killing the lion and the bear. Ah! how glad that we hadn't such wild beasts to frighten, and maybe kill, our sheep and us." The roads in this county were, at one time, noted for their mire and sloughs. In those days a journey was described as follows: " Nothing but mischief! Some trick or other plagued us all the day. Crack goes one thing, bounce goes another; this was the trade from morning till night."

* Pages 254, 302, 317.   † Page 342.

Prince George of Denmark, the husband of Queen Anne, was six hours in going nine miles, and his attendant writes, " We did not get out of our coaches save only when we were overturned, or stuck fast in the mire, till we arrived at our journey's end." Another person, writing of a church near Lewes, says, " I saw an ancient lady, and a lady of very good quality, I assure you, drawn to church in her coach by six oxen," and the reason was, " the way was so stiff and deep, no horses could go in it." Such travelling has ceased in England, but you will be amused to know that in April 1866, I travelled in Italy in a coach drawn by five horses and four oxen.*

There is no port of commercial importance on the Sussex coast, but the fisheries are extensive, that of the brilliantly marked mackerel being amongst the most abundant in England.† One boat once returned with £1000 worth, caught in one night.

Amongst the clay of Sussex Weald, there are thin beds of limestone. This has long been quarried at Petworth, and when polished goes by the name of " Sussex Marble." It is composed of the shells of snails held together by particles of lime. It has been used in ornamental building since the time of the Romans, and forms the tomb of Queen Eleanor in Westminster Abbey, and the throne of the archbishops in Canterbury Cathedral. The Weald is also rich in fossils ; many of those strange monster animals, now in the British Museum, having been discovered here by Dr Mantell.‡

We will now travel through Sussex, from east to west, following the rivers and the waves.

Our first river is the Rother, that rises near the highest hill in Sussex, Crowborough. The view from it is beautiful, and here, in former days, when the Armada was ex-

* Page 328.   † Pages 175, 185, 313.   ‡ Page 291.

pected, the beacon fires were watched, and signalled an
alarm all around.* In this wild but picturesque county
is Mayfield, where there are curious remains of the archbishop's palace, and strange stories about Dunstan, the
wicked bishop, in the reign of poor King Edwy. Here is
one : he found that the church, a wooden one, was not due
east, so he put his shoulder to it, and easily moved the
whole building. Queen Elizabeth once passed right
royally through this valley, and relics of her progress are
still seen.† There still stands at Northiam the old oak-
tree under which she took off her pretty green silk shoes,
which are shown at the castle. Another curious castle
is Bodiam, surrounded by a deep moat, filled with water.
About two miles from the mouth of the river is Rye, one
of the ancient Cinque Ports. It was once walled, and
some old towers still remain. Many French Protestants
settled here after the dreadful massacre of St Bartholo-
mew.‡

A few miles from Rye is Winchelsea, which has altogether lost its Cinque-Port importance. The sea and Winchelsea have never agreed ; old Winchelsea, built on a low
island, was covered by the waves, and new Winchelsea,
built on a hill, with a beautiful harbour, was deserted by
them. Now, there are little more than old grey ruins.
Off here, the English and Spanish ships met, in Edward
III.'s reign. The king was present with his two boys,
the Black Prince and John of Gaunt.§ John was too
little to hold his bow, " but the king had him on board
because he much loved him." Queen Philippa was on
shore, not far off, and anxiously watched the battle. The
English were victorious, and that evening the king landed
at Winchelsea with his young sons, and rode over to his

* Pages 228, 269.   † Page 342.
‡ Pages 175, 338.   § Pages 148, 336.

wife's mansion to comfort her loving heart. Winchelsea has been four times burned down by the French.

Between Winchelsea and Hastings, the marshy land ceases, and a sandstone range of hills appears.* Beneath this, in a very sheltered situation, lies Hastings, and close to it St Leonards. The air here is mild but bracing ; and many delicate people are strengthened by its breezes. On this coast, William the Conqueror's army landed. The remains of a large encampment, said to have been his, are seenon the cliffs above Hastings ; and about seven miles distant is Battle, where Harold and the Saxons were defeated in that combat which placed the Norman duke on the English throne. The battle was undecided, till Harold and his brothers fell, whilst struggling to preserve the Saxon standard, and then the Saxons fled to the woods.† William vowed, if victorious, to build on the battle-field a great abbey. Its remains still exist. One of the privileges that William gave to the abbot, was, that he might pardon any condemned criminal he should meet in any part of England. That Norman conquest seemed, at first, hard for Englishmen, but God overruled it for good, as the union of the quiet perseverance of the Saxon and the bravery of the Norman was destined to form the high character of the Englishman. English boys and girls ! never by cowardly, or idle, or dishonest conduct, disgrace the character of our " dear old England."

A low marshy coast succeeds that of Hastings,—it was once a bay dotted with low islands. Here stand the ruins of Pevensey Castle, the site of Anderida, an old Roman fortress. William the Conqueror landed here, falling on the ground as he leaped ashore. The soldiers said, " A bad sign ! " but he, rising, exclaimed, " I have seized the ground with my two hands ; it is ours ! " From this castle,

* Page 302.   † Pages 45, 102, 315.

during a siege in the time of "the Roses," the earliest letter now existing is dated. It was written by the brave female defender, Lady Pelham, to her "true lord."

Farther west is Eastbourne, a very pleasant, quiet watering-place. Then Beachy Head appears, with its grand rocks. On the adjoining cliffs there are countless sea-birds,* and innumerable chattering jackdaws, but on Beachy Head, I have heard, that two peregrine falcons have always built their nest, and, as these are birds of prey, the others leave them in undisputed possession. Here grows, in great abundance, the samphire, a fleshy flower, used as a pickle. It generally grows on sea-side cliffs, but never within salt-water mark. Now listen to a tale of the preservation of life by the knowledge of this fact. A ship was wrecked off Beachy Head, in a dark tempestuous night. Four sailors were thrown on the ledge of a rock; the tide was rising, the waves were lashing, the rock above was too steep to climb, and they said, "Let us throw ourselves again into the water; the waves may wash us where we may be safe." At that moment one felt his foot slipping, and, to save himself, he caught hold of a weed, which a flash of lightning showed to be samphire. "Let us stay," he exclaimed; "we are above the tide." They remained, and when morning light came they were rescued.

West from Beachy Head is the mouth of the Cockmore. This little river rises near Heathfield, where there is a tower built in honour of Lord Heathfield, the famous defender of Gibraltar. It afterwards passes a curious old priory, now a farm-house, with the crypt made into a dairy, and the roof a dwelling-place for owls. The next little town is Seaford, one of the cinque ports, but, like so many of the others, with its harbour choked up,† and, farther on, at

* Pages 18, 85, 337.   † Pages 337, 338, 340, 348.

the mouth of the Ouse, is Newhaven, the best harbour
between Portsmouth and the Downs.   Vessels sail hence
for Dieppe, in France.*   At Newhaven, in 1848, Louis
Philippe and his amiable queen landed, when they fled from

Boats.

their own country.   They had crossed the channel in an
open fishing-boat.†
   To-morrow we will follow the Ouse, on condition of your
telling me of all the Ouses we have already met with in
Old England.

SUSSEX.—PART II.

Now give me your relation about the Ouses—one, two, three.
   Near the upper part of the Ouse is Horsted-Keynes,
where good Archbishop Leighton spent the latter part of
his life, and where he is buried.   He died in an inn in

* Pages 340, 341.   † Pages 306, 333.

London. He had often said, that if he could choose the place of his death, it should be an inn, "for what is the whole world to a Christian, but a large and moving inn, while he is a wayfarer, tarrying as short a time as possible, and then hastening away to his Father's house." *   In the adjoining parish of Fletching, Gibbon, the historian, died. No hope of a heavenly Father's house cheered his dying hours, for he denied the faith of Christ. Farther down, where the Ouse pierces the South Downs, and very prettily situated, is Lewes, an extremely ancient town, with a castle, a priory, and several churches. In the castle is a museum of Sussex curiosities. At Lewes, in Queen Mary's reign, martyrs were imprisoned and burned alive. The cellar, said to have been their prison, may still be seen. This town is the birth-place of Dr Mantell, the famous geologist. He made the chalk of the Downs, and the clay of the Weald, tell, through their wonderful fossils, many a silent truth of the order of creation. Near Lewes, on Mount Harry, Simon de Montfort and the barons fought a bloody battle against the weak King Henry III., in which the king was defeated.†   The churches on the Ouse have often round towers ; but now we will leave this little stream, when you have found out a Sussex riddle concerning three villages upon it, " Heighton, Denton, and Tarring, all begin with A."

The next town on the coast is Brighton, the largest watering-place in England, having a population of nearly 100,000.‡   It has many streets and squares, and is a gay and lively place. The air is fresh and pleasant from the sea, and the houses are all furnished as in foreign towns, with outside blinds, as the sunlight glare would otherwise be too great, the want of trees causing a want of shade. George IV. made Brighton the fashionable watering-place it has be-

* Contrast pages 53, 190.   † Page 205.   ‡ Pages 56, 334.

come within the last fifty years.* He built a very extra-ordinary kind of palace, called "The Pavilion," very Chinese looking. Queen Victoria did not like Brighton as her sea-side home; so the palace was sold, and the town bought it for public uses. The chain pier is the first that was ever built in England. Brighton is so like the west end of London that one might almost imagine it was that part of the metropolis moved down to the sea-side; and the trains between London and Brighton are so frequent, that many gentlemen living in Brighton are almost daily in London for business.

Farther west, at the mouth of the Adur, is Shoreham, where a great deal of timber is brought from foreign parts, and where ship-building goes forward. From this place, Charles II. embarked after his hiding in the oak-tree at Boscobel, and after many other adventures in crossing the country.†

Now let us find the source of the Adur. It is in St Leonard's Forest, a remnant of the great wood which once covered the county. The tide used to rise as high as Steyning where once there was a harbour, defended by Bramber Castle, the remains of which are few. Its moat is now filled with trees, and covered with prim-roses. The Adur runs hence through a gap in the hills, and passes Old Shoreham, which succeeded Steyning as the harbour, till it was also deserted by the sea. The next bathing-place is Worthing; near it is Tarring, famous for its fig orchard, containing 100 trees, raised from stocks, said to have been planted by Thomas-à-Becket. A little bird, which goes in Italy by the name of the fig-eater, regularly appears here as the fruit ripens, and after remaining five or six weeks flies away over the sea to its warmer home.

* Pages 210, 323. † Page 196,

z

Our next river is the Arun, rising also in St Leonard's Forest, as you will see on the map, running south through the South Downs, just as the Wey goes north through the North Downs. The first town on its banks is Horsham, a small, but busy trading town. Near it the poet Shelley was born; and his greatest amusement, when a boy, was managing a boat on Warnham pond. On the Rother, a little river joining the Adur, is Midhurst, an old-fashioned country town, near which are the ruins of Cowdry Castle, which, like a hall in Derbyshire (name it) used to show, by its preservation of olden usages, how our forefathers lived. It was, however, entirely destroyed by fire, and now only ivy-covered ruins remain.* Farther east is Pet- worth, and near it is Petworth Park, a beautiful place. In the mansion are a great collection of pictures, and very fine carved wood. You can ride fourteen miles round the walls of the park, enjoying extensive views over the Downs and Weald, or watching the deer herding under the fine old clumps of beech and oak trees.

The next interesting place near the Arun is Bignor, where have been found some of the most perfect remains in England of a Roman villa. The Mosaic pavement re- presents all kinds of figures; and the bath-room, the open fire-place, the banqueting apartment, and others may be traced. The house must have been a very large one, as the buildings are 200 yards in length. Do we not wonder who lived there; who wore the fine golden ring discovered there; or who trod on that ancient pavement?† Follow- ing the Arun, we reach North and South Stoke, where yet more ancient things have been discovered—British canoes, hollowed out of the stems of oak trees. Farther on is Arundel, with a very fine castle, belonging to the Dukes of Norfolk. The greater part was rebuilt about seventy

* Pages 145, 265. † Pages 194, 210.

years ago; but the keep is very old, and has seen more than one siege. It is covered with netting, on account of the fine eagle owls there confined. In the church are many very old and beautiful tombs to the memory of the Earls of Arundel. Littlehampton is near the mouth of the river, a nice bathing-place, with pleasant sands. The Arun is famous for its mullet, a kind of fresh-water fish, and, like the birds that visit Tarring for its figs, so the osprey, at the best season, visits the Arun for its favourite fish.

I shall mention only one more sea-side place, Bognor, in a very flat country, which the sea is rapidly overtaking. In this way Selsey Point, our next projecting piece of land, forms a great contrast to Dungeness. The old cathedral of Selsey is now under the waves.* It was built by Wilfred of York, who baptized the Pagan inhabitants, and taught them how to provide food by fishing, when they were starving from famine.

Chichester, our last town, is the county town of Sussex, and has a very fine cathedral. The old walls, with semicircular towers, still surround the city. The walls are lined with tall elm trees, which look very pretty. The houses are chiefly roofed with red tiles. The principal streets form a cross, running north and south, east and west.† The spire of the cathedral was particularly beautiful, but suddenly, a few years since, after a storm of wind, it sank upon its foundation and perished. Excepting York, this cathedral is the broadest in England, and it is distinguished by having five aisles.‡ There are many interesting monuments; one is to the poet Collins, who wrote the famous poem on the Passions, beginning, "When Music, heavenly maid, was young." He was born, and died at Chichester. His life was a very melancholy one.

* Pages 54, 169, 180, 337.   † Page 211.   ‡ Page 83.

Near the cathedral is a campanile, or bell-tower. Not far from Chichester, at the head of a salt-water creek, is Bosham, with a very old Saxon church. A story is told that its bells were carried off by the Danes; that a great storm arose in the creek, and that their weight sunk the ship. Below the water they remain; but when the bells now hanging in the tower chime gladly, the others are heard to chime too. Echo will tell if this is true.*

And now we have reached the borders of Hampshire, of which you shall hear a great deal to-morrow.

HAMPSHIRE.—PART I.

HAMPSHIRE is another beautiful and important county of our native land. It has not the fertility of Kent; because, though the climate is even warmer, the soil is not nearly so rich.† It is, however, well cultivated, and in it is very much to interest us. The map will tell the surrounding counties; the direction of the rivers; and will show you that the coast is not straight, but has headlands running out to the sea. Then you will observe, that there is a strait separating the mainland from the pretty Isle of Wight. This beautiful island shall, however, have a chapter to itself.

The chalky ranges of the North and South Downs unite in Hampshire, and extend across the middle of the county into Wiltshire. You may, therefore, expect to see hills with rounded tops, and sweeping valleys, and roads of a very light colour. Quite in the north of the county, the soil is gravelly, and a good deal of brown heath grows; but near the rivers, there is valuable meadow-land, and frequently in the central part, there are heavy crops of

* Page 66.   † Pages 313, 330.

corn. The principal rivers are the Anton or Test, and the Itchin, uniting to form the Southampton Water, and the Avon, which runs quite in the west of the county. The New Forest lies between the Southampton Water and the Avon. The scenery there is very beautiful,—

Stoney Cross and the New Forest.

the old gnarled oaks and silvery beech trees, with here and there an open stretch of heather, and on the south the sea washing the border. Sometimes there are fires in the forest, the heath and fern burning for days together. The woodcutter's axe is often heard, for the trees are required for the royal navy;* and the swineherd's horn is mingled with the grunting of his 500 or 600 pigs,† that, during October and November roam about, delight-

* Page 208.   † Page 254, 342.

ing in their repast of acorns and beech-nuts. Besides these, there are wild swine, thought to be the descendants of our good, old, domestic pig, but becoming more and more like the wild boar. Their ears stand up, their colour is generally black; the forepart of their body is the thickest, and they have a strong bristly mane.* They usually wander in small herds, led by one patriarchal boar. Dogs are employed to hunt them. Hampshire is famous for its bacon, the people taking much pains in curing it. Another wild animal of the forest is the pony; twenty or thirty ponies are sometimes seen together. The Romans found horses of the same kind inhabiting Britain. There are, also, innumerable squirrels and rabbits, and a great many foxes and badgers. There used also to be deer ranging here, but they have all disappeared. †

Amongst other products of Hampshire, there are plenty of fish in the rivers and sea; good sheep on the Downs; ‡ and very excellent honey. It is not a county for manufactures, but a most important one for ship-building; § as you will find, when I tell you of Southampton and Portsmouth.

Now, you shall hear of some famous people born in this county. One is William of Wykeham, whom I have already mentioned; he was a famous bishop in Edward III.'s time.‖ He did all he could to encourage learning, and was himself an excellent architect; as his buildings at Windsor Castle, Oxford, Winchester, and many other places show. Another is Gilbert White, who wrote the Natural History of Selborne," his native place; tracing, in the care with which everything was made, the goodness, and, in their habits, the wisdom of God, He lies

---

* Page 15.   † Pages 208, 315, 354.   ‡ Page 346.
§ Pages 31, 231, 299.   ‖ Page 244.

in the quiet churchyard, sheltered by the yew-tree he has himself described. Edward Young, famous for his poem, " Night Thoughts," was also born in this county; and Charles Dickens.* But as honourable a name as any of these is that of John Pounds, a cobbler,† a philanthropist, and the originator of ragged schools. I will tell you a little more of him. He lived at Portsmouth. An accident crippled him when fifteen years of age; yet he not only supported himself, but also a little crippled nephew. He thought the boy would learn better with a companion; so he offered to teach the child of a very poor woman, then another, then another, till he had about forty, including twelve little girls. He particularly tried to induce, what he called "the little blackguards" to come; and would go down to the town quay with a roast potato, offering it to them, if they would assemble. The children soon learned to love this kind, good man. He taught them about God; he taught them to read, to cook their own food, and to mend their own shoes. He was their doctor and nurse when they were ill; their playfellow when they played. He died suddenly, on New Year's day, 1839; and the poor children wept, and some even fainted, when they heard that their dear friend was dead. But the cobbler's work died not. Its success was talked of. It was seen that the wildest and most neglected of children could be influenced by kindness. His example was copied; and now there is hardly, I believe, one large town without a ragged school, if it is required.‡

In telling you of Hampshire, we will travel, as in Sussex, from east to west.

Near the source of the Wey, which river I hope you re-

---

* Page 331.　　† Pages 9, 160.　　‡ Pages 50, 272.

member in Surrey, is Selborne, the pretty village of Gilbert White; and farther down is Alton, a market town, in the midst of a hop district, and famous for its ale. The church there saw a bloody fight in the time of Charles I. The brave commanding officer, and 260 out of his 800 men, were killed.* Another market town in this neighbourhood is Petersfield, where there is a fine statue of William III., on horseback; he saved England from the tyranny of James II. South of Petersfield is the ancient forest of Bere, once a royal hunting-ground;† and then comes Portsdown Hill, formed of chalk. Every summer there is here a great fair for horses and cheeses, and on the top of the hill is a monument to Lord Nelson, looking down on the large naval town of Portsmouth.‡

Portsmouth is built on the island of Portsea, lying between two inlets of the sea, Langstone and Portsmouth harbours, and connected with the mainland of Hampshire by bridges. Portsmouth is the chief naval arsenal in England.§ It has become thus important, from its situation in the centre of the Channel coast, with a first-rate harbour, and with the roads of Spithead, where ships can generally ride safely at anchor. The largest men-of-war are moored in the Portsmouth harbour; whilst in the dockyard are dry docks, where the biggest vessels may be repaired and refitted in a very short time. It is a noble sight to see one of these men-of-war, or the great iron-clads, like floating castles resting on the waters. The order and cleanliness of them are perfect. The cannons look out of their portholes, perhaps, as in the *Duke of Wellington*, 131 in number; and their heavy shot, of the exact weight which they are intended to carry, rest piled up behind; whilst, between them, are swung the hammocks

---

* Pages 225, 313. † Pages 208, 315.
‡ Page 184. § Pages 321, 332.

of the brave sailors or marines. Vessels of this size require about 1300 men to man them. One of the most interesting ships at Portsmouth is the *Victory,* where Lord Nelson was killed, at the battle of Trafalgar. The spot where he fell is shown, and also the cabin where he died; and in this is inscribed the celebrated watchword he gave at that great battle, "England expects every man to do his duty." On October 21st, the anniversary of that day of victory, the vessel is always garlanded with laurel. Whilst speaking of ships, I must tell you a sad story of a splendid man-of-war lost in the harbour, when it was crowded with people, and everything seemed safe. This ship was the *Royal George* of 100 guns. The vessel was nearly ready to sail for the Mediterranean, and loaded with guns and shot, which are very heavy. The carpenter found that a new watercock was necessary. The watercock is something like the top of a barrel in the side of the ship, where the well is, from which salt water is pumped to wash the decks. To take the old watercock out, it was necessary to lay the ship so far on one side, that the cock might be above water. This was done by drawing the heavy guns on one side in, and running the others out. Then a sloop, laden with rum, came alongside, and the weight of the barrels of rum, and the seawater, which was coming in at the holes, inclined the great vessel still more to the water. The carpenter saw there was danger, and asked the lieutenant to give orders to right the ship; but the lieutenant was angry, and said, "Sir, if you can manage the ship better than I can, you had better take the command." A few minutes more, and it was too late; the ship turned over, and with all its cannons, its provisions, its officers, its men, and many others, it sank to rise no more. Very, very few escaped; nearly a thousand people are supposed to have perished.

The wreck remained for nearly sixty years, when it was removed, partly by means of men with diving bells, and partly by blowing it up with gunpowder. Another large ship, *The Boyne*, was burnt in Portsmouth Harbour. When the fire reached the gunpowder, it exploded with such a tremendous shock, that it was felt all over the town. The large naval dockyard at Portsmouth is a wonderful place; all the work there is on a gigantic scale. The masts made are sometimes sixty-six yards long; the rope-house is 1000 feet in length; and ropes, with a coloured thread run through, marking them as the Queen's, are made as thick as a man's waist. The "Smithy," or blacksmith's premises, is where anchors, twenty feet long, are forged; whilst in the saw-house, the steam-saws are as busy as can be, cutting stems of trees across, as if they were cheeses, sawing, within half an hour, a huge trunk into seven or eight planks, and preparing the blocks, or oval pulleys, on which the ropes run, that hoist or lower the sails. By the steam-machinery, ten men can do the work of 110, and 130,000 blocks can be easily made in a year. In this dockyard the convicts work in their prison dress, and under care of guards.

The forging of enormous anchors is well described in the following lines :—

As quiv'ring through his fleece of flame, the sailing monster slow
Sinks on the anvil—all about the faces fiery grow,—
"Hurrah!" they shout, "Leap out, leap out;" bang, bang, the sledges go;
Hurrah! the jetted lightnings are hissing high and low;
A hailing fount of fire is struck, at every squashing blow:
The leathern mail rebounds the hail; the rattling embers strow
The ground around; at every bound the sweltering fountains flow,
And thick and loud, the swinking crowd, at every stroke pant "Ho!"

At Portsmouth is also a large gun-wharf, where numbers of guns are stored, ready for the ships that require them. On the opposite side of the harbour, at Gosport, is the great victualling yard, where all that a ship's crew can want is kept. Think of some of the things—water, this is obtained from a well a hundred and twenty yards deep,*— enormous quantities of bread, salt-meat, oatmeal, flour, vinegar, tea, cocoa, wine, rum, tobacco, and clothing. I must tell you something about the bakery, where all the sea biscuits for the navy are made. The wheat is ground by steam into extremely fine flour, twenty stone of which is sent at one time, through a pipe, into the bakehouse. This is mixed with water, and a revolving wheel, set with knives, cuts away the dough, which is at length thrown in lumps under great cylinders like enormous garden-rollers. These roll it and double it and re-roll it until it is quite smooth. Then it is cut in large squares, which are stamped with a frame divided like a honeycomb, thrown into the oven, baked for twelve minutes, taken out, and broken into fifty-two biscuits. Ten tons of biscuits can thus be baked in an hour.

Near Gosport is Haslar Hospital, where about two thousand sick or wounded seamen can be cared for, and which is visited by the best medical men.† Portsmouth and Gosport are strongly guarded by fortifications, said to be the best in Europe; and when one sees the strong stone-work and the many cannons, one feels it would be very difficult for an enemy to approach.‡ How thankful should every English child be that our dear old land is so well defended ; and, trusting in an Almighty Father's care, let us gladly sing

"Rule Britannia ! Britannia rules the waves;
Britons, never, never, never shall be slaves."

Portsmouth harbour runs inland about four miles. On

* Page 333. † Page 332. ‡ Pages 316, 332, 340.

the north of it is Fareham, where small vessels are built, and where there are potteries for converting the clay there found into draining-tiles or flower-pots. Not far distant is Porchester, with its old gray castle. The outer walls are supposed to have been built by the Romans, and it was a place of importance long before Portsmouth was anything but green fields. In later years, it has been used as a prison for captives taken in war, some thousands of Frenchmen having been kept here during the last war with France. They made very ingenious toys and ornaments, and a great deal of fine lace. Now, with thoughts of ships, and guns, and dockyards, we must leave Hampshire to-day. To-morrow, you shall hear of very different things—of abbeys and cathedrals and forests.

HAMPSHIRE.—PART II.

BEFORE we follow the streams that run into Southampton Water, I should like to tell you about some interesting places in the north of the county, which belongs to the basin of the Thames.

First, there is Aldershot, not far from Farnham, in Surrey.* Regiments are sent here, that the officers and men may be trained in the modes of camp life, which they must put in practice, should they march to meet an enemy. The officers' huts are divided into eight rooms, each officer having one, whilst the huts for the private soldiers hold twenty-two men. Here Queen Victoria has a pavilion. The kitchens and offices are below the little hill on which it stands, and the dishes for the royal table are conveyed to the dining-

* Page 303.

room through a glass tunnel, by means of a lift. On this wild common, in Queen Victoria's reign, it is not for the *first* time that soldiers have encamped. Close to Aldershot, on a chalky hill, is Cæsar's Camp, the remains of a military work, belonging to very early English history.*

The river that in the north-east separates Hampshire from Surrey and Berks, is the Blackwater, so called because, running through peat, it is of a dark colour. Not far distant is the Whitewater, of quite a different hue, for it passes through a chalk district. Near this is Odiham, with the remains of an old castle, where David, King of Scotland, was confined. Where was he taken prisoner? † West of this is Basingstoke, a very old town, near to which is Basing House. This house is celebrated for its siege in the time of Charles I. It was defended by the Marquis of Winchester, and was a refuge for many of the Royalists.‡ Oliver Cromwell at length came with a strong force and took it, and the soldiers obtained from it a great deal of plunder, as its furniture was splendid, and its provisions plentiful. One bed was worth one thousand three hundred pounds.

North of Basingstoke is Strathfieldsaye, presented by the nation to the great Duke of Wellington, after the battle of Waterloo.§ Here is buried the duke's celebrated horse, "Copenhagen." During the eighteen hours he rode on the day of the battle of Waterloo, he used no other charger. The faithful animal lies under a clump of elms in the paddock where he spent, in quiet and comfort, his last years, and where he used constantly to be fed with biscuits by the duchess.

Near Strathfieldsaye is Silchester, the remains of an

---

ancient Roman town. Here, it is said, that the Constantine, who was made emperor at the same time as Honorius, was crowned; and there is also a tradition, that Silchester saw the coronation of King Arthur. The walls are as extensive as the old walls of London; but their enclosure is now very different, being only an old church and a farm-house.*

Kingsclere has a fine old church. It is in a very wild district. We read of King John's groom receiving five shillings for killing a wolf here, and even now the district is so thinly peopled, that you may go twelve miles along the banks of the Embourn, the stream that separates it from Berkshire, and only meet with one church.†

Now let us return to the streams running south, first following those that fall into Southampton Water. The most easterly of these is the Hamble river. Near it is Bishops-Waltham, where are the ruins of an old castle of the Bishops of Winchester. Here was a famous chase, which used to be stocked with beautiful deer. These were, however, destroyed by the Waltham Blacks, a set of deer-stealers, who, before they went out on their expeditions, blackened their faces, that they might look fierce and not be known.

On Southampton Water, above the opening of the Hamble creek, is a military hospital, and below this are the beautiful remains of Netley Abbey. The situation is very lovely, with hills behind, and wood around, and water below, and the pretty traceried windows have ivy twining round and round them.‡ Farther north is the mouth of the Itchin, which we will now trace from its source. The first town I would mention is Alresford, not so important as it was in King John's time, when a large pond was formed by the bishop to make the river navig-

---

* Pages 226, 276.   † Page 74.   ‡ Pages 43, 48, 53, 224.

able from Southampton. Near this is Titchbourn, about which a curious story is related. The good Lady Isabelle was dying, and, as she lay on her death-bed, she begged her husband to give her sufficient land, that bread might be doled to all who visited Titchbourn on Lady-Day. Her husband took from the hearth a flaming piece of wood, and said he would give her what she could herself encircle whilst the brand continued to burn. She was then carried out; and, on her hands and knees, crept round several acres, which are still called the Crawles. An old prophecy says, that the house will fall should any descendant cease to give the charity thus obtained. 1900 small loaves used to be regularly distributed, but now, money is given instead.

After passing several small villages, the Itchin reaches Winchester. This is one of the most interesting and ancient towns in England. The Britons had a city here; then the Romans, in whose time temples to Apollo and Concord stood, where the cathedral is now built; then it became the capital of the Saxon kingdom of Wessex, and when Egbert became king over all England, he was crowned here. Alfred the Great and Canute the Great chiefly resided here; and, at one time, it was more important than London.* The removal of the seat of royalty, fires, and civil wars, have all contributed to diminish the importance of Winchester, and now it is comparatively quite a small town. Its cathedral has not, however, lost its beauty, nor has the abbey of St Cross, nor other old buildings. The present cathedral was built in the time of William I., who gave the bishop leave to take as much wood from a forest, higher up the Itchin, as his carpenters could cut and carry in four days and

* Pages 44, 263.

nights. On receiving this permission, he collected every carpenter he could find, and when the king passed, a few days afterwards, the forest was gone. The king was angry at first, but he soon forgave the zealous bishop.* Now, I want you to look out Matthew vii. 7, and inquire if you act as zealously upon the permission you have from the great King of heaven. Winchester Cathedral is one of the handsomest in England, and is longer than any other, being 287 yards in length. Here are buried Canute, William Rufus, Egbert, and several Saxon kings. St Swithin is one of the bishops buried here. It is said, that for forty days continued rain prevented the removal of his body from the churchyard to a golden shrine made for it, and this is the origin of the belief, that if it rains on St Swithin's day, July 15th, it will rain, more or less, for forty succeeding days; and, as this part of the summer is often showery, the saying very frequently comes true. At Winchester is a grammar school, founded by William of Wykeham. It is the most ancient school intended as preparatory for Oxford and Cambridge. Amongst its scholars was the excellent Bishop Ken.† It is said, the favourite song, "Dulce Domum, Home Sweet Home," with its soft plaintive air, was written by one of the boys, who, by way of punishment, was not allowed to go home during the holidays. Having cut a labyrinth among some trees on a neighbouring hill, he laid himself down under an old elm, still known as the Domum Tree, and there from grief of heart he died. There were two castles at Winchester, one built by the bishop, King Stephen's brother, and the other by William the Conqueror; both are ruins now. In the latter, the hall of which is still preserved, the unfortunate Henry III., called Henry of

* Page 153.   † Page 230.

Winchester, was born.* Here is shown King Arthur's Round Table. It has a double rose, red and white, in the middle, above which is King Arthur seated, wearing his crown. From this proceed twenty-four variously coloured rays, each one bearing the name of one of the knights. The painting is believed to have been done in Henry VIII.'s reign; but how old the table really is, I cannot tell.† Under an old abbey that once stood in this city, the great and good Alfred was buried.‡ In the museum here is shown the old Winchester bushel, that, in the reign of the Saxon King Edgar, was made the standard for measuring corn. Charles II. began to build a palace here, but his death stopped its progress, and the part that was finished is now a barrack for soldiers.

A mile below Winchester, on the Itchin, is the Hospital of St Cross, for the maintenance of thirteen poor brethren, and from which weekly gifts continue to be distributed amongst the poor. Here, too, at the Porter's Lodge, "the Wayfarer's Dole" is still given to every person, rich or poor, who asks for it. It is a horn of beer and a slice of bread. The church is very large and handsome, though the tower is low compared with the high roof. The park at Hursley, near Winchester, belonged to Richard Cromwell and his daughters, and in the church, he, who for a very short time reigned as Protector, is buried.§ The vicar of this parish was Keble, the well-known author of the "Christian Year," in which is the beautiful evening hymn beginning "Sun of my soul, thou Saviour dear." Further down the Itchin is Bishopstoke, and where it reaches the Southampton Water, stands Southampton, a town nearly as old as Winchester, to which it formerly served as a port. It was frequently the residence of King

* Pages 205, 352. † Pages 227, 296.
‡ Pages 238, 243, 255. § Pages 265, 282.

2 A

Canute.*   Here it was, that, seated on a chair on the sea-
shore, he commanded the advancing tide not to surround
him, and when it heeded not his words, he turned to the
flattering courtiers standing near, and bade them contrast
his human weakness with that Divine power, which set a
bound to the advancing waves, saying, "Thus far shalt
thou go and no further."

After the Conquest, Southampton was found a very
convenient port to embark for Normandy, and it became a
place of great importance.   The British soldiers who, in
Edward III.'s reign, won the victory of Cressy, and those
who, in Henry V.'s time, won that of Agincourt, sailed
from Southampton.   In the middle ages, it was, so to
speak, the packet station for the Venetian ships, laden
with wines from Italy or Greece, with carpets from
Damascus, and with gold and spices, brought through
Syria from the East.   When the passage by the Cape of
Good Hope was discovered, Southampton lost its importance; but now that the passage to India is again overland,
and that modern energy has constructed great docks for
the ships, which the largest vessels can enter, Southampton has regained its former consequence ; and its increase
during the last few years has been most remarkable. †
Immense steam vessels now sail weekly with the mails
for India ; and mail packets also start for Africa, the
West Indies, North and South America, Lisbon, and
Gibraltar.

The Indian mails are packed in wooden boxes, sometimes weighing twenty tons; and the American mails, in
India-rubber bags.   All kinds of distinguished visitors,
bipeds and quadrupeds, arrive here.   " Foreign monarchs
—royal Bengal tigers,—Indian, African, and Egyptian
princes,—great monkeys, hippopotami, alligators, generals,

* Page 172.   † Pages 97, 105, 230.

admirals, illustrious exiles, Californian bears, colonial governors." The Great Eastern's first voyage was from London to this port. * Some of the old walls, towers, houses, and three of the gates of ancient Southampton still exist. One of the gates is in the very centre of the present High Street; so it would now be of little use as a defensive outwork. One of the oldest hospitals in England still stands in this town. It is called " Domus Dei," or " God's house." The most celebrated person born in Southampton is Dr Isaac Watts, whose beautiful songs almost every child of dear Old England has heard.

To the west of Southampton is the mouth of the Test. The first village on its banks that I shall mention is Laverstoke, with its manufactory for the paper used for Bank of England notes. † Below is Whitchurch, with silk manufactories. The Anton, a richly wooded river, running, however, through a country of bare, chalk Downs, soon joins the Test. On it is Andover, in the time of the Saxons a royal residence, but now a quiet little country town. To the west of it is Weyhill, famous for its fair, where horses and sheep, cheese from Wiltshire, and hops from Farnham, are bought and sold. ‡ The second day is the one for hiring farm-servants, who distinguish themselves thus :—The carters have whip-cord in their hats, the shepherds a piece of wool, and the threshers, an ear of grain. On the hills in this neighbourhood are several mounds and entrenchments, the remains of ancient encampments. The next place of interest on the Test is Romsey, where there once was a nunnery, and where there still remains a very beautiful church. Below it was the house of Lord Palmerston, the great statesman; and not far distant is that of Florence Nightingale, the tried friend and nurse of our brave soldiers in the Crimea.

* Page 299.   † Page 166.   ‡ Pages 304, 358.

On the west side of Southampton Water lies the New
Forest, formed in the reign of William I.*   He is called
the "Father of the wild deer;" for he cared far more for
them than for his people, and made savage laws, by which
any one who injured a stag was condemned to death.   God,
however, cares for the poor; and, though some may say it
was by accident, I think he "took the matter into His own
hands," as the Psalmist says, when two of William's sons
were killed in this very forest.   The spot, called Stoney
Cross, is still shown where William Rufus fell, pierced by
the arrow Sir Walter Tyrell had shot.   His body was that
evening found by a charcoal burner, who conveyed it in a
cart to Winchester.   At the mouth of the Southampton
Water is Calshot Castle, built in the time of Henry the
Eighth.†   Continuing westward, along the shore of the
Solent, the name of the strait separating this part of Hampshire from the Isle of Wight, you see Beaulieu Water, on
which is Beaulieu Abbey, founded by King John.   Here
the unfortunate Margaret of Anjou sought shelter, when
she reached England, on the day of the battle of Barnet.
Here she heard the sad tidings of the death of her
friend the Earl of Warwick; and hence she and the young
and brave Prince Edward marched to the fatal battle of
Tewkesbury.‡   The next stream running through the New
Forest is the Boldre.   Near its source are some splendid
old oak trees, far older, probably, than the forest itself. §
Near one of its little streamlets is Lyndhurst, a sort of
village-capital of the New Forest, where the court is held,
and where a stirrup, said to have belonged to William
Rufus, is shown.   At the mouth of the Boldre is Lyming-
ton, a pleasant bathing-place, in a beautiful neighbourhood.   There are here salt works, from which Epsom salts

* Page 102.   † Pages 338, 341.
‡ Pages 209, 269.   § Pages 157, 304.

are made.* Quantities of wood ashes are found here, which have led people to think the ancient Britons made salt at this place; their manner of doing so being, to set fire to a pile of wood, and on its hot ashes to pour sea water. † Further west is Hurst Castle, built at the end of a narrow bar of shingle which is two miles long. Though exposed to furious storms, and formed of nothing but gravel, the shingle has not moved for hundreds of years. In Hurst Castle, poor Charles I. was confined, after being taken from Carisbrooke.‡ To this succeeds a wide bay, the cliffs of which are crumbling rapidly. On this coast is High Cliff, belonging to Lady Stuart de Rothesay. I will tell you of something at the mansion there which, I think, will make you laugh. It is a case of stuffed animals, arranged to represent the trial of a prisoner. Two wise-looking owls are magistrates, and a weasel is clerk. The culprit is a rat, who has killed a chicken, which its distracted mother presents at court. The policemen holding the prisoner are bantams; and the witnesses and audience are rats, chickens, hedgehogs, and other creatures; amongst them is the rat's wife, holding a baby rat in her arms. Further west, we find an inlet formed by the mouths of the Avon and Stour.

From what county do both these rivers come?

Not far from the Avon, above Ringwood, is Moyles Court. This was the home of the noble Dame Alice Lisle who in James II.'s reign was most cruelly beheaded, by order of Judge Jeffreys, for concealing fugitives, after the battle of Sedgmoor.§

Ringwood is a small and ancient town, noted for woollen gloves and brewing. The next town of interest is Christchurch, which might have been an important place, but

---

* Page 308.   † Page 101.
‡ Pages 258, 287.   § Page 237.

across the mouth of the harbour is a moving bar of sand, which prevents all large vessels entering.* Formerly there was here an important monastery, the church of which still exists. It contains a great deal of curious and beautiful carving, and the tombs of many distinguished people.

Between Christchurch and Bournemouth the trees are chiefly firs, hollies, and evergreens, and consequently do not lose their foliage in winter. They are cut down when young, to make scaffolds for building. The sands are yellow, like those in the deserts of Egypt. Boscombe Chine is very pretty, the little stream making a deep dell for itself through the soft sand, which is overhung by dark green firs. Boscombe is a town without a street, the villas situated in the midst of pine and fir plantations. It is much frequented by people in consumption, as the climate is very mild. And here we must leave the mainland of Hampshire, and to-morrow visit the Isle of Wight.

HAMPSHIRE.—PART III.

ISLE OF WIGHT.

SEPARATED from the mainland by the roadsteads of Spithead and the Solent, is the fruitful, healthful, and beautiful Isle of Wight. It is diversified with hill and valley, with woodlands and fields, with rocks and water. The climate is so mild that many consumptive people go there to escape colder winds, and to breathe warmer air,† and there the myrtle, fuschia, and hydrangia, flourish all winter in the garden, and grow into trees rather than shrubs, so that myrtle stems are sometimes used for firewood. Here, too, butterflies sport that are not seen else-

* Pages 106, 154, 213, 340.   † Page 349.

where in England, and their beautiful scarlet and purple wings look gay in the summer sun. To people who understand the formation of the clays, chalk, and sands, this island is most interesting, and those who know little about these things cannot but remark how the chalk lies over the green sand; and again, how clay, and sands of various hues, and gravel, rest on the chalk. The highest part of the island are the chalk hills, which run in two ranges, one across the middle from Culvercliff on the east to the Needles on the west, and the other across the south part of the island, just above the beautiful district called the Undercliff. The rivers run north. The principal one is the Medina, which divides the island into east and west, up which boats can go as far as Newport, in the centre. We will now begin with Newport, and then on paper we will take a voyage round this pretty island.

Newport is not new. It is a very ancient town; but was once, I suppose, the new port of the still older town of Carisbrooke.* Lace is made here, and tools for husbandry; and it is the chief market town of the island. The most interesting spot in Newport is the tomb of the Princess Elizabeth, the daughter of Charles I. She died in Carisbrooke Castle, about eighteen months after her father. The princess is represented lying in death's stillness under the prison grating, her head resting on God's own book, opened at the words, " Come unto me, and I will give you rest." It is said, she was found dead in this position. Our good Queen Victoria erected this, to show that she loved the princess's virtues, and felt sorrow for her sufferings. Carisbrooke Castle is very near Newport. It is a ruin now with extensive walls from which there are beautiful views. For twelve weary months it was the prison of the unfortunate Charles I. He was fond of read-

* Pages 20, 227.

ing, and passed a great deal of his time in perusing poetry and religious works; and he used to play at bowls on a bowling-green within the castle walls. He twice tried to escape; but without success. There is a very deep well in the castle. A light is lowered till it reaches the surface

Carisbrooke Castle.

of the water, and then you can look down and see its depth. At the side of the well is a huge and ancient wheel. A donkey enters the wheel, standing on the notches of its broad rim. This forms a treadmill; for the donkey tries to climb, and, as it tries, the wheel goes round. As the wheel goes round the bucket of water rises, and in process of time reaches the top of the well, when the donkey marches out. The patient creature is well fed and looks strong. One friend left it a curious legacy—a penny roll every morning.

Near Newport is a prison-reformatory for boys. They are separated from grown-up prisoners; their food is extremely plain; their dress very peculiar; they are not allowed to talk; are taught to work hard; and wear an iron on the leg.* These are some of the sad consequences of sin; but we trust that many a boy leaves that prison reformed, and will yet grow up an honest man. Will you pray for them?

On the eastern side of the Medina is Whippingham, where the Queen goes to church, when she lives at Osborne. Osborne House is a beautiful residence of our dear sovereign, at which she and the royal family spend much of their time.† It is a very handsome building, and looks well from the sea. Beautiful little fairy steamers are frequently employed in crossing the straits conveying members of the royal family to and fro. When the Queen was very young, she used to stay in the Isle of Wight with her royal mother, and there she enjoyed the sands, and delighted the boatmen by being brave and kind.

At the mouth of the Medina is Cowes, separated by the river into two parts, east and west, both of which have castles and churches. It is principally celebrated as being the head-quarters of the Royal Yacht Squadron. Yachts are pleasure ships, which are generally beautifully built and fitted up. It is a pretty sight to watch them either sailing or lying at anchor.

Passing eastward, Ryde is the next town you will see on the map. It is rapidly growing into a very large place. As the sands are quite level, the water is very shallow, and the pier runs out nearly half a mile, before it is deep enough for the steamers to approach at low tide.‡ The town is very pretty; trees and flowers growing amid the villas, and almost reaching the water's edge.

* Pages 325, 359.　　+ Pages 257, 286, 353.　　‡ Page 327.

Near Ryde, at the head of a bay or harbour, is Brading. In its churchyard is buried "Jane, the Young Cottager," whose life has been most sweetly written by the Rev. Legh Richmond. There are many beautiful epitaphs in this churchyard. One that little Jane learnt, I will write for you—

> " Forgive, blest shade, the tributary tear
>   That mourns thy exit from a world like this;
>   Forgive the wish that would have kept thee here,
>   And stay'd thy progress from the realms of bliss.
>   No more confined to grovelling scenes of sight ;
>   No more a tenant pent in mortal clay ;
>   Now should we rather hail thy glorious flight,
>   And trace thy progress to the realms of day.

Another pretty epitaph is on the gravestone of a little child.

> " This lovely bud, so young so fair,
>   Called home by early doom ;
> Just came to show how sweet a flower,
>   In paradise would bloom."

Little Jane had wicked parents and friends ; but God's grace made her early love Him. She died when quite young, saying to her pastor, "Christ is everything to me. Sir, we shall meet in heaven; shall we not? Oh! yes, yes; then all will be peace—peace." A yew-tree was planted beside her grave ; but, like Jane, it soon died. Now, there is a gravestone marking the rest of

> " That child to memory dear, and dear to God."

Farther inland is Arreton, where the " Dairyman's daughter " lived and was buried ; whilst along the coast, forming the eastern point of the chalk hills, is Culver Cliff, where Legh Richmond met the " Negro Servant;" of both of whom he has written in his " Annals of the Poor."

Following the coast, you will observe Sandown, with good sands and a fort for soldiers. Here a frightful occurrence happened not long ago ; a soldier, supposed to be a lunatic, murdered, one by one, his wife and six little children, the youngest, a baby, at its mother's breast. They now lie side by side, in Brading churchyard. Still following Sandown Bay, I must tell you of another pretty village, Shanklin, where a little stream finds its way to the ocean; not in a gentle course, through meadows and cornfields; but leaping and sparkling through the deep clefts of a chine. This is the name given in the Isle of Wight, and along England's south-western coast, to deep chasms in the cliff.* This chine is very beautiful; light green ferns, and dark masses of foliage, brown earth, yellow rock, cottages which almost seem suspended in the air; and the water, like a broken mirror, flinging back the sun's bright rays in each of its sparkling drops, and all writing softly in their loveliness, " God is love."

We now reach what is called the Back of the Island. Near Shanklin commences the Undercliff, so famous for its mild climate and lovely scenery. For many centuries —how long I cannot say—there have been crumblings and breakings of the upper cliffs. In the year 1818, a large portion of the east end thus fell down. This broken soil mixes with the earth below, and becomes very fruitful; nature's hand doing here, what, in other places, the farmer does for his land, when he strews the clay soil with lime.† The high cliff that remains above, protects it from every cold blast of wind. From the foot of this upper cliff, the uneven luxuriant land extends to the verge of the sea, where another cliff abruptly terminates it. The first interesting village is Bonchurch, where a pretty little church stands in one of the most beautiful of churchyards. Trees and hillocks, and quiet nooks are there interspersed with the tombs, or the simple crosses that mark the graves of the dead. On many is written, " Thy will be done ! "

* Page 374. † Pages 174, 189.

Side by side lie a brother and sister, the passion-flowers
twisting round the stone on which is engraved, " He bring-
eth them unto the haven where they would be; then are
they glad, because they are at rest;" and others speak of
the sole foundation of the hope of glory—Christ crucified.
A little farther west is Ventnor, where many invalids go,
especially during winter; and beyond it is the church of
St Lawrence, which used to be celebrated as being the
smallest church in all England, twenty feet by twelve.
Measure that with this room.   It is, however, now enlarged.
At the west end of the Undercliff is Black Gang Chine, a
great contrast to Shanklin, for no trees grow there; no
verdure covers its bare, steep, frowning, darkened rocks.
The scene is very grand, when the wind blows stormily,
and the great waves of the Atlantic roll, sweeping onward,
nothing breaking their force, or arresting their progress,
till they dash with noise like a cannon's roar against the
rocky coast.   There have often been fearful shipwrecks;
but lighthouses are erected, lifeboats built, and brave coast
guardsmen, employed to save life.*   Behind Black Gang
Chine is St Catherine's Mount, one of the highest parts of
the island.   A lighthouse used to stand on its summit;
but a new lighthouse is now built close to the sea; for in
cloudy weather, when most needed, the light on the hill
top could not be seen.   At the end of this chapter, I will
tell you an interesting story of a little lad that went from
this part of the island to sea.   For some distance west of
Black Gang Chine there are no remarkable places; and
the scenery, though pretty, is nothing like the Undercliff.
Again, however, high chalk cliffs rise, and following them,
for a few miles, we at length reach the western extremity
of the island, well known as " The Needles."   The waves
are gradually wearing these chalky masses away; only, as

* Pages 6, 22, 180, 338.

those farthest out to sea disappear, it seems probable others will be separated from the mainland.* Remember, however, all these changes are very, very slow; many years pass, and perhaps no difference can be observed. The bays here are very fine and curious. One, Alum Bay, is celebrated for its different coloured sands. They are placed in vertical or standing up strata, red, black, white, yellow, brown, greenish gray. It is not often the earth displays colours, nearly as bright as those of flowers. On all these cliffs are many sea-birds, which are very difficult to catch. The islanders are tied on a cross stick, held by a rope which is fastened securely to an iron bar, at the top of the Cliff. This rope, with the man thus seated, is let down; and choughs, puffins, or eider-ducks, are taken. In this neighbourhood lived Tennyson, the poet-laureate.†

Keeping round the western end of the island, you will see Yarmouth, on the little river Yare. This stream rises at Freshwater, so near the sea, that in stormy weather the spray of the waves has been dashed across the wall of separation, and has mingled with its source. At Yarmouth, there is one of Henry the Eighth's castles.‡ Yarmouth is a small trading port, at which ships are generally laden with the fine white sand that is found at Alum Bay and along the coast, and which is valuable in making glass or fine china.§

And now you shall hear the story of the sailor-lad. In Queen Anne's reign, a little boy, called Hobson, was born at Bonchurch. He soon became an orphan, and was apprenticed to a tailor at Nitou. One day, several men-of-war were sailing past, and all the villagers ran down to the shore to see the sight. Hobson, on the impulse of the moment, jumped into a boat, rowed to the admiral's ship,

---

and was taken on board as a volunteer. The boat was cast adrift, the boy's hat had been left on the shore, and all thought poor Hobson was drowned. The next day there was a fight with the French. A sailor told Hobson they must fight till the white rag at the enemy's mast-head was struck. He exclaimed, "Oh! if that's all, I will see what I can do." The ships were then covered with smoke, but lying close together; unobserved, he climbed the rigging, crossed over to the French ship, and hauled down the flag. Soon, the British sailors saw the flag was gone, and shouted "Victory!" The French left their guns in confusion; the English boarded the enemy's ships, and took them, when, to the astonishment of every one, Hobson appeared with the French flag round his arm. Because of his bravery, he was promoted, rapidly rose in rank, became an admiral, and was knighted. One day, a party of officers knocked at the tailor's door and begged his wife would prepare them some plain fare. They sat down with the worthy couple to a meal of bacon and eggs. After trying many ways to lead the woman to speak about himself, Hobson, who was one of the officers, at last began a verse of a song which he had often sung in former days. The wife's tears were in her eyes, and she said, "For all the world like our poor Hobby." Then the admiral almost cried, and you may imagine how astonished and glad the tailor and his wife were, and how kind a friend their old apprentice-boy proved to them.

Enough of this fair island of fair England. To-morrow we must travel inland, and visit Wiltshire.

WILTSHIRE.—PART I.

WILTSHIRE takes its name from Wilton, the old Saxon capital. What counties surround it? Its rivers run east, west, and south; the Kennet, joining the Thames; one Avon, after leaving Wiltshire, running through Somerset, to the Bristol Channel; and another, through Dorsetshire, to the English Channel. You remember the Downs that we have spoken of in Hampshire, Kent, and Sussex, and the Chilterns, and the Gog-Magog Hills in Oxford and Cambridge. Now look at the map, and you will see that all these ranges have a common starting-point in Wiltshire, as, also, other chalk hills that stretch south-westward into Dorsetshire. This centre is an elevated table-land, extending over the south of Wiltshire. A large portion of it is called Salisbury Plain, but the highest part is Inkpen-Beacon, in the corner where Berks, Hants, and Wilts meet. It is the highest ground of England east of the Severn and south of the Thames. This district is very bleak, having few trees, and covered with the short smooth grass, which is generally seen on chalk downs. Great numbers of short-wooled sheep feed here, and the air that blows is fresh and bracing.* The north of the county is well cultivated and very fertile. There are rich corn-fields, and fine pastures where the cows feed, from whose milk we have the celebrated Wiltshire cheese. This county is particularly distinguished for its British antiquities, such as the wonderful remains of the Druids' Temple at Stonehenge, entrenched camps, ancient banks and ditches, and sacred circles. The people are big and strong; they speak like their Somersetshire neighbours, a very broad dialect, and their ideas are often very simple.† Besides cheese, the county is noted for good brawn, and for the manufacture of broad cloth and carpets.‡ Amongst famous men born in Wiltshire are, Sir Christopher Wren, the architect;§ the Earl of Clarendon, Lord Chancellor and historian in

* Pages 169, 254, 346, 356.   † Pages 8, 38, 61, 228.
‡ Pages 50, 201, 208, 228.   § Pages 293, 322.

Charles the Second's reign; and Joseph Addison, who wrote papers in the *Spectator*, which are greatly admired for their beautiful composition.

We will now follow the rivers. First, the rivers to the Thames, then the Somersetshire or Lower Avon, and then the Upper Avon that takes us into Dorsetshire. I told you in Gloucestershire, that the branch of the Thames, whose source is furthest from the sea, rises near Cheltenham; and so that is the true source of the great river.* The stream, however, which retains its name till after passing Oxford, is the Isis, and this rises near Crudwell, on the borders of Gloucester and Wiltshire. The first town on its banks is Cricklade, small, but ancient. South of it lies Swindon, a noted station on the Great Western Railway, for every train must stop here for ten minutes, that the passengers may partake of refreshments. Here is a great engine depôt, where the ponderous locomotives stand in their stalls, like horses in a stable. Here is also a house for putting together the various parts of an engine. The men who work here made, for the Great Exhibition in Hyde Park, a pair of the tiniest little steam-engines, which could stand on a shilling, and only weighed three drachms. The workmen have all neat cottages, and a good church and schools have been built for them and their children. The old market town of Swindon stands on a hill.

The Kennet rises in a wild hilly district, where there are the remains of British camps, and ancient burial-places for the dead, and stories of battles between Britons and Saxons, in which the brave British King Arthur fought. Over this wild country large blocks of stone are scattered, which the people call Sarsen stones—Sarsen stands for Saracen, or heathen, the stones having, probably, been used for heathen rites; † or sometimes they call them young

* Page 207.   † Pages 65, 328, 330.

wethers, because they look like sheep. Soon the Kennet passes Avebury, where there are still a few remains of what has been a very large Druidical temple. Once there were about 600 immense round stones, arranged in curious circles; but they have been broken up for roads, cottages, and roadside walls. Not far from this is Silbury Hill, the largest artificial mound in Europe, raised in the shape of a sugar loaf, perhaps to mark a battle-field or the burial-ground of some great hero, perhaps as a representation of something sacred, or as a spot for the promulgation of laws, as the Tynwald mound is now used in the Isle of Man.* Along the Marlborough Downs to the South of the Kennet, extends the Wansdyke, an ancient British wall and ditch, probably used to defend the Britons against the Romans.† We look on these remains of our forefathers with special interest and with thankfulness, too, that we were not born in those days of savage ignorance. The British priests, or druids, looked venerable, with their long white garments, and wreaths of oak-leaves twisted round their brows, and uncut silvery hair. But notwithstanding this picturesque costume, their hands were often employed in bloody deeds. Human beings were offered as sacrifices, perhaps on some of the stones of which I have told you, and their thoughts were as savage, and as far from the true God, as were a few years ago those of the New Zealander, or are in the present day those of the Dahomian or Bornese.

The first town on the Kennet is Marlborough, whence a great deal of butter and cheese is weekly sent to London. It had a castle, where, in Henry III.'s reign, a parliament was held, which made some celebrated laws, known as the statutes of Marlborough. The mound of the keep in the garden of the college is all that now remains. The college is an excellent school, where about 500 boys are educated.‡

* Page 32. † Page 19. ‡ Pages 205, 210, 252, 268, 287, 292, 294, 369.

Near Marlborough is Severnake, a magnificent forest. One tree is called the Creeping Oak, for a huge branch of it stretches along the ground. The avenue of beech-trees, five miles long, is reckoned the finest in England. Near this is Wolf Hall, where King Henry VIII. married Lady Jane Seymour, who became the mother of Edward VI.*

The Lower Avon rises in Branden Hill, and soon passes the old town of Malmesbury, with the remains of its beautiful abbey church. Here lived William of Malmesbury, an old historian, and Oliver of Malmesbury, a man very fond of making experiments. He wished to fly, so having made wings, and fastened them on to his hands and feet, he mounted one of the abbey towers, and commenced his flight. But poor man! he was a weighty bird; he fluttered downwards rather too rapidly; and as he reached the ground, he broke both his legs.

Chippenham is the next town, where a handsome old bridge, of twenty-two arches, crosses the Avon. Alfred the Great held his court here. It is a busy little town, with a famous cheese market, ironfoundry, large tanyards, and silk and cloth manufactories. Its cloth gained the first prize at the Great Exhibition. On a small branch of the Avon is Calne, more famous for woollen manufactures in bygone days than now. St Dunstan once held a synod here; the floor gave way, and all present excepting himself fell into the apartment below. This was thought miraculous, so the priests let him have all that he desired.†

There is a fine seat of the Marquis of Lansdowne's, two miles from Calne, where there are beautiful pictures. West of the Avon is Corsham, where the Saxon Kings of England once lived.‡ Here, too, is a nobleman's seat, with very fine pictures, said to be the oldest private collection

* Pages 267, 322.   † Page 348.   ‡ Page 367.

.

in England. Further down the Avon is Laycock Abbey. It is now a private residence; but some of the abbey ruins yet remain. Laycock has also a curious story of a flight from the top of the church. It is that of a young lady leaping down into her lover's arms. The wind bore up her dress, so that she was unhurt; but he was nearly killed. However, her father, hearing of the leap, gave her leave to marry him, and she became the ancestress of the Talbots, to whom the abbey now belongs. In Laycock church, Bishop Jewel preached his last sermon from the text, "Walk in the Spirit." He left his pulpit for his bed, from which he never rose. Below Laycock is Melksham, a small but busy cloth-manufacturing town. Still further down is Bradford, once very important for its woollen factories; but now rivalled by its namesake in Yorkshire.* The water of the river dyes wool peculiarly well.† The Avon and Kennet Canal passes this town. The situation of Bradford, on the steep banks of the Avon, is very picturesque. This is a beautiful river; and the lofty hills around, the bright green fields, the rich woods, and sparkling streams wandering through each little valley, cause the whole neighbourhood to be greatly admired.‡ South of Bradford is Trowbridge, also an important clothing town. It once had a castle, very little of which now remains. I will only tell you of one place more in Wilts, near this Avon, and that is Box, where the railway passes through a tunnel one mile and three quarters long.§ Near Box there are subterranean stone quarries. The stone not being very hard, is cut with a saw. It is worked below ground, like coal in mines, and sometimes the blocks, which are brought up the shafts to the surface, are very large. Now, leaving the Lower Avon to enter Somersetshire, and thinking of what it will meet with there, we will wait for another

* Page 49.   † Page 213.   ‡ Page 226.   § Page 35, 87.

chapter to commence the course of the Upper Avon.*
I must tell you of one town on the canal between the
Lower Avon and Kennet. This is Devizes, an important
agricultural town, with the largest corn market in the west
of England, and some silk manufactories.† The old castle,
of which very little now remains, was built in Henry I.'s
time. There is written in the market-place the record of
a very awful event. Ruth Pierce and two other women
had agreed to buy amongst them a sack of wheat. One
of the women found the money was not all paid, and she
desired Ruth to give her share. The wicked woman said
she had already done so, and wished she might drop down
dead if she had not. The words had hardly passed her
lips when her feet tottered, her eyes glazed, she fell down
and was dead; whilst her hand yet held the money that
she had concealed. Truly God hateth the lying tongue.

WILTSHIRE.—PART II.

THE sources of the Upper Avon, a famous stream for trout,
lie amongst the hills near Devizes and Marlborough. One
of these, called Roundaway, was the scene of one of the
many conflicts during the civil wars in Charles I.'s time.
Here the Royalists gained a complete victory; the enemy
losing guns, gunpowder, and baggage, and having about
two thousand men killed and wounded. Another village
near which the little stream wanders marks the spot where
Ethelred was slain by the Danes. Again we cannot help
thinking with sadness of so much of dear Old England's
ground having been stained by the blood of her sons!‡
The Valley of Pewsey, through which the stream flows, is
a fertile district between the bleak Marlborough Downs on
one side, and the yet more dreary Salisbury Plain on the

---

   * Page 229.   † Page 51.   ‡ Pages 45, 206, 256, 269.

other. This plain is not a dead level, but rather resembles the waves of the sea, suddenly stilled, and hushed, and solidified. Here stand the extraordinary remains of Stone-henge, on which the traveller looks and wonders. There is little doubt but that it is the remains of a Druidical temple, and also that it was built by the ancient Britons at two different periods; but what ages have rolled be-tween; what scenes, festal or wretched, may there have been acted; who have been the priests, and who or what the sacrifices, we cannot say. Some of the stones, as you will see in the picture, form tri-liths, or three together,—one across two that are upright; and others are huge boulders,

Stonehenge.

standing alone. They are arranged in circles, and in the centre is an altar stone, or, as some have thought, a stone whence the priests observed the sun, moon, and stars; but we cannot tell.*

* Pages 41, 65, 330, 385.

" Pile of Stonehenge, so proud to hint, yet keep
    Thy secrets——"   WORDSWORTH.

A line across these stones would stretch nearly a hundred yards; and some of them are eight yards high, and weigh about seventy tons.

Two miles from Stonehenge, in a pretty wooded valley on the Avon, is Amesbury, where is an abbey built by the wicked Queen Elfrida, to atone for the murder of her son-in-law, Edward.* Near this, covered with a thick wood, is a hill, called Vespasian's Camp;† and here is a beautiful view, and again, the remains of old embankments. Don't you think Wiltshire may be well styled the "antiquarian" county of dear Old England? As the Avon wanders on, more remains of old camps and British villages appear on the hills above, and at length it reaches the site of Old Sarum, the hill on which, in the times of the Romans, Saxons, and Normans, Salisbury stood, where the old cathedral and castle were built, where kings assembled councils and made strong entrenchments. At length, however, the soldiers and the clergy quarrelled, and a new road, which did not pass through Sarum, was made, and a new cathedral was built where Salisbury now is, and old Sarum became more and more deserted, till at the present day it is but a green mound.

Salisbury, or New Sarum, is built at the meeting of three streams, the Avon, the Bourne, and the Wiley. These streams are brought to run in clear little canals through the streets, and look bright and cool. The streets are laid out in regular squares. Some of the houses have curious old-fashioned decorations, with carved gables; but the building that of all others distinguishes Salisbury is the cathedral, with the highest and most beautiful spire in England.‡ The windows are said to be in number equal

* Page 17.   † Page 365.   ‡ Pages 30, 45, 153, 181, 288, 355.

to the days, the pillars to the hours, and the gates to the months of the year. Find out how many there are of each. In the cathedral there are many curious old monuments to various bishops. One is to a boy-bishop. It was the custom, on St Nicholas' day, December the sixth, for the choir boys to elect one of their number as bishop, which title he kept till Innocents' day, December the twenty-eighth. Should he die within this time, which appears once to have happened, he was buried with great honour, in his bishop's robes. Salisbury has been the scene of battles and sieges, in various ages. The last historical event was William the Third's glad entry with his soldiers, when he came to save England from the tyranny of James II.*

Now, leaving the Avon for a little while, we will follow the Bourne and the Wiley. Bleak hills, with British camps, villages, and graves, characterise the country through which these rivers flow. Some of these British graves are very interesting. There was in one a little child clasped in its mother's arms; and in another a young girl, her head still wearing its coronal of beads. Another contained the ashes of a British warrior, with five beautiful arrow-heads of cut flint, round him deers' horns were encircled, and above him were the bones of his faithful dog, that had, perhaps, been slain with his master. But there is no tombstone to mark the Britons' hope in Him who is "the Resurrection and the Life." In this neighbourhood is Ludgershall, a small village, once celebrated for its fine Norman castle. The first market-town, not far from the source of the Wiley, is Warminster. The Lord of the Manor is bound to provide the sovereign and his attendants with one night's lodgings, should he be in the neighbourhood.† George III., with his queen and

* Page 256. † Pages 166, 196.

daughters, claimed the right, and was entertained at Longleat, a very beautiful place, in a lovely neighbourhood, belonging to the Marquis of Bath. Here Bishop Ken died. Near this is Woodhouse, which Lady Arundel defended, in Charles I.'s reign, till, finding she could hold it no longer, she escaped, being carried out secretly in a coffin.* Another town on the Wiley is Heytesbury; but, like many other places in Wiltshire, it is losing its population. After passing many camps and mounds, the Wiley reaches Wilton, the ancient capital of Wessex, now deriving its chief celebrity from the excellent carpets there manufactured. Near it is Wilton House, with ancient armoury, sculptures, and fine pictures. At Wilton, the Nedder joins the Wiley. It rises in a little lake on the borders of Dorsetshire. It soon passes Wardour Castle, a beautiful ruin. It was nearly destroyed during two sieges in Charles I.'s reign. At one time Lady Blanche Arundel, with only twenty-five men, for five days withstood the attack of one thousand five hundred of the enemy. The ruin is very extensive, and there are many curious relics. One is an oaken drinking-cup, supposed to have existed from the time of King Edgar. It will hold two quarts of ale, and inside of it are eight pegs, one above the other, dividing the quantity into half-pints. This was to prevent people drinking too much, as whoever drank below the mark was punished.† Another relic is a lock of Queen Elizabeth's hair, given by her to Sir Philip Sidney, of whom you read in Kent.‡ Near this is Fonthill, the splendid estate that once belonged to Mr Beckford. The festivities here were more like those of an Eastern monarch than of an English gentleman. For a week, three hundred dined at his table daily, and twelve hundred of his tenants feasted on the lawn, thirty thousand

---

* Pages 242, 350.   + Page 131.   ‡ Page 329.

lamps burning nightly in the park. On the borders of Wilts and Dorset is a wide district of wild forest land, called Cranbourne Chase. In some parts, the wood is thick, and in others the bleak but grassy downs extend, now and then crowned by what the country people call a " hat of trees."

On the Avon, near Salisbury, is Clarendon, anciently a royal palace, and noted as the place where some famous laws were drawn up in the reign of Henry II., called the Constitutions of Clarendon. They were to assert British liberty against the encroachments of the Pope.* Here Edward III., with the captive kings of France and Scotland, hunted the deer. Further down the Avon is Longford Castle, where there are remarkably fine paintings. One picture is a portrait by Holbein, of Erasmus, which that learned man sent to his friend, Sir Thomas More: Holbein brought it over himself, with a letter of introduction, and soon the artist became of great repute.

Now, I must cease to tell you about Wiltshire ; but I wish you to remark that not only is it the county of antiquities, but it is a county retrogressing or going backwards in importance, its towns and population nearly stationary. Poor Wiltshire ! it has not the advantages of the sea-shore for trade, nor of coal or iron for manufactures, nor of luxuriant soil for agriculture. However, it has very healthy breezes, and a simple-minded, courteous race of people—health of body and mind is more precious than wealth. This is the last inland county of which I shall speak. To-morrow we must visit the maritime one of Dorsetshire.

* Pages 303, 385.

DORSETSHIRE.

DORSET is not a more luxuriant county than Wiltshire, a great deal of the surface being chalk hills and sandy heaths. It has, however, a beautiful sea coast, and, like Wiltshire, is a healthy, breezy county. Though the climate is one of the mildest in England, the harvests are not early, and as the farmers do not like to give up their old customs, the same improvements have not been made here as in the eastern counties.* There is a great variety of soil in Dorset. The country called the trough of Poole, extending from Poole, westward towards Dorchester, is very sandy and barren. On each side of this are chalk downs, stretching, in the north, from the Cranbourne Chase to Beaminster, and on the south, to Dorchester, where they unite. Throughout the Isle of Purbeck, (not really an island, but a peninsula, to the south of Poole harbour,) and along the coast, is clay, of the same kind as in the Weald of Kent, limestone, most excellent for building, Kimmeridge clay, which the people can burn for fire instead of coal, Portland stone, of which the greater part of St Paul's, in London, is built, and various kinds of Oolite stones and clays. Just as you traced from Wiltshire the different branches of chalk,† so from Dorset you may draw a line through Somerset, Gloucester, Oxford, Northampton, the west of Lincoln and Yorkshire; and in all these counties you will find the Oolite formation of rock, called from a word which means egg, for the large masses of earth or rock have in them the tiniest little globules like the egg, or roe of a fish.

The useful things peculiar to Dorset are building stone, potters' and pipe-clay, grain, potatoes, flax and hemp,

---

* Pages 148, 174, 185, 311.　　　　　　† Page 383.

beer and cider, butter and cheese—the cheeses are not good, for they are made of skim milk*—a great many fish, especially mackerel and oysters, and a great many sheep. Several things are manufactured on a small scale, such as silk and woollen goods, shirt buttons, and gloves.

The chief rivers in Dorset are the Frome and the Stour, both flowing south-west.

First we will follow the Stour, which unites with the Avon in forming the little inlet on which Christchurch, in Hampshire, stands. Its source is very remarkable, being in the midst of the fine park of Stourhead. From some springs called the Six Wells, it flows underground, till it enters a grotto, and comes pouring out of a large urn.† Then it wanders through grounds ornamented with temples and statues, and old or curiously grafted trees, and passes below a hill, on which is Alfred's tower, commemorating the spot where that good king raised his standard, when he determined to fight against the Danes.‡ These grounds are in Wilts and Somerset; but very soon the Stour enters Dorset, and receives a little river which comes from the neighbourhood of Shaftesbury, a very ancient town, going back to the time of King Lud, who is said to have lived B.C. 1000 years; but about whom nothing certain is known.

A nunnery, however, was founded here by Alfred the Great, in which Edward the Confessor's body was enshrined, and which became a very rich place. Shaftesbury is on the top of a high chalk hill, with no springs of water. The supply came from the neighbouring parish of Gillingham. Once a year the Mayor of Shaftesbury used to present to the steward of the manor of Gillingham a large broom, hung with jewels, a calf's head, a pair of gloves, two penny loaves, and a gallon of ale, to

* Page 186.　　　† Page 207.　　　‡ Pages 238, 255.

show how much obliged the town was for the water. The steward used politely to return the broom, which was kept for the next year. Canute the Great died here.*

The Stour next receives the Cale, a little river flowing through the vale of Blackmoor, a marshy fertile valley, with beautiful oak trees, fat cattle, and numbers of pigs. Once it was a forest, where Henry III. hunted a white hart, but compassionating the pretty creature, forbore to kill it.†   Another hand more cruel afterwards slew it, which displeased Henry so much, that the county had to pay a yearly fine, called White Hart Silver.

The river passes some old but small market towns, and through a district where there are remains of Roman camps and earthworks, and at length reaches Blandford, once noted for point lace, now for shirt buttons. It was burnt to the ground in 1731, but is rebuilt a nice cheerful little town, with red brick walls and high roofs. The largest oak tree that, perhaps, ever grew in England once stood here. It was nearly twenty-three yards round.‡

At Wimbourne Minster, a town with a fine old church, the Stour receives the Allen from Cranbourne, an old market-town, near to which is St Giles' Court, where lives the good Lord Shaftesbury, the friend of the poor.§ It is said that, in the garden here the first cabbages were grown in England. ‖

Close to this, is another estate of Lord Shaftesbury's, on which the unfortunate Duke of Monmouth was taken prisoner. The soldiers had sought him the previous day without success, and were just leaving, when one of them saw a man concealed in a ditch, and nearly covered with fern leaves. This was the poor duke, who was taken to London and there beheaded.¶

---

* Pages 367, 370.   † Page 48.   ‡ Pages 157, 164, 259, 386.
§ Page 94.   ‖ Pages 300, 338.   ¶ Pages 237, 286.

Very near the Hampshire border is Poole, built on Poole Harbour, an inlet of salt water, almost like a lake, It has a beautiful island in the centre, where a castle is built, where dark fir trees grow, and where a great deal of potters' clay is found, and sent to the "Potteries,"—in what counties?* Poole is the chief seaport in Dorsetshire. Clay is its principal export; the blue potters' clay for pottery, and a kind that burns white, called pipe-clay, for tobacco-pipes;† small ships and beautiful yachts are made here; and also sails and cordage, and a great number of linen shirts. Many little creeks run inland from the harbour, and the channels being very narrow, the tides, which in most places are very regular, cannot here be depended upon.

The chief river that flows into Poole Harbour is the Frome. Near its source is Wolverton Hall, concerning which an interesting story is told. In Henry VIII.'s reign the King and Queen of Castile, a province of Spain, were driven, by bad weather, to Weymouth, and kindly entertained at Wolverton. The host, Sir Thomas Trenchard, did not, however, understand the language of his royal visitors; so he thought of a young neighbour of his, John Russell, who had lived sometime in Spain. His manners were so pleasing, that the king and queen asked him to go with them to London, and introduce them to the English king. He became a favourite with Henry VIII., who gave him a title and much land; and from him are descended the Dukes of Bedford and the Earls Russell. Dorchester is a pleasant well-built town, noted for its ale. It is a very ancient place, and contains curious remains of British and Roman works. One building, called the amphitheatre, would hold about 12,000 people. In this town sat the wicked judge Jeffreys during the Bloody Assizes, in James II.'s reign. The court was hung with scarlet, to symbolise, I suppose, its cruel deeds, and on one day eighty people were sentenced to death.   At Dorchester, the little Cerne joins the Avon from Cerne Abbas, with an old abbey.   Immediately above it is the Giant's Hill, on the chalky side of which, the turf is removed to leave the figure of a huge man, sixty yards high, holding a great club in one of his hands.   This is said to commemorate the death of a giant; he, having feasted on some sheep, lay down to sleep, but was fastened to the ground by the people, who then traced on the hill-sides his outline !*

Further down the Frome is Wareham, another very ancient town, surrounded by an earth-work, cast up by the ancient Britons.   Here the Frome is joined by the Piddle, on which is Piddletown.   A little streamlet running into this river passes Wilton Abbey, a beautiful place among the hills, with fine carving in the old abbey church—and then it passes Woodbury Hill, near Bere Regis, where there is every year a famous sheep fair. The Frome then becomes the boundary of the Isle of Purbeck.   A natural, huge chalk wall crosses the neck, which joins this so-called island to the mainland.   Only at one place this wall opens, and there stands Corfe Castle, the scene of many a deed of wickedness.   Do you remember reading in history of Queen Elfrida, here causing her step-son, the unsuspecting Edward, to be stabbed?†   Here, too, Edward II. was imprisoned;‡ and here the wicked King John murdered many noble prisoners.   And yet, perhaps, the greatest interest of Corfe Castle, is the wonderfully heroic defence that Lady Bankes made during her husband's absence, in the troublous times of King Charles.§ The Parliamentarians summoned her to surrender, but in vain ; she and her servants, both men and women, mounted the few rude guns that they had.   Again the enemies

* Page 255.   † Page 390.   ‡ Page 214.   § Pages 350, 392.

approached, with two great engines, the " Boar" and the " Sow," and shouted that they would give no quarter ; but still the brave lady was not daunted. Stones and burning ashes were thrown from the walls, which the enemy vainly tried to scale ; and though they were several hundreds in number, they were obliged to give up the siege. Three years afterwards it was again besieged, and captured through treachery. Then the Parliament ordered it to be blown up with gunpowder, which caused the ruined walls, though twelve feet thick, to lean outwards, and moved a tower, which is still in its upright position, three yards below the spot where it formerly stood. The coast of Purbeck Island is very wild and rugged, with grand precipices, large caverns, and cliff quarries, which look like the ancient cavern sepulchres found at Petra and in Egypt.

On the east side is Swanage, a pleasant bathing-place, its bay extending from the white chalk rocks of Foreland Pinnacles, on the north, to the black cliffs of Peveril Point on the south. Look on the map, and you will see Foreland Pinnacles are exactly west of the Needles ; and there is no doubt the line of chalk rock connecting them runs under the sea.* The Dancing Ledge is a curious sloping rock on the south of Purbeck, where, as the wild waves break, they seem to dance and sparkle. The most southern point of the island is St Alban's Head, where the little chapel, built to say mass for the passing sailors, has been changed into a coast-guard station, furnished with ropes and rockets to save those that are perishing.

At Kimmeridge, the black clay, which can be used as coal, is found.† Farther along the coast it forms a cliff, which took fire, and continued to burn for many years— an English burning mountain. I could tell you of many beautiful cliffs and caves, but shall just now only mention

* Pages 319, 380.   † Page 85.

"White Nose," where the white-chalk hills are again seen. On these Downs, the turf has been removed, to represent, on the chalk below it, an enormous figure of George III. on a trotting-horse.

On Weymouth Bay are situated Weymouth and Melcombe Regis—divided from each other by the harbour. They have a delightful beach with smooth sands. This was the favourite sea-bathing place of good old George III. and his family. * Here, there was once a terrible shipwreck of an East Indiaman, the "Abergavenny."† The ship got off the rocks, on which she had struck and the captain hoped to be able to run to the nearest port, but in vain. The water increased rapidly through the leaks that the rocks had made, and at length the ship went down, in water so shallow that the top of the rigging appeared above the waves when the hull touched the bottom. To this many poor seamen clung; some, after passing a night of great cold and misery, were saved; but most were drowned, and in one churchyard are the graves of eighty who were lost.

South of Weymouth is Portland Island. It is famous for building-stone; and for the mutton of the sheep fed on its downs. It is united to the mainland by one of the most extraordinary works of nature in England—a wall of shingle, called Chevil Bank, nearly eleven miles long, and about two hundred yards wide.‡ The waves have no doubt brought the shingle there; but we cannot tell why it was not thrown against the coast. The narrow channel which separates the coast from the bank is called the Fleet. Chevil Bank may be said to commence at Bridport, seventeen miles distant, where it consists of fine sand. This gets more and more mixed with pebbles, then the pebbles become larger and larger, till at Portland they

* Pages 210, 260, 352, 377.   † Page 361.   ‡ Page 733.

are about four inches wide. The inhabitants can tell on a dark night the exact part of the bank on which they are, by the size of these pebbles. The shore is most dangerous in stormy weather; so much so, that the bay on the west is called Deadman's Bay. There is a curious

Quarries in Portland.

story of a ship that sailed across the wall. A dreadful storm was raging—a sloop was drifting among the waves, when a billow of enormous power hove it upwards, and placed it on the top of the bank. Then the crew landed and walked to Portland. The storm passed over, and the ship, uninjured, was launched in the Fleet on the other side. There are about 100 quarries in Portland island; and it is reckoned it will supply stone, at the same rate as now, for 2000 years.* There are cliffs all round the

* Pages 126, 347, 387.

2 c

island, excepting on the north side, opposite Weymouth.
Here a very extensive breakwater is formed, as Portland
has been made a naval station. The stone required, about
2000 tons daily, was close at hand, and the labour was
chiefly performed by convicts, a large prison being here. *
On the overhanging cliff, on the east, is a very curious old
fortress, called the Bow and Arrow Castle, said to have
been built by William Rufus. There are little round holes
pierced in the walls through which arrows might be shot,
and brackets on the top for throwing down stones on the
enemy. Portland Castle, where the bank joins the island,
was built by Henry VIII., who presented it to three of
his unfortunate queens successively.

At the end of the Fleet, near Abbotsbury, are the Decoy
and Swannery. In the Decoy, numbers of wild fowls are
captured by a tame one. In what other county have you
heard of this?† In the Swannery, about 1000 beautiful
white swans find a home. At Abbotsbury are ruins of an
old abbey, built by King Canute, and a castle, whence
there is a fine coast view from the Hurst Point to Portland
Bill. The next town is Bridport, on the little river Bride,
which passes Beaminster, noted for double Dorset cheese,
and two hills, as like each other as they can possibly be,
called by sailors the Cow and the Calf. Bridport has some
commerce, and was once noted for its ropes and twine. It
still sends a number of fishing nets to Newfoundland.

The coast continues very beautiful, with its Golden-cap
Hill and fine Downs, and then another little river, the
Char, is reached, with Charmouth at its mouth. Here
Charles II. was very nearly discovered, before he was able
to embark for France. His horse wanted shoeing, and the
blacksmith observed that the old shoes were fastened in a
North of England fashion. Fortunately, however, the

* Pages 325, 362.   † Page 176.

horse of the trooper, who prepared to follow the king, took the wrong road.*

The last town in Dorsetshire, and one most beautifully situated, is Lyme Regis, where the little river Lyme flows through a deep valley into the sea. Here the unfortunate Duke of Monmouth landed, and waited till about 2000 people joined him.† A little girl, ten years old, called Mary Anning, here discovered the first ichthyosaurus. This colossal fossil animal was found imbedded in the cliff, and is now in the British Museum. When we hear of these enormous reptiles, I think we may thank God that the "great moving creatures" lived at a period before Adam and his children dwelt on the earth.‡ And now, with a promise that our next lesson shall be of one of the largest and most beautiful of English counties, we shall to-day leave the pretty sea-side Dorsetshire.

DEVONSHIRE.—Part I.

DEVONSHIRE is the third largest county in England. Which are larger? It is the fourth in population. Which do you think are more populous?

Now look on the map, and observe how the sea borders it, and how the rivers run through it. The shore extends with its inlets and outlets, on its north side and on its south side, about 212 miles, and the scenery of the coast is magnificent,—fine rocky cliffs continually rising from the water, frequently clothed with wood, or festooned with lovely creepers, but sometimes bleak, and bare, and grand. In the eastern part, the rivers flow south from hills but little distant from the northern shore. In the west, they flow both north and south from land near the centre.

* Pages 196, 353.   † Pages 237, 373.   ‡ Pages 58, 291, 321, 352.

What, therefore, about the high lands of the county may you know, without being told?

The high land in the north-east is called Exmoor, from which starts the range of hills, known as the Mendips, in Somersetshire, and the Cotswold, in Gloucestershire.* It forms the source of the Exe and of many of its tributaries. The high land more in the centre is Dartmoor, and from it you may trace the courses of the Teign, the Dart, the Tavy, the Oke, and the Taw. Exmoor and Dartmoor are very desolate. Exmoor, which forms a home for wild ponies and red deer, is covered with heather, excepting in those parts which, within the last few years, have been culti- vated. Dartmoor is about twenty miles square. It is composed of granite, a very old rock, which, in England, you have only heard of — in what northern counties? † This granite rises in the most whimsical shapes on the tops of all the rising grounds of the moor, and the great rocks it forms are called Tors. Some are like animals, some are like enormous giants, others are like old castles. Each Tor has a particular name. The highest is called " Yes Tor," and, according to their shape, they are "Sheeps' Tor," " Fox Tor," " Lynx Tor," and " Hare Tor." The granite is covered with peat, where heather, reeds, and moss grow; and, in the centre, is an immense bog, which, in many parts, would quickly swallow up the lightest forms that might tread upon it.‡ This bog and others are the sources of the different rivers I have named. Besides the Tors there are on Dartmoor many rock pillars, stone avenues, memorials of those strange superstitions of which I told you at Stonehenge, and hut circles, the stone founda- tions of the houses in which our forefathers lived. They all measure nearly nine yards across, but some of them have a circle beyond; and these outer circles are thought

* Pages 207, 228.   † Pages 69, 89.   ‡ Pages 62, 88.

to mark the mansions of the chiefs. The round enclosures of the villages, or perhaps of the folds for the cattle, may also be traced.* Try and fancy the days, nearly 3000 years ago, when our forefathers lived as the South Sea Islanders do now? Do you know a verse which Isaiah at that time wrote about the distant islands, which is now gloriously fulfilled in our dear old England?† A few huts, covered with straw or green rushes, are still scattered here and there, the inhabitants of which speak a strange mixed language, not easily understood.

The most beautiful scenery in Devonshire is found near these moorlands, amongst the rocky heights which extend from Exmoor along the coast, and amongst the beautiful wooded glens, through which the little streams from Dartmoor leap turmoiling onwards.

Excepting on these moors, Devon is exceedingly fertile; the two districts which are peculiarly so are the vale of Exeter and the South Hams. The latter, lying between Dartmoor and the Channel, is called the Garden of Devonshire, and there the apple grows abundantly, and much cider is made in the Pound-houses, a great deal of which is drunk by the country labourers.‡ Grain is not well cultivated; but the pastures are very rich, and the cows, which are almost all red, and the sheep, which very quickly grow fat, are noted as extremely good. The cream makes excellent butter; but it is more famous for being made into clouted cream, a dainty very much relished, and which is only made in this county and Cornwall. Another famous dish is Devonshire Junket, a mixture of cream, spirit, and spices. Many cheeses are made; but they are not rich, as skim milk only is used. The farmers in Devonshire use oxen very much for ploughing; a man and a boy go with each team, and, as they trudge along,

* Pages 65, 328, 330, 384.　† Isaiah li. 5.　‡ Pages 199, 216, 222.

they chant notes of music, which the oxen like to hear, and which seem to make them draw the plough more willingly.* The ponies on the moors feed in herds.† When they approach a boggy place, they first put down their nose, and then they pat the ground with their little fore-feet, and judge, I suppose, by sound, feeling, and smell, if the ground will bear them.

Devonshire is a county rich below ground, as well as on the surface. You remember our imagining a line drawn From the Exe to the Tees.‡ We have long been east of that line, but now again we are west of it; and we shall hear about mountainous and mineral regions. In this county, as in Dorset, a great deal of potters' clay is found, which is sent to the potteries in Staffordshire, and a little of fine white porcelain clay, used in making fine china. Here there are mines of tin, which you have not heard of before in England; and, also, mines of copper and lead.§ There is also freestone for building, granite, a remarkably hard and durable stone, and slate, as in the Lake districts.|| The county is not a seat for manufactures, but coarse woollen goods, such as druggets, are made, and carpets to imitate Turkish ones; also linen, and beautifully fine lace, called Honiton, and great numbers of shoes, which are sent over the Atlantic to the island of Newfoundland.

Besides these varied farming, mining, and manufacturing riches, the seas of Devonshire supply a great quantity of fish, such as mackerel, soles, turbots, and John Dories. The pilchard is also caught here; but I will tell you more of it when we reach Cornwall. The rivers abound with salmon-trout.¶ In the Dart these are sometimes killed by spearing. This is a kind of salmon-hunting. It is followed

* Page 346.   † Page 358.   ‡ Page 4.
§ Pages 19, 26, 78. || Pages 69, 78.   ¶ Pages 10, 17, 63, 195.

at night, with blazing torches, which discover the retreats of the frightened fish.

From what I have already said, you will see the people of Devon have various employments. Many of them live in the most picturesque little cottages, with thatched roofs, and walls made of cob, a mixture of mud and pebbles, grayish in colour, very warm and lasting. Vines, roses, or fuschias grow over these walls, and outside are the gardens, full of pretty flowers.* Through these villages a clear stream generally flows; for almost every valley has its bright and sparkling river. Though the wages are small, the people are industrious and careful, putting as much of their money as they can into the savings' banks. Instead of coal they generally burn peat, which they cut from the boggy moors, † or wood which they carry slung over a packsaddle on their hardy little ponies.

The climate is remarkably warm, and, for so northern a latitude, it is very equal throughout the year. In some parts on the southern coasts, snow and ice are seldom seen; whilst on the moorlands, the winds from the Atlantic blow very strong, and the air is fresh and bracing.

A great many famous men have been born in this county, especially brave seamen and good painters. Perhaps the sea washing the shores of all the bays and inlets accounts for the seamen, and the exceedingly picturesque scenery for the painters. Of the former there were, in Queen Elizabeth's time, Sir Francis Drake, who made the first voyage round the world, and returned with strange stories of unknown lands, and with new kinds of spices, monkeys, birds, and plants;‡ Sir John Hawkins, one of the admirals that went against the Armada;§ and Sir Walter Raleigh, who gained the queen's notice by throwing

* Page 374. † Pages 62, 77, 172. ‡ Pages 40, 322. § Page 316.

his cloak in the mud, to save the soiling of her shoes, and who afterwards proved both brave and skilful. He brought from America the potato and tobacco, the one as useful as the other is hurtful. Near Dartmouth is seen a part of the chimney-piece against which he is said to have sat when he smoked the first cigar that was seen in England. In Devonshire were also born Sir Humphrey Gilbert, who discovered Newfoundland, and John Davis, who gave his name to the Davis Straits, which you will find in the map of North America. In later days, Devonshire was the birthplace of Admiral Hood, who gained, in George III.'s reign, victories over the French. Amongst the painters, four noted in modern days were born at Plymouth, Haydon, Eastlake, Northcote, and Prout; and another little town, Plympton, is the birthplace of Sir Joshua Reynolds. The greatest soldier born in Devonshire is the Duke of Marlborough, who, in the reign of Queen Anne, gained very great victories over the French.* Amongst Devonshire poets are Gay, who wrote fables, and Coleridge; and amongst literary and scientific men, are Gifford, once a shoemaker's apprentice, but rising by talent and industry, he founded scholarships at Oxford, and was for many years editor of a very clever magazine, the *Quarterly Review;* and Buckland, much noted for his discoveries in the science of geology. Long ago Bodley was born here, who founded the famous Bodleian Library, of which I told you—where?†—and, in later days, Newcomen, once an ironmonger, but giving his mind to mechanics, he made important discoveries in working the steam-engine. Devonshire has also been the birthplace of many men honoured to work for God. At the little town of Crediton, many years ago, Wilfred was born, who went as a missionary to Germany, to make known to the rude tribes there the love of Jesus.

* Page 241.   † Page 245.

He is usually called St Boniface. Two good and learned clergy who lived in Queen Elizabeth's time were born in this county;—Hooker, always known as the judicious Hooker, and Jewel,* the excellent Bishop of Salisbury. The Queen was so pleased with a book which he wrote, that she ordered it to be chained and read aloud in every church in England. A little later, the good John Howe was born; he lived in an age when many conscientious persons suffered much persecution.† One night, Mr Howe had offered prayer in a gentleman's family, in the north of Devonshire, when word was brought that he had been discovered, and would soon be taken prisoner. The night was stormy, dark, and wintry; but it was thought better that he should leave the house. He and his servant soon lost their road on the common. They saw before them a mansion; knocking there, a kind invitation was given for them to remain all night; but on entering Mr Howe found it was the house of the magistrate who had been doing all he could to seize him. He talked long and seriously with him that night. The next morning, he expected to be sent to prison, but, instead of a summons, received a kind invitation to breakfast. That conversation had made the magistrate anxious that his soul should be saved. During an illness afterwards, his anxiety became greater; and after his recovery, he showed himself an earnest Christian and a very warm friend and supporter of Mr Howe. Another learned clergyman born in Devon was Dr Kennicott, particularly noted for his knowledge of Hebrew. There are many more, of whom I cannot now tell you.

* Page 387.　　　　　　　† Page 163.

DEVONSHIRE.—PART II.

WHAT was the last town of which you heard in Dorsetshire? Hoping that this is remembered, I must tell you that west of it, along the coast, there occurred at Christmas, 1839, a wonderful landslip, similar to those of which I have told you in the Isle of Wight.* Cracks in the ground had been observed for about a week, when, on Christmas Eve, the land began to move very slowly, the cracks enlarging. The following night, the great chasm opened, with a sound like the tearing of cloth, and gradually widened, till it was eighty-three yards across. No lives were lost, as the movement was very gradual; some of the trees were killed, but others moved with the soil, or re-rooted themselves; and apples are still gathered from the transported orchard, as if nothing had happened.† The scenery became, however, grander and wilder.

Following the coast, we soon reach the mouth of the Axe, which little river we will track. Axminster is the first town after leaving Dorsetshire. Its famous carpet manufactories have been moved to Wilton. ‡ In this neighbourhood a battle is supposed to have been fought between Athelstane and several Danish and Northern kings. Nine kings are said to have been left dead on the field. In consequence, Athelstane founded the Minster, which still stands, and which is in parts very ancient.

Colyton stands on a little stream, flowing into the Axe, and has many people employed in making lace. Here, also, is a paper-mill, where once a sheet of tissue paper was made, six feet broad and four miles long. It only weighed fourteen stone. On the east side of the river a chain of hills continues to the sea—two of them

* Page 379.　　　　† Page 220.　　　　‡ Page 392.

crowned with Roman camps. West of the Axe, the coast is very beautiful; the cliffs being of great height, and of various colours—bright red sandstone, and white chalk, contrasting. At Beerhead is the last chalk hill we shall meet with in England. We have met it frequently, ever since I told you of—what grand rocky promontory in Yorkshire?*

At Beer, there is a curious sandstone quarry, which goes a quarter of a mile underground. If you had not a guide, you would probably be lost, as there are many passages. Would it not be a famous place for hide and seek? You would require torches and warm dresses, as the caverns are both dark and wet. Beyond this, beautifully situated —hills and valleys, and streams, all mingled in picturesque confusion—is Branscombe. Here also lace is made of the most beautiful kind. Queen Victoria's splendid wedding-dress was made at this little village. More grand cliffs, some of them 500 or 600 feet high, and a lovely Devonshire town is reached, on the shore of one of the rich valleys that opens towards the sea. This is Sidmouth, once a small seaport, but now only a bathing-place, as the harbour is filled with sand and shingle. The collier-ships that arrive, have to empty their cargoes into little boats; so, as you may fancy, coal is dear. The climate is very warm, but rather too damp for invalids. Sidmouth is famous for its beautiful pebbles, green, red, and yellow; and also for its elegant cottages. The most beautiful of these is Knole Cottage. The rooms are all on one floor, and the drawing-rooms one hundred feet long. Within are all kinds of pretty curiosities, and without are conservatories filled with beautiful plants, and aviaries with rare birds, whilst kangaroos and buffaloes sport or range upon the lawn. At Sidford, near this town, Charles II., when he was escaping

* Pages 36, 168, 240, 249, 261, 302, 318, 346, 356, 380, 383, 399.

from his pursuers, hid himself in a chimney.* West of Sidmouth is High Peak, one of the most beautiful red sandstone cliffs on the coast; and a little farther is the mouth of the Otter, so called from the number of otters that abound in it.

We must go a little distance inland for the source of this river; and first, I will tell you of the lovely lanes, for which this neighbourhood, and all Devonshire, is famed. They are deep, and narrow, and hilly; the hedges with their beautiful blossoms, and green banks, carpeted with ferns, and mosses, and starry flowers, stretching upwards to the height of thirty feet. The Otter rises amongst the Black Down Hills, which separate Devon and Dorset. It passes Honiton, from which place the fine lace, of which I have told you, takes its name. It nearly equals the fine point lace of Brussels. It is different to that made in Bedfordshire; as the pattern, instead of being worked with the net, is made by the hand, in separate pieces, and then sewed on net, made by machine.† The vale of Honiton, extending down the river, is celebrated for its butter. In this district is Ottery St Mary, with a beautiful church. Here lived Sir Walter Raleigh. Farther down is Peppleford, which receives its name from the number of oval pebbles there found; and below this is Bicton, where there are gardens beautifully arranged; the collection of trees and shrubs being almost the finest in England. The cottages here seem embowered in myrtles; and the sparkling stream, and pretty pebbles, and finely-coloured cliffs, as the shore is approached, make the scenery very lovely. In this neighbourhood Raleigh was born.

We now reach the mouth of the Exe. Its source will take us to a portion of the bleak region of Exmoor in the county of Somerset, not far from the Bristol Channel.

* Pages 196, 353, 403.   † Page 162.

As it enters Devon at Exbridge, it receives the Barle, a beautiful mountain-stream, flowing through a wild valley, up which no road passes. Here are woods where the red deer hide, and above is purple heather, where they feed. The Exe thus increased, passes onwards and receives a little stream from Bampton. This is a quiet little town, in a wild region; where there are fairs for sheep, cows, and ponies, and near to which are limestone quarries. It is very pleasant to look at the beautiful view from a stone seat in the churchyard, which is sheltered by old yews, whose branches, rent by age, are mended with masonry.

Farther down the Exe is Tiverton. When the bobbin-net machine was invented at Nottingham, there was such opposition that Mr Heathcote, the inventor, was obliged to remove. He came here, and for several years Tiverton was the place where all machine-made net was manufactured. Now, fifteen hundred people are employed in Mr Heathcote's factory.* There are here the ruins of a fine old castle. The Great Western Canal connects Tiverton with Taunton, in Somersetshire. Continuing its bright, pleasant course, the Exe receives the Creedy river from the west. On its banks stands Crediton, a very old town, so old that people say

"Kerty [Crediton] was a market-town
When Exeter was a furzy down."

Shoemaking is the principal trade of this place. In what central county is shoemaking the chief occupation of the people?† On the left the Exe receives the Culmer, on which stands the little market town of Cullompton. Formerly it was noted for woollen manufactures; and a rich clothier, who built part of the church, ornamented the outside with a representation of his machinery for cloth.‡

* Page 137.   † Page 159.   ‡ Page 256.

The Exe, enlarged by many streams, now passes the city of
Exeter, which is the chief town of the county.   Its situation is healthy and beautiful, and it seems rightly called
"The Queen of the West."   It must be a very long time
since Exeter was a "furzy down," for there is no doubt
it is a very ancient place.   Many suppose it was a British
city ; and it is certain that the Romans made it one of their
chief towns.*   In the time of the Saxons, Athelstan here
fought the ancient Britons, driving them farther west;
and, in the time of Charles I., it was besieged in turn
by Royalists and Parliamentarians.   In this troublous
time, whilst the queen stayed in the city, a little princess,
called Henrietta, was born, who afterwards married a
royal duke of France.   The chief building in Exeter is
the cathedral, the western side of which is reckoned
very beautiful.   The "Peter Bell" is one of the largest
in England ;† but what you will like to hear of, is a
very strange old clock, on the centre of which the earth
is represented ; the sun revolving in the outer circle tells
the hour of the day and the age of the moon ; whilst the
moon, revolving in the inner circle, shows, by some machinery, all the real moon's changes, from new to full.
The bishop's throne, of black oak, more than seventeen
yards high, is beautifully carved.   The castle called Rouge-
mont has long been in ruins.   There are stories which connect it with the history of several of our early kings.   It is
said that Exeter is the first town that ever sent a member
to the House of Commons.   Owing to its very fertile soil,
and warm climate, the nursery gardens here are the best
in England.   In one, a fir-tree from California is growing.
If it grows as it does in its native country, it will be larger
than any tree in England, its natural size being giant-like.
   Below Exeter, at Topsham, the Exe receives the Chirt,

* Pages 44, 106, 154, 194, 226, 229, 276, 367.   † Pages 153, 244, 288.

and then it widens greatly and becomes an arm of the sea, but not a useful arm, for a sand-bank stretches across its mouth, leaving a very narrow channel, which, at low water, is only eight feet deep, so that no large ships can enter. The last town on the Exe that I shall mention is Exmouth, situated, as you will guess, at the river's mouth. There are beautiful walks in the neighbourhood, with extensive and varied views. The town is a very favourite bathing-place. Many of the male inhabitants are employed in fishing, and the females in lace-making. In the neighbourhood are some pretty villas. Here is an almshouse for poor old maidens, which is called " Point in View," for it bears this motto, " Some point in view we all pursue." On the other side of the Exe extend the Haldon Hills. They look like mountains from Exmouth. Westward on the coast is Dawlish, a new and very pretty bathing-place.

A little farther west, we reach the mouth of the Teign, one of the rivers that rise in Dartmoor. Its early course is through splendid wildness, passing strange tors, rock pillars, ancient trees—oaks, and beech, and fir, and running beneath a remarkable old granite British bridge. Soon it reaches Chagford, a pretty little town, with fine bracing air from the wild land of Dartmoor. Here, Sydney Godolphin, a leading man amongst the Royalists, was killed. The little river plunges wildly onwards, through Gidleigh Park, rushing over steep rocks, which re-echo the sound of its roar. Here is an ancient Druid temple; but you shall hear more of the Druids anon, for we are now in the neighbourhood of difficult access, where the Britons were driven by England's early invaders.

Farther on, the river passes Spinsters' Rock, about which strange wild stories are told. It is a flat stone on three pillars, so high that you can walk underneath it. Then amidst briars and ferns, and everything wild and beautiful, the river passes a curious logan stone, and reaches Fingle Bridge, considered the most beautiful part of all its beautiful course. Steep wooded hills and rocky precipices shut in the river; and the bridge, covered with ivy, rests on rocks at either side. Then the village of Drews-Teignton is reached, or "Druids' Town on the Teign." Can you fancy the time, when those ancient priests, with white garments and mistletoe wreaths, walked in these solitudes? But they were not solitudes then, for old British castles still crown the hills, that, in this neighbourhood, overlook the river. Turning southward, the merry river hastens on, each portion of its course telling of God's love in making scenery so pretty, and then it passes the little town of Chudleigh, which, like Tiverton and others, was once destroyed by fire. It is famed for the marble rocks that are near it. Half-way up the cliff is a deep cavern called the "Pixies' Parlour." Pixie is a name for fairy. The parlour is roofed with interlaced roots of trees, very suitable for fairies! Farther south, the Teign réceives the Wray, which, with pretty little brooks that have joined it, has its source in Dartmoor. One called the Beckey, rises near High Tor, whence the view over the rich sea-bound land to the south, and the wild dreary moor to the north, is splendid. There granite is quarried, and taken by canal to Teignmouth. Then the little stream passes Hound Tor and Bowerman's Nose, formed by the oddest-shaped stones possible, and, before joining the Wray, it reaches Beckey Fall, a precipice of granite, and tumbles eighty feet down into a deep glen. The other brook is the Bovey, at one time losing itself beneath natural stepping-stones, which consist of great blocks of granite, at another time passing between hills covered with furze, which I have seen described, as resembling an embroidery of gold on velvet of the richest green, and then rushing past groups of rocks, which, according to the animals that lodge there, have names, such as the Raven's Tower, or the Foxes' Yard. One curious rock is called the Nutcrackers. It is balanced, so that the touch of the little finger can roll it from side to side. When moved it touches another rock, and if a nut is placed between them it is cracked very effectually.

Between the Wray and the Teign is Bovey Heathfield; low ground supposed once to have been a lake, to which, in former days, the crumbled granite was brought by the streams from Dartmoor. It now forms very fine clay, fit for the finest porcelain. At the village of Bovey Tracey, are porcelain works, which have an advantage over Worcester or Derby, in having the material close at hand. But though we love the Teign's wild banks, we must hasten on. Newton is an old town,* memorable as the place where William of Orange made his first declaration in England, of his objects as the liberator of the people.

The river widens, and at its mouth is Teignmouth, a large watering-place. Here it is crossed by a bridge, said to be the longest in England, 557 yards, about one-third of a mile in length. As in the Exe, a broad sand-bank nearly crosses the mouth of the river; but the bank here is made useful, for it is a good promenade, and a lighthouse stands at the end.† The people are chiefly fishers, some of them going all the way to Newfoundland. Now remember the Axe, the Otter, the Exe, and the Teign.

To-morrow I hope to tell you more of charming Devonshire.

* Pages 20, 375.　　　　　　† Pages 106, 154, 213, 374.

2 D

DEVONSHIRE.—PART III.

ALONG the coast, south of Teignmouth, you will see on the map a little promontory, the point of which is called Hope's Nose, and farther south is another called Berry Head, between which lies the beautiful, the sheltered, and the interesting Torbay. There is a lovely cave near Hope's Nose; its marble cliffs shining like satin, the sand white and sparkling like glass, and ivy creeping over the rocks as if they were ruined towers. On Torbay stands Torquay, considered by many the best climate in England for consumptive patients. It is a pleasant town, and the houses are handsomely built. Near it is a cavern, called Kent's Hole, where all kinds of wild beasts' bones have been found, like those in—what Yorkshire cavern ?*

Tor Abbey, a ruin now, was once one of the richest in England. On the south side of Torbay is Brixham, a spot of deep interest in English history; for here landed William Prince of Orange, who was God's instrument in delivering England from its unworthy king, James II., thus frustrating his endeavours to bring our dear old country under the Pope's power.† A furious wind from the east had driven the prince rapidly down the Channel past Torbay, and all seemed lost, for William could not land near Plymouth, which was strongly fortified. But God made the stormy wind to cease, and a gentle south breeze to blow; and the ships sailed into the bay, and sixty little boats conveyed the soldiers to the shore. Then a strong northerly gale rose, and met the king's ships, so that they could not follow William. The night was wet and desolate, and the prince slept in a fisherman's little hut, his Orange banner waving from its roof.

* Pages 53, 235.   † Pages 230, 256, 360.

A quantity of fish is caught in Torbay; two hundred trawler boats belong to Brixham. The trawling net is like an immense bag, twenty or thirty yards long, the mouth kept open by a long wooden beam. This is trawled along the bottom of the bay, and is soon filled with various fish. Hill and dale succeed each other very rapidly between Brixham and Dartmouth; and there we reach another river, the Dart, and you must tell me where it rises.

The neighbourhood of its early course brings us to a stranger place than you have yet heard of—Wistman's Wood; a remnant of the ancient forest that probably covered Dartmoor, and which is thought, from its name and situation, to have been the scene of some of the abominable rites of heathenism practised by the Druids. Now it is covered with morass, and with wood—not tall handsome trees, but strange stunted oaks and ash, seldom more than ten feet high, branched and twisted in every form. No human foot can penetrate that forest. It is only a home for serpents and foxes; but we must thank God that the idols and their bloody sacrifices are utterly abolished.* In this neighbourhood is Crewkerne, where, till 1749, the Stannary Parliament was held. This was a meeting of twenty-four gentlemen sent by the different mining districts, to make regulations, and to deal justice. A strange parliament house, the bleak side of a hill, in the very centre of Dartmoor! † Close to Dartmeet, the spot where the East and West Dart join, are very visible remains of an ancient British town. The same kind of old British bridges, made of single enormous stones, span the Dart, as cross the Teign; and there are, in many places, on its bank, traces of tin mines, that have ages ago been worked. A beautiful spot on the Dart is called the "Lover's Leap," where a slate precipice rises straight above the water. The

* Pages 10, 54, 263, 332, 385, 389,   † Page 330.

river afterwards passes near Ashburton, a pleasant town in a cultivated valley, on the outskirts of the moor. Both Ashburton and Buckfastleigh, the next town on the river, have wool factories. The church at Buckfastleigh is reached by 140 steps.* The gravestones look very mournful, being of black marble, of which there are quarries in the neighbourhood.

The next town of interest is Totness, to which place small ships can ascend. The neighbourhood is noted for its fine timber and beautiful marble. Totness is a very old town, with strange, antique houses, and the ruins of a round ivy-clad castle. To the west of Totness is the castle of Berry Pomeroy, hidden in wood, the trees growing even inside its deserted walls. It was partly built by the Duke of Somerset, Protector in Edward VI.'s reign.† The river below Totness is very beautiful, winding in such manner that it looks like a string of lakes, and the banks echo again and again the voice of the traveller. Passing Stoke Gabriel, with its enormous yew-tree, and Dittisham, with its plum-trees, and in the middle of the water, the anchor rock, on which Sir Walter Raleigh used to sit and smoke,‡ it at length reaches the old town of Dartmouth. The harbour, nearly surrounded by land, forms almost a lake. It is, consequently, very safe for ships, which bring coal, wine, and fruit, and take away cider, woollen goods, and corn. The town is built on the side of a steep hill. Look at the picture of the pretty old buildings. One street is on a level with the roofs of the houses of another, and steep flights of steps connect them.§ The old church of St Saviour's is noted for its very rich and curious carvings. There are the ruins of an old castle; whilst a more recent one, of the time of Henry VII., stands beautifully on the edge of a rock, which is washed by the deep blue waves.

* Page 92.   † Page 292.   ‡ Page 407.   § Page 43.

Its tower used to contain a chain, stretched, for defence, across the mouth of the harbour.

The shore westward forms a curve, Start Bay. The cliffs look bright, and in some parts sparkling. They are composed of slate. The bay ends in the Start Point, where stands the lighthouse, whose revolving light is fre-

Old Houses at Dartmouth.

quently the last sign of their native shore that our Indian or Australian-bound voyagers see. On one side of Start Point all is smooth and bright, and on the other dark and rugged; for on the west the waves of the Atlantic beat and fierce winds blow. It is the hardness of the slate and gneiss rocks of which this promontory is composed, that has withstood their force. Prawle Point is the most southern cape of Devonshire, and the other two points of

the promontory are Bolt Head and Bolt Tail.   From Start
Point to Bolt Tail the scenery is grand.   A pretty inlet
lies between, running some distance inland.   The shores
of this inlet are extremely warm, and lemon and orange
trees flourish in the open air; but the surrounding hills are
bleak, and inland the country is not pretty.   Kingsbridge
and Salcombe are the two towns on the coast.   Salcombe
is famous for its white ale, made of hops, flour, and spices.
Along the rough shore many crabs and lobsters are found.
Near Bolt Head is a cave, from which it is said that there
is an underground passage to another cave that opens out
in an adjoining bay.   There is an absurd story of a bull
that went in at one end and came out at the other; but,
strange to say, it went in black and came out white.

Leaving again the coast and its curious crags, we
will find the source of the next river, another Avon.
Count up all the Avons. *   Its source is in Dartmoor.
Near South Brent, a little town on its banks, Devonshire
sand is procured, which is used in sanding paper.   The
bay into which the Avon falls is Bigbury, and at its mouth
is Burr Island, where fishermen employed in the pilchard
fishery reside.

The next river from Dartmoor is the Erme, also a wild,
lonely stream.   In the midst of memorials of the past you
will now see spanning the river and its valley a beautiful
railway bridge, looking fragile among the massive wildness around; and farther down is Ivy Bridge, which,
though but a few yards long, stands in four parishes.†
Farther on is Ermington, with a leaning spire;‡ and near
it Old Modbury, with slate-fronted houses.   West of the
mouth of the Erme the coast continues wild, and grand,
and lonely; and on a low slate crag, an old church stands,
a monument to Him whose power has set to that great

* Pages 121, 228, 384.   † Page 155.   ‡ Page 132.

swelling sea its bounds that it should not pass. ' The next river is the Yealm, noted for the Yealm Bridge Cavern, full of the bones of hyenas, elephants, rhinoceroses, and strange large birds. Near its mouth, on a beautiful rocky inlet, with heathery hills rising behind, are three little villages, called Yealm. There is a sad tale of the ravages of the plague in one of them, which left only seven of its inhabitants alive.*

The coast now brings us to the most important, and, perhaps, the most beautiful of all Devonshire bays, Plymouth Sound. Three rivers fall into it, the Plym, the Laira, and the Tamar; and three large towns stand on it, Plymouth, Stonehouse, and Devonport, which united form one whole—"Plymouth being the business or city part, Devonport the West End, and Stonehouse the part for hospitals and manufactories." There are manufactories of soap, earthenware and ropes, sugar refineries, and various mills; it is a port for ships from all parts of the world, especially for emigrant ships from Australia; but it is chiefly noted as a naval station, for, as at Portsmouth, the arms of the Sound preserve their depth as they run inland, and thus form excellent harbours for large men-of-war.†
Formerly the Sound was not a good anchorage; for when a south-west gale blew, then the large Atlantic waves rolled inwards, and the ships lay in great danger. A famous engineer, Mr Rennie, proposed, however, a plan of raising a stone rampart across the part where the waves rolled in most fiercely. It was to be nearly a mile long, and of such strength that the waves should not destroy it. This was a stupendous undertaking; but it has been, after many years' labour, accomplished; and now ships lie quite safely within this great breakwater. The weight of the stone is reckoned to be equal to that of the Great

* Pages 80, 108, 129.　　　　† Pages 321, 324, 332, 360.

Pyramid of Egypt. The citadel at Plymouth is very strong, and well furnished with cannons. It is on the eastern end of the Hoe, which is one of the most beautiful walks conceivable. The view of land and water, of green trees and white sails, of woods and cliffs, of chimneyed cottages and masted ships, is most beautiful.* From this point the Spanish Armada was discovered; and at Mount Edgcumbe, on the western shore, was lighted the beacon fire that roused Old England's lion.†

"Night sank upon the dusky beach and on the purple sea,—
Such night in England ne'er had been, nor e'er again shall be.
From Eddystone to Berwick bounds, from Lynn to Milford Bay,
That time of slumber was as bright and busy as the day;
For swift to east and swift to west the warning radiance spread,
High on St Michael's Mount it shone—it shone on Beachy Head."

At Stonehouse is the victualling yard, where the Prince of Wales landed, after his memorable visit to America, in 1860. Here provisions are prepared by steam, as they are at Gosport. In the slaughter-house eighty large oxen can be killed at once. Here, too, is a large naval hospital. Devonport is very conveniently and pleasantly built. Here is the dockyard, where steam machinery makes ropes, hammers, nails, cuts wood, and performs various other work, just as it does at Portsmouth. One machine for plaiting a kind of rope, wheels about and turns about so continually, that it is called a Jim Crow. These towns are well supplied with water, brought from Dartmoor by a channel made through the exertions of Sir Francis Drake. What worthy citizen wrought a similar work for London?‡ To Plymouth this channel or leet brought the water thirty miles. When the water first ran its course through the channel, cannons were fired, and the mayor and aldermen, in grand dresses, went to meet it.

Now, for a very short time, we must follow the Plym,

* Page 226.   † Pages 36, 347.   ‡ Page 262.

which rises near Sheep's Tor, the chief home, according to Devonshire story, of the pixies ; and to this day the country people who visit it drop a pin for them. They say that the little fairies have stored in this Tor precious minerals ; and particles of the gold have sometimes been found in the streams below.

For a time, the Plym is called the Cad, and the arm of Plymouth Sound which it enters is Cat Water. Its course is wildly beautiful, dashing over blocks of granite, passing by strangely-shaped rocks, and roaring under ivy-clad bridges. A railway connecting Plymouth and Dartmoor runs nearly parallel with the course of this river, its chief use being the conveyance of huge blocks of granite.

We have had enough for to-day. The beautiful Tamar and all the northern coast must be for to-morrow.

DEVONSHIRE.—Part IV.

THE Tamar, like the Exe, rises very near the Bristol Channel. Its source is in Cornwall, but it receives many feeders from Dartmoor. Almost throughout its course it divides Devon from Cornwall ; the character of its two banks being very different. The eastern one generally consisting of steep craggy rocks, and the western of gently swelling meadows. Just above Lifton, where it is joined by the Lyd, is a bridge, on which, an old tradition says, there used to stand a man with a black bill in his hand, ready to knock down all lawyers endeavouring to go into Cornwall. Why ? I cannot tell. The Lyd is one of the beautiful streams of Dartmoor. On its banks stands Lidford, now a straggling village, but once a very important place, where the trials of the Stannary Courts were held,* and where there was a mint.† Judge Jefferies, the Execrable, held a

* Page 419.   † Page 298.

court here,* and the people who have stories about everything, say, that he sometimes visits the courtyard, in the
shape of a black pig. Here a bridge spans the river,
reckoned one of the most remarkable things in Devonshire.
It is a single arch, over a ravine seventy feet deep, along
which the water rushes tumultuously.† Soon the river
hastens forward to meet a brook, which leaps a precipice
of thirty-seven yards, and throws itself into the Lyd's deep
dell. The Tamar continues its beautiful course, and passes
Endleigh, a lovely cottage-mansion, belonging to the Duke
of Bedford.‡ The grounds are beautiful, particularly the
Dairy Dell. The next interesting place is the grand Morwell
Rocks, which appear towering high above the river; and
here are not only picturesque beauty, but also the signs of
busy life, as this place is the termination of a little canal
from the Tavy. The canal is on high ground, but the barges,
laden with granite or copper ore, are moved with their cargoes to trucks, which slide down a steep railway to the
river-side. The river widens before it reaches the Tavy,
and then it expands so as to appear almost like a beautiful
lake. The Tavy is another Dartmoor stream; its clear
waters foaming over its stony bed. It runs through a district famous for copper mines. One of these, Wheal
Friendship, is very large and deep, and entirely worked by
water, which is guided into all parts of the mine, turning
the immense wheels. In another part there are extensive
slate quarries, and many villages inhabited by miners.
Two of them are called Peter Tavy and Mary Tavy. There
is a story of a judge, a stranger to the county, making a
mistake about a trial, and ordering Peter and Mary Tavy
to appear in court. The largest town is Tavistock. Here
is a large old church, the tower of which rests on arches,
which span a thoroughfare for passengers. There are the

* Pages 237, 373, 397.   † Pages 415, 419.   ‡ Page 411.

ruins of a large abbey, where, in a stone coffin, were found enormous human bones, supposed to be those of a giant, Ordulph, who was so tall that he could stride across a river ten feet wide, and so strong that he could chop off the heads of wild beasts at a blow. Tavistock was once very famous for its woollen manufactures, Tavistock Kersey having been celebrated all over England.* At Double Water, amidst crags and caves, with names such as the Raven Rock, or the Virtuous Lady, the Walkham joins the Tavy. Once more to Dartmoor. Near the early course of the Walkham is Dartmoor prison, where many convicts are employed cultivating the ground. Here the wilderness has been turned into fields of grain or of vegetables. The river winds round Great Mis Tor whose surface is white in parts with granite rock. It passes many hut circles. In one place, when the plague raged in Tavistock, these were used as a market, the country people bringing provisions thus far, which the townspeople carried away, leaving money instead. Do you remember a similar tale amongst the hills of Derbyshire? † Farther down the Tavy, is Buckland Abbey, where there are still many relics of the brave Sir Francis Drake, amongst others the Bible which he carried with him all round the world. Soon the Tavy joins the Tamar, near a very large silver-lead mine,‡ and then the Tamar becomes very wide, and farther down, in the part called the Hamaoze, the great men-of-war lie at anchor.

Now look at the map for the north of Devonshire, and we will follow its most beautiful coast. The first river at the east side is the East Lyn, which runs through Lyndale, a district of wild beauty. At Waters Meet, another little rivulet joins, forming in the deep valley a scene of great loveliness. Lynmouth is one of the most picturesquely

* Pages 175, 189, 237, 256, 305.   † Page 124.   Page 19.

situated villages possible. There the East and West Lyn unite, the West Lyn turmoiling in a succession of cascades, through a very deep dingle, clothed with trees and ferns and moss. Lynmouth seems to be locked in with hills, and all day long the sound of the wildly rushing rivers is there heard to mingle with that of the ocean.

Lynton is built on a height above Lynmouth; and is also a charming village. Near it, is one of the wildest scenes in England;—the Valley of Rocks, where separate masses in

Ilfracombe.

very grotesque shapes rise, and seem ready to fall upon the green grass, or into the blue sea beneath. Here many human bones have been found, marking, it is said, the spot where a large party of Danes were slaughtered. Deep wild glens succeed, and then Comb-Marten comes, where, for more than 500 years, a silver lead mine has, at times, been worked, and where a quantity of lime is burnt. The hills continue beautifully grouped, and the coast full of pretty little caves, where the water looks clear, and where sea-anemones abound, stretching out their tiny arms in their rocky homes. Ilfracombe, with an excellent harbour, is beautifully situated on this hilly coast. It is a favourite bathing-place; and, in the reign of Edward III., was comparatively a large seaport, which you will understand, when I tell you that it sent six ships to Edward III.'s fleet, when the now important river Mersey contributed only one.* Farther west is Bideford, or Barnstaple Bay. At the north point of this bay is Morte Stone, or the Rock of Death, so called from the number of shipwrecks that it has occasioned.† The two principal rivers falling into Bideford Bay are the Taw and the Torridge; one from Dartmoor, and the other from Cornwall. The Taw, from Dartmoor, pursues its early course in the same kind of region as the Teign and the Tavy. Below Chudleigh, a pleasant, little, old-fashioned town, the Taw is joined by the Mole, from the south of Exmoor. In this neighbourhood is Fleton Oak, supposed to have been there since the time of Alfred the Great. It measures eleven yards round. At South Molton, Samuel Baldock—a learned dissenting minister, once a butcher—was born. Do you observe how many English people of humble origin have distinguished themselves by bravery, or learning, or goodness? Near the mouth of the river is Barnstaple, a small commercial town, where ships arrive with coals, groceries, iron, and porter; and take away grain, wool, leather, and earthenware. There are potteries in the town; and many are employed in making lace. There is a large fair every year; on the second day of which a stag is hunted on Exmoor.‡ Triston Quay, a small bathing-place, stands where the Torridge and Taw unite. Let us now

* Pages 97, 154, 337.   † Pages 11, 400.   ‡ Pages 208, 315.

follow the Torridge. It rises in the same bog as the Tamar, in the county of Cornwall; but their distance soon increases, and the Torridge—after running nearly as far as the Tamar, but in the shape of C—enters the sea, not many miles from its source. Hatherleigh, with its thatched cob cottages, and agricultural inhabitants, is the first town on its course. The people have the strange custom of ringing the church-bells merrily, as soon as a funeral is over, saying, "That the dead person is removed from a world of trouble to one of joy;" and such we know is true of those who die in the Lord. Below Hatherleigh, the Okemont joins the Torridge; and this is our last river from the bogs of Dartmoor. Its western branch rises in Cranmere Pool, the lake of Cranes; and its eastern, below Yes Tor, the highest point of Dartmoor, and whence there is a very extensive view. The united streams pass Okehampton, where the picturesque ruins of a fine old castle look down into the dell of the river.

The next town on the Torridge is Torrington. Here, during a battle in Charles I.'s time, eighty barrels of gunpowder exploded, blowing into the air the church, with two hundred prisoners, and their guards. Near Torrington, General Monk, who was the means of Charles II.'s restoration, was born. In the town is a manufactory for gloves. Flowing between pleasantly-wooded banks, the Torridge reaches Bideford, a pretty and a healthy town, with a very fine bridge. Here are potteries, and a good deal of commerce. Near the town is a mine of cannel coal, of the same kind as is found near Wigan,—where ? *

At the mouth of the Torridge is Appledore, a very old little town, with a curious story of a Saxon victory over the Danes, when the Raven banner was taken, which clapped its wings before victory, but remained quiet before

* Page 85.

defeat. At the mouth of the united Taw and Torridge is the Pebble Ridge—a remarkable ridge of stones, two miles long. On one side is short grass, on the other, sand ; but on neither is there a pebble to be found.* Westward, after passing along steep, wooded cliffs, is the fishing town of Clovelly, said to be "the most romantic in Devonshire, and probably in the kingdom." Near it is the park of Clovelly Court, where strangely-bended rocks, rising above the deep blue waters of the sea, are crowned with beautiful old oak-trees. The west point of Bideford Bay is Hartland. It is considered the boundary of the Bristol Channel. The scenery is wild and desolate, with curious rocks, and strange deep chasms, and bright leaping waterfalls. Formerly there stood near this an abbey of some consequence; and now the Abbey Church is very interesting, with its quaint inscriptions, fine carvings, and time-worn stones.

Now, excepting Lundy Island, about which I have an interesting story to tell you, we have finished charming Devonshire. Lundy Island lies north of Bideford Bay. It is very wild and rocky, with only one landing-place, and very many rocky islets around it.† In the days of William and Mary, a ship-of-war with friendly Dutch colours, anchored in the roadstead, and sent a little boat ashore, asking milk for the captain, who was said to be very ill. The kind people gave the sailors milk, who at last told them that the captain was dead, and asked leave to bury him in the little churchyard. "Willingly," said the people, and the coffin was brought ashore. It felt very heavy. Then the sailors said that they must be left alone in the church during part of the ceremony. The islanders waited, and soon Frenchmen, not Dutchmen, rushed out, armed with weapons that had been in the coffin; they

* Pages 373, 400. † Pages 11, 18, 85.

made the poor people prisoners, roamed over the island, throwing the sheep and goats into the sea, laming the horses and bullocks, and then, having stripped their helpless prisoners of their clothes, finding that they could do no more mischief they decamped. Were they not miserable cowards to treat thus treacherously the kind islanders?

Farewell to Devonshire. Cornwall to-morrow.

One exercise on Devonshire might be a skeleton map, marking the rivers and mountains. When this has been accurately drawn, let the towns and places of interest be added.

CORNWALL.—PART I.

WE have at length reached the last of England's counties, the one like the Wellington boot, with a very small toe, and when we arrive at the Land's End, the description of our beloved fatherland must cease.

Now look at the map, and find out four circumstances in the position of Cornwall, which are peculiar to this county.

The sea-coast of Cornwall is very wild and beautiful. It receives the Atlantic waves in all their fury, so that nothing but the hardest kinds of rocks remain—granite, slate, and serpentine.* The latter receives its name from the streaks upon it being thought to resemble those of a serpent's skin. It is a beautiful rock of green and various other colours. In the interior of Cornwall there is a great deal of dry moorland, and in the valleys extensive swamps. On the wild moors huge masses of granite are piled, some by nature, and others by the Druids, who there held their strange gatherings.

* Pages 55, 380, 421.

Do you remember any parts of England where the principal riches are underground ?*   So it is in Cornwall.   Although the climate is much warmer than that of Durham, and there are no volumes of smoke as in the Black Country, yet the ground is so stony that there is little vegetation. Potatoes are the most productive vegetables.   Sometimes the farmer gets two good crops in one year, one in June and the other in October.   The weather, though warm, is generally rainy or foggy.†   Cornish people say, " There is a shower of rain on every week day, and two on a Sunday." It does not, however, rain long at a time.   The fogs there are not cold and gloomy, but have the reputation of putting people into good spirits.   The number of salt particles

Tin Mines.

blown from the surrounding sea prevents the luxuriant growth of trees; but there is little frost, and myrtles and geraniums grow in the open air. ‡

* **Pages 26, 109.**   † **Pages 61, 85.**   ‡ **Pages 349, 374, 394, 407, 414.**

The underground riches of Cornwall are in the lead, tin, and copper mines. The copper mines, which are much the most valuable, have only been worked about a hundred and sixty years. They now supply one-third of the copper used in Europe. At first the miners called it dust, and when they found it they gave up their tin working, saying that the dust had come in and spoilt their tin.

The tin mines have been worked from a very distant period of history. The inhabitants of Tyre planted a colony at Carthage ; these again planted one at Cadiz in Spain, (supposed to be the Tarshish of the Bible,) and the merchants of Cadiz traded with the Britons for tin ; their ships receiving the metal from an island on the coast. Cornwall now furnishes nine-tenths of all the tin used in Europe.

Grains of gold are sometimes found. These belong to the miner, who sells them to the goldsmith. Lead is also found near the north coast. Generally tin lies in granite, lead in slate, and copper at the junction of these two kinds of rocks. The veins of tin and copper run east and west, those of lead north and south.

The only animal produce for which Cornwall is famed is fish, especially the pilchard, which approaches no other county but this and Devon. Pilchards are smaller than herring, and visit the shores of Cornwall during August, September, and October. They are caught by thousands, or rather by millions, in enormously large nets, sometimes three-fourths of a mile long, and worth £170 apiece. They have lead on one side and cork on the other. Can you imagine why? These nets enclose a whole shoal, the presence of the fish being known by the red tinge they give the water. Though the net is so enormous, it is let down in a few minutes, and forms a circle, the ends being brought together; then, if the nets reach the bottom, and it is level, there is no possibility of the fish escaping. Afterwards the tuck net, a smaller one, is let down inside the large, or sieve net, and hauled to the surface with loud shouts of " Yo-she-hoy ! Pull away, boys ! Huzza !" At length it reaches the surface, and thousands of the silvery fish are thrown into the boats waiting outside the large net. Then comes the salting process, which is the work of the women. When the fish number 4,000,000 or 5,000,000, it occupies nearly a week. Afterwards they are packed in barrels, and sent chiefly to Italy and Spain. The numbers are often enormous. There were enough caught in 1847 to encompass the whole world in a band, six fish deep.*

Many sea-birds live on the rocky coast of Cornwall. Sometimes, amongst the cliffs, a rare kind of bird, called the Cornish Chough, is seen. It has red legs and beak, and like the magpie, it is a great thief, stealing all sorts of things. There are also many cormorants, with sooty black feathers, and shrill hoarse voices.†

Most of the Cornish people are employed in mining and fishing. They are simple, honest, and sober. Whitfield's and Wesley's preaching did much good about a hundred years ago, and the benefit is still visible. There are very few public-houses; but a washing-house is attached to all the mines, supplied by the engine with hot water, where the miner changes his dress before he goes home. Many suffer from consumption, to which they seem particularly subject. They are superstitious; believing that fairies are real beings, they won't whistle underground; and if a person has been hurt by any instrument, they keep the weapon clean and bright, thinking that by this means the wound will heal. There is a well, in the water of which they like to have their children baptized, because they

* Pages 10, 183, 347, 406, 419.   † Pages 18, 85, 337, 350, 381.

then imagine that they can never be hanged.*   The
people are generally strong, and are fond of gymnastic
games, particularly wrestling and hurling.   In hurling two
parties try to catch a wooden ball thrown up into the air.
The wages are not high, but the people are careful and con-
tented.   Those who dig the ore are paid according to the
value of what they bring to the surface; so, sometimes, if
they light suddenly upon a rich vein, they become suddenly
rich.   They are very intelligent; and I have read stories
of noble actions that they have done.   One tale I must
tell you.   Two miners were at work at the bottom of a
shaft, preparing the shot for blasting.   Only one could
ascend at a time; so the one left below was to strike the
match after the other was up.   By accident the match
kindled when they were both in the mine.   Both shouted
loudly; both sprang into the basket; but it was impossible for both to ascend together.   Then said Will, who
loved God, and believed that he would be with Jesus if
he died: "Go aloft, Jack, and sit down; away!   In one
minute I shall be in heaven."   Soon Jack was drawn up.
Immediately afterwards the explosion came; and Will,—
where was he?   God wonderfully preserved him; the
blasted rocks formed an arch over him, and he was very
slightly injured.   Now, was not this true courage?

In former days the people spoke Cornish, a language
quite different to English, more similar to Gaelic, Welsh,
and Irish.†   So many of their names begin with the same
syllables, that it is said—

> "By Tre, Pol, and Pen,
> You may know the Cornish men."

Though people cannot now converse in Cornish, some of
the old words are still used.   "Chealveen" answers to the

* Pages 247, 425.   † Page 197.

"bairnie" of Northumberland,* and means little child; and the miners often talk of being wet as a "quilquin," which signifies a "frog."

Amongst great and good men born in Cornwall is the devoted missionary, Henry Martyn. He reckoned neither friends, nor home, nor fame, nor life dear, and, in the midst of strangers, he died, trying to make Christ known among the heathen and Mohammedans.† Howeis, who preached and wrote of the love of Christ, was also born here, as were two brothers, Richard and John Louder, who explored the river Niger. Amongst scientific natives of the county is Adams, the discoverer of the planet Neptune, and Sir Humphrey Davy, whose greatest invention was the safety-lamp, by means of which miners may work in the deep mines without any fear of an explosion. This has saved the lives of thousands. It is said, too, that Cornwall is the birthplace of the famous King Arthur, of whom you have heard so many legends since the time I told you the story of him and his knights being asleep in a mysterious vault at Richmond—in what county?‡—and of whom Tennyson has written in beautiful poetry. Before I finish to-day's chapter, you shall hear about a copper mine, just as you have heard of coal and of salt mines.

THE DESCRIPTION OF A COPPER MINE.

Above ground appears the tall chimney of the immense steam-engine that pumps the water from the mine; rough sheds, where the ore is sorted; platforms, iron chains, and other machinery. The work that the steam-engines perform is immense. In one place, the pumping-rod is the third of a mile long, and one thousand six hundred gallons of water are sometimes pumped in a minute. This water, which below would destroy the miners, when raised above cleanses the copper, and becomes most useful. A

* Page 8. † Pages 122, 169. ‡ Pages 40, 227, 236, 369.

deep shaft leads to the bottom of the pit. The shaft is divided into two parts, one for bringing up the ore, and the other for the ascent and descent of the miners. Whoever goes down the shaft, whether visitor or miner, changes his dress. He puts on a suit of coarse flannel, a white nightcap, and a round hat, hard as iron. Then a lighted tallow candle is fastened against the hat with a piece of clay ; and thus equipped, he begins the descent of the ladder. This is very toilsome, especially in a deep mine, and the ascent yet more so, for the men often take an hour to come up the weary steps, and at length reach the surface wholly exhausted. From the shaft, different galleries branch off, and run underground a considerable distance. Along these galleries or passages, the miners are at work. Sometimes they work alone, and it seldom happens that more than four or five work together. They do not use the Davy lamp, as there is no fire-damp, or danger of explosion, as in coal-pits.* The heat is excessive, especially in the lowest passages ; and the miners work half naked, the perspiration streaming from their bodies. † When a light is held against the ceiling, the ore looks very beautiful ; sometimes it is bright green veined with red streaks of iron. Often the miners are below the sea, and then the sound of the breakers amongst the rocks above is distinctly heard.

A gentleman, **who** descended a mine, near the " Land's End," describes it thus : " After listening for a few moments, a distant unearthly noise becomes distinctly audible ; a long, low, mysterious moaning that never changes, a sound so sublimely mournful and still, so ghostly and impressive, when listened to from the subterranean recesses of the earth, that we instinctively hold our peace, as if enchanted." This was when the sea was calm. When

* Pages 25, 51, 74.   † Page 129.

storms rage, and the waves roll rocks along the ocean's bed, and the breakers lash the cliffs in fury, then even the miners fear, for the noise is exceedingly terrible, and, leaving their work, they hasten to the mouth of the mine. When the ore is raised to the surface, it is separated from the waste matter by washings and crushings, and these are principally done by women and children, who go through their daily labour contentedly and happily. The working hours are too severe to be lengthened, and, after eight hours' labour, the miners return, again put on the home attire, and, joined by their wives and children, with washed faces, they all go to their homes. The ore is sold, and afterwards smelted, the tin ore in Cornwall, and the copper at Swansea, in South Wales. One of the delicacies of Cornwall is a beef-steak broiled on a block of tin fresh from the furnace. 30,000 miners are supposed to be employed in Cornwall and Devonshire. The Prince of Wales is Duke of Cornwall, and receives a share of the profits of the mines.

To-morrow we must traverse Cornwall from the east; but try not to forget either the pilchard fisheries, or the tin and copper mines.

CORNWALL.—Part II.

NEAR the source of the Tamar is Kilkhampton, where Harvey wrote his "Meditations among the Tombs." The first town of interest on the Cornwall side of the Tamar is Launceston, where there are the ruins of an old castle, of an old priory, and of old city walls, and where a very fine church still stands. It was long reckoned the chief town of the county; but now, Bodmin, of which you shall soon hear, takes its place. The Tamar receives several small rivers from the west; but they run through a wild, bleak, barren country, where few people live and where few objects of interest can be seen. As it flows south, it passes, to the west, Kit's Hill, a hill of granite, where Cornish and Devon miners have met to discuss their rights, and where battles between Danes and Saxons have been fought.* Below it is Callington, an old town, where a number of miners live. On the Tamar, amidst lovely scenery, is Cothele, an ancient mansion, which, like Haddon Hall, in Derbyshire, has all its old fittings of Queen Elizabeth's time.† Coats of mail still hang in the hall, tapestry on the walls, and the old hearths for burning wood are ornamented with the queerest figures. The river Tamar below this becomes very broad, with picturesque inlets on each side. Then it narrows, and there stands Saltash, a pretty fishing village, with cottages hanging one above another on the side of a steep hill. Saltash is famous for its boatwomen. They have often gained prizes at regattas, handling the oars with the skill and power of men. Near it is the ivy-grown, red-stone castle of Trematon, where the Stannary Courts used to be held, and farther up a pretty creek is St Germans, now a village, once a cathedral town. The old tower of the cathedral, covered with ivy, looks very pretty. It is partly in ruins, and partly used for a parish church.

The extreme point, at the south-east corner of Cornwall, is Rame Head, surmounted with a ruined chapel, from which you see, thirteen miles south, the far-famed Eddystone Lighthouse. This is built on a rock most dangerous to sailors, for it is covered with water at every high tide. The first lighthouse was erected by a brave and clever engineer —Winstanley. He was, however, too confident of its strength, and measuring his power against God's, wished to be there during the fiercest storm that ever blew. On November

* Pages 155, 211, 238, 255, 314, 430.   † Pages 130, 329, 354.

26th, 1703, he with some workmen, went out to make repairs. Then a terrible storm began to blow. A perfect hurricane swept the ocean; and when the next morning dawned, those who stood on the shore looked towards the boasted lighthouse, and it was gone, not a vestige of it remained. The second lighthouse was wooden; but it was burnt. A third was erected nearly a hundred years ago; it was built of granite, the model being the stem of an oak-tree. No storm has shaken it, and it is so dovetailed into the rock, that it seems as firm as the rock itself, and appears to rise wonderfully from its ocean bed.

West of Rame Head the sands are so white that the bay has the name of Whitesand Bay. The source of a little river, the Seaton, will take us to St Cleer, where there is a well whose waters were thought holy, and capable of curing mad people. In this neighbourhood are several curious stones. One, called the Trevethy Stone, is a large slab laid on six pillars, supposed to be an ancient burial-place. Another group of stones is called the Hurlers; the story about which is, that there was a party of men, who went out to play at ball on Sunday morning, and, like Lot's wife, they were turned into stone. Probably, like Long Meg and her daughters in Cumberland, they are the remains of Druidical buildings.* Another extraordinary rock is the Cheesewring; the little stones are at the bottom and the big ones above. Build a Cheesewring in like manner, with little stones in the garden, and see if you can keep them from falling. The one in Cornwall is eight yards high. Not far distant are large copper mines. South of these, connected with the sea by a canal, is Liskeard, which has, like most other towns in the south-west of England, its story of a battle in Charles I.'s time.† Near it is a well, the water of which newly-married couples

* Pages 65, 330, 385, 389, 416.   † Pages 225, 398, 430.

hasten to drink; for the one who drinks first bears the
rule over the other. The poet Southey wrote a comic
ballad about this, of which the last verse is—

> " I hasten'd as soon as the wedding was o'er,
>   And left my good wife in the porch:
>   But, indeed, she had been wiser than I,
>   For she took a bottle to church." *

At the mouth of the inlet to which the canal passes, are
East and West Looe, extremely pretty fishing villages, with
odd gables, outside staircases, and beautiful gardens. From
this place granite, copper, lead, and tin are exported.

The next river, widening towards its mouth, is the
Fowey. It rises in hills nearer the north than the south
coast, and flows through extensive moors, strewn, like that
of Dartmoor, with blocks of granite. On one of its branches
is St Neot's, with an old church and very curious windows,
representing the wildest legends of St George, St Neot, and
others. How thankful we should be, that in our churches
blessed Bible-truths are now heard, instead of foolish
fables! Farther down the river is Lostwithiel. Near this
town, with its pretty sounding name, is the old castle of
Restormel, with its ivy-covered ruins. Horses were stabled
in its church during the civil wars. Near it is a very
extensive copper mine, which Queen Victoria visited a
few years ago. Many mines are wrought between the
Fowey and the next river westward. In one of them the
men are carried up and down by machinery, which saves
the labour of the ladders. The river Fowey is beautiful,
with its clear broad water and richly wooded banks. The
little town of Fowey, at its mouth, was once one of the
largest ports in England, presenting Edward III. with more
ships than any town, except Yarmouth.† Now it is inhabited by fishers and miners; and a few vessels trade for

* Pages 247, 435.   † Pages 97, 154, 226, 337, 429.

copper-ore and china-clay. The next little river runs through wild Cornish scenery, and passing St Blazey, in the midst of mines, falls into the sea at Par, a busy little town, with a harbour protected by a breakwater. This breakwater, and many other great works in this part of Cornwall, were made entirely at the expense of Mr Trefferry, who spent his riches most wisely and usefully, for his countrymen's benefit.*

The next town and bay are those of St Austell, near which are the celebrated tin mines of Carclase. It is said to have been worked more than four hundred years. The granite had become so soft, that the upper part was quarried instead of mined. The lower part being more compact, the miners can follow the vein of tin underground. The stone is beautiful white granite, so that the mine is said to look like a chasm in a mountain of silver. The granite is useful in the manufacture of porcelain, and for bleaching paper and calico. Its value was quite unknown a hundred years ago. Now, it is worth nearly a quarter of a million of pounds yearly.

Following the rocky rugged coast, a broad inlet is reached on which Falmouth stands. This receives the Fal, the Truro river, and other streams, each of which widens into a beautiful broad river.† Truro is one of the principal towns of Cornwall; there carpets are made and tin is smelted. It has a valuable museum, with rare Cornish birds and specimens of minerals, of the precious stones found in the mining regions, and with old remains of man's handiwork, which were discovered in the neighbourhood.‡ The old town of Penryn, with its fine granite, of which Waterloo Bridge is made,§ and its early vegetables, which supply Covent Garden, before winter is over, is at the head of one of the branches of the harbour. Falmouth has a splendid

* Pages 133, 262.   + Page 423.   ‡ Page 352.   § Page 301.

harbour, in which three hundred ships have together taken shelter. Southampton has of late years taken its place as a packet station for Spain and the West Indies.* Orange and lemon trees are here trained against walls in the open air, and bear beautiful fruit.

The heel of Cornwall now stretches southward ending in the Lizard Point, the most southern part of England. The rock is almost all of beautifully veined serpentine, on which grows a lovely white heath, that only likes a serpentine soil. Generally the country is very barren; but in one or two places the soil changes, and then its fruitfulness is wonderful. There are beautiful coves and caverns all along the coast. One is called the Lion's Den, and when the weather is stormy, and the sea dashes in through an archway, it is like a " huge boiling caldron." Another is Kinnace Cove; the rocks are green, veined with red and purple. In the centre is a little island pierced by a chasm, through which the waves rush tumultuously. The waves seem blown through a monster bellows, and when they have passed, the traveller holds a letter at the post-office —the name of a little opening in the rock. The invisible postman, a current of air, rushes through, and throws it most rudely in his teeth. There is also the Soap Rock, so called because, when touched, it feels soft like soap. North of the Lizard district is Helstone, with strange legends and curious old customs. One custom obliges every one in the little town to keep holiday on May 8th on pain of a ducking in the river Looe.† The day begins with a merry ringing of bells. Near Helstone is a little lake, Looepool, a bar of pebbles separating it from the sea. In very wet weather this requires to be opened, as the slow rate at which it filters through the stones, causes too great a rise in the waters. To do so, permission of the lord of the manor is necessary, which is always asked with the presentation of a leather purse and three halfpence.* The opening is a beautiful sight—the waters of the lake rushing to meet those of the sea, which seem to repel the unexpected intruder.

The bay between the heel and toe of Cornwall is Mount's Bay. On the shore near Penzance, the sea has made great encroachments, and it is believed that the bay was, eight hundred years ago, covered with forests. Here is the village of Marazion, where the Jews held tin markets in olden days. They called it Màre-zion, or bitter Zion. Near it is St Michael's mount, a beautiful rocky island, with a good harbour. The island is at low water joined to the mainland, by an isthmus forty yards broad.† There used to be here a monastery and castle. A little westward is Penzance, the western temination of English railways. It has a good deal of trade, chiefly in tin and fish. One of the dainties of the poor people is a conger-eel pie. The conger-eel is very fierce, and sometimes does battle with the fisherman who siezes it. There is an excellent collection of minerals at Penzance. The winters are so mild that summer flowers bloom at Christmas. One peculiar custom is the lighting of tar barrels, in June, on the eves of St John's and St Peter's days. From these, boys and girls light torches, and whirling them round, run hand in hand through the streets, shouting, "An eye, an eye, an eye!" Then they stop, and the last two raise their arms, forming an eye, through which the long string passes, like the game, which I dare say you know, of "Thread the needle." West of Penzance, a mine was actually sunk in the sea, a kind of chimney rising from the shaft, eleven feet above the water.‡ The coast continues very wild, and is strewn with blocks of granite. One of these blocks is the "Logan

* Page 395. † Pages 10, 400. ‡ Pages 74, 438.

Stone," weighing sixty tons. This was so balanced that it moved with a touch.* A lieutenant in the navy, however, very foolishly dislodged it, with the help of his boat's crew—rather an expensive trick, as government ordered him to have it replaced, which, with great difficulty, was done, but not to balance as before. Now, to-morrow, we hope to reach the Land's End.

CORNWALL—Part III.

THE bay which stretches along the coast on the north-west of Cornwall is Bude Bay. The cliffs, with their various forms and colours, are very fine. Here stand Moorwinstow, with its beautiful old church; and Bude, where lived the inventor of the brilliant Bude light. From this place thousands of horse-loads of sea-sand are taken yearly to be used as manure for the land in the neighbourhood. A little inland, is the old town of Stratton; near which is Stanford Hill, memorable for a great victory the Royalists gained over the Parliamentarians. Much blood was shed; and on the top of the hill may still be observed the mound which marks the soldier's cemetery. South of this runs the Bude Canal, which stretches from Bude into Devonshire, a branch being cut to Launceston. The canal is across ground much higher than the sea. The barges are raised, not in the usual way by locks, but by inclined tramways, about three hundred yards long. Laden with sand or mineral ores, they are put on wheels, and are moved up by a chain. This chain is attached to an enormous bucket filled with water, whose weight descending from the top of the incline into a deep well, pulls the barge upwards, till it reaches the level of the higher canal.†

Following the wild, grand, and desolate coast, the next

* Page 417. † Page 426.

place of interest is Boscastle, with its tiny harbour, where two or three vessels can ride safely, when the sea beyond is all fury. The fissures in the rocks here are very strange. One is underground, the water rushes through, and then, at a distance of nearly twenty yards from the shore, throws up through a deep hole, a grand column of water, sparkling in the sunbeams.* Here a great many seals are caught. The poor creatures lie on ledges in dark caverns, which the boatmen, carrying torches, enter when the sea is smooth, and the seals, startled with the light, are easily made prisoners. Following the coast, a tiny stream is passed, noted for its cascade, which is almost lost amid thick ferns and brushwood. Near it is a ruined cottage, concerning which the country people tell a strange story. Two sisters came to live there—their names, their histories quite unknown. They were gentle but sorrowful, and they never spoke an unnecessary word to any one. No servant tended them, no visitor inquired for them. The people wondered who they were; but every effort to discover anything about them was vain. At last one died; the villagers came to bury her, but the other sister spoke not a word; she only wept and wept in long and dreary silence. Days passed, and when the villagers looked into the room, she was still sitting in the same chair, still weeping—her fragile form wasting day by day. At last one morning a little girl told the villagers that the lady's hand hung strangely, and that she seemed motionless. They went to look, and she was dead, sitting in the same chair, her handkerchief beside her still wet with tears. And thus the sisters died in solitude, and no trace of their history could ever be discovered.

A very little farther westward, and we see the peninsula on which stands Tintagel Castle, a fine old ruin, built on

* Page 6.

the summit of grand towering rocks. Here it is said King Arthur was born, and here he died. He left the castle with his followers in the early morning to fight his wicked nephew, Mordred. They returned at night victorious; but they bore with them the dying body of their chieftain, the beloved hero of ancient British story. The cliffs are formed of slate, some of them hollowed into basin-like holes, which are called by the country people King Arthur's cups and saucers. The scenery is magnificent, and has been often painted, especially by Creswick, a famous artist.*

A bay extends from Tintagel to a point which bounds the only inlet on the north of Cornwall. As a harbour of refuge, it is much spoiled by a bar of sand at its mouth.† This, however, I hope, will soon be removed; and, instead of being hurtful, will become most valuable, for there is so much lime amongst it, that the farmers find it improves their land exceedingly, and so it is carted away in enormous quantities.‡ The sand has, however, nearly buried two ancient churches.§ This inlet receives the Camel. Near the source of the Camel are slate quarries, which have been worked for some hundreds of years, and are said to produce the best slate in the kingdom. The slate is loosened by gunpowder, then separated by wedges, then placed on trucks and raised by chains; then emptied on movable tables, which, when laden, are drawn away by horses. The best slate feels hard and rough, and is of a light blue colour. || Near Camelford, a little farther down the river, was fought the battle in which King Arthur was wounded to death. The place where he is said to have received his wound is still known as Slaughter Bridge. Below Camelford, the Camel receives a little stream through

* Page 304. † Page 417. ‡ Pages 174, 189, 379.
§ Page 184. || Pages 69, 77, 88, 140, 406

the wild and beautiful Hannow valley. In it there stands one solitary tree. A thunder storm broke over the district in the summer of 1847; the rain descended in torrents, and the streams swelled fearfully. A farmer was travelling to Camelford, and was just going to cross a foot-bridge, when the torrent beneath rose so much that he could not proceed, and the plain behind was so flooded that he could not go back. Two trees stood near him; he climbed one, thought it weak, passed to the other, and there he remained, whilst the flood bore down the first tree, and desolated the valley. I hope the farmer felt thankful to God, who had so mercifully preserved him. The Camel next receives the Lank from Brown Willy, the highest hill in Cornwall. It flows through the Hanter Gantick, a valley of rocks, covered with huge square pieces of granite, thrown one over another in the wildest confusion. Not far from the Camel, nearly in the centre of Cornwall, stands Bodmin, a well-built town, where Cornish prisoners are taken to be tried by judges at the assizes. It has a very ancient church. At Wadebridge, the Camel used to be crossed by a fine old bridge of seventeen arches, above one of which a flourishing fig-tree grew.* Here there is some trade, sea-sand being taken inland by the railway, and metallic ores brought down seaward to be shipped. Below this is Padstow, with a very old church and harbour of refuge. The cape beyond the Camel river is Trevose Head with a lighthouse.

The little stream that enters the sea through Mawgan Vale, comes from the wild moors of Tregoss, now bleak and bald, but said to have been once covered with trees, the hunting grounds of King Arthur.† It passes a little market town, St Columb Major, called after one of the missionary bishops sent by St Patrick amongst the ancient

* Page 353.   † Pages 74, 113, 136, 140, 157, 165, 208, 342, 346.

2 F

Britons, and then through the wooded valley to Mawgan, in whose churchyard a boat's stern, painted white, marks the burial place of ten frozen fishermen, who were drifted ashore one cold wintry night. Here there is a Roman Catholic convent, for twenty Carmelite nuns. When they have once taken the vow, they can never see a friend again. They are even hidden from the priest when in the chapel; the very maid-servants must not speak to them; the only person that, under any circumstance, approaches them, is the doctor, and even then the patient's face is, if possible, concealed. How closely guarded a prison in our own free England! And how mistaken a way of serving that God, who said, "Let your light so shine before men that they may see your good works, and glorify your Father which is in heaven."

Farther south, on the coast, is New Quay, a charming little bathing-place, where sand is now hardening into sandstone rock, hard enough to be used in building. Inland from Perran Bay is Perranzabuloe, or Perran-in-the-Sand. Here, covered with sand for a thousand years, have lain the remains of an ancient British church.* It was accidentally discovered a few years since, and is a most interesting monument of the religion of our British forefathers, before the Saxons overran the country. It is a very small and very simple building. The stones are of the rudest kind, and the Britons not then knowing how to make lime, have mixed china-clay and sand together. West of Perranzabuloe is St Agnes' Beacon, a fine hill, where the clay is found with which the miners fasten the candle in front of their hats. Off St Agnes' Head are two rocky islets, called "The Man and his Man." † South and farther inland, in the very centre of the mining district, is Redruth; the surface of the country

* Pages 10, 57, 154, 200, 236, 335.   † Page 402.

is bleak and desolate, but the underground riches are very considerable. About a mile from this town Wesley used to preach to the miners, reasoning with them as the apostle Paul reasoned with Felix, of "temperance, righteousness, and judgment to come." On Whit-Monday the Wesleyans still meet there, and sometimes number more than twenty thousand.* The copper ore from this district is chiefly shipped to South Wales from Portreath, a pretty little seaport on the northern coast. Another populous mining town is Cambourne, which has very recently grown to be of consequence. The coast continues very desolate ; the sand threatening to bury many cottages. A little flower which grows in thick masses and flourishes in sand has, however, been planted, and this humble instrument stays the danger. Remember how great may be the power of *little things*.† Here, too, a small chapel, buried like that at Perranzabuloe, has been found.

The next inlet is from St Ives Bay. Here there stands the busy little seaport of Hayle, where there are great iron foundries, in which immense cylinders have been cast, and sent to different countries. Amongst the mines in its neighbourhood is one where a great deal of silver has been found.‡ At the head of the inlet is an old house, where is shown the first coach ever made in Cornwall. Drawn to church by four beautiful horses, it astonished the people. On the other side of the bay, most beautifully situated, is St Ives, the chief place for pilchard fishing It is thought to be like a Greek town. The chief business of the place is fishing, boat-making, boat-mending, sieve-making, and pickling the pilchards.

The wild desolation of the country seems to increase, and near the little mining town of St Just, on the cliffs overhanging the sea, is the famous Botallick copper mine,

* Page 152.   † Pages 21, 47.   ‡ Page 19.

which I have already described. Not far from the Land's End is a house, on one wall of which, in large letters, the words are written, "This is the last inn in England," and on the other, "This is the first inn in England." The ridge becomes more and more narrow; the cliffs descend, and then the traveller may advance and stand on the farthest point, with the wide ocean washing on either side. As he stands on that narrow promontory, thoughts of time's narrow space and eternity's unfathomable depths may well come into his mind; thoughts like those which Wesley expressed when he wrote—

> "Lo ! on a narrow rock of land,
> 'Twixt two unbounded seas I stand
> Secure, insensible ;
> A point of time, a moment's space
> Removes me to that heavenly place,
> Or shuts me up in hell.
>
> "O God, mine inmost soul convert !
> And deeply on my thoughtful heart
> Eternal things impress :
> Give me to feel their solemn weight,
> And tremble on the brink of fate,
> And wake to righteousness."

Thirty miles from the Land's End, and composed of granite, like that promontory and so much of Cornwall, are the Scilly Islands, forty of which bear grass of some kind; but six only are inhabited. They were discovered by a Greek navigator, called Pythias, and the Greeks called them by a name which meant "tin islands." It is said that they were once connected with the mainland by a tract of country called the Sionope, over which the sea swept. The three largest are St Mary's, Treno, and St Martin's. I will tell you first of St Martin's, as it is the nearest to Cornwall. It contains little more than a hundred people. There are old Druidical remains, and near to it is a cluster of rocky islets of various shapes and colours, which look like beautiful gems set in the dark blue ocean.   On Treno Island lives the lord proprietor, his house built on the ground where the ancient abbey once stood.   Here, too, is the ruin of Charles's castle, and the round tower of Oliver Cromwell's castle, still crowned with cannon.   At the time of the civil wars the Royalists

Land's End.

took here a strong position, and when Cromwell was Protector, they sent out their armed boats to seize the merchant ships entering the Bristol Channel.   A strong force, under Admiral Blake, at length obliged them to yield.* On a neighbouring little islet is the favourite home of the puffins, three hundred of which used, in former days, to be the rental paid for the islands to the king by the monks

* Page 238.

of Tavistock. Where is Tavistock?* The largest island is St Mary's. Most of the inhabitants are fishermen. They are often in danger of being drowned in the stormy seas that lash the shores; and it is said that for one that dies a natural death nine perish by water. Here early potatoes are grown, and sent in great quantities to Covent Garden Market.† Hugh Town is the capital, where Star Castle stands, built in Queen Elizabeth's time, the walls of which, like a star, project from the centre in eight points. There are many stories of shipwreck connected with these islands. The saddest is that of the fleet under Sir Cloudesley Shovel, which was returning from the siege of Toulon, in October 1707. Several of the large men-of-war struck the Gilstone, one of the most western rocks, and were dashed to pieces. Two thousand people are said to have been drowned during that dark and stormy night. Sir Cloudesley had been a poor boy, a shoemaker's apprentice.‡ Then he joined a ship as cabin-boy. In the midst of a fight he bravely swam from one ship to another with a letter from the admiral, for which he was promoted. Being very good and brave, he at last became admiral of the fleet. After the wreck his body was found on the shore, stripped by the islanders; but long afterwards, an old woman, on her death-bed, told the fearful story of his murder. He had escaped the waves, and, wearied and exhausted, came to her cottage for shelter, and fell asleep upon her bed. He wore valuable jewels, and she, tempted by their worth, murdered the excellent man, and took the rings from off his fingers. The Bible has said, " Be sure your sin will find you out;" and truly it did so in the wretchedness of this miserable woman.§ The last story must not, however, be one so very painful, so I will tell you now of an escape from shipwreck, which the merciful

* Page 426.   † Pages 433, 443.   ‡ Page 381.   § Page 44.

providence of God permitted. On an autumnal day, in the year 1840, a wreck was observed drifting into a bay on the south-west of the island. The keel was uppermost. All thought of living passengers was, of course, given over. Think, therefore, of the surprise of the islanders to find within four men and a boy. The ship had been overturned in the Atlantic two days before. These men, in some way, clung to the bottom, and I suppose the ship acted like a diving-bell, the air which filled the hole preventing the water from entering. There the men remained, their heads above the water, which reached to their waists. They tried to make a hole for more air to enter, but fortunately their knife broke; for had they succeeded, the air would have escaped, the water would have risen, and they must have been drowned. Yet, what likelihood was there of reaching land in the midst of the wide ocean, and quite unable to guide their ship? Two pilot-boats fell in with it, and towed it for an hour. They could not bring it to land, for the sea was high; but their course brought it into the current, which drifted it into the bay. Was it not the protecting hand of Him who never sleepeth that directed all these varied circumstances?

And now, from Berwick-upon-Tweed to the Scilly Islands, you have heard about our beloved land. What do you think of the dear old country? I love it very much, and I think you must too. Do you know that they who love their native land are called patriots? And true patriots are not only those who love their fatherland, but who work for it, and pray for it.

When a church is lighted, each little taper has its share in causing the general illumination; when a rainbow spans the sky, each little drop of water helps to form the beautiful arch; when the heavens look glorious on a frosty night, each little star increases its splendour. Even so, dear children, if our land and homes are to be beautiful, do not let the little portion that is yours be neglected ; and if our people are to be honourable and honoured, let no English boy or girl tell a falsehood, or do an unjust or ungenerous action. Yet more,—let English children never forget their God, and their fathers' God—let them honour Him who has cast their lot in so loved an island home ; and let them never cease to ask that He will always be the defence of their " Dear Old England."

The counties touching on the English Channel might, with older children, be historically reviewed. The times of the different lines of kings—Saxons, Normans, Plantagenets, Tudors, &c., being arranged in different columns, in which the places distinguished under each should be inserted. A voyage along the coast would much interest the younger ones ; and an hour might be passed in the evening in finding out a place by questioning thus :—

Willie thinks of Plymouth.

Q. 1. Land or water ? A. Land.
    2. Natural or artificial? A. Artificial.
    3. Ancient or modern ? A. Modern.
    4. Inland or maritime ? A. Maritime.
    5. Important or Unimportant ? A. Important.
    6. Commercial or Picturesque ? A. Both.
    7. Manufacturing or military ? A. Both.
    8. Mercantile or naval ? A. Both.
    9. Is its harbour naturally or artificially protected? A. Artificially.

This leaves no doubt concerning Plymouth, and whoever guesses, must, in his turn, think of a town, mountain, river, bay, cavern, or whatever place he likes.

GAMES FOR ALL ENGLAND.

THE COMMERCIAL TRAVELLER.

Each child having thought of the seat of some manufacture or commerce, the teacher or parent enters the room with a basket of small prizes—pencils, needles, pins, marbles, or ginger-nuts.

Arthur has thought of Sheffield; Ethel of Honiton; Harold of Derby; Rose of Harwich.

Addressing Arthur, the teacher inquires—

T. What kind of town am I approaching ?
A. A smoky and grimy one.
T. In what county ?
A. Yorkshire.
T. On what river ?
A. The Don.
T. With what will Sheffield furnish me ?
A. Knives, scissors, tools, plated goods, &c., &c.

The teacher orders various articles, and Arthur receives payment in marbles from the basket.

In answer to similar questions, Ethel tells that the town is clean, and prettily situated in one of the warmest and most beautiful of English counties; that the manufacture with which she will supply her is elegant and costly; and that, if she wants provender, she can show her butter equal to any in England. The teacher purchases lace and butter at Honiton, and pays in pins or needles.

THE GAME OF THE POST-OFFICE.

Each child selects a friend, to whom he writes, dating his letter from any town or village in England, describing its peculiarities. This is put into a large box, called the Post-office. The teacher, or parent, keeps the key, and opens it once a week. Thus a letter is found from Horace,

2 G

dated Yarmouth, directed to his friend Cave, at Ryde, Isle of Wight. Cave must, the following week, answer the letter, and describe Ryde. Laura writes from Berwick-upon-Tweed to her sister Marion, at St Ives, in Cornwall; and Algernon writes a letter from Richmond, in Surrey, to Evelyn at Richmond, in Yorkshire. This will be found to excite general interest; and the opening of the post-office will be very pleasant on a winter's evening.

THE LORD MAYOR'S TABLE.

The children are all seated in a circle. The teacher commences. The Lord Mayor is providing a very great dinner, with what will you supply him?

Alfred.—With salmon from the Tweed.
Harriet.—Bloaters from Yarmouth.
Alethea.—Oysters from Harwich.
Charlotte.—A conger-eel pie from Penzance.
Lionel.—Whitebait from Greenwich.
Edith.—Mackerel from Shoreham.
George.—Lobsters from Dorsetshire.
Amy.—Pilchards from St Ives.
Kate.—Cockles from the Solway Frith.
Cave.—And a seal from Boscastle !

Meat, vegetables, fowl, game, fruit, and beverages might follow, those paying forfeits who could not supply the Lord Mayor's requirements.

THE END.

PRINTED BY BALLANTYNE AND COMPANY
EDINBURGH AND LONDON

March, 1871.

A SELECTION FROM
JAMES NISBET AND CO.'S
LIST OF PUBLICATIONS.

MEMORIES OF PATMOS; or, Some of the Great Words and Visions of the Apocalypse. By the Rev. J. R. MACDUFF, D.D. With Vignette. Post 8vo, 6s. 6d., cloth.

"Dr. Macduff has given us a volume of beautiful thoughts, and has clothed these thoughts with language which is at once elegant and forcible."—*Rock*.

MOSES THE MAN OF GOD. A Series of Lectures by the late JAMES HAMILTON, D.D., F.L.S. Small Crown 8vo, 5s., cloth.

"Graceful description, imaginative, reconstruction, unconventional, and often very ingenious, sometimes learned disquisition, with the light graceful touch of poetic style and delicate fancy."—*British Quarterly Review*.

LAYS OF THE HOLY LAND. Selected from Ancient and Modern Poets by the Rev. HORATIUS BONAR, D.D. New Edition, with Illustrations from original Photographs and Drawings. Crown 4to, 12s., cloth.

"The Holy Land is a subject to which all great poets have devoted some of their best endeavours, and these are now brought together and adorned by illustrations worthy of such a text. . . . The volume will long remain a favourite."—*Times*.

THE FLOATING LIGHT OF THE GOODWIN SANDS. A Tale by R. M. BALLANTYNE, Author of "The Lifeboat," &c. With Illustrations. Crown 8vo, 5s. cloth.

"As full of incident, as healthy in tone, and as fresh and vigorous in style as any of its predecessors."—*Scotsman*.

LIGHT AND TRUTH—Bible Thoughts and Themes. The Lesser Epistles. By the Rev. HORATIUS BONAR, D.D. Crown 8vo, 5s. cloth.

"The thoughts are seeds, rather than full-grown plants ; but they are, on that account, the more appropriate and the more welcome."—*Freeman*.

A MISSIONARY OF THE APOSTOLIC SCHOOL. Being the Life of Dr. Judson of Burmah. Revised and Edited by the Rev. HORATIUS BONAR, D.D. Small Crown 8vo, 3s. 6d., cloth.

"Very well written."—*Daily Review*.   "Every way readable."—*Nonconformist*.

LITTLE ELSIE'S SUMMER AT MALVERN. By

the Hon. Mrs. CLIFFORD BUTLER. Royal 16mo, 2s.6d. cloth. With Illustrations.
" A pleasing little story."—*Daily Telegraph.*

TOILING IN ROWING ; or, Half-hours of Earnest Con-

verse with my Hard-working Friends. By one who knows and loves them.
Small Crown 8vo, 2s., cloth limp.
" An earnest, affectionate, and practical little book."—*Daily Review.*

A HISTORY OF THE REFORMATION FOR

CHILDREN. By the Rev. E. NANGLE, B.A. With Illustrations, Three
Volumes, 16mo, 4s. 6d. cloth.

PLEASANT FRUITS FROM THE COTTAGE AND

THE CLASS. By MARIA V. G. HAVERGAL. Small Crown 8vo, 2s. 6d.
cloth limp, 3s. cloth boards.
" Will be read with profit and delight."—*Our Own Fireside.*
" Peculiarly well suited for reading at District and Mothers' Meetings, &c."—
Church of England S. S. Magazine.

WHAT SHE COULD, AND OPPORTUNITIES TO

DO IT. By the Author of "The Wide Wide World." With Coloured Illus-
trations. Small Crown 8vo, 3s. 6d. cloth.
" A capital book for girls."—*Daily Review.*
" Clever and interesting little book."—*Glasgow Herald.*

FAITHFUL UNTO DEATH ; or, Susine and Claude of

the Val Pelice. By ANNA CAROLINA DI TERGOLINA. With Coloured
Illustrations. Fcap. 8vo, 2s. 6d. cloth.
" Full of a pathos which will entrance the youthful reader."—*Weekly Review.*

GLEN LUNA ; or, Dollars and Cents. By ANNA WARNER,

Author of "The Golden Ladder." New Edition. With Coloured Illus-
trations. Small Crown 8vo, 3s. 6d. cloth.
" A really good tale."—*Rock.*
" Sure to increase in popularity."—*English Presbyterian Messenger*

THE STORY OF JOB, AND MEDITATIONS ON

PASSAGES FROM THE BOOK OF JOB. By the Rev. A. C. THISEL-
TON, Dublin. Small Crown 8vo, 2s., cloth limp.
" Mr. Thiselton has evidently studied the Book of Job deeply, and brings to
view in an eminently clear and methodical way, the principal lessons intended to be
conveyed by this remarkable writing."—*Dublin Express.*

LOVE FULFILLING THE LAW. Stories on the

Commandments. 16mo, 2s. 6d. cloth.
" Pretty and handy little book."—*Glasgow Herald.*

A PRACTICAL COMMENTARY ON THE GOSPEL

ACCORDING TO ST. JOHN. In simple and familiar language. By
G. B. Small Crown 8vo, 3s. 6d. cloth.
" We cordially recommend them as truly simple, earnest, and faithful com-
ments."—*Our Own Fireside.*

NOTES OF OPEN-AIR SERMONS. By the Rev.

EDWARD WALKER, D.C.L., Rector of Cheltenham. Edited by a Member of the Congregation. Small Crown 8vo, 1s. 6d.,cloth limp.
" Models of sound, faithful, and affectionate gospel preaching."—*English Presbyterian Messenger*.

A TREATISE ON THE PREPARATION AND

DELIVERY OF SERMONS. By the Rev. J. A. BROADUS, D.D., LL.D. With Preface by the Rev. Dr. ANGUS. Post 8vo, 6s., cloth.

THE ATONEMENT ; in its Relations to the Covenant, the

Priesthood, and the Intercession of our Lord. By the Rev. HUGH MARTIN, M.A. Post 8vo, 6s. cloth.
" A volume written with remarkable vigour and earnestness."—*British Quarterly Review*.
" Well worthy of a careful perusal, and we cordially recommend it to all our readers, and especially to ministers and students of theology."—*Evangelical Witness*.

THE SCRIPTURAL ACCOUNT OF CREATION

VINDICATED BY THE TEACHING OF SCIENCE ; or, A New Method of Reconciling the Mosaic and Geological Records of Creation. By the Rev. WM. PAUL, D.D. Post 8vo, 5s. cloth.
" Dr. Paul is entitled to the highest commendation for the extent and accuracy of his knowledge, and for the able, modest, and candid manner in which he applies it to his argument."—*Presbyterian*.

BLOOMFIELD. A Tale by ELIZABETH WARREN, Author

of " John Knox and his Times," &c. Small Crown 8vo, 3s. 6d. cloth.
" A spirited book, and its characters are natural and lively—none the less on this account, but all the more, will its excellent religious lessons reach the heart."—*English Presbyterian Messenger*.

THE LIFE OF THE LATE JAMES HAMILTON,

D.D., F.L.S. By the Rev. WILLIAM ARNOT, Edinburgh. Fourth Edition. Post 8vo, 7s. 6d. cloth. With Portrait.
" We rejoice to recommend this volume as a congenial and worthy record of one of the noblest and most fruitful lives with which the Church of Christ has been blessed in modern days. The editor's work has been done with admirable judgment."
—*Weekly Review*.

A MEMOIR OF THE LATE REV. WILLIAM C.

BURNS, M.A., Missionary to China. By Professor ISLAY BURNS, D.D., Glasgow. Fifth Edition. Crown 8vo, 6s. cloth. With Portrait.
" A more apostolic life has rarely been spent. . . . It is impossible to estimate too highly the good that may flow from this record of Christian life and labour."
—*Sunday Magazine*.

THE LORD'S PRAYER. Lectures by the Rev. ADOLPH

SAPHIR, B.A., Greenwich. Second Edition. Small Crown 8vo, 5s. cloth.
" A work so wide in its range of thought, and so concentrated in its doctrinal teachings, so rich and well packed, yet so simple and interesting, and so clear, pure, and intelligible in expression does not often make its appearance."—*Christian Work*.

CHRIST IN THE WORD. By the Rev. FREDERICK

WHITFIELD, M.A., Author of " Voices from the Valley," &c. Second Edition. Small Crown 8vo, 3s. 6d. cloth.
" Very able and searching applications of spiritual truth."—*Our Own Fireside*.
" Excellent reading for the closet and family circle."—*Watchman*.

THE SHEPHERD AND HIS FLOCK ; or, The Keeper

of Israel and the Sheep of His Pasture. By the Rev. J. R. MACDUFF, D.D.
With Vignette. Tenth Thousand. Small Crown 8vo, 3s. 6d. cloth.
" A remarkably well-written volume, eminently practical and devout in its tone,
and one which spiritually-minded persons will read with both pleasure and profit."—
Journal of Sacred Literature.

ERLING THE BOLD. A Tale of the Norse Sea-Kings.

By R. M. BALLANTYNE, Author of " The Lifeboat," &c. With Illustrations
by the Author. Fourth Thousand. Crown 8vo, 5s. cloth.
" The story is cleverly designed, and abounds with elements of romantic interest ;
and the author's illustrations are scarcely less vigorous than his text."—*Athenæum.*

LIGHT AND TRUTH. Bible Thoughts and Themes—

First, Second, Third, and Fourth Series—1. THE LESSER EPISTLES. 2. THE
ACTS AND THE LARGER EPISTLES. 3. THE GOSPELS. 4. THE OLD TESTA-
MENT. By the Rev. HORATIUS BONAR, D.D. Crown 8vo, each 5s. cloth.
" Rich in matter and very suggestive."—*Christian Advocate.*
" Valuable work. It contains a series of brief expositions well suited for private
use, or for family reading."—*Record.*

LECTURES ON HOSEA XIV. Preached in Portman

Chapel during Lent, 1869. By the Rev. J. W. REEVE, M.A. Small Crown
8vo, 3s. 6d. cloth.
" It would be hard to over-estimate the amount of Gospel truth, practical exhor-
tation, plain speaking, and affectionate interest in the spiritual welfare of his people,
contained in these six lectures."—*Record.*

HE THAT OVERCOMETH ; or, A Conquering Gospel.

By the Rev. W. E. BOARDMAN, M.A., Author of " The Higher Christian
Life," &c. Second Edition. Small Crown 8vo, 3s. 6d. cloth.
" It is an excellent book for reading out on the Sabbath evenings in the family
circle."—*Christian Work.*

THE SPANISH BARBER. A Tale, by the Author of

" Mary Powell " Small Crown 8vo, 3s. 6d. cloth.
" A charming story for young and old, and most charmingly told."—*Rock.*
" An instructive story of missionary work in Spain."—*Christian Advocate.*

SHINING LIGHT. By the Author of " Memorials of

Captain Hedley Vicars," &c. Small Crown 8vo, 2s. 6d. cloth ; Cheap Edition,
1s. cloth limp.
" A clear and vivid exposition of the great outlines of the gospel."—*Christian
Advocate.*

SERMONS. Preached at King's Lynn. By the late Rev.

E. L. HULL, B.A. First and Second Series. Post 8vo, each 6s. cloth.
" This new volume of twenty sermons has all the claims of the first—the same
happy use of Scripture, the same clear and firm grasp of the principle of every text
he selected, the same earnest longing after the beauty and holiness on which he has
now entered, the same play of imagination, the same freshness of thought, and
fitness of utterance."—*Freeman.*

THE TITLES OF OUR LORD; A Series of Sketches for Every Sunday in the Christian Year, to be used in Bible-Class, Sunday School, and Private Study. By the Rev. ROWLEY HILL, M.A., Vicar of Frant. 16mo, 1s. 6d. cloth.

"The idea is excellent. . . . The matter is well arranged, free from repetitions, and in exposition thoroughly scriptural."—*Record*.

HEADS AND TALES; Or, Anecdotes and Stories of Quadrupeds and other Beasts. Compiled by ADAM WHITE, Duddingston. Second Edition. With Illustrations. Small Crown 8vo, 3s. 6d. cloth.

"Full of pleasant anecdotes."—*Times*.
"Amusing, instructive, and interesting."—*Standard*.

STEPPING HEAVENWARD. By Mrs. PRENTISS. Author of "Little Susy's Six Birthdays," &c. With Coloured Illustrations, Small Crown 8vo, 3s. 6d. cloth.

"A faithful diary, recording the experiences of a good and gentle soul in its onward march to a better land."—*Rock*.

THE ROMANCE OF NATURAL HISTORY. First and Second Series. By P. H. GOSSE, F.R.S. New Edition, with many Illustrations, Small Crown 8vo, each 3s. 6d. cloth.

"A very pleasing and attractive work."—*Times*.
"It would be difficult to find more attractive gift books for the young."—*Record*.

BOOKS FOR WAYFARERS. By ANNA WARNER, Author of the "Golden Ladder." 32mo, cloth. 1. WAYFARING HYMNS, ORIGINAL AND SELECTED. 6d. 2. THE MELODY OF THE TWENTY-THIRD PSALM. 8d.

"There is an unction and a beauty about the books that well fit them to be pocket or table companions."—*Freeman*.
"Two little books, beautiful without and within."—*English Presbyterian Messenger*.

HOME THOUGHTS FOR MOTHERS AND MOTHERS' MEETINGS. By the Author of "Sick Bed Vows, and How to Keep Them," &c. Third Edition. Small Crown 8vo, 1s. 6d. cloth.

"We have seen no book which is better fitted to assist the efforts of district visitors, and other Christian labourers among ' the masses.' "—*Record*.

MEMORIALS OF THE LATE JAMES HEN- DERSON, M.D., F.R.C.S.E. Medical Missionary to China. Fifth Edition. With Appendix. Small Crown 8vo, 3s. 6d. cloth. With Portrait. Also, Cheap and Abridged Edition, 16mo, 1s. cloth limp.

"The memorials of Dr. Henderson form as beautiful and exhilarating a little history as it has been for some time our task or pleasure to read. . . . . It is the story of one of those noble lives before which power and difficulty recoil, and give up the contest."—*Eclectic Review*.

MEMOIR AND REMAINS OF THE LATE REV.

JAMES D. BURNS, M.A., of Hampstead. By the late Rev. Dr. HAMILTON. With Portrait. Second Edition. Small Crown 8vo, 5s. cloth.

" It is not often that such sympathy of piety, friendship, and genius, exists between a biographer and his subject. It makes the book very precious—a memorial of the one as much as the other."—*British Quarterly Review.*

NOONTIDE AT SYCHAR; or, The Story of Jacob's

Well. By the Rev. J. R. MACDUFF, D.D. Seventh Thousand. With Vignettes. Small Crown 8vo, 3s. 6d. cloth.

" One of the most attractive of the many pleasant and profitable religious studies published by Dr. Macduff."—*Daily Review.*

DEEP DOWN. A Tale of the Cornish Mines. By R. M.

BALLANTYNE, Author of "The Life Boat," etc. With Illustrations. Small Crown 8vo, 5s. cloth.

" This is just the subject for Mr. Ballantyne, whose stories in connection with that enterprise and adventure which have made England great are amongst the best of modern days."—*Daily News.*

FAMILY PRAYERS FOR FOUR WEEKS. With

Additional Prayers for Especial Days and Occasions. By the Very Rev. HENRY LAW, M.A., Dean of Gloucester. Small Crown 8vo, 3s. 6d. cloth.

" Thoroughly sound and scriptural, and really devotional."—*Christian Observer.*

LIFE OF THE LATE REV. JOHN MILNE, M.A., of

Perth. By the Rev. HORATIUS BONAR, D.D. With Portrait. Third Edition. Crown 8vo, 6s. cloth.

" Written with the elegance, sound judgment, and good feeling which were to be expected from Dr. Bonar ; and being given to a large extent in the autobiographical form, it is, on that account, the more trustworthy and valuable."—*British and Foreign Evangelical Review.*

A COMMENTARY ON ST. PAUL'S EPISTLE TO

THE GALATIANS. With Sermons on the Principal Topics contained in it. By the Rev. EMILIUS BAYLEY, B.D., Vicar of St. John's, Paddington. Crown 8vo, 7s. 6d. cloth.

" Admirable commentary. It is full of well arranged and well digested matter, and without any pedantry, it is scholarlike in its criticisms."—*Record.*

TALES FROM ALSACE; or, Scenes and Portraits from

Life in the Days of the Reformation, as drawn from Old Chronicles. Translated from the German. Third Edition. Crown 8vo, 3s. 6d. cloth.

" We have not for a long time perused a more delightful book. . . . . . we are certain wherever it is read it will be a great favourite with young and old."—*Daily Review.*

A PRACTICAL COMMENTARY ON ST. LUKE. In

Simple and Familiar Language. By G. B. Crown 8vo, 3s. 6d. cloth.

"A gentle trickling rill of practical improvement. . . . The remarks are simple, practical, and in good taste."—*British Quarterly Review.*

A MEMOIR OF THE LATE REV. DR. MALAN,

OF GENEVA. By one of his Sons. With Portrait and Engravings. Post 8vo, 7s. 6d. cloth

"We feel ourselves in this biography brought into contact with an humble but truly saintly man, whom to know is to love, and whom it is impossible to know without being ourselves benefited."—*Christian Work*.

EMMANUEL ; or, The Father revealed in Jesus. By the

Rev. J. CULROSS, D.D., of Stirling, Author of "Divine Compassion," etc. etc. Small Crown 8vo, 2s. 6d. cloth.

"No one can take this small but suggestive volume without a conscious quickening of the intellectual and spiritual life. It abounds with fresh and noble thoughts on a mysterious but absorbing theme."—*Watchman*.

FAMILY PRAYERS FOR A MONTH, with a few

Prayers for Special occasions. By the Rev. J. W. REEVE, M.A., Portman Chapel. Small Crown 8vo, 3s. 6d. cloth.

"Admirably suited for the devotions of a Christian household."—*Rock*.

BEACONS OF THE BIBLE. By the Very Rev. HENRY

LAW, M.A., Dean of Gloucester, Author of "Christ is All," etc. Second Edition. Small Crown 8vo, 3s. 6d. cloth.

"Dr. Law's work overflows with striking and beautiful images, briefly expressed in short, incisive sentences, often musical in their cadence, and melodious as poetry itself."—*Rock*.

THE WORKS OF THE LATE JAMES HAMILTON,

D.D., F.L.S. Complete in Six Vols., post 8vo, each 7s. 6d. cloth.

"More than most men he has embalmed his qualities in his writings. . . They well deserve to be published in a permanent form, and this handsome library edition will be a great boon to many families."—*Freeman*.

THE SHEPHERD OF ISRAEL : or, Illustrations of the

Inner Life. By the Rev. D. MACGREGOR, M.A., St. Peter's, Dundee. Third Edition. Small Crown 8vo, 3s. 6d. cloth.

"The quaint, quiet fancy of the writer, his happy art of illustration, his anecdotes old and new, his fine tenderness of soul, thrilling at the touch of life's manifold sorrows, yet radiant always with Christian joy, give to this volume a singular charm."—*English Presbyterian Messenger*.

OUR FATHER IN HEAVEN. The Lord's Prayer

Familiarly Explained and Illustrated. A Book for the Young. By the Rev. J. H. WILSON, Edinburgh. Fourth Edition with Illustrations. Small Crown 8vo, 2s. 6d. cloth.

"We know no better book of its kind."—*Edinburgh Evening Courant*.

"One of the most interesting and successful expositions of the Lord's Prayer in our language."—*Evangelical Magazine*.

RIGHTS AND WRONGS: or, Begin at Home. By M. M.

GORDON, Author of "Work: Plenty to Do, and How to Do it." Second Edition. Small Crown 8vo, 2s. 6d. limp cloth.

"The purpose of the publication is for circulation amongst the female inmates of cottages and working men's houses, or to be read at mothers' or daughters' meetings. For these ends it will be found exceedingly suitable, and fitted to be widely useful."—*Aberdeen Free Press*.

GATHERINGS FROM A MINISTRY. By the late

Rev. JOHN MILNE, M.A., of Perth. Crown 8vo., 5s. cloth.

"The discourses are all excellent, very practical and searching, clear in style, and pervaded by a lofty spiritual tone."—*English Presbyterian Messenger.*

FROM SEVENTEEN TO THIRTY. The Town Life

of a Youth from the Country; its Trials, Temptations, and Advantages. Lessons from the History of Joseph. By the Rev. THOMAS BINNEY. Fourth Edition. Small Crown 8vo, 1s. 6d. cloth.

"Nothing can exceed the quiet dignity, beauty, and simplicity of style in which this book is written. Not only is it a model of wise scriptural exposition, but we cannot at this moment recall anything that approaches it."—*English Independent.*

THE SABBATH-SCHOOL INDEX. Pointing out the

History and Progress of Sunday Schools, with approved modes of Instruction, etc., etc. By R. G. PARDEE, A.M. With Introductory Preface by the Rev. J. H. WILSON, Edinburgh. Second Edition. Small Crown 8vo, 2s. 6d. cloth.

"The author has succeeded in an admirable manner in producing a work that will stand pre-eminently as the teacher's handbook. We have not found one subject of any importance to the teacher which he has not considered."—*Weekly Review.*

MEMORIES OF OLIVET. By the Rev. J. R. MACDUFF,

D.D. With Vignette. Sixth Thousand. Post 8vo, 6s. 6d. cloth.

"The almost photographic clearness with which every point around Jerusalem is described, and the frequent though unobtrusive illustration of the sacred text from eastern life, together with the vivid realization of the movements of our Saviour during the last few days of his earthly career, make the *Memories of Olivet* a most valuable companion in the study of the preacher and teacher, and in the chamber of the home student."—*Record.*

THE LIFE OF THE LATE REV. DR. MARSH,

of Beddington. By his DAUGHTER, the Author of "English Hearts and English Hands," etc. With Portrait. Seventeenth Thousand. Post 8vo. 10s. cloth; Cheap Edition, Small Crown 8vo, 3s. 6d. cloth.

"We have read this volume with much interest, and can recommend it as an excellent account of Dr. Marsh's life and career, and of the associations connected with them."—*Times.*

MEMORIES OF GENNESARET; or, Our Lord's Minis-

trations in Galilee. With a new and extended Preface, from observations made upon the spot. By the Rev. J. R. MACDUFF, D.D. Twenty-first Thousand. Post 8vo, 6s. 6d. cloth.

"An excellent and exceedingly attractive work. Its character is simplicity, earnestness, and devotedness."—*Witness.*

THE PEARL OF PARABLES. Notes on the Parable

of the Prodigal Son. By the late JAMES HAMILTON, D.D. With Twelve Illustrations by SELOUS. Printed on toned paper, and elegantly bound. Small 4to, 8s. 6d. cloth. Also a Cheap Edition, without Plates, 16mo, 1s. 6d. cloth.

"A book like this is a very rich enjoyment for both mind and heart. A more fitting gift-book for young men could hardly be conceived."—*British Quarterly Review.*

THE DARWINIAN THEORY OF THE TRANSMU-
TATION OF SPECIES EXAMINED. By a GRADUATE OF THE UNIVER-
SITY OF CAMBRIDGE. Second Edition. Demy 8vo, 10s. 6d. cloth.

. "The volume is a work of no ordinary merit. . . . It indicates extensive reading, intimate acquaintance with the whole history of the Transmutation school of thinking, great mastery of the abundant material placed at the disposal of the author, and a large infusion of common sense."—*British Quarterly Review*.

FIGHTING THE FLAMES. A Tale of the London
Fire Brigade. By R. M. BALLANTYNE, Author of "The Lifeboat," "The Lighthouse," etc., etc. With Illustrations. Crown 8vo, 5s. cloth.

"Those who value the welfare of the young and rising generation ought to encourage the circulation of such healthy works as this."—*Edinburgh Evening Courant*.

PLAIN SERMONS ON THE GOSPEL MIRACLES.
By the Rev. ARTHUR ROBERTS, M.A. Crown 8vo, 5s. cloth.

"Plain and simple, without attempt at critical disquisition or philosophical inquiry, they are earnest, scriptural, and attractive. The style, with nothing lofty in it, is pleasant, and the sermons are thoroughly readable."—*Church of England Magazine*.

THE SHADOW AND THE SUBSTANCE. A Second
Series of Addresses by STEVENSON A. BLACKWOOD, Esq. Small Crown 8vo. 2s. cloth limp, 2s. 6d. cloth boards.

"A very thoughtful and thoroughly scriptural view of the Passover. . . . To those who wish for useful reading to adult classes, or to mothers' meetings, we commend this book."—*Record*.

THE PROPHET OF FIRE; or, The Life and Times of
Elijah, and their Lessons. By the Rev. J. R. MACDUFF, D.D. Eighth Thousand. Post 8vo, 6s. 6d. cloth.

"Full of incident, rich in illustration, smooth and pleasing in style, and abounding in practical lessons."—*English Presbyterian Messenger*.

MISCELLANEOUS SERMONS. By the Rev. ARTHUR
ROBERTS, M.A. Crown 8vo, 5s. cloth.

"Incomparably the best sermons for the people with which we are acquainted."—*Our Own Fireside*.

THE PRAISE-BOOK; being "Hymns of Praise," with
accompanying Tunes. By the Rev. W. REID, M.A. Harmonies written or revised by H. E. DIBDIN. Third Edition. Crown 4to, 7s. 6d. cloth elegant.

"This magnificent volume has no rival, at least we know of none published in England. It is a standard book both as to hymns and music."—*Sword and Trowel*.

ST. PAUL; His Life and Ministry to the Close of his
Third Missionary Journey. By the Rev. THOMAS BINNEY. Third Edition. Crown 8vo, 5s. cloth.

"Mr. Binney has elaborated into a volume his magnificent lectures on St. Paul's Life and Ministry. . . Mr. Binney's books need no commendation of ours."—*Quarterly Messenger Young Men's Christian Association*.

SUNSETS ON THE HEBREW MOUNTAINS : or,

Some of the most prominent Biographies of Sacred Story viewed from Life's Close. By the Rev. J. R MACDUFF, D.D. Seventeenth Thousand. Post 8vo, 6s. 6d. cloth.

" Dr. Macduff has rightly appreciated the characters he has described, and has truthfully delineated their features. The points of instruction, too, which he draws from them are apposite, scriptural, and telling."—*Church of England Magazine.*

THE LIGHTHOUSE ; or, The Story of a Great Fight

between Man and the Sea. By R. M. BALLANTYNE, Author of " The Lifeboat," etc., etc. Illustrations. Crown 8vo, 5s. cloth.

" Interesting to all readers."—*Arbroath Guide.*
" A story at once instructive and amusing."—*Dundee Advertiser.*

FIFTY-TWO SHORT SERMONS FOR FAMILY

READING. By HORATIUS BONAR, D.D. Crown 8vo, 6s. cloth.

" These are short plain sermons for family reading, and are admirably fitted for so good a purpose."—*English Presbyterian Messenger.*

THE LIFEBOAT : A Tale of our Coast Heroes. A Book

for Boys. By. R. M. BALLANTYNE, Author of " The Lighthouse," etc. With Illustrations. Crown 8vo, 5s. cloth.

" This is another of Mr. Ballantyne's excellent stories for the young. They are all well written, full of romantic incidents, and are of no doubtful moral tendency ; on the contrary, they are invariably found to embody sentiments of true piety, and manliness and virtue."—*Inverness Advertiser.*

FORGIVENESS, LIFE, AND GLORY. Addresses by

S. A. BLACKWOOD, Esq. Small Crown 8vo, 2s. cloth limp ; 2s. 6d. cloth boards.

" Full of devout earnestness and scriptural truth."—*Church of England Magazine.*
" They are all solemn and searching.—*Morning Advertiser.*

HYMNS OF FAITH AND HOPE. By HORATIUS BONAR,

D.D. First, Second, and Third Series, Crown 8vo, each 5s. cloth. Also, Pocket Editions, Royal 32mo, each 1s. 6d. Also a Royal Edition, printed at the Chiswick Press, and handsomely bound. Post 8vo, 7s. 6d. cloth.

" There is a freshness and vigour, an earnestness and a piety in these compositions, which is very gratifying. The language is highly poetical."—*Evangelical Christendom.*

GOD'S WAY OF PEACE. A Book for the Anxious.

By HORATIUS BONAR, D.D. A Cheap Edition, 6d. sewed, and 9d. cloth limp. In 16mo, 1s. 6d. cloth. Also, a Large-type Edition, crown 8vo, 2s. cloth.

" The best ' book for the anxious ' ever written."—Rev. SAMUEL GARRETT, in *Revival Truths.*

GOD'S WAY OF HOLINESS. A Companion Volume

to "God's Way of Peace." By HORATIUS BONAR, D.D. A Cheap Edition, 6d. sewed ; 9d. cloth limp. In 16mo, 1s. 6d. cloth. Also, a Large-type Edition, crown 8vo, 2s. cloth.

" Our sympathies have been chained to Dr. Bonar's delightful teaching, which, in these times of controversy and apathy, falls upon the spirit like refreshing dew."—*Church Standard.*

THE POEMS OF GEORGE HERBERT. Illustrated

in the highest style of Wood Engraving, by Birket Foster, Clayton, and Noel Humphreys. Post 4to, 12s. cloth elegant.

"There have been many editions of Herbert's Poetical Works. One of the most splendid is that of Nisbet, London."—*Encyclopædia Britannica.*

HELP HEAVENWARD : Words of Strength and Heart-

cheer to Zion's Travellers. By the Rev. OCTAVIUS WINSLOW, D.D. 16mo, 2s. 6d. cloth.

"It is replete with sound, searching, practical remark, conveyed in the winning and affectionate spirit, and with the luxuriant richness of phraseology by which the author is characterized."—*Scottish Guardian.*

ILLUSTRATIVE GATHERINGS FOR PREACH-

ERS AND TEACHERS. By the Rev. G. S. BOWES, B.A. First and Second Series, Small Crown 8vo, each, 3s. 6d. cloth.

"Its tone is thoroughly evangelical and spiritual, and it is fitted to furnish useful hints and illustrations to the Christian teacher."—*Christian Witness.*

ENGLISH HEARTS AND ENGLISH HANDS ; or,

The Railway and the Trenches. By the Author of "Memorials of Captain Hedley Vicars." Small Crown 8vo, 5s. cloth. Also a Cheaper Edition, 2s. cloth limp.

"The Memorials of Vicars and these Memorials of the Crystal Palace Navvies are books of precisely the same type, and must not be overlooked. We recognize in them an honesty of purpose, a purity of heart, and a warmth of human affection, combined with a religious faith, that are very beautiful."—*Times.*

THE EXETER HALL LECTURES TO YOUNG

MEN, from their commencement in 1845-6, to their termination in 1864-5, all uniformly printed, and handsomely bound in cloth, and embellished with portraits of the Friends and Patrons of the Young Men's Christian Association. Complete in 20 vols., price of each volume, 4s. ; or the whole series for £3.

MATTHEW HENRY'S COMMENTARY ON THE

HOLY BIBLE, comprising upwards of 7000 Pages, well printed (the Notes as well as the Text in clear and distinct type) on good paper, forming Nine Imperial 8vo volumes, and handsomely bound in cloth. Price £3 3s. cloth.

*** The work may also be had in a variety of extra bindings, of which a list will be forwarded on application.

THE REV. THOS. SCOTT'S COMMENTARY ON

THE HOLY BIBLE, comprising Marginal References, a copious Topical Index, Fifteen Maps, and Sixty-nine Engravings, illustrative of Scripture Incidents and Scenery. Complete in 6 vols. 4to, published at £4 4s., now offered for £2 10s.

THE BIBLE MANUAL : an Expository and Practical

Commentary on the Books of Scripture, arranged in Chronological Order : forming a Hand-book of Biblical Elucidation for the use of Families, Schools, and Students of the Word of God. Translated from the German Work, edited by the late Rev. Dr. C. G. BARTH, of Calw, Wurtemberg. Imperial 8vo, 12s. cloth.

THE WORD SERIES.

By ELIZABETH WETHERALL and ANNA LOTHROP, Authors of "The Wide Wide World," "Dollars and Cents," etc. Uniform with the "Golden Ladder" Series, with Coloured Illustrations. Crown 8vo, each 3s. 6d. cloth.

"The aim of this series of volumes is so to set forth the Bible incidents and course of history, with its train of actors, as to see them in the circumstances and colouring, the light and shade of their actual existence."

1. WALKS FROM EDEN: The Scripture Story from the Creation to the Death of Abraham.

2. THE HOUSE OF ISRAEL: The Scripture Story from the Birth of Isaac to the Death of Jacob.

3. THE STAR OUT OF JACOB: The Scripture Story Illustrating the Earlier Portion of the Gospel Narrative.

THE GOLDEN LADDER SERIES.

Uniform in size and binding, with eight coloured Illustrations. Crown 8vo, each 3s. 6d. cloth.

1. THE GOLDEN LADDER: Stories Illustrative of the Eight Beatitudes. By ELIZABETH and ANNA WARNER.

2. THE WIDE WIDE WORLD. By ELIZABETH WARNER.

3. QUEECHY. By the same.

4. MELBOURNE HOUSE. By the same.

5. DAISY. By the same.

6. THE OLD HELMET. By the same.

7. THE THREE LITTLE SPADES. By the same.

8. NETTIE'S MISSION: Stories Illustrative of the Lord's Prayer. By ALICE GRAY.

9. DAISY IN THE FIELD. By ELIZABETH WARNER.

10. STEPPING HEAVENWARD. By Mrs. PRENTISS. Author of "Little Susy."

11. WHAT SHE COULD, AND OPPORTUNITIES. A Sequel. Tales by ELIZABETH WARNER.

12. GLEN LUNA; or, Dollars and Cents. By ANNA WARNER.

13. STORIES ILLUSTRATIVE OF THE PARABLE OF THE SOWER. By ANNA WARNER (In the Press.)

14. THE DRAYTON FAMILY. Stories Illustrative of the Beatitudes. By ALICE GRAY. (In the Press.)

THE ONE SHILLING JUVENILE SERIES.

Uniform in size and binding, 16mo, Illustrations, each 1s. cloth.

1. CHANGES UPON CHURCH BELLS. By C. S. H.

2. GONZALEZ AND HIS WAKING DREAMS. By C. S. H.

3. DAISY BRIGHT. By EMMA MARSHALL.

4. HELEN; or, Temper and its Consequences. By Mrs. G. GLADSTONE.

5. THE CAPTAIN'S STORY; or, The Disobedient Son. By W. S. MARTIN.

6. THE LITTLE PEATCUTTERS; or, The Song of Love. By EMMA MARSHALL.

7. LITTLE CROWNS, AND HOW TO WIN THEM. By the Rev. J. A. COLLIER.

8. CHINA AND ITS PEOPLE. By a MISSIONARY'S WIFE.

9. TEDDY'S DREAM; or, A Little Sweep's Mission.

10. ELDER PARK; or, Scenes in our Garden. By Mrs. ALFRED PAYNE, Author of "Nature's Wonders."

11. HOME LIFE AT GREYSTONE LODGE. By the Author of "Agnes Falconer."

12. THE PEMBERTON FAMILY, and other Stories.

13. CHRISTMAS AT SUNBURY DALE. By W. B. B., Author of "Clara Downing's Dream."

14. PRIMROSE; or, The Bells of Old Effingham. By Mrs. MARSHALL.

15. THE BOY GUARDIAN. By the Author of "Dick and his Donkey."

16. VIOLET'S IDOL. By JOANNA H. MATTHEWS.

17. FRANK GORDON. By the Author of "The Young Marooners." And LITTLE JACK'S FOUR LESSONS. By the Author of "The Golden Ladder."

THE EIGHTEENPENNY JUVENILE SERIES.

Uniform in size and binding, 16mo, with Illustrations, each 1s. 6d. cloth.

1. AUNT EDITH ; or, Love to God the Best Motive.

2. SUSY'S SACRIFICE.   By Alice Gray.

3. KENNETH FORBES ; or, Fourteen Ways of Studying the Bible.

4. LILIES OF THE VALLEY, and other Tales.

5. CLARA STANLEY ; or, a Summer among the Hills.

6. THE CHILDREN OF BLACKBERRY HOLLOW.

7. HERBERT PERCY ; or, From Christmas to Easter.

8. PASSING CLOUDS ; or, Love conquering Evil.

9. DAYBREAK ; or, Right Struggling and Triumphant.

10. WARFARE AND WORK ; or, Life's Progress.

11. EVELYN GREY.   By the Author of "Clara Stanley."

12. THE HISTORY OF THE GRAVELYN FAMILY.

13. DONALD FRASER. By the Author of " Bertie Lee."

14. THE SAFE COMPASS, AND HOW IT POINTS. By Rev. R. Newton, D.D.

15. THE KING'S HIGHWAY ; or, Illustrations of the Commandments.   By the same.

16. BESSIE AT THE SEASIDE.   By Joanna H. Matthews.

17. CASPER.   By the Authors of " The Wide Wide World," etc.

18. KARL KRINKEN ; or, The Christmas Stocking.   By the same.

19. MR. RUTHERFORD'S CHILDREN. By the same.

THE EIGHTEENPENNY JUVENILE SERIES—*Continued.*

THE SELECT SERIES.

Crown 8vo, each 3s. 6d. cloth.   Bound by BURN.   Most of them with Illustrations.

1. DERRY.   A Tale of the Revolution.   By CHARLOTTE ELIZABETH.
2. THE LAND OF THE FORUM AND THE VATICAN.   By the Rev. NEWMAN HALL, LL.B.
3. THE LISTENER.   By CAROLINE FRY.
4. DAYS AND NIGHTS IN THE EAST; or, Illustrations of Bible Scenes.   By the Rev. HORATIUS BONAR, D.D.
5. BEECHENHURST.   A Tale.   By A. G., Author of "Among the Mountains," etc.
6. THE HOLY WAR.   By JOHN BUNYAN.
7. THE PILGRIM'S PROGRESS.   By JOHN BUNYAN.
8. THE MOUNTAINS OF THE BIBLE; Their Scenes and their Lessons.   By the Rev. JOHN MACFARLANE, LL.D.
9. THROUGH DEEP WATERS; or, Seeking and Finding.   An Autobiography.
10. HOME AND FOREIGN SERVICE; or, Pictures in Active Christian Life.
11. LIFE.   A Series of Illustrations of the Divine Wisdom in the Forms, Structures, and Instincts of Animals.   By PHILLIP H. GOSSE, F.R.S.
12. LAND AND SEA.   By P. H. GOSSE, F.R.S.
13. JOHN KNOX AND HIS TIMES.   By the Author of "The Story of Martin Luther," etc.
14. HOME IN THE HOLY LAND.   By Mrs. FINN.
15. A THIRD YEAR IN JERUSALEM.   A Tale Illustrating Incidents and Customs in Modern Jerusalem.   By Mrs. FINN.
16 & 17. THE ROMANCE OF NATURAL HISTORY. By P. H. GOSSE, F.R.S.   First and Second Series.
18. BYEWAYS IN PALESTINE.   By JAMES FINN, Esq. F.R.A.S., late H. M. Consul of Jerusalem and Palestine.
19. HEADS AND TALES; or, Anecdotes and Stories of Quadrupeds and other Beasts, as connected with the Histories of more or less distinguished men.   Selected and written by ADAM WHITE, Duddingston.
20. BLOOMFIELD.   A Tale by ELIZABETH WARREN, Author of "John Knox and his Times," &c.
21. TALES FROM ALSACE; or, Scenes and Portraits from Life in the Days of the Reformation, as drawn from old Chronicles. Translated from the German.
22. HYMNS OF THE CHURCH MILITANT.   By the Author of "The Wide Wide World."

Henderson, Rait, & Fenton, Printers, 23, Berners Street, Oxford Street.

Im The Story
personalised classic books

JANE
IN
WONDERLAND

LEWIS
CARROLL

"Beautiful gift, lovely finish.
My Niece loves it, so precious!"

Helen R Brumfieldon

☆☆☆☆☆

UNIQUE GIFT

FOR KIDS, PARTNERS
AND FRIENDS

Timeless books such as:

Kids

Alice in Wonderland · The Jungle Book · The Wonderful Wizard of Oz
Peter and Wendy · Robin Hood · The Prince and The Pauper
The Railway Children · Treasure Island · A Christmas Carol

Adults

Romeo and Juliet · Dracula

Highly Customizable

Change Books Title

Replace Characters Names with yours

Upload Photo for inside page

Add Inscriptions

Visit
Im The Story .com
and order yours today!

CPSIA information can be obtained
at www.ICGtesting.com
Printed in the USA
BVHW081602120819
555665BV00013B/1023/P